Psychosocial Responses to Sociopolitical Targeting, Oppression and Violence

This book will prepare social wo[illegible] [illegible] and counselors for psychosocial work with individuals a[illegible] [illegible] are experiencing distress and trauma resulting from historical a[illegible] [illegible] sociopolitical oppression and violence.

Sociopolitical oppression is a sustained, systematic catastrophe, which results from social targeting and discrimination such as racism, sexism and misogyny, homophobia, and anti-immigrant fervor. The consequences are profound and debilitating. In some ways, they are similar to reactions to a single event disaster (e.g., hurricane, earthquake, terrorist attack) but even more insidious because the social targeting and harassment have been ongoing and will continue.

As a guide for direct clinical practice, this book offers new models for understanding the nature and consequences of sociopolitical disasters as well as guiding a range of interventions – clinical, psychoeducational, advocacy, and social justice – for use on a micro, mezzo, and macro level.

Drawing on indigenous and BIPOC knowledge and scholarship and using case studies from around the world, it criticizes while also adapting and integrating knowledge and theory from the fields of disaster mental health, psychosocial capacity building, trauma therapy, psychodynamic theory, cognitive behavioral theories, and theories of resilience and positive psychology, linking them to an understanding of historical and social oppression, social justice, and intergroup conflict and reconciliation. The book offers critiques of dominant Western, Eurocentric visions of personhood and models of intervention and questions assumptions about the roles of "client" and "worker," proposing more egalitarian, collaborative relationships and extensive use of training of trainers.

It will prepare graduate students and practitioners across the helping professions for work that promotes the collective and individual strength and efficacy of affected people, while also responding directly to vulnerability, stress, and trauma.

Joshua L. Miller is Professor Emeritus of Social Work at Smith College, United States. He is co-author of *Racism in the United States: Implications for the helping professions* (3rd ed.) 2021, NY: Springer Publishing and author of *Psychosocial capacity building in response to disasters* 2012, NY: Columbia University Press.

Psychosocial Responses to Sociopolitical Targeting, Oppression and Violence

Challenges for Helping Professionals

Joshua L. Miller

LONDON AND NEW YORK

Cover image: Getty Images

First published 2023
by Routledge
4 Park Square, Milton Park, Abingdon, Oxon OX14 4RN

and by Routledge
605 Third Avenue, New York, NY 10158

Routledge is an imprint of the Taylor & Francis Group, an informa business

British Library Cataloguing-in-Publication Data
A catalogue record for this book is available from the British Library

ISBN: 978-0-367-89790-1 (hbk)
ISBN: 978-0-367-89794-9 (pbk)
ISBN: 978-1-003-02116-2 (ebk)

DOI: 10.4324/9781003021162

Typeset in Sabon
by Apex CoVantage, LLC

Contents

Figures

Boxes

Preface

All books have a story about why they were written, and I will briefly share what led me to write this book. In order to do that, I need to begin with my own struggles throughout my 50-year career as a social work practitioner and educator. I was educated in social work in the 1970s, taught as a full-time professor at Smith College School for Social Work for the past 30 years, and have practiced as a social worker in the United States, United Kingdom, Ireland, Sri Lanka, China, Uganda, Haiti, and Canada. Central to the focus of my work has been a deep commitment to antiracism and dismantling White supremacy, social justice, and decolonizing education and practice, which includes naming and questioning the dominance of Eurocentrism in my field. My struggle has been that I am a White, cis-gendered, heterosexual middle-class male having lived in the United States, United Kingdom, and Ireland and that I have been a member of a profession – one of the "helping professions" – for all of my career. By virtue of my privileged social identities, where I have lived and been based, where I was educated, where I worked and taught, the professions that I joined, and the journals that published my articles, I have been immersed in the very milieu which I have sought to change.

When I was a beginning social worker, working for a "local authority" in London in the 1970s, I realized that something was wrong as I worked with "clients" from Uganda, Pakistan, Nigeria, Guyana, India, Scotland, Jamaica, Ireland, Wales, as well as local English clients – White and of color. My direct practice – my caseload – was supposed to be separate from social advocacy and social change. Somehow, the understanding of personhood (what it means to be a person) that I was taught, what it meant by a "normal" family, and the theories of human development and practice which I was exposed to were held to be universally valid for families from all over the world, with a tremendous range of social identities and experiences of privilege and oppression. Already, early in my career in London, I questioned this fallacy.

When I attended the Institute of Family Therapy in London for training, I learned about family psychodynamics, structure, systems, roles, communications, behaviors, and interventions which were also presented in a decontextualized, universal manner. When the field of family therapy began to "discover" in the 1980s that ethnicity and culture mattered, the early books and articles were written from a White perspective – the worker was assumed to be White and had to learn about working with families with different cultural orientations; White was normal, and cultural differences were viewed as "different." And the emphasis was on cultural differences, not differential exposure to colonialism and White supremacy, with many assumptions made about heteronormativity and little attention to misogyny and male dominance.

While I was working in London with a young Black man from a West Indian country, who needed to go into "care" (a group home), I had to call a clearing house for group homes used by social service organizations around the country that would then place social work clients. The first question I was asked was "what color is he?" I spluttered and asked why I was being asked that and I was lectured about how of course it was important because certain group homes catered to "colored" adolescents and others to English (which meant White). I had to place my client that night, so I shared his racial identity, but I also filed a complaint with the national race relations board. Within a few weeks, while on vacation, I was notified by the director of my office that she was aware of the complaint and that the director of social services for the borough where I worked was mortified that I had filed it without going through the regular channels and that my desk had been searched and we would talk about this when I returned. I was nearly fired and admonished for my irresponsible rogue behavior. I did receive support, however, from the workers at the race relations board, who could not protect me but encouraged my whistle blowing.

Fast forward to early in my career as a professor, where I immediately began team-teaching a course about racism in the United States, always with a colleague of color. What I quickly began to realize was that despite my liberal values and willingness to call out racism, and even though there was historical trauma in my Jewish family, I had a lot of work to do with my whiteness (as well as many other aspects of my identity) – my internalized sense of privilege and my assumptions about the world and my place in it. I was fortunate – I co-taught this course for over 20 years with a number of different colleagues, who invested in expanding my awareness and my growth as a professor, despite the fact that this was not their job and I imagine was at times painful for them. Eventually, I collaborated with some of them, and we co-authored the book *Racism in the United States: Implications for the helping professions.*

My professional practice in the 1990s began to focus on helping individuals, families, and communities to recover from "disasters" – natural, technological, and human-caused – and I joined local community teams, the American Red Cross and immersed myself in "disaster mental health" and developed a course at Smith College with that title. The prevailing mythology at that time was that disasters affected everyone equally, regardless of social positions and identities, that there were common reactions in response to disasters, and universal, "evidenced based" interventions to be made. Of course, none of this is true, which I eventually came to understand.

In the mid-2000s, I had the opportunity to respond to the Asian Tsunami in Sri Lanka for two months. I worked with communities of Tamil Hindus, Tamil Muslims, and Sinhalese Buddhists. I remember running a workshop with my British wife (also a social worker) early on in a Tamil Muslim community, where men sat on one side and women on the other, and hearing about how all of the young women in the village would never be married because the tsunami had destroyed their dowries. Reflecting on this I thought: "all that you think that you know about helping people recover from disasters may be irrelevant and wrong, and may even cause harm in this context." It stopped me in my tracks and was a turning point in my career where I began to question everything that I had learned and thought that I knew. That work and my subsequent work in Northern Uganda in response to a long-standing armed conflict with my colleague Joanne Corbin led to my discarding the model of disaster mental health and instead developing (with Joanne, Yoosun Park, and others) the model of psychosocial capacity building in response to disasters based on an understanding of social ecology and an emphasis on intersectionality.

I was invited to work in China after the 2008 earthquake in Sichuan Province and ended up teaching at Beijing Normal University as a visiting professor for a decade. My colleague Xiying Wang and I responded to the survivors of the earthquake, co-taught courses together, and also published together. She and others impressed upon me how China responded to a major disaster, with a much greater emphasis on the community, collectivity, and groups, which was different from my experience responding to U.S. disasters. While Xiying and I were collaborating, we kept thinking about whether or not disaster response should be a distinct field of practice and wondered about the relationship to what we initially called "social disasters" – ongoing societal oppression – and realized that although there were major differences between a disaster and unrelenting racism, religious persecution, and so on, there were also some aspects in common. I explore this in the first chapter of the book.

I have shared some of my personal story because it is still a journey in progress, and despite my work and writing, the gravitational pull of coloniality, White supremacy, and Eurocentrism is always a force that I have to contend with – outside of me in the institutions where I have worked and the theories of helping that are used – and inside of me as I strive to unlearn so much of how I was trained and even what I taught others. But it is what has led to this book and rather than present myself as objective, detached, or taking some sort of universal, expert stance, I wanted to briefly situate myself so that readers can take what I have written in the context of my experience, and yours.

My goals in writing this book are to grapple with how people in "the helping professions" can work with people experiencing social oppression due to history and the structure of society, guided by an imperative to decolonize Eurocentric theories and practices, decentralize Eurocentric views of personhood, and to value and strive for liberation, collective action, and the ability of helpers to intervene on multiple levels. I seek to interrogate the existing paradigms of human service practice while expanding the reservoirs of knowledge, wisdom, and practices that hold lessons for healing. In this process, I have tried to put the collectivity at the forefront without losing sight of families and individuals. While I shared part of how I got to this point, the ethics, values, and work described in this book are part of a collective movement, led by BIPOC and indigenous scholars and practitioners. The scholars referenced in this book, as well as the people mentioned in the acknowledgments, have taught and inspired me and strongly influenced how I have approached this topic. This has involved not only rethinking theories about human development and practice but questioning traditional roles and the terms used to describe "helper" and "client," which I discuss in the first chapter. What I seek is a framework for collaboration, not a practice manifesto with me in the role of expert. I have drawn on the scholarship of others, made suggestions, and shared understandings and insights that accrued during my career. My hope is that by offering both a critique of current practice and possible pathways forward, readers will take, discard, criticize, and rework what I have written, based not only on what I say, but knowing a bit about who I am.

I have taken a position in this book that questions universal visions of personhood, assumptions about what people think and feel, and prescriptions about what people need in order to protect themselves, reduce and alleviate their suffering, and thrive. In the context of coloniality, which is explained in the first chapter, White, European visions of what it means to be a person, and what is seen as normal and abnormal, have structured the systems of service response and delivery, centered certain epistemologies over others, influencing what is validated and invalidated, what is viewed as "evidenced based," and what is considered merely mystical and intuitive. Despite centuries of healing practices and traditions in many indigenous societies and religious practices, modern psychology and psychotherapy are often presented as the gold standard of what it takes for people to recover from adversity and wounds and thrive. I challenge this notion throughout the book.

In order to contrast what I interrogate and question with many sources of knowledge and insight that have been marginalized and downgraded, I have, at times, had to use broad strokes, for example, to compare Western with indigenous societies and practices. As my colleague Christian Rangel emphasized to me, there are always nuances, contradictions, and exceptions. Repression does not only take place in Western societies. Despite the ravages of capitalism on many peoples and the planet, other economic systems have also been oppressive. There are no utopias – past and present; all societies have engaged in targeting and oppression to some extent. While racism in the United States takes the form of White people oppressing people BIPOC people, in China, a similar process occurs with Han Chinese dominating and subjugating Uighurs and other ethnic minorities. And, as I acknowledge throughout the book, although I question many of the precepts of modern psychotherapeutic practice, there are many insights and useful understandings offered by mainstream Western psychology which should be integrated with other practices, although never imposed.

I take as my point of reference the world that we currently inhabit, shaped by coloniality and White supremacy, dominated by capitalism, threatened by climate change, characterized by profound inequality between and within societies, riven by conflict, genocide, and forced migration, and the shadow of Western nations hovering over the standards and practices of the helping professions. I offer this book with humility as one small voice in a chorus of a broader global effort to reimagine, rethink, and reconfigure how to challenge what is dominant and to work toward a more just, life-affirming, equitable, and inclusive planet, valuing its many societies, cultures, and people, and for helping professionals/volunteers to play a constructive role in this process.

Acknowledgments

I have been blessed during my 50-year career, having worked with inspirational colleagues, students, and collaborators. They have taught me so much and their insights and wisdom have guided much of my writing of this book, although any mistakes or problems are mine alone. Much of my work and writing over my career has focused on anti-racism, confronting societal oppression, dismantling White supremacy, psychosocial capacity building, and responding to disasters of all sizes in the United States and around the world. I am a White, heterosexual, male, an older professional, and middle class with many unearned privileges. Although I am ethnically Jewish, I am spiritually Buddhist. Thus, I am indebted to so many people who have helped me throughout my career to understand and appreciate historical and collective trauma, racism, coloniality, and the complex dynamics of power, privilege, and oppression.

I cannot mention every colleague and former student by name, but I would like to recognize some people who contributed to my thinking about this book over the past few years. My colleagues at Smith College School for Social Work continue to engage in a brave and inspiring commitment to confront endemic White supremacy in their program as well as working to decolonize the curriculum. This includes Dean Marianne Yoshioka, Associate Dean Megan Harding, Associate Dean Irene Rodriguez Martin, and the following full-time professors: Kenta Asakura, Loren Cahill, Rory Crath, Annemarie Gockel, Alberto Guerro, Hannah Karpman, Shveta Kumaria, Brandyn McKinley, Ora Nakash, Peggy O'Neill, Marsha Kline Pruett, and JaLisa Williams. I learned a great deal from co-facilitating a seminar for faculty called Pedagogy and Diversity over the years with Mamta Dadlani, Ann Marie Garran, Hye-Kyung Kang, Tanya Greathouse, Raymond Rodriguez, LaTasha Smith, Ruth Spencer, Rani Varghese, Keisha Williams, Lisa Werkmeister-Rozas, Nichole Woffard, and the late Deb Fauntelroy. My colleagues Mary Gannon and Mareike Every have always been a role model of authentic White allyship in the struggle against racism. My collaborations with the Smith College School for Social Work Field Office were where the theoretical met the applied realities of student internships and practice: I am appreciative of Katelin Lewis Kulin, Katya Cerar, Arianne Napier White, and Maria del Mar Farina. A conversation with adjunct professor Christian Rangle in the gym helped to clarify some of my thinking about culture and society. I appreciated my talks with Anna Miller, who helped me to reflect on my Jewish ethnicity and how it might relate to this book.

I am part of a scholarly collective that produced the book *Racism in the United States: Implications for the Helping Professions* and owe a deep debt of gratitude to my co-authors Ann Marie Garran, Hye-Kyung Kang, and Lisa Werkmeister Rozas. I would also like to give a shout-out to my academic colleagues in China and Hong Kong with whom I have frequently collaborated, notably Xiying Wang, Cecelia Chang, Xiulan Zhang, and Qianwen Xie. I have been working closely with colleagues in Uganda over the past decade and would like to thank Father Obol Remigio, Patrick Okello, Mary Auma Alai, Monica Akello, Jacqueline Olanya, and Susan Alai, who have taught me more than I can ever adequately acknowledge. Ann Markes, Matt Kane, Linda Cohen, Meg Carmel, Vicki Weld, Janet Namono, Maria Torres, Leah Cantler, Eileen Giardina, David LaLima, Sally Deans Lake, Sandy Kobalarz, Pam Cavanaugh, Ashley Brant, and others have been part of the U.S. team working in Uganda, whose work is shared in this book, and were great collaborators. I also am grateful to Joanne Corbin, who was responsible for introducing me to my friends and colleagues in Uganda and taught me a great deal about psychosocial capacity building. Collaborating with Yoosun Park and Bao Chau Van on research about the effects of Hurricane Katrina on the Vietnamese population in Biloxi expanded this understanding even further.

Jean Pierre Louis, the Executive Director of CapraCare, brought me to Haiti after an earthquake and was a great colleague and collaborator. I owe a great debt to Dishani Jayweera and Jayantha Senaviarthne, who invited me to Sri Lanka after the Asian Tsunami and helped me to recognize the problems with exporting Western clinical notions of healing and recovery to a non-Western population. My colleagues in Calgary with Alberta Health Services and their consultants were an important part of my learning journey – particularly Debbie Grey, Cheryl Gardner, Tina Nash, Patricia Watson, Elizabeth Dezgois, Kathy GermMan, Tavia Narzarko, and David Turner. I would also like to express my gratitude to the members of the Stoney Nakoda First

Nation and Siksika First Nation, who deepened my understanding of coloniality, and the interaction of historical trauma with present-day sociopolitical oppression.

I always learn from Agnes Umutesi, Mia Deonate Fuentes, and Ben Thompson who are like family as well as my friend Jamie Daniels. I would like to give a shout-out to Andrea Schmid of the Pioneer Valley Workers Center, who spearheaded a state-wide effort in Massachusetts to ensure that undocumented immigrants are able to have a driver's license. I have great respect for the Western Massachusetts Critical Incident Stress Management team of which I am a member and have gained many insights from my first-responder colleagues.

Amy Kahn and Karen Rowe taught me how to adapt EMDR to different sociocultural contexts. I am very indebted to Melissa Lopez and Peggy O'Neill for looking at drafts of part of the manuscript and giving me feedback. This book would not have happened without the encouragement of my editor at Routledge, Claire Jarvis, who invited me to consider a book on this topic and has been patient and forbearing throughout the process. I would also like to express my appreciation to Sully Edwards, and Jayachandran Rajendiran for their excellent work with the editing and production of the manuscript.

We all have mentors in our life and a few deeply shaped me as a professional: Irving Miller, Sidney Miller, Richard Cloward, Frances Fox Piven, Alex Gitterman, Stanley Ofsevit, and Ann Hartman, as well as many of my professors along the way. I worked in Springfield, Massachusetts, as a community organizer between 1988 and 1992 where many people supported and guided me as we worked to dismantle institutional racism in the city, including Henry Thomas, Norma Baker, Herbie Flores, Paul Doherty, Ben Jones, Susan Fentin, Peter Negroni, Al Tervalon, Neil McBride, Ben Jones, Jeannie Bass, and Dora and Frank Robinson.

Last but not least, I would like to acknowledge and thank my family for their love and support – my sister Abby, my step-daughter Lucy and her husband Justin, daughters Corina and Sophie and her partner Chris, and grandchildren Xan, Otto, and Fig. And of course, my wife and life partner, friend and colleague, Davina Miller has been my greatest support and a constant font of love and caring.

1 Psychosocial Responses to Sociopolitical Targeting, Oppression, and Violence

Challenges for Helping Professionals

Introduction

African Americans and Black people and their allies in the United States protest against police brutality after waves of murders of unarmed Black people by police officers, most of whom are white. They do not feel that they or their friends and family are safe – not while driving, walking, or sleeping in their beds at night. They are disproportionately affected by the COVID pandemic with much higher rates of infection and mortality due to the long-term effects of racism and unequal access to medical services that are often racially biased. Their right to vote is, once again, being challenged as one major political party in the United States, the Republican party, composed of mostly white voters, attempts to suppress the Black vote in multiple states – e.g., closing down polling locations in Black neighborhoods or changing locations at the last minute, curtailing voting hours, spreading misinformation, forcing former convicted felons to pay outstanding fines before being allowed to vote, and in the state of Georgia, even prohibiting serving food or water to people waiting on line to vote.

A small group of women in Beijing publicly demonstrate against misogyny on International Women's day by placing stickers on busses and subway cars. They are arrested, interrogated, imprisoned, and once released, they and their families remain under ongoing surveillance. They suffer from the symptoms of trauma and have panic attacks every time there is a knock on their door.

Members of a First Nation in Canada experience a huge flood and their community takes longer to rebuild than neighboring White communities affected by the same flood. A regional public health and social service agency reaches out to them to see if they can help. What they find is that members of the tribe do not distinguish between

DOI: 10.4324/9781003021162-1

the consequences of the flood, the legacies of coloniality, historical trauma, and their ongoing social, political, and economic exclusion due to racism and White supremacy.

Undocumented students in the United States have experienced fear, trauma, family separation, a lack of trust in the U.S. government, and a sense of insecurity. While this has been true under both Democrat and Republican administrations, they have felt demeaned, dehumanized, and threatened by President Trump and his unceasing anti-immigrant of color rhetoric. They have relatives who tried to enter the United States and had their children taken from them; some do not know where their children are. The COVID pandemic sweeps the nation, and many are unable to attend schools in person: some have access to sufficient technology to take classes online and some do not. Some have access to health care, while others not only do not have health-care insurance but are also fearful that if they go to a health facility they may be picked up by U.S. Immigration and Customs Enforcement. Many have family members working in high-risk, high-exposure occupations. Some have trouble sleeping and live with a constant sense of dread.

These examples take place in developed nations, but the experience of being targeted socio-politically occurs throughout the world. Intergroup conflict and its consequences – genocide, ethnic cleansing, enslavement, human trafficking, armed conflict, pogroms, concentration camps, economic exclusion, social targeting, and political repression – have occurred in every region of the world throughout human history; this is more consistently the human condition than peace and prosperity. Today, sadly, in many if not most parts of the world, this is the experience of many people, accelerated by the effects of climate change contributing to massive human migration, famine, poverty, intimate partner violence, sexual exploitation, vulnerability to disease, police and military brutality, and terrorism (at the hands of the state and other actors such as militias and cartels).

What does it mean to be socio-politically targeted? I use the term to describe people who are members of racial or ethnic groups, tribes, and religions and who face multiple threats: violence, social denigration, cultural erasure, social and economic exclusion, bullying, and harassment. In many contexts, this also applies to women and people targeted due to their gender and/or sexual orientation. Often, this is a pattern that has lasted for centuries but is manifested in a unique historical moment. Wherever there is sociopolitical targeting, people are exposed to multiple sources of oppression and repeated threats, often multiple times a day, which lead to major psychosocial consequences – feeling unsafe, constant states of vigilance and activation, and an inability to calm and soothe oneself, depression, social isolation, feelings of hopelessness, and much more. Sometimes the threats are overt and violent, but they can also be expressed through social exclusion and discrimination, stereotypes, and microaggressions.

This book is intended for helping professionals who work with targeted people but what does it mean to be a helping professional? The term usually refers to social workers, psychologists, psychiatrists, nurses, counselors, and public health workers, as well as other related professions. Many are considered therapists, counselors, and coaches. All these professions require training and credentialing. Helping professionals are more prevalent in developed nations than in developing nations. The term also implies that there is a client or consumer who will be helped, immediately creating a hierarchy between the helper and the helped: one has training and expertise and is often being paid for their work, while the other *receives* help, implying a certain degree of dependency. This reified dichotomy also leaves out many people who play a helpful role in the community: volunteers, religious leaders, formal and informal community leaders, and others. Recognizing this problematic, for the purposes of this book, I will often use the term "helping professionals/volunteers," who are in a position to offer psychosocial support to individuals, families, and communities. I will also use the term "psychosocial worker" to denote the person offering the help, although sometimes the worker is engaging in the work on a volunteer basis. Comas-Diaz and Rivera (2020) describe workers as *accompanists*, as the worker is alongside of the person receiving support rather than leading or above them. Witness is another term that they use which I will also employ.

I am uncomfortable with the common term's client and consumer, as these are too passive and imply a dependent, receptive state, reflecting the professional practices and organizational structures of developed countries. Instead, I will use words like associate, collaborator, partner, and group/community members as they imply a more active partnership with the person/people offering support. I will also use the term "affected people," as this denotes people within socio-politically targeted groups.

Disasters, Catastrophes, and Pandemics and Their Consequences

Sociopolitical targeting and marginalization share some similarities to a cascading, at times unending disaster. Thus, I will briefly consider the psychosocial impact of major disasters, as they overlap with some of the psychosocial costs for people facing sociopolitical oppression, but there are also important differences, which I will consider.

There have always been and always will be disasters, catastrophes, and pandemics. Rosenfeld et al. (2005) describe six of their characteristics:

1. There is a sizeable, identifiable "footprint" – a locality or region experiences an overwhelming event that leads to substantial loss of life and property.
2. There is an identifiable beginning and end, often with a sudden onset, with long-lasting effects.
3. Large numbers of people are negatively affected.
4. The scope is so broad that there is a public dimension to the impact and consequences of a disaster.
5. The experience for people of a disaster is outside of their normal, everyday experiences.
6. There are psychological consequences of disasters such as stress, anxiety, depression, and trauma.

I have (Miller, 2012; Miller & Pescaroli, 2018) stressed the psychosocial consequences of disasters, which go beyond psychological reactions – e.g., the loss of social networks, neighborhoods, collective efficacy, social trust, and social cohesion. Summerfield (2000) talks about the loss of sociocultural worlds. All disasters occur within a "social ecology" (Figure 1.1) – the sociocultural context that shapes vulnerability, access to resources, power, privilege, differential outcomes, meaning-making, and what constitutes help and recovery (Miller, 2012; Miller & Pescaroli, 2018; Park & Miller, 2006).

Most disaster theorists note that there are different types of disasters (e.g., Halpern & Tramontin, 2007; Miller, 2012; Rosenfeld et al., 2005; Van den Eynde & Veno, 1999). One common category is that of natural disasters, such as floods, earthquakes, and tsunamis, sometimes referred to as "acts of God." A pandemic would fall within this category. Technological disasters are viewed as occurring due to human negligence, such as an oil spill, fire, or chemical explosion. And armed conflict, terrorism, and military attacks on civilians are characterized by human intention and malfeasance – one group is intentionally trying to harm members of another group.

But such categories are too rigid and essentialist and rarely are there clean-cut distinctions between types of disasters (Miller, 2012; Van den Eynde & Veno, 1999; Park & Miller, 2006). For example, the

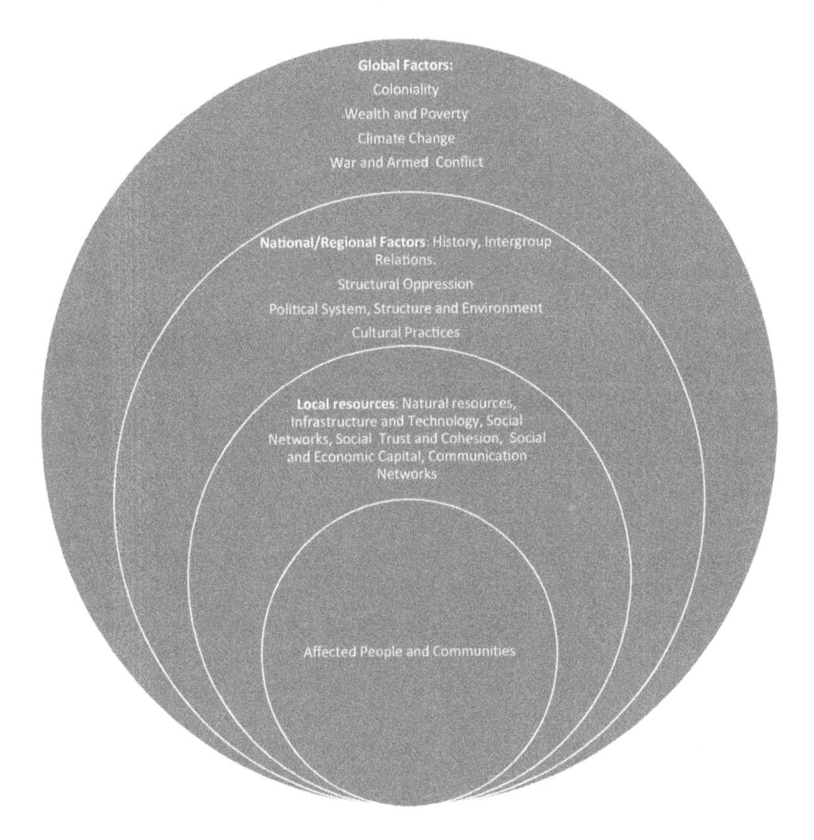

Figure 1.1 Social Ecology

hurricane in Hurricane Katrina was a "natural" event, but climate change resulting from human activity has increased the strength and frequency of hurricanes, and where people live when hurricanes strike and their consequent vulnerability, as well as who receives help and to what extent, are shaped by historical and contemporary racism (Park & Miller, 2006). For a long time, there was a mantra among disaster responders that disasters affected anyone living in a disaster area; all were vulnerable regardless of socioeconomic status and class. But this is not accurate – the social ecology of the disaster very much influences who is most vulnerable, who is socially targeted while they try and seek help (such as Black people in New Orleans who were not allowed to flee to certain neighborhoods and were sometimes viewed by authorities as criminals rather than victims), who is deemed worthy or unworthy of disaster relief, who does and does not have access to resources, and how quickly or slowly people are able to rebuild and recover from a disaster (Miller, 2012; Park & Miller, 2006).

An important dimension of disasters is the scale of destruction and scope of affected people (Miller, 2012). Quarantelli (2006) and Alexander (2000) argue that the most destructive disasters are catastrophes, destroying infrastructure, community resources, the mechanisms of government, social networks, and disrupting everyday routines that constitute communal life. Pescaroli and Alexander (2016) call the rippling effects of huge disasters "cascading disasters." For example, when there is an initial catastrophe, such as the massive Wenchuan earthquake in China in 2008, there are undulating effects: power grids fail, roads are blocked, communication systems are disrupted, and dams break leading to floods. Global pandemics such as COVID-19 can be viewed as cascading, catastrophic disasters – e.g., affecting the entire world, shutting down economies, overwhelming health-care systems, curtailing travel, and influencing and disrupting migration patterns.

Disasters are often not isolated events, separate from whatever else is going on, and there are often interacting disasters. In the United States in 2020, there was the COVID pandemic, interacting with historical and structural racism and white supremacy, a consistent pattern of police brutality directed toward Black and Brown people, economic collapse, and political ineptitude and divisiveness that contributed to the needless loss of tens of thousands of lives (Miller, 2020). Any of these catastrophes would have been destructive by themselves, but their interaction amplified their damaging impact, particularly for people of color and poor people. There were not only many deaths but folks also lost their jobs and homes, found their relationships with family and friends suspended, and due to political divisions and opportunism, people were misinformed, divided from one another, and further targeted by inflammatory political rhetoric.

Disasters lead to social isolation by disrupting and destroying social networks. They undermine a sense of safety and security. Community cohesion can dissipate. Individual and collective efficacy is often replaced by resignation and hopelessness. Affected people become emotionally activated and psychologically wounded. There are threats to people's health, cognitive processes are scrambled, feelings are heightened and may seem unmanageable, anxiety and depression commonplace, interpersonal relationships strained, and often there are the symptoms of trauma: hypervigilance, extreme agitation or numbing, flashbacks and ruminations playing in recurring loops, intrusive thoughts, as well as maladies such as depression and sleep and eating disorders. And yet people and communities are resilient and, despite the destructive impact of disasters, are able to not only survive but also grow and find new sources of strength and meaning (Miller, 2012, Miller & Pescaroli, 2018; Walsh, 2003).

A major driver in modern-day disasters is globalization and its many affects: global travel, interconnected economies, global communication networks, interpenetrating cultures. What remains constant are the legacies of colonialism that have shaped where wealth and power reside, the rules and structures of trade and economic development, which countries extract resources and money, and those (former colonies) that are plundered and despoiled of natural resources lose human capital and are blocked from achieving economic prosperity. Some of the ongoing consequences of modern globalization in the context of coloniality (Grousfoguel, 2013; Quijano, 2000) are mass migration, stateless people, human trafficking and exploitation, and modern slavery and economic servitude (Kara, 2017; Kochenov, 2019). All of this is accelerated and exacerbated by climate change.

Sociopolitical Targeting

Sociopolitical targeting is similar to a major disaster in that it is often overwhelming for targeted people and may lead to many detrimental outcomes – poor health, depression, trauma, chronic stress, social fragmentation, mistrust of authorities, low self-esteem, anger, alienation, and many of the negative consequences that occur in the wake of disasters. And as with disasters, there is a collective dimension; the targeting affects groups of people based on their social identities – e.g., race, gender, sexual orientation, socioeconomic class, and religion. But a major difference is that sociopolitical targeting is ongoing and built into the structure of society and its political discourses and is unrelenting. It occurs on a daily basis and is continuous, without a visible endpoint.

There can be official targeting – such as government-sanctioned harassment or violence – but it can also be unofficial, such as residents of a neighborhood trying to keep out people from particular racial and ethnic groups. An example of this was in Florida in 2012 when George Zimmerman spotted Trayvon Martin, a young African American man, walking through his neighborhood. Zimmerman followed Martin, confronted him, and then killed him. His rationale for racial profiling and violence was that he was protecting his neighborhood. He was acquitted by a jury. A similar pattern emerged in the assassination of Ahmaud Arbery in 2020, a Black man who was killed by three white men while jogging in Brunswick, Georgia.

As mentioned earlier, sociopolitical oppression is a sustained, systematic assault on personhood by virtue of perceived or actual membership in a social group (e.g., race, ethnicity, gender, religious, sexual orientation, political affiliations, etc.), which results in social targeting, discrimination, devaluing, loss and erasure of rights, harassment, and violence. Racism, sexism and misogyny, homophobia, and anti-immigrant fervor are all examples of sociopolitical oppression. This dynamic occurs in many countries representing a wide range of cultures, social structures, varied legal and civil rights and protections or lack thereof, religious traditions, and political systems. What is common among different types of sociopolitical oppression internationally is an "us vs. them" dynamic, which has often been shaped by colonialism and its legacies. These are some central themes that characterize sociopolitical oppression [much of this is taken from Miller and Wang (2017)] (Box 1.1).

Box 1.1 Characteristics of Sociopolitical Targeting

1. There is a hierarchy of human value.
2. Systematic targeting of people based on their social identities (e.g., race, ethnicity, religion, caste or class, gender, sexual orientation).
3. People and groups with targeted identities are harassed, bullied, attacked, excluded, and erased, lack equal opportunity, are denied rights that other identities have, and are often subject to state-sanctioned and/or unofficial violence, surveillance, and discipline.
4. Threats are ongoing and people who are socio-politically targeted must maintain vigilance, which can lead to an ongoing state of hyperarousal.
5. The erosion of social trust and a belief in the safety and fairness of society, members of other groups, and government.

- There is a hierarchy of human value and worth (Stanley, 2018). For example, White lives matter more than Black lives when pulled over by the police for traffic violations in the United States.
- People with certain social identities are systematically targeted. In any society, some identities are valued and privileged while others

devalued, but when there is sociopolitical oppression, the scope and degree of marginalization can lead to criminalization (e.g., "driving while Black"), social exclusion (e.g., segregation, ethnic cleansing), and dehumanization (e.g., not having full social or political rights).

- People with targeted identities are bullied, harassed, attacked, socially and economically marginalized, and erased, lack equal opportunity, lack rights that other groups have, and are often subject to state-sanctioned and/or unofficial violence, surveillance, and discipline.
- Victims are constantly aware of the ongoing threats that they face and therefore lack a sense of safety and security.
- Since the threats are ongoing, targeted people must maintain their vigilance, which can leave them in a perpetual state of hyperarousal.
- Social trust erodes as those who experience recurring social oppression have to constantly weigh up whether a person with power and privilege is trustworthy and expend energy decoding social interactions that may or may not betray underlying bias or patterns of inequality.

(See Box 1.2 for a summary of the consequences of sociopolitical targeting.)

Coloniality and Its Discontents

Coloniality is a historical-conceptual framework that traces our modern world through 600 years of colonialism and domination by the West (Europe and North America) (Grousfoguel, 2013; Quijano, 2000). The system of coloniality has privileged whiteness, wealth, maleness, capitalism, and Christianity over all other sociocultural ways of organizing society. Chavez-Dueñas et al. (2022) describe how indigenous Latina women suffered and continue to suffer interacting, simultaneous forms of oppression (racism, sexism, colonialism) which they term "racial-gendered colonialism." Diverse and heterogeneous indigenous societies were "collapsed" into categories of "other" – e.g., non-white, heathen, Indian, and Black (Quijano, 2000). This has dominated every facet of life: how labor is paid for or not paid for (e.g., slavery), who receives the profits from other people's labor, what is considered modern and civilized, and even how people think and what knowledge, epistemologies, and discourses are viewed as being legitimate or illegitimate. An insidious feature of coloniality is that it has a point of view that privileges particular ways of organizing society, its economic systems, gender roles, and racial hierarchies, but this is presented as a universal positionality, without acknowledgment that it is but one point of view (Grousfoguel, 2013; Mignolo & Walsh, 2018), one that sustains international and domestic hierarchies. It is viewed as the "natural" way of things (Quinjano). It becomes the immutable social norm of how society is structured (Sidanius & Pratto, 1999).

The inevitability and invisibility of coloniality inhabit people's minds and structure human relationships. It defines personhood (Summerfield, 2004) – what is collectively considered normal, healthy, professional, reasonable, rationale, and feasible – and becomes part of people's inner cognitive maps of the way the world is and should be, which in turn influences how people behave with members of their own groups and those of others. This defines who gets to be a full person and who is considered "other," marginalized and subordinate (Fanon, 1963; Gilroy, 2006; Miller & Schamess, 2000).

Coloniality dominates higher education and professional graduate schools. They reflect a geopolitics of knowledge and epistemology, with dominant narratives about how the world is and should be, intrinsically privileging the Western version, while marginalizing, erasing, and ignoring local histories and ways of knowing and understanding (Shahjahan et al., 2022). This not only shapes global discourses but also dominates who is worthy of help and how help is proffered, and who is socially positioned to offer and determine the nature of services. Coloniality has shaped curricula, the content of classes, how history, knowledge, and practice are framed, and how it is taught and has defined the hierarchical roles of teachers and students (Shahjahan et al., 2022).

Coloniality, therefore, shapes human services and clinical interventions (Miller, 2020). Where are clinicians and other human service workers trained? Who are their teachers? What do they read? What theories and conceptual frameworks are employed? What is considered "normal" and "healthy" human functioning? What modalities are privileged – e.g., "talk therapy"? What interventions are funded or not funded? Which organizations offer services? Who conducts evaluation about the efficacy of interventions and what is considered "evidence-based"? Who benefits from conducting such research and its "findings" (Silva et al., 2022)? Where are the professional associations that sanction licenses and practices located and who are their leaders? When answering these questions, it can help to compare countries such as the United States or United Kingdom with Sri Lanka and Uganda.

Human services and clinical interventions are in many ways the soft diplomacy of coloniality. A social order – domestically or internationally – is maintained either overtly or covertly; it teaches people how to be people and professionals how to help them be the right kind of person and it reinforces the social hierarchies that define who is privileged and who is targeted in society. Even for those who are well-intentioned, who have developed a critical consciousness about privilege and oppression, and who are committed to challenging hierarchies of social dominance, simply by living in a certain part of the world, by having citizenship in a developed nation, by having been trained in certain schools and being part of legitimized professional societies, by earning incomes common to developed nations, by living lifestyles that are "normal" to certain sectors of society or particular countries (however, moderate or humble), by having access to certain services (decent medical care, highways, Internet, banks, etc.) are socially situated, often in a different social location than those being helped. And what is always present is that some people, by virtue of their social identities, positions, where they live, and what they have access to are at risk, individually and collectively, physically, socially, emotionally, and psychologically

So, what is to be done about this? How can people living in developed nations or who have privileges within their countries practice in a way that does not reinforce existing hierarchies and boundaries of coloniality? How can people who are socially targeted or who live in developing nations be empowered without giving up their personhood? What can be salvaged, modified, reconfigured, and reimagined from Western psychology, psychiatry, social work, counseling, and public health, and what needs to change? What does liberatory practice look like?

Engaging with these questions is the core of this book. There are no simple answers, and complex interventions and antidotes are called for.

Challenges Posed by Coloniality for Helping Professionals

Coloniality therefore poses a number of challenges for helping professionals.

Box 1.2 Challenges Posed by Coloniality for Helping Professionals

1. Establishing trust and empathy when working from different social locations
2. The power of historical, cultural, and collective trauma and their legacies
3. The limits imposed by a system that pays professionals, who are often not part of a community, to work with individuals (rather than with communities)
4. Exporting the hegemony of Western coloniality and imposing this vision of personhood, epistemology, value, and validating on the rest of the world

Establishing Trust and Empathy From Different Social Locations

Trust is the foundation for all psychosocial interventions, and this is true for all forms of intervention. It is the foundation that allows a helping professional to engage with those in need – change often involves taking risks, experiencing difficult feelings and emotions, trying new behaviors, revisiting and reprocessing painful and traumatic experiences, and facing daunting challenges – trust is essential to embarking on this journey. Trust is essential to a meaningful relationship, which also involves feeling seen, heard, understood, respected, and believed in, which are all components of empathy. Trust needs to be earned and does not happen automatically as a result of good intentions.

All helping professionals are aware of the importance of trust and the vast majority work to establish a secure and trusting relationship with consumers. But there are many things that can get in the way. One is differences in personhood, mentioned earlier. This is not just recognizing that there are "cultural differences." Personhood (Miller, 2012, 2020; Miller & Pescaroli, 2018; Summerfield, 2004) is, as the term implies, what it means to be a person. What constitutes a sociocultural world? What is the meaning of history, all aspects of social identity, relationship to family, what is a crisis and what is not, what is healthy and normal, what progress looks like, what do we seek help for, and who do we go to? How does all of this shape what we think and feel and how we act?

It is not only about *differences* in personhood. Personhood is a passport to power, respect, prestige, and being treated as a full person for some and a set of limits, restrictions, and threats for others. We know that not all forms of citizenship are equal (Kochenov, 2019). For example, U.S. citizenship entails many more rights and privileges than being a citizen of Uganda, including where passports do or don't take us, access to resources, and how people are treated. Some examples of citizenship questions help to establish this (Kochenov):

- Can you be with people whom you love or are you forced to be separated from them?
- Can you speak your mind or face violence or legal sanctions for your opinions?
- Can you safely vote for your beliefs and values?
- If you require urgent medical care, can you access it?
- Can you move to wherever you would like to live?
- Can you decide what being in a family means to you in a way that is legally recognized?
- Are there legal protections for being a woman, queer, or a member of a particular racial or ethnic group, and are people with these identities socially and politically safe?

Inequalities in personhood track inequalities of citizenship. Those with passports of power and privilege, whether formal or informal, carry certain assumptions about how safe, fair, predictable, and manageable the world is, whether conscious or not. Much of this corresponds to one's social identities and the value that society places on these identities, but it is also a function of education, employment status, and one's role – such as being a helping professional. Thus, there is almost always an understanding and empathy gap needing to be bridged when some people, particularly professionals, are trying to help others. Even with the best of intentions, the most open of minds and hearts, this chasm exists. And whether helping professionals are comfortable with the hierarchies that go with their work, they are part of this social ecology, which shapes relationships with "consumers."

When there are shared aspects of social identity between the helper and their associates – e.g., race, ethnicity, social class, nationality/region, gender, and sexual orientation – there might be a higher expectation for empathic understanding, although this is not inevitable. And it is rare that any helping professional or volunteer shares the exact same social identities as the person in need, so there are almost always obvious differences as well as subtle distinctions. But the very process of coloniality that structures our differences in the first place makes it more likely that those offering help enter the relationship from a social position that involves greater power and privilege. Thus, the very presence of helping professionals and the interventions that they employ further the project of coloniality!

Another factor that interferes with establishing trusting working alliances is that helping professionals may evoke collaborators' negative associations with authority, lack of caring, arrogant entitlement, representing agents of social control, and activating fear of being exploited or brutalized. Helping professionals are not simply individuals while only their partners can be clustered and categorized into groups, being a helping professional and carrying certain social identities is also symbolic and representational; affected people may have good reason to not only mistrust but fear helping professionals, despite the best of intentions.

The very notion that certain kinds of problems – depression, trauma, family violence, and problems with thinking or working – require professional assistance is yet another assumption that imposes and privileges one version of personhood; a benefit of citizenship that is not universally shared around the world and within societies. And many things come with professionalism – boundaries, roles, regularity of contact, coverage, and paying for services, to name a few. Not only is professionalism a part of an internal sense of self, but it is also part of the structure of society, encoded in laws and regulations, such as licensing, legitimizing what is considered evidence-based, and what constitutes malpractice. I am not suggesting that these are inherently problematic – they serve to protect many people from ill-intentioned, irresponsible, and iatrogenic affects – but if we are going to decolonize what helping looks like, the taken-for-granted rules of engagement need to be interrogated and examined.

I will consider ways of challenging these hierarchies, crevasses, and imbalances between professionals and citizens later in the book, but structurally, this is a common pattern: those in a position to help often come from developed countries with greater resources or if working within their country enjoy greater privileges by virtue of their social identities (e.g., class, race, gender, etc.) and (even for those with similar social identities to their partners) due to their access to educational and organizational capital. And this in turn poses challenges to forming relationships, alliances, and developing trust.

The Power of Historical, Cultural, and Collective Trauma and a System that Pays Professionals to Work With Individuals

Trauma is often viewed in individual terms – someone has a traumatic experience and is left with a traumatic reaction and symptoms. But trauma is also historical and collective and often both; intergenerational trauma usually stems from historical trauma that was experienced collectively (e.g., the Jewish Holocaust; genocide of indigenous people in the Americas, chattel slavery, ethnic cleansing throughout the globe). Even when trauma is within a family – e.g., child maltreatment – it frequently reflects historical and collective trauma experienced by parents and their ancestors, as well as state/societal violence and oppression that are historical and/or contemporary (Heberle et al., 2020). For example, the complex web of anti-Black racism that stems from chattel slavery that extends through segregation, voter suppression, Jim Crow, the intricate web of institutional racism, and current police brutality toward Black people has traumatic consequences that are often viewed through the lens of individual pathology (Garran et al., 2021; Heberle et al., 2020). These ideas will be developed further in Chapters 2 and 3.

And yet human service professionals, by virtue of being professionals, expect to be paid for their work, and the system of payment is geared toward working with individuals. Mental health agencies, social service organizations, and private practitioners rely on predictable major sources of funding: public allocations, specific governmental support for programs, foundational grants, reimbursement from private and public insurance programs, and out-of-pocket payments by individuals. While there are grants from the government and foundations that support psychosocial interventions for families, or "at-risk" groups [the term "at-risk" locates the problem with the group and not the society that places the group at risk!], as well as neighborhood support, development, and empowerment, the preponderance of responses to trauma occurs through the mental health system, which is dominated by insurance reimbursement. What is a historical, collective, and societal process that shapes collective oppression and its consequences becomes an individual problem, requiring diagnoses, professional interventions, and third-party payment.

Exporting Coloniality

This system of conceptualization and reimbursement exists in developed nations, but it is being exported to developing nations. When social work or psychology emerged in developing or non-Western areas of the world, even when it seeks to maintain a sense of uniqueness – e.g., as social work emerges in China as a profession there is a mantra that it is *Chinese* social work – the coloniality of the West kicks in. The theories of human development and personhood, the locus of intervention (usually individuals and families), the ways of helping, and the techniques of intervention are only the tip of this process. Programs that train helping professionals in developed countries often partner with schools in developing countries or those where professions are newly emerging – sending professors, using their textbooks, and adapting their syllabi.

Helping professionals are taught by professors, trainers, and supervisors and require credentials to engage in professional work. Professors seek job security and tenure, and this requires publishing in "high-impact" journals. Even in a powerful, proud country like China, with its long-standing historical record of withstanding Western exploitation and domination, academics are respected, promoted, and gain job security through publishing in Western-based high-impact journals. I taught for a number of years in a Chinese University's social work program and developed scholarly partnerships with a number of my colleagues; the rating of a journal's impact where we published our articles was a much greater factor for their careers than mine. And the professional associations and codes of ethics for professions in developing countries are often viewed in comparison to those existing in developed nations.

How Can We Navigate These Challenges and Barriers?

Although I have described historical and contemporary challenges to the very project of being helping professionals, I am a helping professional and believe that there is a constructive role for us. This involves addressing what I have presented as challenges in this chapter as well as reimagining a pathway forward that does not replicate hierarchies, does not place consumers at risk or in danger, does not further coloniality, where indigenous knowledge and practices are reclaimed, and that offers a framework that is collaborative and generative. And a related task is to critique and reconstruct the language that we use to describe "helping professionals" and "clients," "patients," and "consumers."

When working with socially targeted population, either as a paid professional or volunteer, there are principles and practices which help to decolonize the process of offering psychosocial support and foster collaboration and social justice, which will be developed throughout this book and are summarized here (Box 1.3).

Box 1.3 Decolonizing Psychosocial Work

1. Radical transparency between psychosocial workers and the person with whom they are collaborating.
2. Engaging collaborators as full partners in any process of change with equal rights to determine the direction of the work.
3. Constant attention to the dynamics of power and hierarchy and society and how they are manifested in the relationship between the worker and their collaborator.
4. Collaborative training of local and indigenous people to better enable them to help their own communities.
5. Liberatory psychosocial work should lead to mutual transformation.
6. Understanding interlocking oppressions and intersectional identities.
7. Understanding and integrating historical and structural factors when working with a person's inner world.
8. Recognizing the historical and collective context in which an individual exists.
9. Valuing "pluriversal" (Mignolo & Walsh, 2018) ways of knowing, including blending Western and indigenous knowledge.
10. Recognizing both the destructive power of historical trauma and the collective and individual resilience, wisdom, strength, and beauty necessary for survival.
11. Avoiding therapeutic neutrality, sharing values, motives, social commitments, and personal/professional goals.
12. Consider and analyze the role of the state in maintaining systemic oppression.
13. Engaging in multilevel and multisystemic interventions.
14. Collaborating with clients and engaging in advocacy and collective action.
15. Utilizing a psychosocial capacity-building approach, building on strengths, cultural practices, and resilience.

Radical Transparency

Radical transparency means that there is a contract between the worker/volunteer and their collaborator/partner where the worker commits to sharing their assumptions, agendas, reasons for asking certain questions, any hypothesis that they are developing about what is happening, what might help, and negotiating these with the partner (Miller, 2020). Comas-Diaz and Rivera (2020) describe this as "radical openness." This is ethical practice in general but is essential when working with people who are consistently being targeted, are at risk, and may understandably be wary of offers of support.

Engaging Collaborators as Full Participants

In order to prevent unnecessary hierarchies from forming, which can replicate patterns of power and helplessness, those people being supported should be considered full participants and co-authors of the work. This is not informed consent but rather active, agentic, and egalitarian collaboration (Miller, 2020; Rivera & Comas-Diaz, 2020). It entails stepping out of the role of "expert" and reconceptualizing the process of psychosocial support and intervention as not only a shared one of alliance and partnership but also where the worker displays what Comas-Diaz (2020) calls "radical humility," where there both parties are open to experiencing the full spectrum of life experiences.

Constant Attention to Power and Hierarchy

The foregoing points require that psychosocial workers consistently see, recognize, understand, and are responsive to how power is manifested and the hierarchies that it creates. This involves developing a critical consciousness and putting it into action (Kang & O'Neil, 2018). Rivera and Comas-Diaz (2020) draw on Paolo Freire's insights when making this point. People who experience oppression not only encounter a web of barriers, threats, and constricted opportunities but often have internalized these social arrangements. The same is true of those with privilege, who are often unaware of how they are amassing and employing power, including well-intentioned efforts to support those with less social privileges. Agency and control are central to this and thus the need for an egalitarian, collaborative approach. But this will not occur without ongoing praxis and attention to and vigilance about how power and hierarchy are present.

Whenever Possible Utilize Training of Trainer Approaches

One way of engaging collaborators as full associates and reducing hierarchies is to share knowledge and skills held by the helping professional so that people who are indigenous to the targeted group can adapt and rework them to be used with their group members. Helping professionals may, therefore, have less of a direct intervention role but serve as a mentor, resource, trainer, and consultant to those from the affected community who are the main drivers of interventions (Miller, 2012, 2020; Miller & Pescaroli, 2018).

Liberatory Psychosocial Work Should Lead to Mutual Transformation

Lack of safety is part and parcel of being a member of a socially targeted group. Liberatory psychosocial work aims for liberation and transformation and is geared toward strength and empowerment; the process involves a certain degree of vulnerability as people explore feelings, thinking, behaviors, and relationships. In order for this to occur, the person who is offering services and support should also be open to being vulnerable and transformed by the process so that risk and change are mutual. A characteristic of coloniality-informed psychosocial engagement is that the worker is more detached, objective, and taking fewer risks than their "client." Liberatory psychosocial practice means viewing the goal of intervention as emancipation and liberation from the psychological, emotional, institutional, and other structural shackles that have accrued over centuries of coloniality and white supremacy, which requires workers and volunteers to also shed the remnants of coloniality that shape who takes the risks, who is open to change, and who will be transformed. Comas-Diaz (2020) makes a similar argument – when therapists or other psychosocial workers engage in their work from this perspective, there is the potential for mutual liberation.

Interacting Oppressions, Intersectional Identities

Oppression involves interlocking forces – e.g., stereotyping, social exclusion, differential power and privilege, unequal opportunity, respect for some but not for others – that differentially have an impact on people. Intersectionality refers to the ways that we all have complex social identities, which often carry a mixture of privileges and oppression, and these identities interact, rather than being standalone aspects of personhood; the effects of interacting oppressions are not additive but cumulative (Garran et al., 2021). For example, people who are Black, transgender, and poor in the U.S. experience a far greater level of vulnerability and violence than do those who are White, cis-gendered male, and wealthy. These interacting systems of oppression are endemic to social institutions (Heberle et al., 2020; Rivera & Comas-Diaz, 2020). Psychosocial work with oppressed populations necessitates an understanding of interacting oppressions and intersectional identities.

The Inner and the Outer Are Inseparable

Oppression and its consequent trauma and psychosocial needs are always an interaction of psychological factors, both individual and collective, with systemic and structural realities (Chavez-Dueñas et al., 2022; Garran et al., 2021; Miller, 2012; Miller & Pescaroli, 2018; Rivera & Comas-Diaz, 2020; Quinones-Rosado, 2020; Brave Heart & DeBruyn, 1998). When responding to people's psycho-emotional needs, the coloniality tendency has been to act as if these can be considered separately from the historical and structural forces that have shaped those needs. They are never separate! Failure to integrate the structural with the intrapsychic not only does not lead to emancipation, but it also continues a process of dependency, subordination, and individual blame and self-blame.

The Individual Exists in a Historical and Collective Context

All of us are shaped by our histories, and for members of oppressed groups, the history of oppression and resilience is particularly salient. Historical, collective, and intergenerational experiences and trauma all converge in the present moment (Garran et al., 2021; Heberle et al., 2020; Miller, 2012; Quinones-Rosado, 2020; Rivera & Comas-Diaz, 2020; Brave Heart & DeBruyn, 1998). The welfare of the individual is inextricably linked to that of the collectivity. This has important implications for the locus of intervention – individuals are helped by work that leads to greater group and collective efficacy; grieving losses from the past while recognizing intergenerational resistance is relevant to helping people as they confront their present-day circumstances. For example, as Brave Heart and DeBruyn, Brave Heart et al. (2020), and Marsh et al. (2015) argue, if trying to help an indigenous person grappling with chemical dependency, family, and interpersonal violence, it is critical to consider how this is related to chronic racism and oppression and unresolved, historical/intergenerational trauma and grief.

Blending Indigenous and Western Practices

There are many excellent ideas about how to help people experiencing psychosocial suffering that emanated from Western psychology, psychiatry, and social work, e.g., putting the client front and center, theories about intrapsychic growth and development, understanding trauma, a range of intervention methodologies, family systems theory and family therapy, theories of groupwork and group therapy, and much more. These professions and the concepts that they use have helped millions of people. However, they are not the only source of knowledge about helping people to recover from crisis and catastrophe, and nor are they as universal as they have been presented over time. Although Western psychology and its cousins have embraced the idea of cultural sensitivity and responsiveness, they have not centralized the range of personhood and epistemologies that exist in the world. How we understand ourselves and what sense we make of the world is critical to healing and resilience. There is no objective, neutral way of approaching this, and yet most Western psychosocial interventions present themselves in this manner. The evidence in "evidence-based practices" is not universal: what evidence is collected and who collects and interprets it is not neutral and reflects the legacies of coloniality and Western dominance. Knowledge comes from a situated subject position and is never complete and what is often thought of as evidence is the knowledge that comes from above rather than below (Lykes & Távara, 2020).

When I use the term "indigenous," I mean local to a given population and reflective of historical collective sociocultural practices. As mentioned earlier, personhood is shaped by these practices, as well as coloniality. Thus, many practitioners and researchers working with populations that have been historically oppressed and marginalized and continue to face similar threats argue that interventions and research should reflect a blend of Western and indigenous traditions (e.g., Brave Heart, 1998; Brave Heart et al., 2020; Brave Heart & DeBruyn, 1998; Comas-Diaz, 2020; Lykes & Távara, 2020; Marsh et al., 2015; Miller, 2012; Miller & Pescaroli, 2018; Rivera & Comas-Diaz, 2020). Mignolo and Walsh (2018) describe this as "pluriversal" ways of knowing; Western ideas are included in a pantheon of epistemologies but are not privileged. Marsh et al. quote Chief Charles Labrador as calling this "Two-eyed Seeing." As Brave Heart and DeBruyn, Braveheart et al., and Marsh et al. argue, when working with Native Americans, it is harmful to only focus on the internal struggles of individuals in the present moment without understanding the historical sources of grief, and to value extended family, community, shared history, and collective survival as essential for healing and recovery.

Where There Is Historical Trauma There Is Also Resilience

In the next chapter, I will consider historical, intergenerational, and collective trauma in greater detail. Any model of recovery, healing, and well-being must consider the terrible cost of coloniality, white supremacy, pervasive sexism and misogyny, heterosexism, ableism, and religious oppression passed down structurally and interpersonally over generations when working with the consequent "soul wounds" (Brave Heart & DeBruyn, 1998; Marsh et al., 2015). But alongside of historical trauma, there is collective and individual resilience and survival as well as strength and beauty. Ortega-Williams et al. (2021) offer an epigraph by Kazru Hega: "If we carry intergenerational trauma (and we do) then we also carry intergenerational wisdom. It's in our genes and our DNA."

There Is No Such Thing as Therapeutic Neutrality

Therapeutic neutrality is a fiction (Miller, 2020). There is no neutrality in a world shaped by structural forces that delineate psychosocial services and interventions. Everyone is embodied and socially located, and psychosocial workers rely on theories and concepts that reflect their training, which if left intact and uninterrogated replicates colonial Eurocentric dominance. What are the worker's identities? Their personhood? How is the worker socially situated? What are the worker's values and beliefs, how were they trained, and how does this influence their approach to their work? Partners should understand and have access to worker subjectivity and the ways that this interacts with their personhood and subjectivity. Abandoning neutrality also means sharing political and social commitments so that associates can decide for themselves whether or not there is sufficient alignment for them to benefit from a particular worker.

Actively Consider the Role of the State

In different countries, communities, and contexts, the role of the state in promulgating oppression and violence varies. This is of course shaped not only by history but also by the dynamics of intergroup conflict and current power arrangements. Does the state consider some citizens to be worthier of human rights and access to resources based on race, ethnicity, religion, gender, or sexual orientation? Are there legal protections for targeted and vulnerable populations? If there are legal rights and protections are they being fairly administered or undermined or ignored? Does the state have social welfare policies, benefits, resources, and protections available to people?

Sadly, the state is often the perpetrator of violence, such as racialized police violence and brutality and separating children who are migrants from their families in the United States (Heberle et al., 2020). Thus, the role of the state in placing associates at risk or failing to protect people must be assessed when working with people who are members of oppressed groups. And the positionality and relationship between the psychosocial worker and the state must also be critically assessed, as this will influence what is and is not possible. Is the worker at risk? Is the worker protected while their collaborators are in danger?

Multilevel/Multisystemic Interventions

Psychosocial workers need to include a structural analysis to accompany micro-interventions, such as counseling and therapy and be willing to intervene at the structural level as well as working with consumer's internal worlds. Since the "trauma" experienced by people who are socially and politically targeted is an interaction between inner wounds and interpersonal factors with structural and systemic realities, then interventions should reflect that reality. The hard boundary between doing intra-psychic work and walling that off from systemic interventions serves workers and their professions but does not necessarily meet the needs of people experiencing chronic, multisystemic oppression. The Interagency Standing Committee, which is an international organization that has developed best practices for disaster response and which advises the United Nations has said that while some people require specialized counseling and therapy in the wake of catastrophes, the majority need economic security, safety, social networks, and group and family interventions (Bragin, 2014).

Advocacy, Agency, and Collective Action

As mentioned earlier, worker neutrality is a fiction when trying to support people suffering from sociopolitical oppression. Although "therapeutic neutrality" was a principle that was enshrined with the development of psychoanalysis, spreading to other forms of psychotherapy, this principle grew out of a privileged, white bourgeois milieu. When clients are experiencing police brutality directed toward Black people, or continuing to suffer from the intergenerational effects of state-mandated boarding schools for indigenous children, or are terrified that they and their families will be harassed or locked up by the government because they have expressed their political beliefs, they do not seek therapeutic neutrality. Rather they need full-throttled advocacy – both directly and toward the sources of their systemic oppression.

Related to this, it is important that affected people are in charge of the efforts to confront the sources of their oppression, with psychosocial workers as allies. Given what was said earlier about not replicating hierarchies of power and privilege, having the workers/volunteers "take charge" dampens the agency of affected people. And collective action is always more powerful than individual action (Comas-Diaz & Rivera, 2020), not only exhibiting solidarity and strength but also fostering social networks of resistance as well, which leads to a greater sense of safety and empowerment.

Using a Psychosocial Capacity-Building Model

Psychosocial capacity building incorporates all of the aforementioned points (Miller, 2012; Miller & Pescaroli, 2018). It is a model that integrates internal reactions with external realities and psychological processes with structural factors. It focuses on building the capacity of individuals, families, systems, and communities and is strengths-based, recognizing that individual and collective healing are inextricably connected. History, culture, and personhood are central to understanding what has gone wrong and what is needed to recover. Indigenous leadership and practices are prioritized whenever possible. And in a world of helpers informed and structured by coloniality, psychosocial capacity building is cautious and wary about the iatrogenic effects of intervention.

Conclusion and Outline for the Book

In this chapter, I have described how coloniality and structural oppression not only place targeted people and populations in constant danger but how this has also shaped the structure, dynamics, and hierarchies present in psychosocial interventions. I compared the similarities and the differences between the impact of disasters and catastrophes and sociopolitical oppression; as the latter is ongoing, it can leave people in a consistent state of dread, threat, and activation. The concept of coloniality was presented as a central historical framework for considering who is oppressed and privileged, who helps and who is being helped, and how this has relied on a one-dimensional vision of personhood, erasing indigenous knowledge and significant cultural differences about what it means to be a person. Given this, I explored the challenges for helping professionals who do not want to collude with or collaborate with the oppression of the people who they seek to help. I then shared 14 principles to guide decolonized, liberatory psychosocial work, derived from my experiences and past writing (e.g., Garran et al., 2021; Miller, 2012, 2020; Miller & Pescaroli, 2018) noting when there were similarities with the approach of liberation psychologists (e.g., Comas-Diaz & Rivera, 2020), who independently came to similar conclusions.

These themes will now be explored and deepened in the following chapters.

Chapter 2 – Historical and Collective Trauma and Their Consequences

The roots of oppression are manifold, and the consequences are profound. Two interacting factors are historical/collective trauma and structural oppression. Having introduced these concepts in Chapter 1, they will be explored in greater depth over the next two chapters. In Chapter 2, I will consider the similarities and differences between intergenerational trauma, historical trauma, collective trauma, and cultural trauma. How have these processes shaped the experiences of oppressed groups in many different social contexts? The concept of "social ecology" (Park & Miller, 2006; Miller, 2012; Miller & Pescaroli, 2018) will be developed as a helpful framework for understanding the factors that lead to a unique constellation of sociopolitical and cultural variables that influence the consequences of historical and collective trauma.

Chapter 3 – The Collective, Interpersonal, and Intrapersonal Consequences of Structural Oppression

This chapter is Part 2 of the preceding chapter, as historical and collective trauma did not end, rather the forces that contributed to this continue to plague and act to subjugate socio-politically targeted groups. How is structural and systemic oppression consistently manifested and how are they also shaped by social ecology? And how does contemporary structural oppression interact with historical and collective trauma and what are its consequences for individuals, families, communities, and social groups? The concepts of social identity and intersectionality will be central to this exploration.

Chapter 4 – Violence

Chapter 4 considers degrees of violence – from ongoing microaggressions to armed conflict and torture – and the specific consequences of being exposed to direct or indirect violence. "Violence" is a term that is used to describe a range of violent and aggressive actions directed toward individuals and groups. There are different forms of violence – physical, political, interpersonal, intergroup, emotional, and psychological. All forms of violence have an impact on individuals, families, groups, and communities, and often there are multiple forms of violence occurring at the same time – e.g., police shooting an unarmed Black man while calling him racial epithets. And violence is also witnessed by others – such as the man's child seeing the aforementioned shooting.

I will present a conceptual frame – the spectrum of violence – which will illustrate similarities and differences between varying types of violence. There will be a consideration of who is most vulnerable to different types of violence and information about which organizations try to help affected people and what they offer. The barriers and impediments to helping people who are still in the midst of sociopolitical catastrophes – such as an armed conflict – will be described and the implications for offering response services considered. All forms of violence will be covered in this chapter, although the more extreme forms of violence – e.g., armed conflict, physical assaults, torture – will receive the most attention.

Chapter 5 – Liberatory, Decolonial Psychosocial Capacity Building: Guiding Ethical Principles

As my approach to psychosocial capacity building is collaborative and seeks to decolonize, this chapter articulates ethical principles that help to inform this work, without being overly proscriptive. It offers a scaffolding of non-hierarchical partnerships. It establishes the foundation for a framework discussed in the next chapter.

Chapter 6 – Liberatory, Decolonizing Psychosocial Capacity Building: A Framework for Collaboration

This chapter offers a framework for what workers/volunteers can actually do when working with their collaborators. It draws from the work of indigenous scholars and practitioners and enumerates tasks for the helping professional/volunteer. It discusses the importance of critical social awareness by the worker/volunteer when engaging in psychosocial capacity building and elaborates on, expands, and develops the intervention approaches discussed in this chapter.

Chapter 7 – Responding to Critical Psychosocial Needs

Sociopolitical targeting results in many psychosocial challenges to individuals, families, and communities. This chapter considers critical psychosocial needs, such as creating a sense of safety and responding to trauma, and how to respond to them. It cautiously examines how Western interventions can be integrated with indigenous knowledge and wisdom. I suggest the use of activities in addition to psychotherapeutic interventions and also share helpful mindfulness strategies. Sustaining hope and maintaining efficacy are key themes.

Chapter 8 – Collective Resilience While Facing Oppression

A great deal has been written about sources of individual resilience, but given that this book is considering sociopolitical targeting and oppression, it is important to weave these insights into an exploration of the sociocultural factors that make groups and individuals resilient. How can psychosocial workers foster, incubate, and stimulate such resilience? How does collective resilience interact with individual resilience? This will include a consideration of the importance of social networks, social cohesion, and social trust. I will consider impediments to fostering sociocultural resilience as well as ways of navigating such challenges.

Chapter 9 – Psychosocial Support for Immigrants and Refugees

Climate change, war, violence, and sociopolitical repression are strong drivers of immigration. Coloniality continues to shape global responses to migrants, refugees, and asylum seekers. The perils of migration and immigration combined with prior exposure to conflict and terror and the subsequent experiences of ongoing social oppression in the new country create a unique mix of threats and challenges for people. In addition to the types of stress, vulnerability, and trauma described in earlier chapters, there is also the dislocation and disorientation of being in a different culture, society, and physical and political environment. I consider the challenges and threats experienced by immigrants with targeted social identities before, during, and after embarking on their immigration journey, particularly for refugees and asylum seekers. This chapter will consider important factors that need to be considered by helping professionals and offer suggestions about ways of working that build on migrant agency, resourcefulness, strength, and wisdom.

Chapter 10 – Collective and Individual Self-Care and Critical Awareness

This chapter reviews the risks and challenges for helping professionals/volunteers in general and particularly when working with people experiencing social targeting and oppression. I consider how people can prepare themselves for this work and care for themselves and others while engaged with their collaborators. In addition to examining self-care for individuals, I consider the ethical obligations of organizations and employers to support self-care. Self-care is also a collective issue and responsibility and collective self-care and individual self-care are intertwined. As with other chapters, I critique a strictly Western, Eurocentric view of self-care. I also argue that self-care and critical awareness are closely related and give examples of two programs that illustrate this: the critical conversations model (Kang & O'Neill, 2018) and witness to witness model (Weingarten et al., 2020).

In all of the chapters, I include vignettes and case illustrations often drawn from examples shared by scholars and practitioners of color as well as from my own domestic and international work. I hope that readers will draw on this book to critique hegemonic Western ways of understanding people and how to help them when they are in need, to integrate an understanding of historical and sociocultural factors when dealing with psychosocial issues, and evince a willingness to integrate indigenous, non-Western wisdom and practices in their work in order to maintain a pluralistic understanding of the complexity of human suffering and well-being in a range of sociocultural contexts. And more than anything, I hope that the book contributes to human professionals/volunteers approaching our work with humility, critical self-awareness, and a commitment to collaboration and sharing.

References

Alexander, D. (2000). *Confronting catastrophe*. New York: Oxford University Press.

Bragin, M. (2014). Clinical social work with survivors of disaster and terrorism: A social ecological approach. In J. Brandell (Ed.). *Essentials of clinical social work* (2nd ed., pp. 366–401). One Thousand Oaks, CA: Sage Publishing.

Brave Heart, M.Y.H. (1998). The American Indian holocaust: Healing historical unresolved grief. *American Indian and Alaska Native Mental Health Research*, *8*(2): 56. DOI: 10.5820/aian.0802.1998.60

Brave Heart, M.Y.H., Chase, J., Myers, O., Elkins, J., Skipper, B., Schmitt, C., Mootz, J., & Waldorf, V.A. (2020). *Iwankapyia* American Indian pilot clinical trial. *Psychotherapy*, *57*(2): 184–196. DOI: 10.1037/pst0000267

Brave Heart, M.Y.H., & DeBruyn, L.M. (1998). The American Indian holocaust: Healing historical unresolved grief. *American Indian and Alaska Native Mental Health Research*, *8*(2): 60–82. DOI: 10.5820/aian.0802.1998.60

Chavez-Dueñas, N.Y., Adames, H.Y., & Perez-Chavez, J.G. (2022). Anti-colonial futures: Indigenous Latinx women healing from the wounds of racial gendered colonialism. *Women & Therapy*. DOI: 10.1080/02703149.2022.2097593

Comas-Diaz, L. (2020). Liberation psychotherapy. In L. Comas-Diaz & E.T. Rivera (Eds.). *Liberation psychology: Theory, method, practice and social justice* (pp. 169–185). Washington, DC: American Psychological Association Press.

Comas-Diaz, L., & Rivera, E.T. (2020). Conclusion: Liberation psychology-crossing borders into new frontiers. In L. Comas-Diaz & E.T. Rivera (Eds.). *Liberation psychology: Theory, method, practice and social justice* (pp. 283–295). Washington, DC: American Psychological Association Press.

Fanon, F. (1963). *The wretched of the earth*. New York: Grove Publishing.

Garran, A.M., Werkmeister-Rozas, L.M., Kang, H.K., & Miller, J. (2021). *Racism in the United States: Implications for the helping professions* (3rd ed.). New York: Springer Publishing.

Gilroy, P. (2006). *Postcolonial melancholia*. New York: Columbia University Press.

Grousfoguel, R. (2013). Decolonizing post-colonial studies and paradigms of political-economy: Transmodernity, decolonial thinking, and global coloniality. *Transmodernity: Journal of Peripheral Cultural Production of the Luso-Hispanic World*, *1*(1). https://escholarship.org/uc/item/21k6t3fq

Halpern, J., & Tramontin, M. (2007). *Disaster mental health: Theory and practice*. Belmont, CA: Thompson Learning.

Heberle, A.E., Obus, E.A., & Gray, S.A.O. (2020). An intersectional perspective on the intergenerational transmission of trauma and state-perpetrated violence. *Journal of Social Issues*. DOI: 10.1111/josi.12404.

Kang, H.K., & O'Neill, P. (2018). Teaching note – Constructing critical conversations: A model for facilitating classroom dialogue for critical learning. *Journal of Social Work Education*, *54*(1): 187–193. DOI: 10.1080/10437797.2017.1341857

Kara, S. (2017). *Modern slavery*. New York: Columbia University Press.

Kochenov, D. (2019). *Citizenship*. Cambridge, MA: The MIT Press.

Lykes, M.B., & Távara, G. (2020). Feminist participatory action research: Coconstructing liberation psychological praxis through dialogic relationality and critical reflexivity. In L. Comas-Diaz & E.T. Rivera (Eds.). *Liberation psychology: Theory, method, practice and social justice* (pp. 111–130). Washington, DC: American Psychological Association Press.

Marsh, T.B., Coholic, D., Cote-Meek, S., & Najavits, L.M. (2015). Blending aboriginal and Western healing methods to treat intergenerational trauma with substance abuse disorder with aboriginal peoples who live in Northeastern, Ontario, Canada. *Harm Reduction Journal.* DOI: 10.1186/s12954-015-0046-1

Mignolo, W.D., & Walsh, C.E. (2018). *On decoloniality: Concepts, analytics, praxis.* Durham, NC: Duke University Press.

Miller, J. (2020). The four pandemics. *Smith College Studies in Social Work.* DOI: 10.1080/00377317.2020.1832944

Miller, J., & Schamess, G. (2000). The discourse of denigration and the creation of other. *Journal of Sociology and Social Welfare, 27*(3): 39–62.

Miller, J., & Wang, X. (2017). When there are no therapists: A psychoeducational group for people who have experienced social disasters. *Smith College Studies in Social Work.* DOI: 10.1080/00377317.2018.1404293

Miller, J.L. (2012). *Psychosocial capacity building in response to disasters.* New York: Columbia University Press.

Miller, J.L., & Pescaroli, G. (2018). Psychosocial capacity building in response to cascading disasters: A culturally informed approach. *International Journal of Disaster Risk Reduction, 30*: 164–171. DOI: 10.1016/j.ijdrr.2018.04.018

Ortega-Williams, A., Beltran, R., Schultz, K., Henderson, Z.R., Colon, L., & Teyra, C. (2021). An integrated historical trauma and posttraumatic growth framework: A cross-cultural exploration. *Journal of Trauma & Dissociation.* DOI: 10.1080/15299732.2020.1869106

Park, Y., & Miller, J. (2006). The social ecology of Hurricane Katrina: Rewriting the discourse of "natural" disasters. *Smith College Studies in Social Work, 76*(3): 9–24.

Pescaroli, G., & Alexander, D. (2016). Critical infrastructure, panarchies, and the vulnerability paths of cascading disasters. *Natural Hazards, 82*: 175–192.

Quarantelli, E.L. (2006). Catastrophes are different from disasters: Some implications for crisis planning and managing drawn from Hurricane Katrina. *Items: Insights from the Social Sciences.* https://items.ssrc.org/understanding-katrina/catastrophes-are-different-from-disasters-some-implications-for-crisis-planning-and-managing-drawn-from-katrina/

Quijano, A. (2000). Coloniality of power and Eurocentrism in Latin America. *International Sociology, 15*(2): 215–232.

Quinones-Rosado, R. (2020). Liberation psychology and racism. In L. Comas-Diaz & E.T. Rivera (Eds.). *Liberation psychology: Theory, method, practice and social justice* (pp. 53–68). Washington, DC: American Psychological Association Press.

Rivera, E.T., & Comas-Diaz, L. (2020). Introduction. In L. Comas-Diaz & E.T. Rivera (Eds.). *Liberation psychology: Theory, method, practice and social justice* (pp. 3–13). Washington, DC: American Psychological Association Press.

Rosenfeld, L.B., Caye, J.S., Ayalon, O., & Lahad, M. (2005). *When their world falls apart: Helping families and children manage the effects of disasters*. Silver Springs, MD: NASW Press.

Shahjahan, R.A., Estera, A.L., Surla, K.L., & Edwards, K.T. (2022). "Decolonizing" curriculum and pedagogy: A comparative review across disciplines and global higher education contexts. *Review of Educational Research*, *92*(1): 73–113. DOI: 10.3102/00346543211042423.

Sidanius, J., & Pratto, F. (1999). *Social dominance: An intergroup theory of human oppression*. New York: Cambridge University Press.

Silva, J.M., Fernandez, J.S., & Nguyen, A. (2022). "And now we resist": Three testimonios on the importance of decoloniality within psychology. *Journal of Social Issues*, *78*: 388–412. DOI: 10.1111/josi12449.

Stanley, J. (2018). *How fascism works: The politics of us and them*. New York: Random House Publishers.

Summerfield, D. (2000). Childhood, war, refugeedom and "trauma": Three core questions for mental health professionals. *Transcultural Psychiatry*, *37*: 417–433.

Summerfield, D. (2004). Cross cultural perspectives on the medicalisation of human suffering. In G. Rosen (Ed.). *Posttraumatic stress disorder: Issues and controversies* (pp. 233–247). New York: John Wiley.

Van den Eynde, J., & Veno, A. (1999). Disastrous events: An empowerment model of community healing. In R. Gist & B. Lubin (Eds.). *Response to disaster: Psychosocial, community and ecological approaches* (pp. 167–192). New York: Brunner/Mazel.

Walsh, F. (2003). Crisis, trauma, and challenge: A relational resilience approach for healing, transformation, and growth. *Smith College Studies in Social Work*, *74*(1): 49–71.

Weingarten, K., Gavlven-Duran, A.R., D'Urso, S., & Garcia, D. (2020). The witness to witness program: Helpers in the context of the Covid-19 pandemic. *Family Process*, *59*(3). DOI: 10.1111/famp.12580.

2 Historical and Collective Trauma and Their Consequences

Introduction

As I write this chapter in June of 2021 in London, during the COVID pandemic, I have running water, a sewer system, electricity, broadband WIFI, paved streets and sidewalks, a grid of street lights at night, and a network of public transportation that includes an intricate subway and a richly saturated bus network. Although there are many homeless people in London from all over the UK and the world, most permanent residents live in brick flats or houses. If I bicycle past Hyde Park corner, with monuments celebrating Wellington's victory over Napoleon, I can go to museums such as the British Museum or the Victoria and Albert museum (both containing "treasures" from many civilizations all over the world) and pass many statues of royalty, military heroes, and statesmen (many fewer of stateswomen). I am able to afford the cost of living here because I am employed by Smith College in the United States, which generously has given me a sabbatical in order to write this book.

There are many people who struggle to afford to live in London. Some come from London or other parts of the UK, and many come from Eastern Europe, Africa, Asia, Latin America, and the Middle East. People can be found begging for a living on Oxford Street, while some sleep in subterranean tunnels beneath glitzy Park Lane (Judah, 2016). London is one of the most cosmopolitan cities in the world and is also very unequal – economically and socially. The imagined "threat" of non-British immigrants "flooding" England was one of the strongest drivers for the UK to vote to leave the European Union, as part of Brexit, and is still a daily topic of most major media outlets. This is the country where a former MP, Enoch Powell, in his "rivers of blood" speech in 1968, threatened that if immigrants of color

DOI: 10.4324/9781003021162-2

continued to migrate to the UK *from former British colonies* (italics mine), it would destroy the UK.

When I go to Gulu, in Northern Uganda every year to engage in collaborative psychosocial and medical capacity building, I stay in a hotel that now has electricity (although it often goes off in the middle of the night), but most of the roads are still unpaved and there is only one block near my hotel that has streetlights. There is internet but it is much slower than in London or the United States. When I do my work in "the bush," there are no paved roads and with very rare exceptions, the only electricity comes from small, single-pane solar generators, which can charge a cell phone and power one light at night. Most people cannot afford the generators and rent charging for their phones from those who can. There is no running water nor a sewer system in the bush – everyone has to draw water from wells, which often involves walking long distances, waiting in line, and carrying heavy plastic yellow jerry cans. Most people live in circular mud and thatched huts in clan-based compounds.

Although my work in Uganda is collaborative, the U.S. team members have all been educated in U.S. universities, often receiving MDs, and a range of Ph.D. and master's degrees, and are earning salaries that support living in the United States. Our passports allow us to travel unimpeded to almost anywhere in the world and most of us can afford to do so. We have health insurance and reasonable health care, including access to hospitals that have the highest standards of supplies and equipment.

My Ugandan colleagues survived (or their parents experienced) a 20-year armed conflict involving the Ugandan government and The Lord's Resistance Army. Most people in the region were forced to live in internally displaced persons (IDP) camps, which fragmented the social fabric, loosened ties to traditional community networks, ties, and sources of resilience. People were prohibited from farming their land, which is how most make their living. The levels of extreme violence from all parties to the conflict were directly experienced by everyone living in the area. Most of my colleagues are from the same tribe (Acholi), and some have left their community to visit the country's capital, Kampala, but very few have left their country or the African continent. If they do travel internationally, they often go through a time-consuming, uncertain process to obtain a visa.

My Ugandan colleagues are among the most skilled, dedicated, committed, and compassionate people with whom I have ever worked. They speak not only English but also their native Luo as well as other tribal languages. They have not only been trained in Western medicine, psychology, and psychosocial work but are also steeped in indigenous rituals, knowledge, and customs that the U.S. team struggles to grasp. Many are part of a valiantly dedicated workforce for a very under-resourced public health network. There are a couple of hospitals in Gulu, one private, which most people in the bush cannot afford, and one public, that is deeply devoid of equipment and supplies. There is no public transportation system, and thus many people in the bush do not have the time or means to be able to make it to the hospital, particularly when very ill or going into labor.

And yet, despite a commitment to work collaboratively between the U.S. and Ugandan teams, emphasizing mutual respect, inquisitiveness, and respecting one another's wisdom and knowledge, and despite the best intentions to avoid hierarchies, there is always an implicit one. There are a number of reasons for this. Members of the U.S. team have been educated in Western medicine, social work, physical therapy, and public health, and Western standards dominate how health care is delivered around the globe. The U.S. team has a greater ability to access resources, use the Internet, travel, and meet. Members of the U.S. team are used to having enough control over their lives to predict and manage their time: if there is a meeting scheduled at 9 in the morning, they have the infrastructure, resources, stability, and predictability to be there at 9. The U.S. team is able to access donations and grants to cover the costs of travel, training, and basic equipment, and members have paid jobs in the United States so that we can donate our time. The U.S. team goes to Uganda every year to support our Ugandan colleagues; our Ugandan colleagues do not come to the United States to support us!

But it goes beyond these present-day advantages. The U.S. team is mostly (although not exclusively) White, and the Ugandan team is entirely Black. The legacies of white supremacy and racism still haunt the world, including this region. The U.S. team comes from a country that was a colonial state and still is an imperial power; the Ugandan team lives in a country that only became independent from Great Britain in the 1960s. Uganda was not a country before it became a British colony and its artificial boundaries include many tribes, some of which were privileged by the British occupiers while others were suppressed. The armed conflict that I mentioned was not a spontaneous explosion of conflict or the consequence of a demented psychopath, but one that has its roots in desperate poverty and need and the tribal competition fostered by the colonial occupiers, which is true of most conflicts in sub-Saharan Africa. Ironically, because of the many tribes and languages spoken in Uganda, English is the official language of the state, although many of its citizens don't speak it.

Roads are being built, bridges repaired, dams constructed, and power lines established in this region, and I often pass Ugandan road crews being supervised by Chinese engineers, part of China's "belt and bridges" campaign. China, like the British before them, also covets Uganda's natural resources. China even invites people from all over sub-Saharan Africa to attend Chinese universities, where they can take classes in English, and receive master's degrees in a field such as Chinese public policy, virtually for free.

I have tried to describe a tiny slice of what coloniality looks like today, wherever one is situated in the world. We are all embedded in "the colonial matrix of power" (Mignolo & Walsh, 2018). Historical and collective oppression and trauma are shaped by coloniality, which is why I summarize some of its relevant factors before considering historical and collective trauma.

Coloniality and Personhood

One reason that I began this chapter with this vignette is to try and illustrate a central point from Chapter 1, the effects of coloniality are very real and palpable; only people who have benefitted from and are privileged by coloniality can act as if psychosocial suffering is an internal reality that reflects an individual's personal life experiences, values, choices, and behaviors, and that somehow the therapist and consumer can create a space where the legacies of coloniality do not exist. All of us are enmeshed in coloniality and none of us can step outside of its web of unequal power (Mignolo & Walsh, 2018). I will go further and say that psychosocial workers who willfully ignore coloniality and its consequences are denying their complicity in this historical/structural process and therefore are in a position to inflict harm on others, despite the best of intentions. If their work with affected people ignores this, then it runs the risk of encouraging those they are trying to help to *internalize*, what are external structural realities, which can foster self-blame and shame. In doing this, helpers are inviting associates and collaborators to be complicit in the helper's unawareness – or, to adapt a current expression, to enact a form of clinical "gaslighting." If consumers refuse or struggle to engage in this, this is, in many ways, an act of resistance and an attempt to retain or reclaim one's full personhood.

I am not a coloniality scholar and yet before considering historical and collective trauma think that it is important to review some key themes of coloniality that are relevant to this discussion. Much of what I share is based on the thinking of Quijano (2000), Grousfoguel (2013), and Mignolo and Walsh (2018).

Box 2.1 Coloniality of Power

1. Centuries-old system of coloniality has led to "developed nations" (former colonial powers and centers of empires) and poorer "developing nations" (usually former colonies). This relied on the systematic dehumanization of "others" which led to stealing indigenous lands, enslaving people, ethnic/racial subjugation, ethnic cleansing, genocide, creating "nations" based on the interests of colonial powers, privileging some ethnic/religious groups over others, and extracting raw materials which enhanced the wealth of colonial powers.
2. "Developed Nations" have the wealth, resources, and infrastructure to continue to extract raw materials from "developing nations," generating greater wealth for themselves, and creating greater global inequality.
3. "Developed Nations" have institutions, resources, and capacity that support the wealth of their citizens, health, adequate food, and infrastructure (e.g., electricity, running water, roads, reliable food supply, etc.) that positions them to be better able to withstand the effects of climate change and extreme planetary events (e.g., earthquakes, hurricanes, tsunamis, fires, flooding, drought, etc.).
4. "Developed Nations" have the power to intervene militarily with other nations and "defend" their borders against immigrants, and their citizens have the ability to travel to other nations with minimal restrictions.
5. "Developed Nations" impose their epistemology and personhood on other parts of the world and engage in knowledge privileging and hoarding, dominate research, education, and professional standards and determine what is considered true, valid, and normal.
6. Institutions such as the World Bank and International Monetary Fund help to maintain the patterns described earlier and enforce the divisions wrought by coloniality that persist today.

7. There are different rules for "developed" and "developing" nations over who has the right to use military force and who is held accountable by international institutions of justice such as the International Criminal Court.
8. Within "Developed" nations, there are dominant ethnic/racial/religious groups. In the Americas, Europe, and Australia, these are usually White and Christian, in China, Han people, and in the Middle East, Central and South Asia, and sub-Saharan Africa, certain tribes/ethnic/religious groups usually dominate (or contest for power).

Ideas taken from Grousfoguel, 2013; Heinrich, 2020; Kochenov, 2019; Mignolo & Walsh, 2018; Miller, 2012; Quijano, 2000; Summerfield, 2004.

- The centuries-old system of coloniality has created wealthier, more powerful nations, often referring to themselves as "developed"[1] nations, where there is affluence (relative to the rest of the world) and resources that are zealously hoarded. One needs to look no further than the campaign to vaccinate against COVID-19 and compare the rates of the richest nations (the former colonial powers) with others. The desire to protect the patents of pharmaceutical companies has meant that insufficient vaccines are available for a large swathe of the world.
- The "developed" world has not only wealth but also infrastructure (roads, electricity, etc.), education and research capacities, health-care systems, and industrial and agricultural capacities that far outstrip other nations. Thus, it was predictable that the major COVID vaccines would be developed by the United States, United Kingdom, Europe, China, and Russia.
- The wealth of the "developed" world depended on subjugation and (in many instances) the extermination of indigenous populations. It was also reliant on the ability to extract raw materials and resources from countries that were colonized. And the cheap supplies (e.g., cotton) generated by the unpaid labor of enslaved people helped to create the industrial might of all regions in the United States, the United Kingdom, and other parts of the world.
- The "developed" world continues to extract raw materials and cheap labor from the "developing" world (most of which were former colonies). But the draw bridges have been raised when it

comes to immigration from those countries experiencing poverty, war, and the consequences of climate change (literally fueled by the industrial might of "developed" nations).

- International organizations such as the G7, International Monetary Fund, World Bank, patent protection organizations, and others maintain and protect the dominance of coloniality. For example, despite stealing and hoarding the wealth and resources of colonized countries and enslaved people for centuries, "developed" nations ensure that "loans" are paid back by struggling "developing" nations, despite their limited ability to do so, and the huge share such debt is of the national budget of poorer nations.
- "Developed" nations have greater military might and periodically invade "developing" countries if they feel that it is in their strategic interests.
- Many "developed" countries have racial, ethnic, and religious groups that are dominant (e.g., White people in the United States, United Kingdom, and Europe, Han Chinese in China, ethnic Russians in Russia, and Jews in Israel), while other groups are oppressed, targeted, marginalized, and minoritized in most aspects of living (e.g., BIPOC people in the United States, United Kingdom, and Europe; Uighurs in China; Chechens in Russia; and Arabs in Israel).

It is important to acknowledge that the aforementioned points do not reflect the full complexity or diversity of world history and international relations. For example, where do countries such as Romania, India, Thailand, South Africa, and Brazil fit into this discussion? They are not as wealthy as the United States or Germany, nor are they as poor or vulnerable to exploitation as South Sudan, Honduras, or the Philippines. Regional inequalities and the dominance of certain ethnic/racial/religious groups in countries occur in non-Western countries such as India (Hindu dominance) and China (Han dominance). There are many complexities, and each country and region have their own unique history, although empire and colonialization figure prominently in shaping these dynamics (Shahjahan et al., 2022). But the aforementioned points do describe a tendency and pattern of how power and privilege have been and continue to be distributed throughout the world.

I have particularly focused on economic, political, and military power in this discussion, and thus included China and Russia, for example, in the group of "developed" nations. As important as these structural factors are, another critical variable is the privileging of

Western epistemologies (Mignolo & Walsh, 2018), presenting them as universal ways of knowing, understanding, and validating the world and the ways that they construct a particular vision of personhood that lingers as one of the most insidious consequences of coloniality that continues to haunt psychosocial interventions. A hierarchy was created and still exists of what is considered superior or inferior knowledge (Grousfoguel, 2013). Thus, historical trauma was an understandable consequence of the project of coloniality privileging Western civilization, culture, and institutions while at the same time erasing and debasing indigenous knowledge and personhood; reducing them to "inferior" beings and societies (Quijano, 2000). As Fanon (1963) argued, the systematic degradation and negation of personhood, humanity, and culture leave people with either accepting the distorted vision that others have systematically tried to impose on indigenous, non-Western peoples – existing as a perpetual "other" and inferior outsider – or struggling with a loss of individual and collective identity, which I will develop further in the next section.

Historical and Collective Trauma

Psychosocial trauma refers to a very distressing, painful, and overwhelming experience that often has profound affects on feelings, thoughts, behaviors, relationships, and our health and well-being. It can undermine our sense of trust, shake our faith in other people and the world, and lead us to rethink our values and the meaning of our lives. Trauma can break people but also be a source of resilience, growth, and strength.

Trauma is most often thought of in individual terms. The notion of post-traumatic stress disorder (PTSD) has assumed a dominant position in how trauma is publicly portrayed and understood and treated by professionals. And yet trauma has historical and collective dimensions, which is what I will consider in this section. However, it is helpful to first briefly summarize the more traditional understandings of individual trauma.

Post-Traumatic Stress Disorder, Acute Stress Disorder, Complex PTSD

According to the National Health Service (NHS, 2021) of the United Kingdom, PTSD is caused when a person experiences either an overwhelming, terrifying event or has prolonged exposure to a trauma-inducing situation. Examples of such precipitating events and situations are wars, exposure to violence, torture, domestic abuse, near-fatal accidents, and sexual abuse. The major symptoms listed by the National Institute of Mental Health (NIMH, 2021) in the United States are clustered into four categories: re-experiencing, avoidance, arousal, and cognition/mood. Re-experiencing includes flashbacks, bad dreams, and frightening thoughts. In my experience working with police officers, firefighters, and emergency medical technicians, re-experiencing feels as if one is actually back in a stressful situation and the body responds with elevated heartbeats, sweating, stomach tightening, and so on. Avoidance can mean staying away from places or things, or thoughts and information that evoke the experience of the event. I worked with women who were arrested by the government in the country where they lived for protesting against misogyny outside of a subway station and over a year later some were still afraid to go near the station. Arousal can be manifested by being easily startled, not allowing oneself to sleep, or being hypersensitive or prone to angry outbursts. I worked with a young man after the Haitian earthquake who would try not to let himself fall asleep, particularly if he was inside. The same man blamed himself for his fiancée's death in the earthquake, felt hopeless about his future life, and would withdraw into dark rooms and watch graphically violent videos: all of which are examples of PTSD cognition and mood symptoms.

People with PTSD are easily "triggered" by something, usually sensory, that evokes the traumatic event; for example, if someone escaped a major fire, the smell of smoke from leaves burning can be the precipitant of flooding and re-experiencing. Van Der Kolk (2014) argues that PTSD is encoded in a part of the brain that is not amenable to logic, reason, and consequently traditional talk therapy. It might be that this occurs because fear-based memory fragments are neurologically encoded but without a coherent self-narrative to make sense of the threats (Bryant, 2018). (Self-narratives are central to many forms of talk therapy.)

In 1994, the Diagnostic and Statistical Manual, which is published by the American Psychiatric Association and is the bible of psychiatric diagnoses, added the diagnosis of "Acute Stress Disorder" (ASD); if PTSD was not applicable as a diagnosis until at least one month after a psychosocial trauma, then how to account for severe symptoms immediately after exposure, and more importantly, what should be done to help people in that situation (Bryant, 2018)? The diagnosis of ASD included PTSD symptoms but added symptoms of disassociation, such as depersonalization and a decreased awareness of one's surroundings (Bryant).

And yet it is only a minority of people exposed to catastrophes who experience PTSD. The NHS (2021) estimates 1/3. In my review of PTSD literature, I found that the range is from 5% to 30% (Miller, 2012). Blanco et al. (2016) in their review of the literature on PTSD have found instances as low as 1.5% despite exposure to collective violence. Bryant's (2018) review of the research on both PTSD and ASD found four distinct trajectories in the wake of exposure to traumatic events: (1) resilience, with low or no trauma symptoms; (2) recovery from trauma symptoms; (3) worsening trauma symptoms over time, including delayed trauma reactions; and (4) living with chronically high levels of trauma symptoms. While PTSD and ASD are helpful medical categories used by helping professionals, they are clearly not a straightforward reaction to trauma exposure, often do not occur or when they do, and are part of a matrix of many other psychosocial reactions, such as grief, anxiety disorders, depression, and chemical dependency.

PTSD and ASD are concepts that were generated in Western developed countries and then applied to people living all over the world who encountered traumatic events. As Summerfield (2000, 2004) has written, this led to the "medicalization of human suffering" and ignored the sociocultural contexts that predated exposure and continue to shape meaning, reconstruction, and healing. And a problem with diagnosis such as PTSD is that it is often ahistorical – not in the sense of personal history but of the collective history of groups in the context of coloniality – and they focus on the individual rather than the collective experience of people with similar identities – such as the experience of racism for BIPOC people in North America and Europe. This can lead to a psychological diagnosis by locating problems within an individual, which inadvertently pathologizes them for being members of groups that have experienced historical and collective trauma (Heberle et al., 2020; Williams-Washington & Mills, 2018).

An interesting evolution of these concepts was the development of the notion of "complex PTSD," which in my view offers a link with historical and collective trauma. The International Classification of Diseases, compiled by the World Health Organization (WHO), identified Complex PTSD (CPTSD) as a distinct syndrome (DeJongh et al., 2016; Ho et al., 2021; Karatzias et al., 2019). CPTSD refers to trauma that accrues from repeated exposure to overwhelming and distressing events, such as childhood maltreatment, domestic violence, child soldering, genocide, slavery, and torture (Karatzias et al., 2019). The symptoms not only overlap with PTSD but also include what are referred to as "disturbances in self-organization" (DSO), which includes dysregulated affect, negative self-concept, and disturbances in relationships (Ho et al., 2021; Karatzias et al., 2019). DeJongh et al. (2016) also adds problems with attention, the shattering of belief systems, and somatic complaints as examples of DSO.

There is a link between historical and collective trauma and CPTSD because the diagnosis of CPTSD recognizes that trauma goes beyond single events and can be caused by repeated exposure, leading to even greater psychological distress than PTSD. Bryant (2018) found in his review of research on ADS and PTSD that a factor determining whether a person experiences profound trauma or not is exposure to ongoing stressors; thus, it is not simply the precipitating event of a critical incident. CPTSD is a diagnostic category that explicitly recognizes how repeated exposure to violence of all types, including psychological and emotional violence, may have profoundly negative consequences, which is an essential quality of historical and collective trauma. But all of these syndromes – ASD, PTSD, and CPTSD – look at the traumatic consequences of stressors and precipitating events on individuals. And none of them consider the historical and contemporary power of genocide, enslavement, Jim Crow, and much more (Williams-Washington & Mills, 2018). This is why historical trauma and collective trauma are such important concepts: social oppression affects individuals because their social identities are based on assigned membership in groups that are targeted and the consequences affect not only the individual but also the group.

Historical and Collective Trauma

Three forms of trauma that go beyond the individual are intergenerational, historical, and collective. They overlap and can all be part of the same group experience, such as racial trauma which has elements of all three categories, but there are also differences. Cultural trauma also bridges the categories and will be explored in the following sections. I will consider all of these processes separately, defining them, anchoring them in coloniality, examining their consequences, and considering general ideas of what helps groups and individuals experiencing these types of traumas which will be developed further throughout the book. I believe that it is important to be unflinchingly clear about the disastrous, deleterious affects of historical trauma while also recognizing the strength and resilience – personal, familial, cultural, and collective – that enabled people to survive (Ortega-Williams et al., 2021a); thus survival, resistance, and resilience should be part of any discussion of historical/collective trauma.

Intergenerational Trauma

In the aftermath of World War II and the Jewish Holocaust, there was an increasing awareness in the fields of psychology, psychiatry, and social work that trauma could be experienced by people in a family who did not directly experience the traumatic events. Intergenerational trauma was the term used to describe when the traumatic events experienced by one generation are inherited by the next generation (Cerdena et al., 2021; Heberle et al., 2020; Isobel et al., 2021; Yehuda & Lehrner, 2018).

How does this happen? There are multiple pathways. The consequences of the parent's traumatic experiences affect their emotional, cognitive, and psychological states, which in turn influences how they parent. For example, anxiety can be viewed as an individual predisposition or genetic inheritance. But for Jews who either directly survived the Jewish Holocaust or Jews who were alive during that period and experienced vicarious trauma knowing that they and their relatives were the targets of extermination, anxiety was grounded in a harsh, existential reality. Their children became members of families where anxiety was part of a strategy of care, protection, and survival, and to view it as simply an individual trait out of this context would miss much of its meaning and why it was passed down as an emotional inheritance. I witnessed this in my own family and that of many of my Jewish friends, where anxiety and a sense that the world could always hold terrible possibilities were taken for granted. Like with individual forms of trauma, there were triggers that could precipitate a state of activation, affecting emotions and relationships and serving as filters through which present-day experiences were understood.

Yehuda and Lehrner (2018) have found evidence to support the idea that such transmission has biological consequences (e.g., hormonal and neurological) as well as influencing behaviors and can therefore even affect offspring not only prior to birth but prior to conception! This is not the consequence of genetic inheritance but is an epigenetic process of multiple determinants that can become a biological as well as psychological legacy (Waters et al., 2011). Intergenerational trauma also has an impact on family communication styles and processes, which are not only a group phenomenon but also become family maps and templates internalized by individuals.

Alexander (2016) notes how genocide that is passed down intergenerationally is also a form of "cultural trauma," as what is valued within a given culture was the target of genocidal erasure. This adds the dimension of identity and thus has implications for how members of a family or group view the world, influencing their values and morals, as well as their optimism or pessimism about the future. This holds true as well for historical trauma.

Brave Heart and DeBruyn (1998) made the connection between the literature and research about intergenerational trauma from the Jewish Holocaust with the experiences of indigenous people in North America. This is a bridge from intergenerational trauma to historical trauma. Intergenerational trauma is conceptualized as being directly passed down from one generation to another generation. It may be part of a historical process of centuries, but there can be families where there is intergenerational trauma – say as an outcome of a traumatic family tragedy – where this is not the case (Mohatt et al., 2014). And intergenerational trauma does not necessarily mean that people with certain social identities are experiencing social oppression in the present. As we move to a consideration of historical and collective trauma, what are distinguishing characteristics are that these processes involve groups of people sharing social identities, that there can be trauma transmission spanning multiple generations, that this usually involves cultural trauma, and that it has not ended: the historical conditions that generated trauma are manifest in the present day.

Historical Trauma

Historical trauma is when there has been a systematic pattern of events directed at people who share an identity as members of an ethnic, racial, religious group or tribe where the intent is genocide, ethnic cleansing, enslavement, seizure of land and the means of survival (such as farm land and food sources), and cultural destruction and erasure leading to massive group trauma (Brave Heart & DeBruyn, 1998; Brave Heart et al., 2020; Heberle et al., 2020; Johnson-Henderson & Ginty, 2020; Mohatt et al., 2014; O'Neill et al., 2018; Waters et al., 2011). A distinguishing aspect of historical trauma is that people (not all of whom are biologically related) experience it collectively and that the negative consequences of coloniality accumulate over time, often centuries, spanning generations (Mohatt et al., 2014; Ortega-Williams et al., 2021a). And a secondary wound is the consistent denial of the history that precipitated historical trauma (Ortega-Williams et al., 2021b) (Box 2.2).

Historical trauma is, in my view, inextricably linked to coloniality, which spawned white supremacy and European dominance. Kirmayer et al. (2014), citing Hartmann and Gone, summarize the "Four Cs" of Indigenous historical trauma: (1) conquests, subjugation, dispossession, and other injuries perpetrated by colonial settlers; (2) collective

Box 2.2 Historical Trauma

1. Caused by violent appropriation of land, destruction of the means of livelihood, enforced and unpaid labor, genocide, ethnic and tribal exclusion and targeting, cultural annihilation, devaluing, and denigration of a group's personhood.
2. Experienced by a group sharing a collective, targeted, sociopolitically excluded social identity.
3. Generates enduring structural and psychosocial effects.
4. Has profound consequences for group members including grief, shame, emptiness, depression, and a sense of being devalued. Historical trauma can be manifested by drug use, suicide, interpersonal violence, and medical and psychosocial vulnerability.
5. Disrupts and dislocates traditional, familiar cultural practices that have sustained groups in the past.
6. The dominant group imposes their epistemology, values, social practices, and vision of personhood on others and excludes or prohibits alternatives.
7. Groups resist historical trauma through their survival, endurance, remembering, reclaiming, resurrecting, and reconstructing collective and individual resistance.

experiencing of these wrongs leading to damage to identities, cultures, and social interactions; (3) cumulative, cascading historical effects of ongoing oppression and subjugation; and (4) the cross-generational impact of unrelenting tyranny and cruelty. The literal survival and the collective cultural survival of a collectivity have been under threat due to the forces of coloniality, and these threats continue (Ortega-Williams et al., 2021a).

It is difficult to scientifically establish causal links between historical trauma and current psychosocial problems. There is always a mixture of historical antecedents, the current dynamics of oppression, environmental influences, and unique individual and family factors. Sometimes the historical legacies are clear, such as the terrible legacy in North America of forced boarding schools on indigenous families and communities' generations later (Barnes & Josefowitz, 2019; Brave Heart et al., 2020). And yet there are also structural and psychosocial consequences from the enslavement of African Americans, the 19th-century Chinese Exclusion Act or the Japanese incarceration during

World War II, or the complex legacy of centuries of U.S. meddling and Imperialism over the centuries and its impact on Latinx people who are both immigrating to and living in the United States. And as the dynamics that led to historical trauma are still in place through the logic of coloniality, white supremacy, and Eurocentrism, historical trauma is not simply history. Indigenous people still live on "reservations" on continents that were originally theirs while national parks occupy their stolen land (Treuer, 2021). Pipelines owned by major corporations, cross indigenous land against the will of local people, and resources are still extracted from reservations by mining companies, despoiling the environment, exposing people to toxins, and bringing in an influx of outside workers (Kirmayer et al., 2014, Waters et al., 2011). The "structural vulnerabilities" of immigration status and labor force participation due to one's social location continue as the system of coloniality shaped the conditions of the country that Latinx people migrated from, the treacherous journey to a more 'developed' country, as well as their social conditions in the new country (Cerdena et al., 2021). Even for Latinx people living in the United States since before the Spanish-American war, there has been unrelenting discrimination, and vigilante and state-sponsored violence (Cerdena). This is why Chapter 3 will consider how contemporary structural oppression interacts with historical trauma.

Racial Trauma

Racial trauma is a form of historical and collective trauma. Carter (2007) described "race-based traumatic stress." Although the main focus was on current systemic racism and its traumatic impact, he situates this in the context of historical racism; they are inseparable. Hartmann et al., 2019) explicitly make the connection between racial and historical trauma. Leary, as cited by Mohatt et al., 2014), coined the term "post-traumatic slavery syndrome." Williams-Washington and Mills (2018) note that since the era of slavery, there have been unremitting, multiple destructive periods and experiences that collectively injured people's bodies, minds, and spirits. Racial trauma has been harmful to not only individuals and families but also communities, which is the case for all forms of collective trauma. I will explore the conditions that generate racial trauma in greater detail in the next chapter.

Collective Trauma

All forms of historical trauma are also collective trauma. Although there can be collective trauma that is not necessarily historical – e.g., an entire village that has survived a devastating fire or hurricane where there was significant mortality – most collective trauma, particularly the kind that this book is concerned about because it is a consequence of sociopolitical targeting and oppression, descends from historical trauma.

As with historical trauma, collective trauma results from intentional acts of domination, subjugation, violence, and harm toward a collective group of people based on the identities of both the targets and perpetrators of the acts of aggression (Blanco et al., 2016). These patterns are grounded in historical, macro processes that reflect an international social order (Blanco et al., 2016). The matrix of coloniality not only is between international states but is also represented and recreated within each state. For example, there is tremendous racism in the United States and Europe directed at migrants fleeing from poverty and violence in Africa and Central/South America (a legacy of coloniality), but the racism extends to residents and citizens of the United States and Europe who are Black and Brown. And yet in most Western nations, helping professionals treat the individual internalized disorders that stem from these larger social forces. However, the individuals being treated are acutely aware that much of their suffering comes from their social identities, which are negatively valued by their societies (Blanco et al., 2016).

Kira et al. (2018) make a distinction between personal identity trauma (PIT) and collective identity stressors/trauma (CIDT). A major distinction between PIT and CIDT is that with the latter, not only are the sources of the trauma macro institutions and groups, but they are also ongoing throughout a person's life. And they are not accidental – the intentionality of the oppression is part of the trauma – you know that your group is devalued and that people with different identities see you as "less-than," and wish you harm if not destruction (Blanco et al., 2016; Miller, 2012; O'Neill et al., 2018). This not only causes personal harm but can also lead to collective grief (Brave Heart & DeBruyn, 1998), a loss of collective culture (Brave Heart & DeBruyn, 1998; Marsh et al., 2015), and a breakdown in social cohesion and social trust.

Pathways for the Transmission of Historical and Collective Trauma

There are many ways that historical trauma is passed down although it can be difficult to "scientifically" establish direct links and correlations. However, the very concept of historical trauma is a way of constructing a meaningful narrative (Kirmayer et al., 2014) that gives coherence to the horrors of the past and sheds light on current struggles, while creating a map for the future. Such narratives pay tribute to the extraordinary courage, strength, and resilience needed to have defied attempts of genocide, resisting centuries of subjugation, and confronting contemporary structural oppression. And yet the sources of the trauma never ended and are a structural and social reality experienced today (Garran et al., 2021; Ortega-Williams et al., 2021a).

For indigenous people in North America, coloniality introduced social, cultural, and political frames of reference that were new and unfamiliar, such as private property, Christianity, and capitalism (Grousfoguel, 2013). Spanning centuries there was genocide, broken treaties, ethnic cleansing, destruction of food sources, and appropriation of land (Garran et al., 2021). Over the past 100 years, indigenous children were forcibly sent to white boarding schools to "kill the Indian" inside of them, which meant stripping children of their culture, social supports, and family, which literally did kill many of them – some buried in unmarked graves at the schools – and left a "soul wound" in their hearts and those of their families. Although this was resisted by many indigenous people, there was also a process of silencing; silencing by a larger White society that didn't acknowledge this process of cultural erasure and social destruction and silencing because of the terrible pain of talking about and reliving this collectively traumatic experience (O'Neill et al., 2018).

But historical trauma is not limited to indigenous people in North America; it has occurred throughout the world. There are many examples of historical and collective trauma that come from former British colonies, particularly in Africa and South Asia. Uganda is a case in point, illustrating how coloniality spawned ethnic conflict, violence, repression, displacement, and chronic social, political, and economic insecurity.

Uganda had been ravaged by slavers before becoming a British "sphere of influence" after an agreement between Great Britain and Germany in 1890 (Ingham, 2021). It was "administered" by the Imperial British East Africa Company until formally becoming a "protectorate" in 1894. The region included many tribes, with different linguistic, cultural, and political systems. As in many British colonies, some tribes were favored over others and given special privileges while others were fiercely subjugated. Agricultural crops, such as cotton and coffee, were developed for British plantation owners, and a steady supply of raw materials was extracted to feed British trade and industry. Laborers from India (another British colony) were brought to Uganda to build railways; some of them settled in Uganda.

Since the nation of Uganda was granted independence in 1962, there have been coups, wars between ethnic groups, and authoritarian regimes. There has never been a democratic election that led to a peaceful transfer of power. The "post-colonial" history included the dictator Idi Amin, who expelled all East Asians from the country in 1972 (Ingham, 2021). The armed conflicts, coups, and civil wars have killed tens of thousands of Ugandan civilians and disrupted social and economic development.

The most severe conflict was a civil war (which I referred to in the introduction to this chapter) in Northern Uganda involving the Lord's Resistance Army (LRA) and the government which lasted for over 20 years until the mid-2000s and led to an estimated 100,000 deaths. Children were abducted and turned into soldiers, with females being sexually assaulted and forced into becoming concubines for soldiers. Abductees were required to commit atrocities, including murdering and mutilating their own family members. Over 90% of the population was resettled into IDP camps by the government, where they were terrorized and assaulted by both the LRA and the government. They were not able to maintain their clan-based system of agriculture, tribal governance, cultural practices, and rituals. Many people in the area are Christians (Catholics and Church of Uganda) and priests and their lay clergy (catechists) were unable to practice, were murdered, and were displaced. Neither the Lord's Resistance Army nor the government has significantly been held accountable for their atrocities, and there have not been any meaningful large-scale peace, reconciliation, restitution, or healing processes. I have been doing psychosocial work in the area since 2007 and have never encountered a person who was not personally affected – meaning having been attacked, maimed, and witnessed murder, having lost a close family member, and having been abducted, raped, and brutalized. Nearly everyone describes themselves as having "trauma." Cultural rituals and traditions have been lost, and many younger people are not familiar with them. There are violent land disputes, high levels of depression, suicide alcohol and drug abuse, and domestic violence. Social cohesion has fragmented, and most people in the area are mistrustful of and alienated from the government. And yet, as with other examples of historical and collective trauma, the community has demonstrated incredible resilience, even during the COVID-19 pandemic, which hit the region particularly hard. Despite the consequences of coloniality, both long and short term, there are many efforts to help to rebuild the community, care for people, and improve their lives despite the many psychic, physical, and communal wounds.

Consequences of Historical and Collective Trauma

There are consequences of historical and collective trauma at many levels: individual, family, group, tribe/ethnic group, community, and nation. When considering these outcomes, it is important to be cautious about generalizing: there are many variations intrapersonally, interpersonally, and institutionally. It is helpful to use an intersectional lens, one that recognizes that intersectionality occurs institutionally, within groups, and within individuals (Garran et al., 2021). Historically and institutionally, the system of coloniality privileged certain identities over others and baked these inequities into legal systems, religious and cultural practices, family relationships, economic access and systems, access to social welfare benefits, political rights, vulnerability to state tyranny, and more. This system of intersectionality constructed categories and then hierarchies of race, nationality, socioeconomic status, gender, sexual expression, citizenship, legal rights, personhood, and religion, and determined who owned or managed land and systems of labor, employment, and the levers of state power and government.

Intersectionality also refers to social identities and how we view ourselves and others. Although some aspects of our social identities are chosen – e.g., whether I am a Buddhist, atheist, or Christian – are socially constructed and determined. What are the options for gender in a society? Do queer people have social, political, legal, and domestic rights? Do people of any race have the same experience when stopped by the police? Are wealthy people more exempt from taxes than poorer people? We know that the answers to these and similar questions vary considerably by society, nation, form of government, and also by the era when they are asked. We also know that power, status, written and unwritten social rules, and cultural norms mean that there is no equity in society and people differentially have access to resources, social space to live their lives as they would like, and the ability to be safe and protected from violence, illness, poverty, and many other threats to well-being. Thus, as we consider the consequences of historical and structural oppression, intersectionality is always a potent influence. And one final point about intersectionality – the impact of having denigrated social identities is not simply additive – e.g., being a woman in a religious minority – but cumulative – the risks of both being a woman and religious minority interact and magnify the overall threats to a person and group (Garran et al., 2021).

I have already described how there have been increased levels of drug use, interpersonal and intimate partner violence, suicide, and unresolved trauma and grief in Northern Uganda since the armed conflict. These symptoms correspond to those identified as affecting indigenous people in North America (Brave Heart et al., 2020; Brave Heart & DeBruyn, 1998; Mohatt et al., 2014; Waters et al., 2011). Other symptoms that have been identified are anxiety, feelings of guilt and shame, self-blame, withdrawal, depression, and social marginalization, along with increased health risks and medical vulnerability (Barnes & Josefowitz, 2019; Blanco et al., 2016; Brave Heart & DeBruyn, 1998; Waters et al., 2011). Many of these are also present in Northern Uganda. I believe that when historical trauma has occurred that it damages a group's sense of pride, efficacy, trust in themselves, trust in the world, and overall sense of security.

Socially, historical and collective trauma toward indigenous people in North America negatively affects family communications and relationships and disrupts traditional social and cultural practices (Brave Heart & DeBruyn, 1998; Kirmayer et al., 2014; Waters et al., 2011; Williams-Washington & Mills, 2018), all of which I have observed in Northern Uganda. Historical trauma shapes how people view the present (Heberle et al., 2020) and can make it more difficult for people to discern and discriminate between the levels of threats they are experiencing, which can leave a person in a highly activated and aroused state (Williams-Washington & Mills, 2018), scanning the environment for potential threats and evaluating what is picked up. Much of the impact of historical trauma is shaped and mitigated by current sociocultural conditions experienced by group members as well as the intersectional differences in social identities described earlier. Once, when I was working with an indigenous community in North America that was in the throes of recovering from a natural disaster, I was taught by the tribe that it was not possible to isolate the effects of the recent disaster from colonialism, the trauma of forced boarding schools for indigenous children, and the current experience of racism and social oppression.

Interestingly, ascribing present-day psychosocial problems to historical trauma can be helpful for those who are directly affected. It can lessen a sense of individual failure and shame. A person or group can view their struggles as part of a long and larger process of historical injustice (Kirmayer et al., 2014). The focus is no longer on individual pathology but on social targeting and oppression (Ortega-Williams et al., 2021a). Triumphalist dominant narratives that minimize historical suffering and erase white supremacy – such as the movement by the Republican party in the United States to demonize critical race theory and for the state of Texas to not teach about its history of slavery – serve to deepen historical trauma and often increase in intensity in reaction to electing BIPOC leaders, enforcing civil rights and voting laws and discussing coloniality and reparations. But despite (or *in spite of*) such counter-reactions, it is important to honor narratives of historical trauma, which can connect with the present experience of oppression providing context, shedding light on its origins, and helping people to historically and collectively situate themselves in the sweep of a larger arc (Mohatt et al., 2014). This can act as a corrective to repressive narratives of superiority while also serving as a narrative of resistance (Mohatt et al., 2014).

Grief

Before turning our attention to the resilience needed to survive historical and collective trauma, it is important to acknowledge grief. While there is understandably an emphasis on current psychosocial functioning, the need to mourn and grieve cumulative losses is critical (Miller, 2012). It is all the more difficult to grieve when losses are unacknowledged, erased, or minimized, what Doka (quoted by Brave Heart & DeBruyn, 1998) calls "disenfranchised grief." As I write this, many First Nations people in Canada are asking to elevate Indigenous People's Day as a holiday while lowering the status of Canada Day in light of multiple discoveries of the remains of children at Anglo boarding schools and the questioning of the symbolic meaning of celebrating a day that marks the genocide of indigenous peoples (British Broadcasting Corporation, 2021).

As Brave Heart and DeBruyn (1998) argue, the need for indigenous people to mourn genocidal losses is similar to the need for Jews to mourn and memorialize the Jewish Holocaust, both stemming from "historical unresolved grief." However, the Jewish experience, with an unequivocal acknowledgment by the German government of genocide and their willingness to make reparations, and the memorials constructed at Auschwitz and other death camps stand in stark contrast to the inability of nations in the Americas to openly discuss, confront, and make reparation for the genocide of indigenous people who had and have been living on these continents or to acknowledge how the wealth of these countries was possible because of the unpaid labor of enslaved Black people. But while the German government has not only acknowledged German culpability in the Jewish Holocaust but also paid reparations to Israel and Jewish families, it has been resistant to adequately admitting responsibility for an earlier genocide against the Herero and Nama people living in what is now Namibia between 1904 and 1908 (Hambira & Gleckman-Krut, 2021). Although it has apologized and paid some money to Namibia, many descendants of those who were killed or survived massacres feel that it is insufficient and pales in contrast to what has been paid for the Jewish Holocaust and there have not been payments to individual families.

In the United States, there was a beautiful memorial constructed in memory of the 168 people killed in the Oklahoma City bombing in 1995, five years later. And yet between 70 and 300 African Americans were killed by a white mob in 1921, rampaging through the Greenwood District of Tulsa, Oklahoma, and there still is no memorial on the scale of Oklahoma City, although there are exhibits in the Tulsa Historical Society and Museum and some reconstruction of the historic Greenwood District. And unlike Oklahoma City, an entire neighborhood and Black community was destroyed and there has been no restitution nor reparations; when certain tragedies are recognized and memorialized and others involving white supremacy and racism are minimized or efforts to memorialize and repair are met with resistance, collective grief only deepens.

An interesting counter-point to this is the establishment of the Forks in the Road memorial in the Natchez National Historical Park, in Natchez, Mississippi (Mendoza, 2021). The memorial acknowledges that Natchez was a center for the buying and selling of enslaved people from 1833 to 1863 and was established by local residents, state and national administrators, and political leaders, with the assistance of historians. The people who worked on this were of many different races, ethnicities, and political orientations and were able to link the wealth that led to the mansions of Natchez coming from the unpaid labor of enslaved people. One memorial such as this does not heal all of the wounds caused by colonialism and white supremacy, but it does recognize the crimes against humanity that were committed, which is partially healing for at least some people.

Strength, Beauty, and Resilience in Response to Historical/Collective Trauma

As I have mentioned, despite the horrific consequences of genocide, white supremacy, femicide and misogyny, homophobia and hatred toward GLBT people, religious persecution and "ethnic cleansing," and more types and instances of group-based historical/collective trauma, we have witnessed tremendous collective strength, resilience, and fortitude in response to these threats. And in collective resistance, the beauty and pride of those who have survived, endured, and have never given up are inspiring.

One theme that occurs repeatedly in the literature about what helps to mitigate historical trauma is the power of restoring and reclaiming traditional rituals that have been lost, obscured, or suppressed (Henderson et al., 2021; Marsh et al., 2015; Ortega-Williams et al., 2021a). This offers great potential to reject colonial, white supremacist myths while instilling pride in one's own culture, tribe, and identity, forming a kind of survival map (Ortega-Williams et al., 2021a). Transitional pathways are links with our past, including the collective past, and shine a beacon toward our future; the present gains meaning from both the wisdom of the past and our future hopes and aspirations (Landau, 2007; Landau & Saul, 2004). Coloniality is a process that valorizes one history, one culture, and one way of knowing and intentionally diminishes, demonizes, and destroys challenges to this epistemological and ontological hegemony. Thus, psychosocial responses for oppressed people must include a decolonizing framework; this allows for historical and collective resilience to re-emerge from the shadows.

In my work in Northern Uganda, I have learned how traditional rituals, cultural practices, and respect for elders who hold deep knowledge all diminished during the armed conflict while people lived in IDP camps. In our efforts, while working with clan and religious leaders to help reestablish traditional Acholi practices – such as healing and restorative practices when violence or murder has been committed – I have learned that while we can draw from the past although we can never completely recover the past; rituals and practices need to be adapted and modernized and integrated with current sociocultural and political realities if they are going to engage many people, particularly younger members of a tribe. Franz Fanon (1967) recognized this 70 years ago as he talked about the importance of rejecting white distortions and stereotypes of Black people that he and others had internalized but how he could not also return to pure, indigenous traditions that he had not experienced in the modern world.

Ultimately, the goal is to recognize and build individual resilience from the construction and reconstruction of collective resilience (Ortega-Williams et al., 2021a). This challenges individualism, which is a cornerstone of the project of coloniality, with an ethos of collective well-being and solidarity; an individual's suffering in the present can be absorbed into a historical narrative of strength and survival, fostering communal power (Ortega-Williams et al., 2021a).

What Helps in Response to Historical/Collective Trauma

The model that I propose to guide psychosocial workers who are attempting to support people who have experienced historical and contemporary oppression will be presented in Chapters 5 and 6. In this section, I will review some important insights gleaned from a number of people who have worked with people who have experienced historical and collective trauma, which will be amplified in Chapter 5 (Box 2.3).

A consistent finding, in my own work (Miller, 2012; Miller & Pescaroli, 2018) and others (Brave Heart et al., 2020; Brave Heart & DeBruyn, 1998; Heberle et al., 2020; Marsh et al., 2015; O'Neill et al., 2018; Ortega-Williams et al., 2021a), is the importance of integrating traditional cultural practices with western psychosocial interventions. Marsh et al. (2015) refer to this as a "two-eyed approach." Indigenous models of healing and restorative justice are particularly important, and integrating them with grieving and collective memorializing is essential. Although Western-oriented psychosocial interventions – such as

Box 2.3 Resisting and Healing From Historical Trauma

1. Integrating traditional cultural practices with compatible, modern psychosocial interventions.
2. Achieving a relative sense of safety. Although complete safety is not achievable, collective practices and interventions can help to construct a shared sense of social support and efficacy.
3. Integrating psychosocial interventions with social action, advocacy, and collective resistance, working toward sociopolitical change.
4. Generating collective narratives that recognize and validate historical suffering while honoring resistance, resilience, and survival.
5. Reconstructing and reconnecting with past sources of strength and wisdom through engagement with elders, storytelling, and reclaiming rituals.
6. Working to achieve post-traumatic growth individually and collectively.

cognitive behavioral treatment – as well as Eastern-derived practices – such as mindfulness and calming techniques – can be very useful in many sociocultural contexts, caution is always needed, particularly with Western-style interventions. One reason for this is that many, if not most white practitioners and the agencies that employ them, use Western psychology and psychotherapy as their main modalities, but these are the very people and systems that groups who have experienced historical and collective oppression are understandably mistrustful or fearful of (Heberle et al., 2020). These can undermine traditional forms of healing and recovery when offered on their own. And when the government is the source of oppression and is targeting groups based on identity or political activities, then added to the mistrust is a profound lack of safety in the present (Miller & Wang, 2017). Safety is an essential foundation for recovery (Bryant-Davis, 2005; Hobfoll et al., 2007; Miller, 2012; Miller & Pescaroli, 2018; Miller & Wang, 2017; O'Neill et al., 2018) and how to deal with an ongoing lack of safety will be considered in Chapters 5–7.

A second shared insight is the importance of collective interventions that engage people so that there is a sense of social support (Heberle, 2020; Johnson-Henderson & Ginty, 2020; Marsh et al., 2015; Miller, 2012; Miller & Pescaroli, 2018; Miller & Wang, 2017; Ortega-Williams et al., 2021a). One of the biggest problems with using Western, psychotherapeutic interventions with survivors of historical and collective trauma is that there is so much focus on individual work. While there is a place for this, collective injuries require collective responses, which are often not supported programmatically and financially. Collective healing and individual healing are always inseparable when there have been disasters (Miller & Pescaroli, 2018) and this is even more the case when groups have experienced collective trauma (Brave Heart & DeBruyn, 1998).

A third area of consensus is the importance of integrating psychosocial interventions with social action, advocacy, and social change (Heberle, 2020; Marsh et al., 2015; Miller, 2012; Weyerman, 2007). This is a key point in my psychosocial model: psychosocial work involves integrating inner change with social change. Land restoration and reparations for enslavement are two examples of goals of social movements that can be integrated with other psychosocial interventions (Ortega-Williams et al., 2021a).

A fourth recommendation is that there be a focus on the construction of narrative, where there is not only a recognition of collective historical wrongs but also stories of resistance and survival (Alexander, 2016; Garran et al., 2021; Miller, 2012). In many ways, this is a form of externalization, helping individuals to share a sense of guilt, shame, and culpability for the wounds of historical trauma (O'Neill et al., 2018). And it connects present-day realities to traumatic historical events (Mohatt et al., 2014). Brave Heart and DeBruyn (1998) stress the importance of extended kinship networks that both connect people to their collective culture but also foster a sense of positive identity. This enhances a sense of belonging, reconnecting with core cultural values, and a history of confronting overwhelming adversity with strength, courage, and the will to survive. There needs to be a balance: the excruciating pain of genocide, loss of land, and other major historical losses not only needs to be acknowledged but also publicly grieved and memorialized (Brave Heart & DeBruyn, 1998; Miller, 2012; O'Neill et al., 2018). But this should be combined with a focus on strength, rights, valuable cultural lessons, and a connection to a liberating and empowering cosmology and way of being (Brave Heart & DeBruyn, 1998; Corbin & Miller, 2009; Henderson et al., 2021; Miller, 2012).

A fifth suggestion is reconnecting people to their historical and cultural past through engagement with elders, parents, spiritual leaders, and other cultural knowledge and wisdom holders (Brave Heart et al., 2020; Corbin & Miller, 2009; Henderson et al., 2021; Marsh et al., 2015; O'Neill et al., 2018; Ortega-Williams et al., 2021a). Connecting with the past gives meaning to the present and opens up pathways for the future (Blanco et al., 2016; Landau, 2007; Landau & Saul, 2004; Miller, 2012; Ortega-Williams et al., 2021a). This often involves non-talk means of expression, including the arts, storytelling, visual and audio installations, games and sports, drum circles, traditional songs, healing circles, rituals, and other non-verbal activities (Brave Heart et al., 2020; Bryant-Davis, 2005; Miller, 2012; O'Neill et al., 2018; Ortega-Williams et al., 2021a). It is exciting and empowering to think of intergenerational ways of responding to a form of intergenerational trauma and to build on indigenous modalities of expression!

A sixth recommendation is to link individual and collective resistance and healing with post-traumatic growth (Blanco et al., 2016; Ortega-Williams et al., 2021a). In their model of post-traumatic growth in response to historical trauma, Ortega-Williams et al. (2021a) have developed a model with the following collective strategies: focusing on collective strengths and power, seeking collective spiritual change, connecting to ancestors and cultural roots, examining new possibilities for the group's future, and appreciation of the lives of the group's members in the present. This model recognizes the importance of strengthening social cohesion and the power of mutual aid.

Conclusion

In this chapter, I have expanded the understanding of trauma from a purely individual experience and pathology to recognition of the historical, collective, and structural roots of trauma. Coloniality is a theoretical framework that sheds light on the intersectional construction of social identities, personhood, in which groups of people were and continue to be denied their full humanity and rights and privileges. I considered how the construction and meaning of historical narratives reframe intergenerational trauma from conceptualizing it as individual and family experiences to recognizing that trauma for members of targeted and oppressed sociopolitical groups stems from historical, structural, and political forces. This also involves an acknowledgment that alongside of historical/collective trauma, there is tremendous strength, resilience, and beauty. Psychosocial well-being entails recognition, grieving, and memorializing profound losses while drawing on cultural epistemologies and practices that facilitated survival in the past and offer maps for future transformation and collective well-being. It is important to judiciously integrate insights from Western psychosocial traditions with the many sources of indigenous wisdom and approaches to healing. While the sources of oppression are structural, the impact is inscribed on people's bodies, health, souls, and psyches; thus, psychosocial approaches should also blend attention to intrapersonal factors with working at the group, tribal, and collective levels leading to advocacy, activism, and engagement with social movements that seek to enact social policies and transform societies. Individual and collective healing are inextricably intertwined!

Note

1 The use of the words "developed" and "developing" runs the risk of echoing the hierarchies of coloniality – civilized/uncivilized, superior/inferior – and erases the violent, intentional processes that created these dichotomies; thus I put them in quotes.

References

Alexander, J.C. (2016). Culture trauma, morality and solidarity: The social construction of "Holocaust" and other mass murders. *Thesis Eleven*, *132*(1): 3–16.

Barnes, R., & Josefowitz, N. (2019). Indian residential schools in Canada: Persistent impacts of aboriginal students' psychological development and functioning. *Canadian Psychology*, *60*(2): 65–76. DOI: 10.1037/cap0000154.

Blanco, A., Blanco, R., & Diaz, D. (2016). Social (dis) order and psychosocial trauma: Look earlier, look outside and look beyond the persons. *American Psychologist*, *71*(3): 187–198. DOI: 10.1037/a0040100.

Brave Heart, M.Y.H., Chase, J., Myers, O., Elkins, J., Skipper, B., Schmitt, C., Mootz, J., & Waldorf, V.A. (2020). *Iwankapyia* American Indian pilot clinical trial. *Psychotherapy*, *57*(2): 184–196. DOI: 10.1037/pst0000267.

Brave Heart, M.Y.H., & DeBruyn, L.M. (1998). The American Indian holocaust: Healing historical unresolved grief. *American Indian and Alaska Native Mental Health Research*, *8*(2): 56. DOI: 10.5820/aian.0802.1998.60.

British Broadcasting Corporation. (2021, July 1). *Canada day: Discovery of more unmarked graves fuels call to cancel holiday*. www.bbc.co.uk/news/world-us-canada-57674682.

Bryant, R.A. (2018). The current evidence for acute stress disorder. *Current Psychiatry Reports, 20*: 111. DOI: 10.1007/s11920-018-0976-x.

Bryant-Davis, T. (2005). *Thriving in the wake of trauma: A multicultural guide*. Westport, CT: Praeger Publishing.

Carter, R.T. (2007). Racism and psychological and emotional injury: Recognizing and assessing race-based traumatic stress. *Counseling Psychologist*, *35*(5): 1–93.

Cerdena, J.P., Rivera, L.M., & Spak, J.M. (2021). Intergenerational trauma in Latinxs: A scoping review. *Social Science and Medicine*. DOI: 10.1016/j.socscimed.2020.113662.

Corbin, J., & Miller, J. (2009). Collaborative psychosocial capacity building in Northern Uganda. *Families in Society*, *90*(1): 103–109.

DeJongh, A., et al. (2016). Critical analysis of the current treatment guidelines for complex PTSD in adults. *Depression and Anxiety*, *33*: 359–369.

Fanon, F. (1963). *The wretched of the earth*. New York, NY: Grove Press.

Fanon, F. (1967). *White skin, Black masks*. New York, NY: Grove Press.

Garran, A.M., Werkmeister-Rozas, L., Kang, H.K., & Miller, J. (2021). *Racism in the United States: Implications for the human professions*. New York, NY: Springer Publishing.

Grousfoguel, R. (2013). Decolonizing post-colonial studies and paradigms of political-economy: Transmodernity, decolonial thinking, and global coloniality. *Transmodernity: Journal of Peripheral Cultural Production of the Luso-Hispanic World*, *1*(1). https://escholarship.org/uc/item/21k6t3fq

Hambira, K., & Gleckman-Krut, M. (2021, July 8). Germany apologized for a genocide. It is nowhere near enough. *The New York Times*. www.nytimes.com/2021/07/08/opinion/germany-genocide-herero-nama.html?action=click&module=Opinion&pgtype=Homepage

Hartmann, W.E., Wendt, D.C., Burrage, R.L., Pomerville, A., & Gone, J.P. (2019). American Indian historical trauma: Anticolonial prescriptions for healing, resilience and survivance. *American Psychologist*, *74*(1): 6–19. DOI: 10.1037/amp0000326.

Heberle, A.E., Obus, E.A., & Gray, S.A.O. (2020). An intersectional perspective on the intergenerational transmission of trauma and state-perpetrated violence. *Journal of Social Issues*. DOI: 10.1111/josi.12404.

Heinrich, J. (2020). *The WEIRDest people in the world: How the West became psychologically peculiar and particularly prosperous*. New York: Farah, Strauss, Giroux.

Henderson, Z.R., Stephens, T.N., Ortega-Williams, A., & Walton, Q.L. (2021). Conceptualizing healing through the African American experience of historical trauma. *American Journal of Orthopsychiatry*, *91*(6): 763–775.

Ho, G., et al. (2021). Complex PTSD symptoms mediate the association between childhood trauma and physical health problems. *Journal of Psychosomatic Research*, *142*. DOI: 10.1016/j.jpsychores.2021.110358.

Hobfoll, S.E., Watson, P., Bell, C.C., Bryant, R.A., Brymer, M.J., Friedman, M.J., Friedman, M., Gersons, B.P.R., De Jong, J.T.V.M., Layne, C.M., Maguen, S., Neria, Y., Norwood, A.E., Pynoos, R.S., Reisman, D., Ruzek, J.I., Shalev, A.Y., Solomon, Z., Steinberg, A.M., & Ursano, R.J. (2007). Five essential elements of immediate and mid-term mass trauma intervention: Empirical evidence. *Psychiatry*, *70*(4): 283–315.

Ingham, K. (2021). Uganda. *The Encyclopedia Britannica*. www.britannica.com/place/Uganda

Isobel, S., McCloughen, A., Goodyear, M., & Foster, K. (2021). Intergenerational trauma and its relationship to mental health care: A qualitative inquiry. *Community Mental Health Journal*. DOI: 10.1007/s10597-020-00698-1.

Johnson-Henderson, N.A., & Ginty, A.T. (2020). Historical trauma and social support as predictors of psychological stress responses in American Indian adults during the COVID-19 pandemic. *Journal of Psychosomatic Research*. DOI: 10.1016/j.jpsychores.2020.110263.

Judah, B. (2016). *This is London: Life and death in the world city*. London: Picador.

Karatzias, T., et al. (2019). Psychological interventions for ICD-11 complex PTSD symptoms: Systematic review and meta-analysis. *Psychological Medicine*, 1–15. DOI: 10.1017/S0033291719000436.

Kira, I.A., Shuweikh, H., Al-Huwailah, A.H., Lewandowsky, L., Alawneh, A.W.N., Abou-Mediene, S., Al Ibrahim, B., & Aljakoub, J. (2018). The central role of social identity in oppression, discrimination and social-structural violence: Collective identity stressors and traumas, their dynamics and mental health impacts. *Peace and Conflict: Journal of Peace Psychology*, *25*(3): 262–268. DOI: 10.1037/pac0000363.

Kirmayer, L.J., Gone, J.P., & Moses, J. (2014). Rethinking historical trauma. *Transcultural Psychiatry*, *51*(3): 299–319.

Kochenov, D. (2019). *Citizenship*. Cambridge, MA: The MIT Press.

Landau, J. (2007). Enhancing resilience: Communities and families as agents of change. *Family Process*, *41*(1): 351–365.

Landau, J., & Saul, J. (2004). Facilitating family and community resilience in response to major disaster. In F. Walsh & M. McGoldrick (Eds.). *Living beyond loss* (pp. 285–309). New York: Norton Publishing.

Marsh, T.B., Coholic, D., Cote-Meek, S., & Najavits, L.M. (2015). Blending aboriginal and Western healing methods to treat intergenerational trauma with substance abuse disorder with aboriginal peoples who live in Northeastern, Ontario, Canada. *Harm Reduction Journal*. DOI: 10.1186/s12954-015-0046-1.

Mendoza, B. (2021, July 3). How a slave market became a national park service site. *The New York Times*. www.nytimes.com/2021/07/03/us/forks-of-the-road-national-park.html

Mignolo, W.D., & Walsh, C.E. (2018). *On coloniality: Concepts, analytics, praxis*. Durham, NC: Duke University Press.

Miller, J.L. (2012). *Psychosocial capacity building in response to disasters*. New York: Columbia University Press.

Miller, J.L., & Pescaroli, G. (2018). Psychosocial capacity building in response to cascading disasters: A culturally informed approach. *International Journal of Disaster Risk Reduction*, *30*: 164–171. DOI: 10.1016/j.ijdrr.2018.04.018

Miller, J.L., & Wang, X. (2017). When there are no therapists: A psychoeducational group for people who have experienced social disasters. *Smith Studies in Social Work*, *88*(1): 39–58.

Mohatt, N.V., Thompson, A.B., Thai, N.G., & Tebes, J.K. (2014). Historical trauma as public narrative: A conceptual review of how history affects present-day health. *Social Science and Medicine*, *106*: 128–136.

National Health Service. (2021). *Causes-post-traumatic stress disorder*. www.nhs.uk/mental-health/conditions/post-traumatic-stress-disorder-ptsd/causes/

National Institute of Health. (2021). *Post-traumatic stress disorder*. www.nimh.nih.gov/health/topics/post-traumatic-stress-disorder-ptsd/

O'Neill, L., Fraser, T., Kitchenham, A., & McDonald, V. (2018). Hidden burdens: A review of intergenerational, historical and complex trauma, implications for indigenous families. *Journal of Child and Adolescent Trauma*, *11*. DOI: 10.1007/s40653-016-0117-9.

Ortega-Williams, A., Beltran, R., Schultz, K., Henderson, Z.R., Colon, L., & Teyra, C. (2021a). An integrated historical trauma and posttraumatic growth framework: A cross-cultural exploration. *Journal of Trauma & Dissociation*. DOI: 10.1080/15299732.2020.1869106.

Ortega-Williams, A., Crutchfield, J., & Hall, J.C. (2021b). The colorist-historical framework: Implications for culturally responsive practice with African Americans. *Journal of Social Work*, *21*(3): 294–309.

Quijano, A. (2000). Coloniality of power and Eurocentrism in Latin America. *International Sociology*, *15*(2): 215–232.

Shahjahan, R.A., Estera, A.L., Surla, K.L., & Edwards, K.T. (2022). "Decolonizing" curriculum and pedagogy: A comparative review across disciplines and global higher education contexts. *Review of Educational Research*, *92*(1): 73–113. DOI: 10.3102/00346543211042423.

Summerfield, D. (2000). Childhood, war, refugeedom and "trauma": Three core questions for mental health professionals. *Transcultural Psychiatry*, *37*: 417–433.

Summerfield, D. (2004). Cross cultural perspectives on the medicalisation of human suffering. In G. Rosen (Ed.). *Posttraumatic stress disorder: Issues and controversies* (pp. 233–247). New York: John Wiley.

Treuer, D. (2021, May). Return the national parks to the tribes. *The Atlantic*. www.theatlantic.com/magazine/archive/2021/05/return-the-national-parks-to-the-tribes/618395/

Van der Kolk, B. (2014). *The body keeps the score: Brain, mind, and body in the healing of trauma*. New York, NY: Penguin Books.

Waters, K.L., Mohammed, S.A., Evans-Campbell, T., Beltran, R.E., Chae, D.H., & Duran, B. (2011). Bodies don't just tell stories, they tell histories. *Du Bois Review*, *8*(1): 179–189.

Weyerman, B. (2007). Linking economics and emotions: Towards a more integrated understanding of empowerment in conflict areas. *Intervention*, *5*(2): 83–96.

Williams-Washington, K.M., & Mills, C.P. (2018). African American historical trauma: Creating an inclusive measure. *Journal of Multicultural Counseling and Development*. DOI: 10.1002/jmcd.12113.

Yehuda, R., & Lehrner, A. (2018). Intergenerational transmission of trauma effects: Putative role of epigenetic mechanisms. *World Psychiatry*, *17*: 243–257.

3 Collective, Interpersonal, and Intrapersonal Consequences of Structural Oppression

Introduction

In the previous chapter, I considered the nature of historical and collective trauma, suggesting that all historical trauma is collective and that collective trauma has historical roots. The legacies of coloniality are structural oppression, hierarchies based on the construction of social identities, unequal personhood and citizenship within and between nations, and a highly unequal global economic and political system, reflecting which countries were colonized and which were the colonizers. Helping professionals/volunteers must therefore consider how coloniality and structural oppression have collective consequences (e.g., on community cohesion and trust, social networks, access to power and resources, cultural dominance and erasure), interpersonal consequences (e.g., relations within families, family roles, dynamics of workplace interaction, how people interact in public places), and intrapersonal consequences (how structural oppression affects health and well-being throughout the life course, identity and one's sense of self, thinking, feelings, behaviors, and the options people believe that they have for how they choose to live their lives).

Structural oppression and social targeting affect all aspects of people's lives; the nature of their society and neighborhoods, where they can and cannot live, what educational and occupational opportunities do and do not exist, access to formal and informal political power, cultural centrality or marginalization, pressures on people to conform to certain categories and roles of gender and sexuality, norms and expectations for parenting and childrearing, as well as the range of psychosocial consequences mentioned in Chapter 2. Therefore, when working with socio-politically targeted populations, there is an array of ways to intervene, often in combination. Thus, helping professionals can

DOI: 10.4324/9781003021162-3

try to influence politics, advocate for laws and social policies, work with communities to strengthen collective efficacy and generate social capital and economic resources, run groups for people with shared social identities, engage in relationship counseling, and work as therapists, life coaches, and mentors with individuals. But because of the way professional helping services are organized, particularly within developed nations, helping professionals are expected to specialize in one level or one aspect of intervention; service systems reflect specialization and atomization while people's lives are holistic and interconnected. This in turn influences how professionals are educated and how they practice, which reinforces the isolation of clinical work from organizing and advocacy. It is important to hold this conundrum – between the way professional services are offered and the reality of people's lives – as a persistent tension for those engaged in psychosocial practice. In this chapter, I will describe the nature of structural oppression and then review three levels of psychosocial consequences of structural oppression: (1) social and collective; (2) interpersonal; and (3) intrapersonal, as well as ways that people resist. In Chapter 4, I will consider the impact of extreme and persistent violence, before devoting the remainder of the book to explicating a model of psychosocial intervention.

The Nature of Structural Oppression

In order to collaborate with people who are experiencing collective, structural oppression, and to minimize the potential for harm, it is important to explore how oppression operates. A critical dimension of structural oppression is the social construction of unequal social identities. Identity is often thought of as something that evolves developmentally and volitionally; we can choose our religion, our political affiliations, and for some where we live. Particularly, but not exclusively, in Western countries, there are values about individualism; creating one's own life course and having opportunities to make choices about who we are and what we do with our lives that buttress this view of identity. But much of social identity is proscribed by society. During the European invasion of North America and the founding of the United States, only White people were viewed as fully human and entitled to human rights. This status did not apply to indigenous people or enslaved persons from Africa; they could not *choose* to be white. In the clan-based society of Northern Uganda, one is born into a tribe and cannot decide to change tribes. In Xinjiang, China, ethnic Uighurs cannot claim to be Han Chinese. Such categories are both real in the sense that not only they are the basis for social segregation and targeting, but they are also social constructions that create rigid categories to explain and justify social inequality, often appealing to biological or cultural explanations for alleged differences between people. These categories differ depending on the social ecology where they are constructed as well as the historical period when they arise. The categories are both accepted, particularly by those with privilege, and contested, particularly by those who are denigrated and disparaged by virtue of their social identities.

Social mores determine who is considered abled or disabled, gender categories and roles, what is considered "normal" sexuality, and who is considered a citizen with full rights. In Uganda, it is a crime to be Queer and homosexuality can lead to arrest and draconian punishments. In North American cities, such as New York, San Francisco, and Toronto, there are many people who are gender non-conforming and/or transgender, but the social space for such identities is constricted in many other parts of North America and the world or even prohibited. Such social and cultural limitations are often resisted and contested and social identities are not fixed or static.

Garran et al. (2021) have defined social identity as how we see ourselves in relation to other people, based on groups that we are members of or identify with, and how we are in turn understood by others and labeled and positioned within a sociocultural milieu. All of us have multiple identities – e.g., gender, sexual orientation, race, ethnicity, religion, socioeconomic class – that interact and intersect. Garran et al. note some important aspects of social identity:

- Social identities change over time for some people. While certain aspects of our social identity are consistent and stable and some people live in social contexts or historical periods where there is greater stability and less fluidity, for many people, there are shifts in aspects of their social identity. For example, someone may be born in a working-class or agricultural family and through education become a professional and increasingly more economically secure, while their race and gender remain consistent. Or a woman married in a heterosexual relationship might become single and perhaps then live with a woman or in a Queer polyamorous situation.
- Some of our social identities are chosen, some imposed, and often a combination of the two. For example, racial categories have and still are imposed on BIPOC folks by formal and informal policies and practices, while religion may be chosen.

- We are aware of some aspects of our social identities all of the time while others only at certain moments or in specific situations. The context in which we find ourselves highlights or minimizes aspects of our social identities. If I am the only man in a group of people, I will probably be aware of my gender but if I am having dinner with a small group of heterosexual couples and I am also heterosexual, I might take my sexual orientation and the social advantages that it carries for granted.
- Conflict, oppression, and being socially targeted highlight our social identities – we are often, if not always aware of them – while having the privilege and being part of a majority contributes to social identities appearing to be "normal" and thus less visible. For example, white people often will describe a person of color as "an African American man" or "Latina woman" while referring to white people as just a man or woman.
- This last point highlights another important aspect of social identities – they are not just different but also carry differential power and privilege. In the United States today, being a cis-gendered, heterosexual, middle-class white male carries an inordinate amount of social power compared to people with other social identities. This does not necessarily mean that a person *feels* powerful or privileged, but if we examine statistics of certain indicators, such as health, arrest records, being targeted by violence, net worth, and access to resources, this person is more likely to occupy a higher place in a social hierarchy. Sociologically, having identities with social privilege makes a huge difference to life chances and opportunities and how a person experiences the world: particularly a sense of centrality, belonging, and safety. Some people have many privileged aspects of their social identities while others have very few, while others have a mixture of social identities carrying differential power and privilege. As mentioned earlier, we often are most aware of those identities that are targeted but less aware of privileged aspects of our identity because those identities are considered "normal" and "central" and are mirrored by society and reflected by social institutions. Thus, the identities of dominant social groups are validated, while those of socially targeted groups are stereotyped and distorted; those with privilege are like fish who do not notice the water in which they swim while those who are oppressed need to constantly navigate rip-tides and are often swimming against the current.
- Lastly, none of us are solely one part of our social identity although some parts are either particularly meaningful for the person or are very salient for society, or both. Social identities are intersectional,

> and this is cumulative, not additive. If I am a queer South Asian woman of a lower caste, depending on where I live I am probably a minority within a minority within a minority when it comes to social targeting, social status, and the ability to live my life as I choose. Intersectionality reflects interacting structural oppressions but is an embodied experience for individuals and groups of people with shared identities.

Having briefly sketched the concept of social identity, I will discuss how structural oppression and social identity interact.

Structural Oppression and Social Identity

Exploitation and Resource Hoarding

Tilly (1998) described "durable inequalities" that are constant and consistent between groups with different social identities, with resource hoarding being central to their maintenance. A few examples of modern-day exploitation are wealthy nations extracting minerals and precious metals from poor nations, hiring low-wage workers from neighboring countries without granting civil or citizenship rights, and hiring poor women to clean middle-class homes without offering benefits. Resource hoarding is maintaining access to certain resources (e.g., living in certain neighborhoods, children of alumni legacy having preferential treatment for admissions in elite universities, offering COVID booster shots in developed nations while most people in developing countries have not received any vaccinations) and through formal or informal means, ensuring preferential treatment for people with certain social identities (e.g., White people, men, straight couples) and barriers and exclusions for targeted and marginalized social identities (e.g., BIPOC persons or non-White/Western countries.

Differential Access to Infrastructure Needed for Success and Upward Mobility

Infrastructure is a specific example of resource hoarding – e.g., roads, schools, efficient transportation networks, electricity, running water and sewage, access to food, health care, employment opportunities, and high-speed Internet. Infrastructure provides the river bed for the flow of opportunity, growth, and success. Those with superior infrastructure continue to benefit from unequal opportunities, which increasingly become intergenerational advantages.

This Influences a Sense of Power and Entitlement

While clinicians work to help targeted people feel a sense of agency and empowerment, the message from society is the opposite. Do people feel as if they belong, are safe and secure, can achieve their goals, and have hope for the future, or are they constantly fighting for their full personhood? Many people are able to experience a sense of empowerment despite structural oppression, but this involves tremendous effort and requires support from family, friends, and social networks, and hovering over achievements is a persistent sense of economic and social precariousness.

Control Over Your Group's Narrative

One aspect of a sense of power is the ability to tell your own story and not have others tell their story about you (Berman, 1994). The vast majority of the written history of North America unabashedly and unreflectively tells the story of the United States and Canada from the perspective of the colonizers (Mamdani, 2020). Indigenous people are often portrayed as "uncivilized, violent, uneducated, untrustworthy" (which when considering the level of violence enacted upon indigenous people more aptly describes the colonizers). When a group experiences genocide, ethnic cleansing, and other forms of violence and then finds themselves as distorted stereotypes in someone else's narrative, there is then a secondary wound to grieve and recover from.

Valued or Devalued Personhood

One consequence of not having control over one's narrative and experiencing historical and structural oppression is having to fight for one's full personhood. Whether it is by virtue of race, gender, class, or sexuality, those who are members of more dominant social groups are not called upon by society to justify their personhood, ways of thinking and understanding the world, and their worth as human beings. This is yet another example of how clinicians may work to help people feel valued while society conveys the opposite message.

Webs of Oppression Are Systematic, Comprehensive, and Cumulative

It is not only being unable to afford to live in a neighborhood (or excluded from a neighborhood for other reasons) but also how this affects access to schools, infrastructure, social networks, banks, shops, jobs, and so on. Thus, people usually do not experience only one or two aspects of webs of oppression, but rather the entire web is connected and the consequences are cumulative. There is a cascading historical toll: webs of oppression did not just spring from the present but are the legacies of historical processes that have been advantaging and depleting different groups of people over time. When White immigrants to the United States were eventually able to buy a starter home, it was usually in a neighborhood where their property values grew over time, allowing the family to accumulate intergenerational assets, which is very different from Black people in the United States who were often restricted to purchasing homes in neighborhoods that lost value over time (Garran et al., 2021; Shapiro, 2004).

Multiple Levels, Formal and Informal

As was mentioned earlier, structural oppression is multifaceted and occurs on multiple levels – macro, mezzo, micro – so that it can affect people economically, socially, and interpersonally and is internalized cognitively, emotionally, and behaviorally. These are not separate planes of experience but rather are seamlessly connected and thus need to be addressed holistically. They reflect not only formal attempts to exploit and resource hoard but also habits, patterns, and tendencies. Segregated neighborhoods in North America were constructed through formal policies – such as who was eligible or ineligible for mortgage loans or the GI Bill after World War II – but also informal practices – e.g., real estate agents redlining neighborhoods that were only shown to White or Black people, or restrictive covenants where people in a White neighborhood agreed not to sell their homes to Black people (Garran et al., 2021).

Parameters Influencing Structural Oppression

As psychosocial workers assess how to help people experiencing structural oppression, there are important societal differences that not only shape the contours of oppression but determine the means and possibilities of resistance.

The History and Form of Structural Oppression

If we look at various forms of structural oppression, they are determined by many variables. If we scan the globe today, we see Uighurs being incarcerated and under surveillance in Xinjiang, China. In the United States, police violence and criminal justice racism is particularly directed toward Black and Brown people. In Northern Nigeria, the state has been unable to protect children from being abducted by Muslim militants from the North. The Hazara ethnic minority in Afghanistan is facing attacks and possible genocide by the Taliban. All of these examples involve ethnic/racial targeting and all involve a range of violent measures – e.g., incarceration, ethnic cleansing, murder, genocide, and abduction – but the historical antecedents and modern structural variables are different. There are unique factors that need to be considered for each of these situations by a psychosocial worker or volunteer – e.g., when does violence occur, what resources exist for protection, and what can people do to protect themselves – and there are also common psychosocial factors about the psychosocial consequences of unrelenting exposure to violence, which will be covered in the next chapter. It is also important to reflect on what forms of resistance have been successful in the past and how things have shifted over time. For example, while white supremacy has been part of the DNA of the United States since its inception, the abolitionist and civil rights movements achieved significant accomplishments, and yet it also remains determining force in today's U.S. society.

The Political Context in Which Sociopolitical Targeting Takes Place

Do the targeting and oppression occur in a constitutional democracy or in a totalitarian state? Is the source of repression directly from the state, from parts of the state (e.g., states in the United States trying to limit the right of BIPOC people to vote), other actors, or some kind of combination? What kinds of protections exist for civil and political rights? This should not be thought of in binary terms but more as a spectrum between elected and accountable governments to overtly repressive, totalitarian regimes, from countries with individual rights and protections to those with group rights. This is of course not fixed, and nations and societies go through different phases of openness and repression. Nor am I suggesting that Western democracies are a better form of government – many Western democracies have sordid and reprehensible histories of colonialism and imperialism, genocide, ethnic cleansing, and slavery.

The Social Ecology of a Given Society or Region

I introduced the concept of social ecology in Chapter 1, and there are many factors to consider. Are populations extremely heterogenous or homogenous? Has one ethnic/racial group consistently held power or is this contested and fluid? How does the unique history of the country shape current forms of social oppression? What are the dynamics of power, privilege, and intergroup relations for this region? Is there an independent media and freedom of access on the Internet? What cultural norms and values influence the dynamics of oppression?

Narratives

How oppression is storied has an influence on how it is understood and conceptualized. Usually, there are multiple narratives, often incompatible, such as those between Jewish Israelis and Palestinians. Sometimes, the group(s) with power and privilege have a narrative that justifies their social position, such as genetic theories of white supremacy or notions of the superiority of certain religions, but often members of groups with societal advantages cast themselves in the role of victim, such as Donald Trump and the Republican party in the United States today who further white supremacy through an ideology of grievance.

Resistance

How have members of groups that have experienced historical oppression resisted? What has worked and what led to a worsening of conditions and greater targeting and repression? What has been the role of coloniality in shaping present-day subjugation and persecution?

The Psychosocial Consequences of Structural Oppression

Structural oppression divides people. There are those who regularly experience it, those who are unaware of it (willfully or unseeingly), and those who are actively or passively part of the apparatuses of repression. Intersectionality, as I have discussed, makes this more complicated. There are people with interacting social identities tilting toward having many social privileges, those facing multiple sources of structural oppression, and for many people a mixture of privileged and oppressed aspects of social identity. The consequences of social oppression are collective and communal, affecting families, and affect individuals in a myriad of destructive ways. While it is difficult to separate out the different levels of psychosocial consequences because they are intricately intertwined, I will describe three broad categories: collective, community, and cultural; family/interpersonal; and individual (Box 3.1).

Box 3.1 Psychosocial Consequences of Structural Oppression and Social Targeting

Collective, Community, and Cultural Consequences

Segregation – leading to social isolation and lack of access to infrastructure, jobs, and services

Lack of political power – leading to policies and practices that target and harm rather than serve and empower

Lack of economic opportunity – whether through lack of access to quality education, jobs, careers, or owning homes where property values diminish rather than grow, there is less access to what is needed for economic security and success

Lack of control and authorship over public group narrative – which leads to groups being defined by those with greater power, including being the target of stereotypes and denigration

Cultural erasure and appropriation – undermining collective strength and connections with the past, leading to collective and cultural trauma

Undermining social cohesion and trust – which can weaken in-group solidarity, rupture social networks, and isolate groups from the larger society

Workplace discrimination, exclusion, and erasure – leading to:

1. Formal and informal policies that favor some and disadvantage and oppress others
2. Enduring microaggressions, stereotypes, and interpersonal aggression
3. Lack of access to organizational power
4. Insufficient resources dedicated to social justice and equity

Social isolation – which impacts friendships and relationships and limits social networks

Family Consequences

Direct and vicarious experiences of social oppression by family members – which place stress on family relationships

The inability to protect loved ones due to the consequences and violence of social oppression
Leading to a sense of lack of safety and security in the family
Grieving – Over losses and the costs to the family of social oppression

Individual/Interpersonal Consequences

Physical, medical, psychological, and emotional harm – which includes poorer health, lower life expectancy, higher infant mortality, and threats to child well-being
Living in a constant state of alertness and hypervigilance – which creates chronic stress and tension and diminishes the ability for flourishing and self-care
Enduring attacks on one's character, identity, and personhood – denying people social validation and mirroring
Mourning and grieving collective, family, and individual losses
Increased vulnerability and stress for helping professionals with targeted and minoritized identities

Collective, Community, and Cultural Consequences

Segregation

Segregation is a cornerstone of sociopolitical oppression and targeting and has cascading consequences. It leads to a lack of access to good schools and jobs, higher concentrations of social isolation, poverty, and less services and resources. This affects the ability to start and run small businesses and there may be fewer pathways to jobs in larger corporations and organizations. Crime rates are higher, police protection lower and attacks by law enforcement, government, and vigilante groups are more common. In the United States, most white people live in neighborhoods where housing values and equity rises while many African Americans live in neighborhoods where property values decline (Garran et al., 2021; Logan & Stults, 2011; Shapiro, 2004). Overall, segregated neighborhoods offer less access to capital, wealth, knowledge, and cultural resources. There is greater exposure to environmental hazards and toxins, scarcer sources of healthy food, fewer spaces for recreation, and less health-care options.

This is not only true for racial segregation in the United States but for people segregated wholly or partially due to aspects of their social identity or who live in different parts of the world. In Afghanistan, as in many countries that were created by colonial powers, there are competing ethnic groups and tribes vying for power and dominance. Hazaras, an ethnic minority who are Shiite, have been consistently targeted for assassinations and attacks on schools and neighborhoods and are gathered in certain towns, regions, and neighborhoods in Kabul, due to social exclusion but also in an attempt to create zones of safety. With the retaking of control of the country by the Taliban, they have faced even greater threats and possible genocide.

Also, in Afghanistan, women have been segregated from many aspects of public life as well as having to conform to norms about social roles and dress. This has affected their life-chances and opportunities in many of the same ways as racism proscribes opportunities in the United States. Should women challenge these norms, they face violence, social ostracism, family pressure, and violence – in other words, their safety is consistently threatened. I am using Afghanistan as an example, but this pattern persists in many countries and global regions.

Lack of Political Power/Being Politically Targeted

This is often aligned with segregation but is a factor in its own right. Power in society resides in many sites – e.g., industry, the military, the media, among the wealthy – as well as within grassroots resistance and social movements (Garran et al., 2021). Political power is most overtly represented in government and politics. In the United States, political power was denied to all people of color, including the country's indigenous inhabitants, as well as women and poor white men at its inception. While the right to vote has been granted to all of these groups since there are current efforts to strip this right away from people. The most recent example is the wave of voter suppression and election nullification laws being passed by Republican-controlled legislatures at the state level, aided and abetted by the gutting of the Voting Rights Act of 1965 by the Supreme Court in 2014 (Berman, 2015; Garran et al., 2021; McIlwain & Caliendo, 2014). Much of this has been funded by wealthy white men trying to increase their hold on power and ability to exploit the environment for their own gain (Mayor, 2021). The Supreme Court further magnified the power of the wealthy to influence elections with a decision in 2010, allowing political action committees to spend unlimited amounts of money to influence elections and not having to identify the sources of donations (Vandewalker, 2015).

The consequences of past and current voter suppression, as well as gerrymandering and other ways of denying democratic representation are far fewer elected people who are BIPOC, women, LGBTQIA, and disabled than their share of the population of the country. This is true of all levels of government but becomes a more profound pattern at the highest levels of government. There has only been one BIPOC president in the United States in its history and never a woman or LGBTQIA person. Ultimately, there is a vicious cycle of suppressing the vote, allowing unlimited money to influence elections (and whose candidates support tax laws that disproportionately benefit the wealthy), which results in a minority of white people maintaining political control at all levels of government, and giving them the power to appoint judges (e.g., six of the nine Supreme Court Justices), who favor their efforts to limit and restrict democratic voting rights.

I have described the lack of political access in an economically developed nation. Not only does this take place in countries at all stages of development but also leads to people holding political power to subjugate and threaten other groups overtly (e.g., through force to control people, attacks, lack of protection, police brutality, racial profiling, patronage) and covertly (e.g., political exclusion, twisting rules and regulations to benefit those in power, running elections with the veneer of democracy where the rules are rigged in favor of those in power). And in its most extreme forms, unequal political power and lack of fair representation are expressed through state efforts that foster chronic subordinate status (e.g., Arabs in Israel), ethnic cleansing, and genocide.

Lack of Economic Opportunities

The first two collective consequences interact with exclusion from economic opportunities. There are many ways that this occurs. One is the lack of capital and resources to begin small businesses. I know a driver in Kampala, Uganda, who must always rent a van if he is escorting tourists or NGO workers, which leaves him with little profit. His ability to pay for his own van is severely limited by his lack of access to loans and capital. Although his situation is true of many people trying to start a business in developing countries, which is a legacy of colonialism, he is not a member of a socially targeted group. I use this example to illustrate how much harder it would be if he was! Women have very little access to loans and capital in many parts of the world and are prohibited from schools and many jobs. Governments can choose ethnic winners and losers and through formal and informal practices make it harder for people with certain ethnic or religious identities to access the resources needed for economic endeavors.

It is also true about larger companies and corporations, where social networks count far more than merit, and many people with socially targeted identities do not have access to those social networks. This was an informal pattern of racial segregation in many U.S. corporations for many years (Garran et al., 2021). There are also neighborhoods with few companies and corporations to work for and the same discrimination based on gender and sexuality described earlier applies as well. This is also exacerbated by mismatches of skills needed for jobs and what people are learning from local schools and community colleges, as well

There are also interacting interpersonal factors. In his book *In search of respect* (1995), Philippe Bourgois follows two LatinX men who are drug dealers in New York City who are astute small businessmen in charge or their own work. They have decided to take the risks of running an illegal business because of their experiences of feeling marginalized, ridiculed, and disrespected when holding low-level corporate jobs. Cose (1993) has conducted research with middle-class Black employees who find that they are expected to conform to White norms of dress, behavior, communication, and recreation despite having degrees from prestigious institutions. Employees with targeted identities also experience microaggressions, where they, on a regular basis, experience interaction with white colleagues that betray stereotypes, prejudice, aversion, disrespect, and marginalization (Garran et al., 2021; Sue & Spanierman, 2020). All of this leads to lower rates of promotion and upward mobility (Pager & Western, 2012) and greater work stress (which will be considered below), resulting in the bleaching of the more senior work force as a disproportionate number of white people are in higher level, leadership positions. This also accentuates who are role models and who sets the tone for the company culture, which invites some people in and leads others to feel like tokens or perpetual outsiders. What goes on the workplace interacts with what occurs in neighborhoods, affecting economic and social capital.

Social Cohesion

Facing adversity can increase social solidarity and cohesion, which I will consider in the following section on resistance to social oppression. But the social exclusion, discrimination, and lack of opportunity described in this section can also leave residents of neighborhoods feeling isolated, mistrustful, despondent, constantly under siege, unsafe, disrespected, and devalued, all of which can undermine social cohesion. Social cohesion is when a group of people feel connected, and intertwined with one another, forming a distinct entity (Petrosino & Pace, 2015) such as neighborhood and block identities. Strong social cohesion involves a sense of collective efficacy, the belief that people can affect changes on behalf of the community, setting goals, and being able to achieve them (Sampson et al., 1997, 1999; Wilson, 2011). Collective efficacy relies on a sense of social trust and an ability to articulate and work toward common collective goals (Putnam, 2000). One of the most insidious aspects of social oppression is the erosion of social trust, undermining social cohesion and collective efficacy. This contributes to collective trauma, weakened social status, and collective malaise (Saleem et al., 2020).

Being the Object, Rather Than Author of Public Narratives About Your Group

People with social identities that are socially targeted struggle to be able to present themselves in their own voices as they want to be seen. Instead, they are often the objects of collective stereotypes, disinformation campaigns, and lurid stereotypes that dehumanize groups of people and place people in a precarious position. Who has the ability to reach many people to tell a story and the power to influence people about its veracity – an immigrant from Mexico or President Donald Trump? President Trump used his bully pulpit and access to social media to terrorize immigrants of color residing in the United States by controlling the public narrative about them. Trump was not only able to demonize people (e.g., referring to them as "rapists" and "criminals") but had the power of his office and the military behind him, while at the same time, he put forth a narrative that white supremacists were "decent people" (Baker & Haberman, 2020; Miller, 2020). When a group no longer can control their own narrative that explains who they are, what they need, and the values that they stand for, then they are at the mercy of divisive demagogic politicians, such as Trump and his many brethren around the world.

Cultural Erasure and Trauma

Related to the lack of control over one's group narrative is the erasure and marginalization of the cultures of groups who are experiencing social targeting. Examples of this are the stereotypes and distortions of Indigenous peoples in the United States, branding feminists demonstrating against misogyny in China as being against the state, or when promulgating a one-sided, partial narrative, limited narrative – lionizing one tribe and denigrating others – after a war between ethnic groups in an African country. This particularly occurs in the wake of colonialism and the many armed conflicts that accompany colonialism and the legacy that it bequeathed to the present.

Alexander (2016) has noted that cultural trauma occurs when a "horrendous event" has happened with a group sharing a collective identity, leading to "indelible marks" on group consciousness, memory, and collective identity. An example in the United States of the impact of attacks on collective well-being, culture, and personhood is that of Japanese Americans incarcerated during World War II because of their race and ethnicity (Nagata et al., 2015). Despite some members of the group living in the United States for years and generations, with many people having served in the armed forces on behalf of the United States, all Japanese Americans were rounded up and jailed, which did not happen to German Americans while the United States was at war with Germany at the same time. The response to this injustice by those affected was often silence instead of expressions of anger, trying to assimilate rather than reasserting one's culture, what Danieli has referred to as a "conspiracy of silence" (Nagata et al., 2015). This led to ulcers, depression, and premature death (which will be considered in the following section on individual consequences of social oppression), and initially a loss of cultural pride and efficacy. Thankfully, collective efforts, often spearheaded by a younger generation that had not directly experienced the atrocity seeking justice and reparations helped to overcome shame and unite, mobilize and reconnect people with their sense of belonging and cultural personhood (Nagata et al., 2015).

Workplace Consequences

The same forces that affect families also influence and shape workplace dynamics, social circles, and friendships. In the office, the dynamics of social privilege and oppression are often manifested in four ways (Garran et al., 2021): (1) formal and informal policies; (2) interpersonal relationships; (3) access to organizational power; and (4) resource allocation.

As Tilly (1998) argued about "durable inequalities," if they exist in society at large, they are emulated and replicated in all subsets of society, such as organizations. In liberal democracies, unfair and discriminatory policies are often covert, while in other contexts, there is outright discrimination against women, sexual minorities, or people from specific ethnic/racial/religious groups. Hiring and retention practices are often tilted toward people with particular social identities (e.g., young, white, cis-gendered, male), and once a pattern is established, it often reproduces itself. For example, in the United States, applicants with white-sounding names are more likely to be called in for interviews than applicants with African American-sounding names, even though people are equally qualified (Block, 2016). Many people hear about jobs through social networks, so if the staff of a company is mostly white, the informal social channels of communicating openings are likely to mirror this social identity (Garran et al., 2021). Also, from the applicant's side, people are more likely to be attracted to a workplace where they can see other people like them.

There are many other ways that social oppression affects workplaces. Due to discrimination, which affects where people go to school and who has the best access to quality higher education, it is more likely that those with social privilege will have stronger credentials when applying for jobs. Also, workplace cultures usually reflect the way groups with privilege talk, interact, inscribing their worldview and values; this is viewed as the way things are and everyone is expected to conform to this assumed way of doing things. Cose (1993) interviewed many African American professionals who felt compelled to play golf – a sport that they had not grown up with – in order to fit in with their companies' culture.

If someone is a minority in a workplace – e.g., a woman among mostly men, a person of color in a predominantly white organization – they often experience microaggressions – interactions that reflect internal stereotypes and biases that are demeaning, alienating, devaluing, and painful (Garran et al., 2021; Pierce et al., 1978). They can occur whenever there are people with more social power interacting with those who have targeted or minoritized identities (Sue & Spanier, 2020). Microaggressions are often subtle and those who enact them may be unaware that they are doing so, because of their socialization and how their beliefs and behaviors seem "normal." But they are unrelenting and have a cumulative impact, like thousands of paper cuts (Garran et al., 2021). There is a vicious cycle, where those who experience microaggressions may also feel an inordinate amount of pressure to disprove the stereotypes that they are experiencing, which Steele (2011) has called "stereotype threat." Steele conducted research illustrating how stereotype threat and the heightened fear and anxiety that accompanies it can undermine academic and workplace performance. Another part of this dynamic is if a woman confronts gender stereotypes or a transgender man responds to cis-gender privilege, they are often accused of being too sensitive or always and only thinking about their targeted identities or of "misunderstanding" others' intentions: in other words, implying that they don't really understand their own experience, while those with privilege do. These dynamics often influence employee evaluations and promotion prospects.

Another classic way that workplace discrimination operates is through expectations and policies that make it more difficult for people to maintain their jobs because of obligations outside of the workplace. This includes policies about maternity and paternity leave, allowing people with caretaking responsibilities to respond to emergencies at home, and having promotion policies that fail to consider the need for some employees to care for others (e.g., children, elderly, and those with medical needs). Women in all parts of the world find that they are disadvantaged if they have children or caretaking obligations.

All of these factors influence interpersonal relations within workplaces and effect who becomes more senior and where organizational power resides. Within offices, there are often informal groupings of people who share certain social identities. This is not negative per se – it can serve as a protective social network and support system – but it can also lead to isolation and some social networks being more connected with the workplace culture and those in power than others. One of the dilemmas for people with minoritized identities is that they are criticized for whatever strategy they pursue. If they hang out with people like themselves, they are open to the criticism of being cliquish and not being open to others, and yet as Tatum (1997) has written about, such social groupings can buffer people from microaggressions and other workplace stressors. If people confront the stereotypes and microaggressions, or unfair and unequal policies, they are open to the accusation of being a difficult person to work with or a troublemaker. And if they keep their head down, try to ignore or deflect what is going on around them, they can be called out for being withdrawn or antisocial. Coloniality continues to manifest itself through workplace arrangements and cultures, further perpetuating the dynamics of inequality and exploitation.

This has consequences for promotions and bonuses and leads to unequal salaries for people doing the same jobs. For example, college professors of color earn 75% of what their white colleagues make while holding the same rank (Renzulli et al., 2006). This can also reflect what is valued in academia and is used as criteria for promotion – what has been called a "white logic" – contributing to a white racial hierarchy (Moore, 2020). This pattern holds true for other professions and occupations as well.

Organizational power accrues from the patterns that I have been describing and this also determines where resources are allocated. With some rare exceptions, the further one looks at the top of an organizational pyramid, the whiter and more cis-gendered male it looks. In the United States, 90.6% of chief executives are white (Bureau of Labor Statistics, 2020). Only 8 of the 102 chief executives of the top U.S. companies are people of color ((Park et al., 2016). This pattern is also evident when examining who enters and is successful in high-status and high-paying professions – e.g., 89.6% of lawyers and 85% or architects in the United States are white (BLS). Women of all races are severely underrepresented in similar ways, although the rates for women of color are even lower (Garran et al., 2021).

In summary, it is much harder for people with minoritized identities to enter the workplace, far fewer supports to help them succeed, and when they are present, they encounter stereotypes and microaggressions, less opportunities for professional advancement, are paid lower salaries for the same work, and are constantly expected to conform to the culture of those who are members of the dominant group and hold a great deal of power.

Social Relations, Networks, and Friendships

The pattern that takes place in the workplace is also evident in social relations outside of the workplace. Piecing together the dynamics of segregation with the mechanics of coloniality and patterns of dominance/privilege and targeting/oppression, it is not surprising that this shapes who socializes with whom and where people socialize. If anything, social life is more segregated than workplace life. Friendship groups, which people hang out with to socialize and which parts of public places are inhabited by folks, are sometimes referred to as "micro-ecologies" (Dixon et al., 2008). While residential, educational, and occupational patterns of racial segregation have been well documented, there has been less research about the patterns of social connection and exclusion in people's personal lives, and yet in my professional experience, this is where much of the drama of in-group/out-group is played out. Why this happens is probably due to a complex process – Dixon et al. suggest prejudice and its patterns, how people categorize themselves, and "meta-perception," how people think that they are perceived. They have also observed in their review of

U.S. research and their own studies in South Africa that the patterns of racialized hierarchies replicate themselves in how people interact in public places – e.g., how close people stand next to one another, who moves to the front of a line, and where people sit on busses. But I believe that there are other factors as well.

Intergroup research about how people construct who is part of their in-group and who are members of out-groups echoes the notion that people sort themselves out by virtue of their social identities in their private lives. Peer and social groups offer people a sense of identity and belonging, shared understandings of the world, emotional and practical support, and a feeling of security (Garran et al., 2021). The downside of this is that by having an in-group, there is the tendency to displace and disown undesirable qualities onto those who are different, projecting these disavowed tendencies onto a screen of a generalized vision of the other, as well as misattributing motives to the out-group (Miller & Schamess, 2000; Volkan, 1988). This is more likely to happen when there is less contact between groups, described in what is often referred to as "group contact theory," which postulates that the more contact people have together, the more they are able to break down stereotypes, fears, and reservations (Garran et al., 2021; Miller, 2012; Stephan, 2008). Sharing overarching goals (Brewer, 2001), expanding the vision of "us" (Dovidio et al., 2016), and having public leaders who foster healing and reconciliation (Staub, 2001; Whillock, 1995) can all contribute to better intergroup relationships.

This is why the structural patterns of segregation in macro contexts (residential, educational, occupational) and micro-ecologies (public spaces, social networks, friendship groups) – where people congregate with people with shared identities – continue the process of "othering." This is a pattern observed throughout the world and is not only a contributor to ongoing social subjugation but also armed conflict, ethnic cleansing, and genocide. And it can be based on many different aspects of social identity – race/ethnicity, religion, gender, sexuality, caste/class, and more. And so, a vicious cycle ensues where groups with dominant social identities exclude those with minoritized identities in the ways described in this chapter, which in turn creates unrelenting stress and physical and emotional energy having to be expended in warding off threats, distortions, and attempts at subjugation. Stereotypes are reinforced by those with power, targets of social oppression are blamed for their situation, and privilege is not only unexamined but often rendered invisible. An example of this is the fact that the majority of white people in the United States believe that so-called "reverse racism" against white people is a greater problem than racism

(Gonyea, 2017), which is astonishing considering the history of racism in the United States and the mountains of evidence of present-day white supremacy and racism. Ultimately, it leads to a lack of empathy by those with power and privilege for those who they (sometimes unknowingly) socially oppress. When this happens, it is difficult to generate political will for public policies and practices that direct and redistribute resources and empower people, families, and communities who have their life chances constrained by structural oppression. Helping professionals are always swimming upstream as we try to counteract this pervasive, multilayered dynamic.

Family Consequences

Structural, collective, and community consequences influence and shape how people relate to one another, in families, friendships, and the workplace. Norms and expectations about gender roles and sexuality affect the structure, negotiation of power, and dynamics of families. Racial and ethnic segregation impacts who are neighbors, friends, and who people interact with in the workplace and how they interact. Interpersonal relations are the nexus between structural, macro factors and internalized, psycho-emotional reactions. In this section, I will assume that readers have knowledge and understanding of family systems and interpersonal dynamics and will specifically focus on the effects of social oppression on these relationships.

There are many different kinds of families. In certain parts of the world, family means heterosexual, two-parent families with biologically related children. In other parts of the world, there are Queer families, intentional families (where people choose who is in their family rather than having blood ties), polyamorous families, families without children, with adopted children, multiple generations of family living in the same household, and many other configurations. There are places where members of families tend to come from the same ethnic/religious group, while in others, there are multi-racial/ethnic/cultural/religious families. And families are not fixed, rigid, or static entities; there are life cycles and they are always developing, forming, and reforming. The possibilities and variety of what constitutes a family are endless, and it is important to be cautious about generalizing. In this section, I am considering all possible family forms.

Within family units, structural oppression is experienced directly, but also vicariously – as discussed in Chapter 2 through intergenerational and historical transmission, but also by witnessing and experiencing the impact on loved ones, as well as exposure to public events, such as the police assassination of George Floyd in Minneapolis. While what happened to George Floyd was a specific event involving individual police officers, it was part of a pattern of racialized police brutality and white supremacy, where BIPOC people do not feel safe in their own country (Kelly et al., 2020). This leads to not only fear but also feelings of shame and humiliation (Kelly et al., 2020). The toxicity of ensuing bodily and emotional reactions (discussed below) influences the way that people in a family interact with, respect, understand, and care for one another. There are a lot of social injuries to take in, and while the family can be a shock absorber for societal threats and violations, the cumulative nature of social oppression can wear and tear the ability of families to buffer against oppression.

Families facing social oppression are also confronted with the terrible knowledge that they cannot protect their loved ones from emotional, social, and physical harm. Adults try to protect their partners, children, siblings, and aging parents but when there are armed conflicts, ethnic cleansing, targeting by the state, or ongoing police brutality, it is not possible to exert total control and insulate loved ones from a range of violence. Children also witness their parents suffering and are powerless to ameliorate it, as well as feeling unsafe themselves. In African American families in the United States, there is often "the conversation," where parents work to counteract negative stereotypes, microaggressions, and structural violence (Coates, 2015). Kelly et al. (2020) have identified three strategies: (1) teaching children about how the "racial rules" of society work so that they can better protect themselves; (2) encouraging children to be strong performers and to upend social and cultural stereotypes; and (3) instilling a sense of racial pride and connection to the collective struggle to counteract negative depictions of being Black.

Structural oppression places more pressure on domestic partnerships and romantic and sexual relationships. This can be due to race-based traumatic stress (Carter & Pieterse, 2021) or religious assaults on Queer families. Externally, there are limits to access to opportunities and resources (e.g., due to policies and benefits that privilege heterosexual marriages, meaning that same-sex couples cannot access the same benefits as straight couples), while internally there can be challenges toward maintaining a positive sense of self in the face of pervasive social onslaughts. The constant warding off of sociopolitical threats can lead to a constant state of hypervigilance, and physical and emotional depletion, which makes it more difficult to connect with, care for, and commit to others. Conversely, such threats can bring people more closely together as they empathically understand their mutual experience of social marginalization and within the family and social groups people can try to offer social support and cushion negative consequences. But overall, helping professionals/volunteers need to appreciate that social oppression places additional heavy burdens on families, above and beyond the usual sources of strain and impasses.

There is also a sense of grief and loss in families because of the impact of social oppression. Children see parents who cannot achieve their goals or fulfill their dreams, which in turn affects the child's sense of the trajectory of their own lives. Coates (cited by Wade, 2021) laments that BIPOC people are robbed of time – lost moments of joy, connection, quality time, and lost years of good health.

Individual, Interpersonal Consequences

All forms of oppression involve dehumanization of those who are socially targeted. Many people have had overwhelming, traumatic, and stressful experiences in their lives, but this is not the same as facing repetitive, unyielding, and unrelenting societal targeting and oppression. Writing about the wave of police killings of African Americans in the United States, Watson et al. (2020) note that the entire project of white supremacy and racism in the United States involved a conscious, intentional effort to dehumanize African Americans from the beginning of their arrival in North America and the formation of the United States as a nation endorsing chattel slavery. Thus, when the brutality and debasement continue through all of the forms of racism mentioned thus far in this book and in particular through the disproportionate violence and mobilization of the criminal justice system toward Black people, it is not only what is going on in the present, but the present is informed by the unremitting tide of history that has led to this moment. Knowing this involves not only the recognition that centuries of assaults on personhood and human rights have not ended but also realizing, and dreading, that this will continue in the future.

When there is a tide of oppression that flows like a torrent, there is no safe harbor from which to rebuild and recover.

> The cumulative effects of horrific beatings, rape, family separation, body experimentation, and other unimaginable brutalities endured in slavery followed by lynching and terror during Jim Crow to present day murder by the police have made it extremely challenging for Black individuals and families to fully recover and heal.
>
> (Watson et al., 2020)

Or as Goosby et al. (2020) put it, "threats to social inclusion are threats to survival."

This is true of so many groups of people who are experiencing social oppression across the globe. Undocumented immigrants around the world not only experienced desperate social and economic conditions that led to their risking their lives to leave their countries but arrive in countries where they are not wanted and treated like criminals and fiends rather than friends in need of help. The countries that reject these immigrants – many of whom are former colonial powers – contributed to the conditions that impoverished and destabilized the home countries of the immigrants while enriching themselves in relation to their former colonies through systematic resource extraction and human exploitation; dehumanization both then and now. Women in Afghanistan know that they will not be treated as full human beings by the Taliban. Queer people throughout the world know that they are viewed as deviant or abnormal by many, often those who hold power. So, as I explore the individual costs of dehumanization in this section, often using racism in the United States as an exemplar, there is a dehumanization tax levied on all people who experience social oppression.

I will consider the physical and psychological impact of oppression that never ends, the stress and trauma reactions that this leads to, and the loss of faith and grieving that are part of this process. So often these reactions are understood in individual, if not pathological terms, and yet they are socially determined psychosocial reactions (Carter & Pieterse, 2021).

Physical, Medical, Psychological, and Emotional Consequences

When anyone is facing threats to their personhood and well-being, the hypothalamus in our brains identities the sources of risk and danger and activates the sympathetic nervous system and the pituitary and adrenal glands, and the hormone cortisol (the body's primary stress hormone) is released (Goosby et al., 2020). This is because the brain is protecting the person by anticipating future assaults – that can be not only physical but also social and psychological (Goosby et al., 2020). We know that even a single exposure to overwhelming threats to one's life and health can result in trauma and that the parts of the brain designed to identify threats and mobilize the body are activated while the parts that engage in complex, deliberate thinking are deactivated (Van der Kolk, 2014). What is the impact on a person's body, spirit, and psychological well-being when such threats are constant, unremitting, and without the hope that they will cease?

When a person is constantly hypervigilant and cortisol is sluicing through the body, there are profound long-term health effects. There is a high "allostatic load" (wear and tear) that can lead to high blood pressure and hypertension, cardiovascular problems, obesity, and diabetes (Goosby et al., 2020). Carter and Pieterse (2021) add ulcers and migraine headaches, as well as a greater tendency to smoke, which in turn exacerbates health problems. When President Trump instituted his "Muslim ban", U.S.-based Muslims had not only more stress-related health-care problems but also more missed medical appointments (Abdelaziz, 2021), illustrating how social oppression from the top weakens social trust in institutions. To make matters worse, people of color continuously experience discrimination, microaggressions, misdiagnosis, under prescribing pain medication, and other facets of racism in the medical profession and health-care system (Garran et al., 2021). And mistrust of the health-care system is based not only on current mistreatment but also on centuries of medical abuse and exploitation of African Americans and other people of color by the medical profession, where people were not only denied treatment but intentionally infected with diseases for "research purposes" (Washington, 2007).

The physical stress of social oppression accumulates over a lifetime and begins before birth and shortens life. When parents are in a constant state of arousal, cortisol is in mothers' bodies and passed down to the babies that they are carrying (Goosby et al., 2020; Heard-Garris et al., 2018; Stenson et al., 2021). Not only are babies born with higher reactivity to stress as a result but there are also more premature births and low-birthweight babies (Abdelaziz, 2021; Goosby et al., 2020; Heard-Garris et al., 2018).

The health risks of social oppression continue throughout the lifespan and are cumulative, and the negative impact on young children predisposes adults to experience more severe diseases (Carter & Pieterse, 2021; Goosby et al., 2020; Heard-Garris et al., 2018). Children experience social oppression, such as racism, either through their direct experiences, witnessing the impact on their parents, or having an awareness of its impact on the community (Heard-Garris et al., 2018). Such sociopolitical stress for children correlates with higher blood pressure, blood glucose problems, weight problems, and having an over-taxed, constantly inflamed immune system (Goosby et al., 2020). And parents who are experiencing social oppression are more likely to be suffering from depression, trauma, exhaustion, demoralization, and depletion and thus despite their best efforts unable to mitigate the impact on their children (Heard-Garris et al., 2018; Miller, 2012). As discussed earlier, another toll of social oppression is the weakening of social supports for parents and their children, further exacerbating the levels of stress and isolation.

While some cultures separate psychological/emotional consequences from physical/medical reactions, many do not. Clearly, there is a relationship between them, whatever epistemological model is being employed to understand them. Even in Western contexts, where the fields of psychology and psychotherapy mostly evolved, there is a greater recognition of the interconnectedness between the body, brain, heart, and soul. The term "behavioral health" acknowledges this shift in thinking. The medical conditions described earlier in this section clearly affect a sense of well-being, hormonal and neurological functioning, and our cognitive and emotional experiences.

With this in mind, there are some clear psychological/emotional reactions to chronic societal targeting and oppression. Stress and trauma are prominent (Kelly et al., 2020). It is important to consider trauma as not being synonymous with post-traumatic stress disorder (PTSD). PTSD is a predominantly Western concept that has been applied to people around the world regardless of their sociocultural reality, which is problematic (Miller, 2012; Summerfield, 2004). Caution is warranted for terms that imply psychological or psychiatric pathology for syndromes and behaviors caused by sociocultural factors, as this misplaces the locus of responsibility to the affected person, rather than the social conditions that fostered the trauma (Carter & Pieterse, 2021; Watson et al., 2020).

Socioculturally induced trauma has certain common characteristics. Using racism as an exemplar, psycho-emotionally, there is often hypervigilance and arousal, intrusion, avoidance of stressful situations, psychic numbing, rumination, depression, and anxiety (Carter & Pieterse, 2021; Saleem et al., 2020; Watson et al., 2020). There are also thoughts of self-blame, feelings of guilt and shame, fear, and anger and rage (Barlow, 2018; Carter & Pieterse, 2021; Garran et al., 2021; Goosby et al., 2020). Behaviorally, this can lead to substance abuse (Heard-Garris et al., 2018) as well as aggression directed toward self or others. All of this can have a profound impact on the ability to form relationships as well as the quality of intimate relationships (Carter & Pieterse, 2021).

Barlow (2018) notes that when Black people experience physical violence, their character is also attacked. This is a critical point – targets of sociopolitical oppression know that there are others, often those with greater sociopolitical power, who not only see their lives and well-being as less valuable but also want to do them harm. People often resist and fight back, while at other times, this knowledge is internalized and affects one self-concept as well as one's sense of hope for the future (Miller, 2012). Thus, social oppression threatens not only one's body, emotions, behaviors, and one's family but also one's sense of self (Carter & Pieterse, 2021). Do I have agency and some control over my life? Am I able to achieve my goals and protect those whom I love? Do I experience respect from other people, do they view me compassionately, are they concerned for my well-being, or do they wish me harm? Even though the answers to these questions clearly reflect socio-structural factors and dynamics, they are often experienced by a person as being due to their personal failings or mistakes – e.g., how did I let this happen to me or to someone whom I love? This can lead to feelings of self-blame, shame, and guilt (Carter & Pieterse, 2021). Part of this also results from inevitable social comparisons with members of dominant social groups. For example, knowing that one might be pulled over, jailed, or harmed for a minor traffic infraction, or face many years of prison time for minor theft or drug use, while wealthy, white, men who scam corporations and/or their clients for great sums of money are often never caught and when they are, spend a year or two in less dangerous federal prisons specifically designed for white-collar criminals. As Wade (2021) suggests, personhood is a collective process, and BIPOC people's personhood is stolen from them.

Race-based traumatic stress happens when a person experiences something as threatening or harmful, the event was unanticipated, and a person has no control over what is happening (Carter & Pieterse, 2021). So, it is not the reality, or even the intention, that is most important but rather one's subjective experience. And the reality is that one cannot control what the police will do in a given situation nor what a co-worker might say at a meeting, which can then lead to an unexpected physical, emotional, or psychological assault. Anticipating such threats can be both positive and negative: on the one hand, a person is not caught by surprise and can prepare themselves, but on the other hand, the knowledge that they will occur can be demoralizing. Physically, the constant preparation and exposure to societal violence tax the immune system and wear the body down (Goosby et al., 2020). And while social support can be experienced within one's social group, the discrimination and opprobrium of dominant social groups excluded people from society at large and denies them the benefits of social support (Goosby et al.).

Grief

Social exclusion, attacks on one's personhood, the inability to keep oneself and loved ones safe, knowing that society values you less and treats you not only without compassion but with hostility, is a narrative of loss: lost opportunities, lost moments of pleasure, lost hopes and dreams, and lost economic and social well-being. As Coates says (cited in Wade, 2021), for BIPOC people time is lost irrevocably, including quality time for relationships. Wade (p. 37) adds that White children, unlike Black children, have time to be children: "White parents are often able to protect their children from the consequences of history such that their children do not have to bear the weight of their ancestor's mistakes." There is a lot to grieve.

Grieving is not only about the loss of loved ones but is also a process of mourning collective losses, often multi-generational. This includes sorrow about what happened to ancestors, sadness over the lack of justice, and lamenting the lack of compassion and empathy from others. I have also found in my work responding to major disasters and catastrophes that when one is faced with overwhelming stresses, threats, and pressures, the need to try and survive and cope closes down the space for grieving and mourning; mourning is secondary to survival (Miller, 2012). Thus, many people facing social oppression need to prioritize survival, which may mean that they carry a great deal of unresolved grief, which does not dissipate but rather contributes to chronic sadness and feelings of inhabiting a bleak world.

Impact on Helping Professionals

Chapter 10 considers the impact of psychosocial work with socially targeted and oppressed people on helping professionals/volunteers, but I would like to briefly mention some effects of responding to collective trauma, particularly when the helpers share social identities with those receiving services and interventions. Weinberg and Fine (2020) have done research in this area and have identified a number of sources of stress due to racism: witnessing acts of oppression toward clients and having vicarious reactions; experiencing oppression directly; having clients with different identities refuse to see them; experiencing microaggressions from co-workers; experiencing cultural and epistemic dominance and hegemony, which devalues their way of understanding and knowing (and which inhibits their application of their learned life experiences and wisdom with clients); experiencing institutional racism (as I have argued, in a society structured by racism, every institution has some of this in their DNA); less promotional opportunities and receiving lower pay; and not receiving affirming and culturally responsive supervision (often feeling as if they need to protect their clients from their supervisors). And for helpers in this position, there is always the ambiguity of intention, meaning, and how to respond: was that really racism; why did that just happen; do I have the energy and safety to respond? And if a person does not respond, what residual feelings are left for them to carry?

Resistance

I have been focusing on the negative consequences of social oppression as I build a foundation for decolonized, liberatory psychosocial responses. The collective and individual psychosocial costs of oppression are profound. And yet, those who encounter social oppression on a daily basis have also developed wisdom, skills, and strategies which have enabled them to survive and even thrive (Carter & Pieterse, 2021).

Black families in the United States have resisted racism by countering the distortions and stereotypes about Black people with their children as well as preparing them for encounters with structural and interpersonal racism. As was mentioned earlier, Kelly et al. (2020), citing Berrey, describe three common strategies: (1) teaching children racial norms and expectations to minimize their risks when they find themselves in racist situations; (2) stressing the importance of performance and not conforming to racist stereotypes; and (3) instilling racial pride and self-acceptance. This is a form of active resistance.

As social oppression affects collectivities, in my experience, communal forms of resistance are the most effective. Collective struggle pools resources, can lead to social movements, and creates closer social ties between resisters. As Heinrich (2020, p. 74) states, "working together on a shared goal deepens group solidarity and strengthens interpersonal connections." It is healing and empowering to join with others having similar experiences. As was discussed in the previous chapter, collective resistance also links people with their ancestors who were part of the struggle against domination and oppression: there is a horizontal connection between those engaged in collective resistance as well as a vertical dimension linking people in the present with their progenitors.

An example of this process is Collective Healing Networks (CHN) for those recovering from and fighting back against the same sources of oppression (Barlow, 2018). The CHN described by Barlow sponsors

Emotional Emancipation Circles for Black people. These are places where people "work together to overcome, heal from, and overturn the lies of white superiority and Black inferiority: the root causes of the devaluing of Black lives." This form of collective confrontation is part of a liberatory process that aims to shed internalized societal stereotypes and untruths and reconstruct a sense of full humanity. It is both intergenerational and very much a response to present conditions. Shared personal stories are woven into a larger historical and social narrative, where cultural practices are reclaimed and previous struggles for liberation are recast into present-day practices of resistance. It involves a form of collective journaling, whether written or oral. This practice unites internal strategies of resistance – healing, shedding internalized racism – with external actions – forming coalitions and connections with others (Werkmeister-Rozas & Miller, 2009).

Collective healing and action are a form of buffering – where members of a socially targeted group avoid situations where they are vulnerable to assault and instead form spaces where they can protect and support one another (Garran et al., 2021; Tatum, 1997). Such buffering also contributes to reinforcing and supporting positive aspects of social identity, which counteracts the undermining of one's sense of self-described earlier (Carter & Pieterse, 2021).

Collective social action is an important form of resistance. As people learned from their participation in the French Resistance during World War II, struggle, even against severe threats and facing daunting odds, offers a sense of freedom; a sense that we are not passive victims but active agents articulating our cherished values, confronting injustice, and protecting ourselves and others. In South Africa, the force of apartheid seemed overwhelming, and yet it was overthrown. That involved not only a long-term struggle within South Africa but also mobilizing the world to help to create the conditions where apartheid could no longer survive. Sometimes there are newer short-term movements of social activism in response to changing events – such as the response to the election of Donald Trump, a racist and authoritarian president: local groups formed Rapid Organizing Responses to resist his agenda, demonstrating agility, the capacity to quickly form and engage in activism, and to adapt to shifting needs and conditions (Garran et al., 2021).

While struggle can unite people and feel liberating, it can also be activating as it can necessitate a great deal of energy and emotional investment. It can also incur the wrath of others, including the state, as feminists in China found when they demonstrated against public misogyny and sexual harassment. Thus, self-care is essential as is generating compassion for oneself and others. This will be discussed further in Chapter 10.

Summary and Conclusion

This chapter has zeroed in on the negative consequences of social oppression, how it affects all aspects of the lives of people who share minoritized and targeted social identities. A basic understanding of the ways that social oppression undermines communities, families, and individuals is important for helping professionals to keep in focus whenever offering psychosocial interventions to those seeking support. This necessitates a grasp of the nature of structural oppression, the role of socially constructed identities, and the factors that shape social identities for individuals and groups. The chapter reviewed Tilley's concepts of exploitation and resource hoarding and how this contributes to segregation and the consequences for neighborhoods, workplaces, families, and individuals.

On the community-societal level, I explored not only how social cohesion can be weakened by persistent social targeting and exclusion, isolating and alienating people from important social institutions, but also how struggle and adversity can strengthen social connections and bonds for those working together to resist and confront social oppression. The persistence and unrelenting nature of social oppression has profound physical, medical, psychological, emotional, and social consequences for families and individuals, beginning before birth and continuing throughout the life course. Using racism as a template, which I believe can be adapted to other forms of social oppression, I considered Carter and Pieterse's (2021) concept of "Race Based Traumatic Stress" and how this is socially caused trauma, not an individual psychiatric condition, devoid of a historical and socio-structural context.

This chapter focused on those who experience the brunt of social oppression, and although I did discuss strength and heroic resistance, I emphasized the negative psychosocial consequences. I believe that it is important to be clear about destructive social targeting and oppression are and how helping professionals must always integrate an awareness of this with any psychosocial interventions; it is harmful to de-couple individuals from this social ecology and context. However, in order for social justice to be achieved, there also needs to be ways that people with dominant identities, including those who are members of groups who actively oppress others, can explore, confront, work on, and take accountability for the harmful affects of their power and privilege on other people. This will also be explored in Chapter 10.

While all types of social oppression are forms of violence, in the next chapter, I will consider the consequences of armed conflict and extreme state violence before moving to chapters that elaborate on a model of psychosocial intervention.

References

Abdelaziz, R. (2021, August 4). Trump's Muslim ban harmed Muslim Americans health, study finds. *The Huffington Post.* www.huffpost.com/entry/trumps-muslim-ban-harmed-muslim-americans-health-study-finds_n_610a9a86e4b039aafa11de3a

Alexander, J.C. (2016). Culture trauma, morality and solidarity: The social construction of "Holocaust" and other mass murders. *Thesis Eleven, 132*(1): 3–16.

Baker, P., & Haberman, M. (2020, August 31). Trump fans strife as unrest roils the U.S. *The New York Times.* www.nytimes.com/2020/08/31/us/politics/trump-kenosha.html?action=click&module=Top%20Stories&pgtype=Homepage

Barlow, J.N. (2018). Restoring optimal Black mental health and reversing intergenerational trauma in an era of Black lives matter. *Biography, 41*(4): 895–908.

Berman, A. (2015). *Give us the ballot: The modern struggle for voting rights in America.* New York, NY: Farrar, Straus & Giroux.

Berman, P. (1994). Introduction: The other and almost the same. In P. Berman (Ed.). *Blacks and Jews: Alliances and Arguments* (pp. 1–28). New York: Delacorte Press.

Block, C. (2016). The impact of color-blind ideology on maintaining racial disparities in organizations. In H.A. Neville, M.E. Gallardo, & D.W. Sue (Eds.). *The myth of racial color blindness: Manifestations, dynamics, and impact* (pp. 243–259). Washington, DC: American Psychological Association.

Bourgois, P. (1995). *In search of respect.* New York, NY: Cambridge.

Brewer, M.B. (2001). Intergroup identification and intergroup conflict: When does ingroup love become outgroup hate? In R.D. Ashmore, L. Jussim, & D. Wilder (Eds.). *Social identity, intergroup conflict and conflict resolution* (pp. 17–41). New York: Oxford University Press.

Bureau of Labor Statistics. (2020, January 17). Usual weekly earnings of wage and salary workers fourth quarter 2019. *U.S. Department of Labor.* www.bls.gov/news.release/pdf/wkyeng.pdf

Carter, R.T., & Pieterse, A.L. (2021). *Measuring the effects of racism.* New York: Columbia University Press.

Coates, T. (2015). *Between the world and me.* New York: Spiegel and Grau Publishers.

Cose, E. (1993). *The rage of a privileged class.* New York, NY: HarperCollins.

Dixon, J., Tredoux, C., Durrheim, K., Finchilescu, G., & Clack, B. (2008). The inner citadels of the color line: Mapping the micro-ecology of racial segregation in everyday life space. *Social and Personality Psychology Compass*, *2*(4): 1547–1569. DOI: 10.1111/j.1751-9004.2008.00123.x.

Dovidio, J.F., Gaertner, S.L., Ufkes, E.G., Saguy, T., & Pearson, A.P. (2016). Included but invisible? Subtle bias, common identity, and the darker side of "we." *Social Issues and Policy Review*, *10*(1): 6–46.

Garran, A.M., Werkmeister-Rozas, L., Kang, H., & Miller, J. (2021). *Racism in the United States: Implications for the helping professions* (3rd ed.). New York: Springer Publishing.

Gonyea, D. (2017). Majority of white Americans say they believe whites face discrimination. *NPR*. www.npr.org/2017/10/24/559604836/majority-of-white-americans-think-theyre-discriminated-against

Goosby, B., Cheadle, J.E., & Mitchell, C.M. (2020, October). Discrimination and African American health inequities. *IRP Focus*, *36*(3): 26–37.

Heard-Garris, N.J., Cale, M., Camaj, L., Hamati, M.C., & Dominguez, T.P. (2018). Transmitting trauma: A systematic review of vicarious racism and child health. *Social Science and Medicine*. DOI: 10.1016/j.socscimed.2017.04.018.

Heinrich, J. (2020). *The WEIRDest people in the world: How the west became psychologically peculiar and particularly prosperous*. New York: Farrar, Straus & Giroux Publishers.

Kelly, S., Jeremie-Brink, G., Chambers, A.L., & Smith-Bynum, M.A. (2020). The Black lives matter movement: A call to action for couple and martial therapists. *Family Process*, *59*(4): 1374–1388. DOI: 10.1111/famp.12614.

Logan, J.R., & Stults, B.J. (2011). *The persistence of segregation in the metropolis: New findings from the 2010 census* (Census Brief prepared for Project US2010). Providence, RI: Brown University. https://s4.ad.brown.edu/Projects/Diversity/Data/Report/report2.pdf

Mamdani, M. (2020). *Neither settler nor native: The making and unmaking of permanent minorities*. Cambridge, MA: Belknap Press.

Mayor, J. (2021, August 2). The big money behind the big lie. *The New Yorker*. www.newyorker.com/magazine/2021/08/09/the-big-money-behind-the-big-lie

McIlwain, C.D., & Caliendo, S.M. (2014). Mitt Romney's racist appeals: How race was played in the 2013 presidential election. *American Behavioral Scientist*, *58*(9): 1157–1168.

Miller, J.L. (2012). *Psychosocial capacity building in response to disasters*. New York: Columbia University Press.

Miller, J.L. (2020). The four pandemics. *Smith College Studies in Social Work*. DOI: 10.1080/00377317.2020.1832944.

Miller, J.L., & Schamess, G. (2000). The discourse of denigration and the creation of other. *Journal of Sociology and Social Welfare*, 27(3): 39–62.

Moore, W.L. (2020). The mechanisms of white space(s). *American Behavioral Scientist*. DOI: 10.1177/0002764220975080.

Nagata, D.K., Kim, J.H.J., & Nguyen, T.U. (2015). Processing cultural trauma: Intergenerational effects of the Japanese American incarceration. *Journal of Social Issues*, *71*(2): 356–370. DOI: 10.1111/josi.12115.

Pager, D., & Western, B. (2012). Identifying discrimination at work: The use of field experiments. *Journal of Social Issues*, *68*(2): 221–237.

Park, H., Keller, J., & Williams, J. (2016, February 28). The faces of American power: Nearly as white as the Oscar nominees. *The New York Times*. www.nytimes.com/interactive/2016/02/26/us/race-of-american-power.html

Petrosino, C., & Pace, J. (2015). Social cohesion, collective efficacy, and the response of a cape Verdean community to hate crime: Learning a new reality. *American Behavioral Scientist*, *59*(13): 1681–1697. DOI: 10.1177/0002764215588818.

Pierce, C., Carew, J., Pierce-Gonzalez, D., & Wills, D. (1978). An experiment in racism: T.V. commercials. In C. Pierce (Ed.). *Television and education* (pp. 62–88). Beverly Hills, CA: Sage.

Putnam, R. (2000). *Bowling alone: The collapse and revival of American community*. New York: Simon and Schuster.

Renzulli, L.A., Grant, L., & Kathuria, S. (2006). Race, gender, and the wage gap: Comparing faculty salaries in predominately White and historically Black colleges and universities. *Gender and Society*, *20*(4): 491–510.

Saleem, F.T., Anderson, R.E., & Williams, M. (2020). Addressing the "myth" of racial trauma: Developmental and ecological considerations for youth of color. *Clinical Child and Family Psychology Review*, *23*: 1–14. DOI: 10.1007/s10567-019-00304-1.

Sampson, R.J., Morenoff, J.D., & Earls, F. (1999). Beyond social capital: Spatial dynamics of collective efficacy for children. *American Sociological Review*, *64*: 633–660.

Sampson, R.J., Raudenbush, S.W., & Earls, F. (1997). Neighborhoods and violent crime: A multilevel study of collective efficacy. *Science*, *277*: 918–924.

Shapiro, T.M. (2004). *The hidden cost of being African American: How wealth perpetuates inequality*. New York, NY: Oxford University Press.

Staub, E. (2001). Individual and group identities in genocide and mass killing. In R.D. Ashmore, L. Jussim, & D. Wilder (Eds.). *Social identity, intergroup conflict and conflict resolution* (pp. 159–184). New York: Oxford University Press.

Steele, C. (2011). *Whistling Vivaldi: How stereotypes affect us and what we can do*. New York, NY: W.W. Norton.

Stenson, A.F., van Rooij, S.J.H., Carter, S.B., Powers, A., & Jovanovic, T. (2021). A legacy of fear: Physiological evidence for intergenerational effects of trauma exposure on fear and safety signal learning among African Americans. *Behavioural Brain Research, 402*. DOI: 10.1016/j.bbr.2020.113017.

Stephan, W.G. (2008). Viewing intergroup relations in Europe through Allport's lens of prejudice. *Journal of Social Issues*, *64*(2): 417–429.

Sue, D.W., & Spanierman, L.B. (2020). *Microaggressions in everyday life* (2nd ed.). New York: Wiley Publishing.

Summerfield, D. (2004). Cross cultural perspectives on the medicalisation of human suffering. In G. Rosen (Ed.). *Posttraumatic stress disorder: Issues and Controversies* (pp. 233–247). New York: John Wiley.

Tatum, B. (1997). *"Why are all the Black kids sitting together in the cafeteria?" and other conversations about race*. New York, NY: Basic Books.

Tilly, C. (1998). *Durable inequality*. Berkeley: University of California Press.

Van der Kolk, B. (2014). *The body keeps the score: Brain, mind and body in the healing of trauma*. New York: Viking Publishing.

Vandewalker, I. (2015). Outside spending, dark money dominate toss-up Senate races. In D.R. Reiner, J. Lyons, E. Opsal, M. Terrell, & L. Glaser (Eds.). *Democracy and justice: Collected writings* (Vol. VIII, pp. 15–17). New York, NY: Brennan Center for Social Justice.

Volkan, V. (1988). *The need to have enemies and allies: From clinical practice to international relationships*. Northvale, NJ: Jason Aronson Publishing.

Wade, B. (2021). *Grieving while Black: An antiracist take on oppression and sorrow*. Berkeley, CA: North Atlantic Books.

Washington, H.A. (2007). *Medical apartheid: The dark history of medical experimentation on Black Americans from colonial times to the present*. New York: Doubleday Publishing.

Watson, M.F., Turner, W.L., & Hines, P.M. (2020). Black lives matter: We are in the same storm but not the same boat. *Family Process*, *59*(4): 1362–1373. DOI: 10.1111/famp.12613.

Weinberg, M., & Fine, M. (2020). Racisms and microaggressions in social work: The experience of racialized practitioners in Canada. *Journal of Ethnic and Cultural Diversity in Social Work*. DOI: 10.1080/15313204.2020.1839614.

Werkmeister-Rozas, L., & Miller, J. (2009). Discourses for social justice education: The web of racism and the web of resistance. *Journal of Ethnic and Cultural Diversity in Social Work*, *18*(1–2): 24–39. DOI: 10.1080/15313200902874953.

Whillock, R.K. (1995). The use of hate as a stratagem for achieving political and social goals. In R.K. Whillock & D. Slayden (Eds.). *Hate speech* (pp. 28–54). Thousand Oaks, CA: Sage Publications.

Wilson, W.J. (2011). *When work disappears: The world of the new urban poor*. New York, NY: Vintagze.

4 Violence

Introduction

In Northern Uganda, there was an armed conflict that lasted for 20 years between 1986 and 2006 (Mugizi & Matsumoto, 2021), which I referred to in Chapter 2. Its roots and causes are complex, but it is relevant to this chapter. There were the legacies of colonialism that created a nation, a geographic space, and a government apparatus that brought together many ethnic groups, tribes, and clans under the nationalist umbrella of being Ugandan. During the colonial period, some of these tribes were elevated, while others were subjugated, patterns that continue to shape Ugandan politics. Certain tribes were offered access to specific roles – e.g., police, army – while others were denied these opportunities. There were interacting, at times, conflicting identities: Ugandan, regional, and tribal (Branch, 2010). There were also religious identities: Catholic, Protestant, Muslim, and those associated with tribal customs and practices. Tribes with linguistic, cultural, and social affinities were separated by the new nationalist borders set by departing colonial powers. As with many former European colonies in Africa, since independence, Uganda has been marred by violent coups that continually upset or reify the balance of power and status between tribes.

As I mentioned in Chapter 2, in the North of Uganda, the dominant tribe is the Acholi tribe, who were subjugated by the British and economically and politically marginalized (Mugizi & Matsumoto, 2021). It is the poorest region in Uganda, exacerbated by the armed conflict (Nannyonjo, 2005). The unique constellation of colonial and post-colonial factors that I have briefly summarized coalesced in a Civil War that ultimately was between The Lord's Resistance Army (LRA), an Acholi-identified rebellion led by Joseph Kony, and the national government of Uganda, under President Yuseri Museveni. During the

DOI: 10.4324/9781003021162-4

peak of the armed conflict, nearly all of the Acholi population in Northern Uganda were displaced and forced by the Ugandan government to live in internally displaced persons camps (Kiconco & Nthakomwa, 2018). This meant that people could not engage in their clan-based, subsistence farming and became dependent on government and NGO largesse. Rates of illness soared and health declined. Cultural and religious practices were abandoned, and clan-based kinship networks were strained. When people foraged for food in "the bush," they were often attacked, maimed, raped, or killed by both LRA and government forces. The LRA kidnapped children, turning girls into concubines and boys into child soldiers, who were forced to commit atrocities, often against their own families. It is estimated that over 100,000 people were killed during the conflict and tens of thousands of children were kidnapped (Neiman, 2020).

I have been engaged in collaborative psychosocial and medical capacity building in Northern Uganda since 2006, working with a team of U.S. doctors and social workers and a Ugandan team of doctors, nurses, midwives, religious leaders, clan elders, farmers, and government officials. What I have witnessed is the devastating impact of this period of extreme violence that continues 15 years after its cessation. People have returned to their homes, but in an area where few people have deeds to their land and which has been farmed by their clans for generations, there are fierce and deadly land disputes and conflicts. There are high rates of drug and alcohol use, suicide, domestic violence, teen pregnancy, and depression. There is still social mistrust, exacerbated by so many former child soldiers now living in their communities. Former female abductees have faced rejection and are viewed as unmarriageable or carrying a social stain (Kiconco & Nthakomwa, 2018). Many people carry the physical scars from the war and everyone – *everyone* – holds psychic and emotional wounds, often some form of trauma. When engaged in training, people are easily triggered and sometimes disassociate. Adults complain that cultural traditions have been lost and social networks, including those within clans, are still frayed from the conflict.

This brief vignette describes a community subjected to some of the most intense instances of violence that can be part of the human condition. Sadly, this can be said about many global conflicts now and in the past. Ethnic conflict is the norm, not an exception, when there are different ethnic groups living in proximity and many such conflicts, while exacerbated by colonialism, also predated it (Bergman & Crutchfield, 2009). Colonialism was in itself an extreme form of violence and planted the seeds of ongoing ethnic/racial/religious conflict that plagues most of the world. Whether it is racism in North America, the treatment of Uighurs in China, or the Taliban's brutality toward ethnic and religious minorities (such as the Hazara) in Afghanistan, the roots of colonialism continue to shape the trees of nationhood. I shared this example as an introduction to this chapter because it not only highlights the theme of coloniality, which is a through-line in this book but also illustrates how the legacies of coloniality and extreme violence continue with profound psychosocial consequences. In this chapter, I will explore the many forms that violence takes and its deep and troubling impact.

The Spectrum of Violence

Violence is central to an exploration of the impact of historical and structural oppression. Indeed, violence is the epitome of othering, dehumanization, social targeting, exclusion, and oppression. What is meant by "violence?" What are the different types of violence? Are there qualitative differences between these different forms of violence? Are the consequences the same for all kinds of violence? Who is most vulnerable to violence and who are often the perpetrators? Although there are some commonalities, the answers to these questions vary considerably between people and societies. In order for violence to occur, there is a process of dehumanizing and othering, which is an essential ingredient in coloniality and systemic oppression. I have considered violence in my exploration of historical and structural trauma in the previous two chapters, and I will now focus on the dynamics of extreme violence and its consequences. I will explain what I mean by extreme violence and connect it to all forms of violence because, in my experience, they are not separate but rather form a continuum, a spectrum of violence.

The World Health Organization (2002, 2014) defines violence as the intentional use of force and power that is threatened or enacted against individuals (including oneself), groups, or communities that results in destruction, injury, death, deprivation, or psychological/emotional harm. What stands out in this definition is *intentionality*, *power*, and *the use of force*. The WHO subdivides violence as self-directed, interpersonal, and collective. Self-directed refers to self-harm and suicide. Interpersonal can be divided into family/intimate partner violence (IPV) and community violence among unrelated people. I also think that is important to distinguish between collective violence that is perpetrated by the state and that caused by non-state actors. Figure 4.1 diagrams this spectrum of violence.

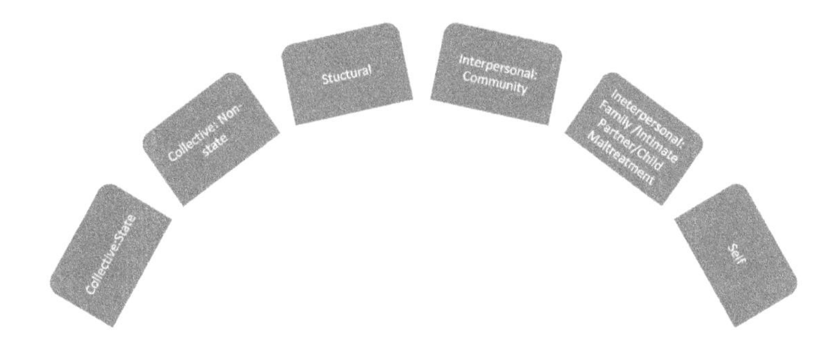

Figure 4.1 The Spectrum of Violence
Source: *World Health Organization (2002, 2014)*

There are situations when all three levels of violence are simultaneously occurring in relation to one another. When a Mexican drug cartel such as the Zetas films extreme killings of people suspected of collaborating with a rival cartel (Perreda, 2021), they are engaged in collective violence as they terrorize a community and interpersonal violence as they literally torture people and broadcast their videos to vicariously terrorize those who are watching. I suspect that the combination of collective and interpersonal violence in this context also fuels more self-directed violence among people who feel trapped, helpless, and unable to protect themselves.

The WHO (2002, 2014) further divides collective violence into social, political, and economic, while acknowledging that often all forms are present and that they are related. Examples of social violence are mob attacks, violence by hate groups, and in the United States, activities associated with organizations such as the Ku Klux Klan, the Proud Boys, and right-wing militias. Political violence includes war and armed conflict, ethnic cleansing and genocide, slavery, and human trafficking. Political violence can be perpetrated by state actors (e.g., governments, official militias, police forces) or by non-state but powerful groups attacking other groups. Examples of economic violence include destroying the means of production, denying access to essential economic resources, and intentionally creating economic disruption and destruction. I would add that this includes access to land, credit, and the ability to live in chosen communities. Economic violence also links with IPV as it makes women more dependent on men, generating greater vulnerability to domestic violence.

All three forms of collective violence are often linked. In Afghanistan, the Taliban re-took control of the country in 2021. They immediately prohibited women from many jobs and schools, which is a form of identity-based gender violence. They have directly attacked or allowed others to attack ethnic/religious minorities, such as Hazaras, reflecting both social and political violence. In the United States, former President Donald Trump fomented political violence in the service of his lies about winning the 2020 election and his attempts to remain in power, leading to the January 6 insurrection that attempted to overthrow the election results and resulted in injuries and deaths. Prior to that, while still President, he exhorted people to "liberate Michigan" in response to the Governor's attempts to protect people from COVID-19, which contributed to a plot by a right-wing militia to kidnap and possibly kill the Governor. And by repeatedly attacking governors who sought to implement COVID protections for his own political gain, he fomented social mistrust in science, medicine, and the government's capacity to protect people, which may have led to 450,000 unnecessary deaths according to The Lancet when comparing the U.S. COVID death rate with that of developed countries in Europe (Beer, 2021).

Figure 4.2 diagrams the different categories of violence with examples of each type. I will now briefly describe them before turning to their psychosocial consequences and the implications for helping professionals.

All types may be linked, and individuals can experience all forms at various times or at once.

Collective Violence

There are many factors that contribute to collective violence and many different sectors of society are complicit in fomenting as well as resisting mass violence; intentions and motives are complex (Gerlach, 2006). Gerlach notes nation formation, racism, and the social disruptions of capitalism as major contributors to collective violence. An important contributor that is often omitted from discussions about intergroup

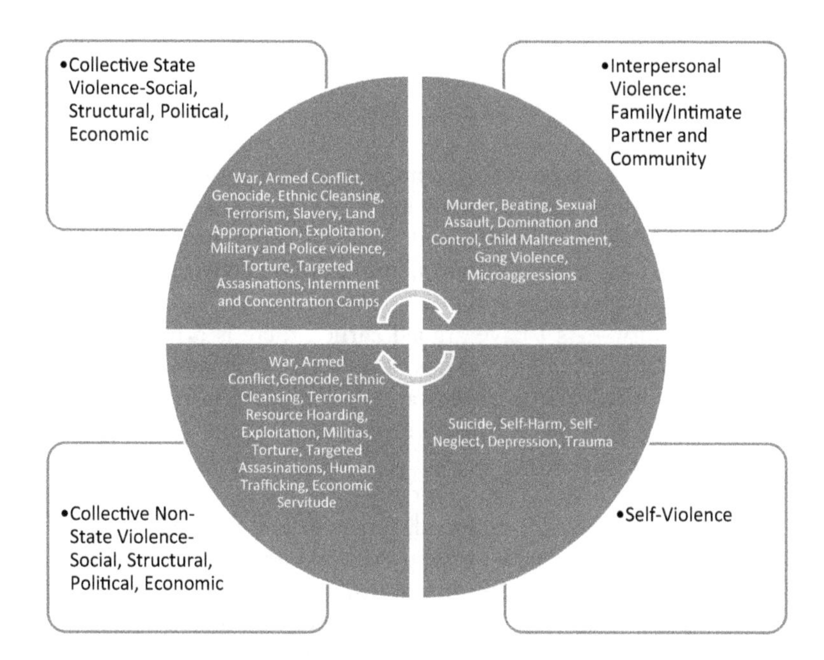

Figure 4.2 Types of Violence

conflict and mass violence is the legacy of colonialism. The WHO does not consider colonialism in its definitions of collective violence despite its centrality in structuring collective violence between and within states. As Volpato and Licata (2010) argue, colonialism "has left its mark on international relations, social relationships within nations, and the ideologies and imaginaries of virtually all the peoples of the world." As discussed in previous chapters, colonialism has shaped the unevenness in global wealth and power, relationships between indigenous people and settlers in countries like the United States and Australia, and persists as developed countries fortify their borders against immigrants from former colonies. Colonialism has shaped the tribal politics within countries in much of Africa, and today's violence and corruption cannot be understood without acknowledging the fountainhead of coloniality. This includes the vignette at the beginning of this chapter. The collective memories and emotions that are legacies of colonialism are a major factor in conflictual intergroup relations, which dominate collective violence in our contemporary world (Volpato & Licata, 2010).

Collective violence is often between groups with differing racial, ethnic, and religious identities, and Wimmer (cited by Bergman & Crutchfield, 2009) has delineated important factors that influence the shape of these forms of collective violence:

1. Complexity – There are often more than two ethnic/racial groups involved in the conflict, involving interconnected political, legal, and economic institutions, and there are often a range of actors (ranging from warlords, gangs, and militias to civic groups committed to nonviolence and peace).
2. Individuality – As I have argued earlier, there is a unique social ecology for every conflict. Thus, while there are attempts to generalize, it is important to understand the unique histories and structural forces that shape collective violence.
3. Depth – With ethnic, racial, and religious conflict, there are groups aligned with and centralized by the state and there are other groups that are excluded, targeted, and marginalized. This not only leads to conflict over power and access to resources but also affects identity, roles, and status.
4. Persistence – Different groups and actors contest when a collective conflict began, with differing narratives about who precipitated the conflict. The longer a conflict persists, the more that it changes and reconfigures institutions, behaviors, social norms, and expectations.

Collective violence is often perpetrated by the state, although it can also occur between non-state actors, such as rival ethnic groups or between gangs. In fact, more often than not there is a confluence between state and non-state forces that coalesce when there is extreme collective violence (Gerlach, 2006). Examples include militias, warlords, and paramilitary groups (Karstedt, 2016) as well as gangs and drug cartels. The intention is to advance a particular social, economic, or political agenda (WHO, 2002, 2014). The combination of state and non-state forces contributes to wars, genocide, ethnic cleansing, enslavement, land theft and appropriation, internment and concentration camps, targeted killings, assassinations, terrorism, and disappearances.

All of these forms have occurred in the United States (see Chapter 3 of Garran et al., 2021 for a more detailed description of this). Indigenous people were nearly exterminated over a 300-year period by European settlers and their land and means of survival (e.g., hunting, growing crops) were permanently stolen. Their children were forced into boarding schools where they were deprived of their culture, shorn of their hair and identities, abused, killed, and secretly buried (Reveal, 2022). Indigenous people were also forced into slave labor although it was the system of chattel slavery of people involuntarily brought from Africa that became a cornerstone of U.S. economic legal and political systems. The brutality of chattel slavery cannot be overstated – murder, beating, torture, family separations, deprivation of basic human rights and needs, unrelenting cruelty, pernicious and pervasive sexual assault of Black women by White slaveholders and White overseers, maiming of bodies, summary executions, and a constant, intentional atmosphere of fear and terror directed at Black people. The wealth created by the system of unpaid labor producing cotton propelled all of the United States, as well as European countries such as Britain, into international positions of power that have never been relinquished. The political system of the United States was shaped by genocide and slavery, determining who could and could not vote, the apportionment of power giving undue political influence to white, rural areas, spawning unrelenting efforts by political parties to suppress Black votes, throughout the era of Democrat Jim Crow voter suppression by southern states to our present moment as states controlled by Republicans pass laws intending to suppress the votes of Black people. Ethnic cleansing was central to the burgeoning White dominance of the United States, ranging from forcing indigenous people from their land, preventing Chinese people from immigrating to the United States at a time when immigration from Europe was being encouraged, to the imprisonment of Japanese Americans during World War II.

Since all forms of collective violence were central to the founding of the United States, they are part of its DNA and beget present-day legacies, such as the disproportionate numbers of African Americans in the criminal justice system and ongoing police brutality that has led to the deaths of unarmed adults and children. When a nation is founded on violence and racial supremacy, it becomes "normal" and is internalized by people, particularly White people, as the way that things have been, are, and will continue to be. These notions, often unconscious, of racial superiority, in turn coalesce in the form of stereotypes and cognitive maps representing feelings of superiority, privilege, centrality, and entitlement. This leads to an interpersonal form of violence – microaggressions. Microaggressions, which were covered in the previous chapter, are interactions that are hostile, demeaning, alienating, and devaluing to socially targeted people, often perpetrated without the conscious awareness of White people (Garran et al., 2021; Pierce et al., 1978; Sue & Spanier, 2020). Although microaggressions might not appear to be violent on the surface, they reenact and reinforce historical and structural oppression and cause psychological and emotional harm, which will be considered when I consider self-violence. They are part of, not separate from, the spectrum of violence that ranges from systematic, collective atrocities to consistent interpersonal assaults, which may seem minor at the time but are so pervasive as to be a form of psychological violence. They are both predictable in that they regularly occur and also unpredictable, as they can also happen in unanticipated situations or emanate from trusted people, leaving the targets of microaggressions inhabiting unsafe social and public spaces and experiencing inner states of protectiveness, emotional activation, and hyperarousal.

Another form of collective violence links to structural oppression and is manifested in exclusionary systems and behaviors, and institutional neglect and mistreatment, often referred to as structural violence. As described in Chapter 5 by Garran et al. (2021), there is a web of institutional racism that BIPOC people encounter, which pervades every aspect of society. What is particularly insidious about the web of institutional racism is that it stems from the original racial contract (Mills, 1997) that underpinned the formation of the United States – i.e., only white people were deemed to be fully human and deserving of human rights – and seems so normal to most white people that despite its pervasiveness and that it is consistently empirically confirmed, it is invisible to the very people who benefit from it (Garran et al.). As described in the previous chapter, the web of institutional racism is fortified by residential segregation, which is still a powerful dynamic in the United States, which in turn affects access to quality public education, access to jobs and transportation, public safety, and the ability to accumulate wealth and to enjoy upward mobility. The web also involves job discrimination and less access to medical and psychological health services and neglect and differential treatment from health and mental health professionals.

Most governments shape who does and does not receive full human rights, often based on ethno-racial-religious categories, gender, sexual orientation, social class/caste, and norms and practices that define ableism. Citizenship is another category that determines rights (Kochenov, 2019), ranging from being able to reside in particular land territories, having political and social rights, or the creation of permanent minorities based on linguistic, ethnic, racial, and religious citizenship. Often this is formal, such as having state religions; this is true in 20% of the world's countries with another 20% having preferred religions (Sherwood, 2017). The countries range from Middle

Eastern countries where Islam is the state religion, Israel, where Jews enjoy greater rights than non-Jews, or Christian countries in Europe where there is sometimes greater state aid to Christian organizations than those of other religions (Sherwood). In the aftermath of 9/11, the United States engaged in state-sponsored terrorism against people from the Middle East or who were Islamic through its "enhanced interrogation" of suspected militants, which was essentially torture (Svendsen, 2008). State-initiated collective violence is often the cause of wars and campaigns of armed conflict, which can be between countries or within countries, where the government attempts to violently suppress uprisings or other threats to the state.

As mentioned previously, collective violence is also perpetrated by non-state actors. As with all forms of collective violence, one group is perpetrating violence on another group (WHO, 2014), although in my experience, the perpetrators often feel like victims and refer back to historical assaults by the other group or the threat of an attack by that group. One example of a non-state form of collective violence is "terrorism," the meaning of which is often contested. One reason that it is disputed is that the ability to label a group and its actions as part of a project of terrorism is determined by who has the power to apply such labels. Most liberation uprisings were labeled as terrorism by the government in power or the colonial power at the time. But terrorism certainly can be enacted by non-state organizations and groups. Svendsen (2008) citing Richardson lists some common characteristics of terrorism:

1. The act is politically motivated.
2. The act involves violence or the threat of violence.
3. The aim of the act is not to defeat the enemy but to convey a message. (In my view, it is also done to achieve aims, which include defeating an enemy.)
4. There is symbolic as well as literal significance.
5. The act consciously targets civil victims, as with 9/11 (although the Pentagon was also attacked).

An insidious aspect of all acts of violence, although particularly for terrorism, is that victims are aware that the intention was to harm them. Hurricanes, floods, earthquakes, and mining disasters are overwhelming, often traumatic events, but they were not intentional. Knowing that pain and suffering are the result of a conscious attempt to harm you and people like you adds another layer of pain, a deeper level of wound (Miller, 2012).

Fear accelerates when it is clear that a group or someone wants to harm you due to your social identities (e.g., race, ethnicity, religion, gender, sexual orientation). Building on this fear, both state and non-state actors exert power and dominance through disappearances and disfigurement. During the reigns of military dictatorships in Chile and Argentina, many people (estimates in Argentina are 30,000) went missing and were even called "the disappeared" (Blake, 2019). Half a century later, many are still unaccounted for. Related to this, children were stolen from the families of murdered people and secretly adopted (Blake). This practice occurred in other conflicts, such as World War II (DW, 2017). Disfigurement and dismemberment are extreme forms of violence meant to instill fear and are discussed in the following section on dehumanization of victims.

Interpersonal Violence

According to the WHO (2014), interpersonal violence is when force is threatened or intentionally used by a person or small group of people that can lead to death, injury, physical or psychological harm, deprivation, or can limit a person's development. It can involve coercion and is a means of exerting power and control over someone else.

IPV, family violence, and child maltreatment take place in the context of a family or domestic relationship. Violence can be between partners and spouses, directed at children, between siblings or extended family, or focused on older or disabled people by other members of a family. What is critical is that there is a relationship and often kinship ties between people. Thus, it always involves a betrayal of the bonds of love and affection. Some societies have laws prohibiting this type of violence and means of investigation and prosecution, while in other societies, the primacy of the family takes precedence over state intervention, often leading to secrecy and the avoidance of scrutiny or recognition. And cultural, religious, and social mores influence what is considered permissible and unacceptable, particularly regarding gender roles and expectations and norms about what parents are allowed or not permitted to do with their children. In China, the notion of "filial piety" (loyalty and obligations to parents) can lead not only to not reporting or confronting child sexual abuse by parents but also leave victims with intense conflicts and doubts about what actually happened, leading to a psychosocial veil of self-inflicted gaslighting (Xie & Miller, 2018).

Zooming in on IPV, it is important to see how this is informed by history, sociopolitical context, and a spectrum of harassment, targeting, and violence toward women (Aymer, 2021). What I mean by a spectrum of violence toward women are the intersections and linkages ranging from harassment in the workplace and in public, informed by gender stereotypes and traditional roles, cultural norms, and ideologies, structural factors such as hiring and promotion, control (ranging from economic, psychological to physical), emotional and psychological antagonism, sexual and physical assaults, and in its most extreme form, death.

What has been deemed acceptable within this spectrum has varied considerably throughout history, and there are marked differences in norms, expectations, and laws between and within cultures and nations. Male hierarchy and power are central to all of this, as are institutions such as marriage and its many definitions and meanings (Aymer, 2021). Another central concept is personhood – ranging from full civil, economic, and political rights to being considered subhuman and property. While IPV can occur in any political economy, particular economic systems and political systems offer opportunities for some and barriers for others and can cultivate the conditions for IPV. What are the expectations for gender roles within a given economic and political structure? Who is responsible for child rearing and domestic responsibilities? Social welfare institutions and laws can lessen or promote IPV. Are there laws prohibiting IPV or legitimizing it? Are there institutions and agencies that will investigate and have the power to act and protect and mitigate? And it is important to note that within any given sociopolitical system, there is rarely a consensus about these issues and questions; rather, gender roles and gender-based violence are fiercely contested. Aymer also stresses the importance of social movements – such as the Civil Rights, Women's Rights, and Battered Women movements in the United States: they can open up new possibilities, demand new realities, and lead to new laws, policies, and practices.

Aymer (2021) shares two models that have been dominant in the field of IPV – the Power and Control Model developed by Pence and Paymar and the Cycle of Violence, established by Walker. As was mentioned earlier, all types of violence are extreme ways of exerting power and control over others to achieve a person or a group's aims. Pence and Pramer's model breaks down the ways that this is done with IPV. As mentioned earlier, economic systems and proscribed gender roles, reflecting hierarchies and power dynamics, are important contributors to IPV. The Power and Control Model identifies how such structures and practices are amplified at home, such as expecting women to do domestic chores, often in an extreme, rigid, perfectionist, and brutal manner. Other examples are economic control and exploitation – seizing all family assets and controlling how they are used so that the targeted person is increasingly dependent and has to ask their partner for money as if her partner is doing them a favor that requires gratitude. Increasing social isolation makes this easier, limiting access to people and resources that are potential sources of support. With increased isolation, there is greater dependency. With greater social isolation and dependency, there is more space for intimidation, blaming, coercion, and emotional, sexual, and physical abuse. Other strategies include minimizing abuse and blaming the victim for her situation and the perpetrator's behaviors and using children as bargaining chips to further maintain dominance and control.

The Cycle of Violence fits well with the Power and Control model as it brings in the notion of phases, rupture, repair, and further ruptures. The three main phases of this model are tension, leading to violence followed by a honeymoon period. In my work with women experiencing IPV, I have witnessed this cycle and found that there is such relief if a phase of violence is followed by apologies, forgiveness, and better behavior that the pattern of dominance and control remains in place; the perpetrator is not confronted and the survivor's hopes can lead to unrealistic expectations that the couple has rounded a corner and that this time things will be different. I have often witnessed women who have left during periods of violence – often finding themselves to be isolated and bereft of resources – returning home after entreaties and promises offering a new chapter in a relationship, only to be met with another cycle of tension, threats, and violence. The subsequent violent episodes can escalate to more deadly forms of violence, and if the woman has left and returned, there is often a sense of betrayal and a greater urgency felt by perpetrators to reestablish control and isolation by accelerating the violence. Tragically, I have worked with a number of women and this has resulted in their deaths. And of course, the impact on children who at the very least are witnessing this or often are experiencing the same pattern directed at them is profound and often life-long.

Intersectionality is a term that I have used in earlier chapters and as Aymer (2021) points out, it is important to consider IPV through an intersectional lens. Racism, hostility to immigrants, poverty, and being members of queer and transgendered families increase the level of social oppression, lack of power and control, access to resources, and being less likely to experience resonant helpfulness when reaching out for support. I have used a male/female dichotomy to describe IPV because of my own experiences and it is the most prevalent form throughout the world, but IPV can occur in any kind of family and be directed at anyone, regardless of gender and occurs in queer and transgendered, gender non-conforming, and polyamorous families.

The distinction between IPV and interpersonal violence in the community is both real and overly dichotomous. Violence within the home certainly has its own dynamics and does not necessarily mean that survivors are facing violence in the community. Conversely, there are forms of community violence that are sometimes separate from domestic violence, such as gang attacks in neighborhoods. But there are also many situations where both occur and have a relationship with one another. For example, when there is gender-based violence at home, it also often occurs in the community and in public. Some of the forms of community-based interpersonal violence that are mostly outside of the home are organized crime, gang violence, sexual assault and networks of human trafficking, forced prostitution, and economic servitude (Kara, 2017). Whenever people are in vulnerable situations due to their race, caste, religion, gender, sexual orientation, economic situation, and age and disability status, they are prone to experience greater levels of interpersonal violence in the community; what is key is a less power and resources to protect oneself and one's family. The social ecology of the community – its history, social structure, available resources and opportunities, and cultural practices shape the forms and nature of community interpersonal violence.

Interpersonal violence in the community also occurs through omission and commission by those in power. For neighborhoods that have little police or government presence, then vulnerability increases by the lack of protection offered by the state. But authorities can perpetrate violence and although patterns of such human rights violations are a form of collective violence, there can also be smaller pockets of interpersonal violence directed at people by corrupt, dishonest, or severely prejudiced people in authority. I want to be clear – when there is a pattern of police violence, it is structural and institutional and narratives that focus on "a few bad apples" obscure this. But there are also bad apples, and they inflict violence and harm by abusing their power.

Self-Directed Violence

The WHO (2002, 2014) includes self-directed violence in its description of worldwide violence. This includes suicide, self-harm, and self-abuse. At first blush, this may appear to be separate from the topic of this book, but I think that it is relevant. Self-violence can be a way or responding to socio-political targeting and being surrounded by collective and interpersonal violence. As described in Chapter 3, the toll of structural oppression is cumulative and allostatic, and there are profound psychosocial consequences to constant exposure to dehumanization, negative stereotypes, and the knowledge that because of a person's identity, one is not safe. As described in the earlier chapters, if a person lives in a society where they witness violence and assaults on people who they identify with and in concert with this, the experience of social mirroring is like the distorted reflections encountered in a house of mirrors in an amusement park, it is understandable that this leads to self-denigrating internalizations and feelings of worthlessness. It can also contribute to difficulty with modulating moods and emotions, as there is a sense of being unable to control one's destiny or even being out of control. All of this can result in feeling worthless, depressed, or wanting either not to exist or to blame and punish oneself for constant pain and suffering.

Dehumanization, Perpetrators, Victims, and Bystanders When There Is Collective Violence

I want to briefly comment on the process of dehumanization and the relationship between perpetrators, victims/survivors, and bystanders when there is collective violence. In my domestic and international practice, I have found that it is important to consider all three roles when working with collective and interpersonal violence. All three are in social relationship with one another and play a critical role in fomenting or mitigating violence. The dynamics of intergroup conflict and violence are complex, and an in-depth exploration is beyond the scope of this chapter, but I will try to extract some key aspects in order to contextualize psychosocial work with victims of violence.

As has been stated, violence can be perpetrated collectively by state and non-state sectors as well as by individuals, who can also be state actors (e.g., police) or civilians. There has been a great deal of research, particularly by social psychologists, about the dynamics of intergroup conflict. As Volpato and Licata (2010) point out, this has often ignored colonialism and thus is historically decontextualized. With this in mind, it is still helpful to examine the intergroup dynamics of collective violence.

Often, violence by one group toward another is justified by denigrating members of the other group (Miller & Schamess, 2000; Staub, 2019) – e.g., "they are dangerous, not fully human, responsible for and deserving of their fate." This involves a complex psychological process of building up the virtue of the group perpetrating violence and projecting and displacing violent impulses or negative qualities onto the group being targeted: creating an objectified and stereotyped "other," elevating high in-group esteem in comparison with the disparaged out-group (Miller & Schamess, 2000; Staub, 2019). What further complicates this is that the group targeted by the violence can shift from being the victim to the aggressor, justifying violence because of what was done to them (Miller, 2012). Both groups see themselves as victims and therefore rationalize violent behavior, creating what Botcharova described as a cycle of revenge, where each group claims virtue and separate, mutually exclusive vindicating narratives are developed by each group (Miller). There are countless examples of this: two modern ones are the dynamics of Israel/Palestine (Jew/Arab) and the ethnic, genocidal conflict between Hutus and Tutsis in Rwanda. Bramsen (2017), by analyzing pictures of violent interactions during the Arab Spring, has found that violence breeds violence: there is a patterned dance that emerges between perpetrator and victim, often of escalating violence, which can be symmetrical, or if one party is able to dominate the other, asymmetrical. Such escalating conflicts are deemed to be intractable and long-standing. But as Bergman and Crutchfield (2009) point out, it is not only the histories of intergroup conflict that shape collective violence but collective fears of the future – what might the other group do to one's own group! The threats are magnified if a group has already inflicted harm on the other group; the perceived threats thereby justify violent actions toward others as a self-protective intervention.

The treatment of African Americans by White people in the United States illustrates many of these points. There was an asymmetrical process of violence – white people enslaving and torturing Black people that was central to the founding of the United States. Thus, great harm as a consequence of violence was inflicted by White people on Black people. This continued through the Jim Crow era and Civil Rights era and continues to this day with the disproportionate numbers of Black people imprisoned and attacked and/or killed by the police and many other forms of structural racism. All of this has involved a process of White people dehumanizing Black people and justifying violence toward Black people because they are perceived as violent. This is not simply a matter of individual attitudes and behaviors but is an institutional pattern of interactions that structures intergroup violence (Garran et al., 2021).

Stoking fears of the future is instrumental to reify in-group solidarity by demonizing the "other." Donald Trump focused on the threats that Brown and Islamic immigrants posed to White Americans, tapping into well-trodden channels of racialized anxiety, and was rewarded with support from some White people who feared that they were being marginalized or "replaced" by people of color. In an interview with VOX reporter Sean Illing (2019), Duke political scientist Ashley Jardina argues that if White people are already worried about declining economic and political power, appealing to their White identity being under threat, as Trump repeatedly did in both of his Presidential campaigns, amplifies their fears and mobilizes them as a political force. As Jardina states: "Deep down it's about this fear that America isn't going to look like them anymore, that they'll lose their majority and with it their cultural and political power."

Another example is Zeta's use of graphic, videotaped extreme violence, intended to intimidate rivals, terrorize communities, and demoralize the government. While directed at the out-group – another cartel – it also serves to strengthen the organizational commitment of in-group members, reminding everyone of their shared goals, roles, and rituals, and fosters group solidarity and belonging (Perreda, 2021) through a combination of fear and shared, diffused moral transgressions.

It is significant to note that collective violence is never static – it evolves and changes, often escalating and expanding. As Braithwaite and D'Costa (2016) state, "violence cascades across space and time from one kind of violence to another": crime can be a prelude to war; war ripples into greater violence and crime, while spreading to other locales, which can eventually lead to state-sponsored atrocities, such as disappearances and torture. There are many international examples of this. While Braithwaite and D'Costa focus on Sri Lanka as a case example another illustration is how gangs formed in Los Angeles prisons of young men from Honduras, the violent criminal behavior metastasized to Honduras, exploding into government corruption, drug dealing, and violence in response (Anderson, 2021). All of this has led to such a dangerous and intolerable situation for many people living in the country that it has sparked major migration to the United States, where children have been separated from families by the U.S. government and subjected to a psychosocial form of torture. Thus, criminal gang violence cascaded into behaviors by two state governments where they committed atrocities.

Staub (2019) points out that historically there are "challenging conditions" that propel intergroup violence: economic decline, political instability, and substantial and rapid social and environmental changes. Gerlach (2006) adds that appropriation (or perceived appropriation) of what belongs to "other" groups is often a motivator for intergroup violence. These factors can pave the way for the rise of authoritarian leaders, such as Donald Trump in the United States, Viktor Orban in Hungary, and Jair Bolsonaro in Brazil. All elevate certain groups (e.g., Whites, ethnic Hungarians) and create frightening and disparaging narratives about the politically constructed "other" (e.g., violent immigrants, indigenous people) who are portrayed as threatening the elevated groups' purity, welfare, families, and economic prosperity. Thus, complex societal changes and problems are distilled down into simplistic either/or thinking blaming the scapegoated group, which makes those who identify with the authoritarian leader and regime feel better about themselves and heightens a sense of in-group solidarity (Staub).

Ultimately, what this leads to is mutual dehumanization. Victims/survivors are dehumanized by perpetrators, but in order to inflict violence on others, one must dehumanize not only the target of violence but also oneself. Engaging in violence involves denying, stifling, or walling off empathy for others and this hurts perpetrators as well as victims. This can leave perpetrators in an emotionally deadened state or can also lead to profound guilt, shame intrusive images, nightmares, interpersonal difficulties, and regrets. In some instances, as with graphic cartel murders, it literally disfigures victims, shares their defiled bodies through videos, and uses them as symbolic signposts, while those who engage in this dehumanizing behavior have crossed a line together through their moral transgressions, which binds them to one another but alienates them from society at large, their families and themselves. This leads to a "downshifting" of empathy toward the other group and ultimately morality (Cehajik-Clancy & Bilewicz, 2020). Boudreau (2021), who saw active combat in Iraq, has written about the experience of "moral injury," where soldiers are asked to commit violence against others and are then haunted and harmed by this experience. He points out that military organizations have a vested interest in making this a personal weakness or problem, when in fact it results from collective, organizational, and political decisions where individuals were asked to harm others.

Everyone does not agree with the dehumanization hypothesis. Mariot (2020), using testimonies of German perpetrators during the Jewish Holocaust, has argued that there was no dehumanization by citing examples of when killers could identify with being a parent as a child was murdered or in some instances knowing the people who they were killing. I think that he is viewing dehumanization as an absolutist, either/or proposition, which it is not. There are varying degrees of dehumanization – ranging from complete dehumanization (e.g., "parasites," "cockroaches") to not extending sufficient empathy to a person whom you are harming, where you can see bits and pieces of yourself but not a full other person worthy of compassion, dignity, and respect. Melenotte (2020) points out that violence can involve dehumanization and distancing but can take place in a context of proximity and even intimacy. Thus, there is, in my view, a spectrum of dehumanization. There is also a temporal dimension to this where under certain conditions, circumstances, and contexts, there is severe dehumanization which is less apparent at other times and other settings. And dehumanization is not static and evolves – violent language can move to violent acts over time; it involves a developmental component (Melanotte). Violence and the process of dehumanization can continue after death, as the use of mutilated bodies by drug cartels illustrates: they serve as symbolic and discursive mechanisms of intimidation through dehumanization (Melanotte).

However, Mariot (2020) raises areas worthy of further inquiry, going beyond seeing perpetrators as bigoted monsters. He cites Browning's questions about diffusion and thus absolution of responsibility, breaking down violence into specialized and/or standardized tasks, the role of peer pressure, and the desire to conform. He also wonders about how cognitive dissonance works, which I believe is part of the process of having both a relationship with people at certain times and under certain circumstances while harming them at others; this pattern not only occurs in IPV but can also occur when there is group or mass violence. Mariot also wonders about "pluralistic ignorance," which is when one assumes that others in a group committing violence are on board with the task, helping to justify one's own participation and may be part of the need to conform. And he also raises the dynamic of creating new norms, where the tolerance of a level of violence escalates and then plateaus into a new normal. This is of particular concern in the United States as I write this where former President Trump and many in the Republican party endorse levels of violence, such as attacking or killing political rivals that would have been unthinkable and intolerable a few years ago.

Concepts such as pluralistic ignorance lead to a consideration of the roles of perpetrators, victims, and bystanders (Sanderson, 2020). As I have argued, dehumanization is a critical aspect of collective and interpersonal violence. And although there are clearly perpetrators and victims/survivors in a particular act or chapter in a history of violent interactions, I have also discussed how victims can become perpetrators and vice versa. Violence at any level rarely occurs in a situation where there are only the perpetrators and victims. In my work with domestic violence victims and survivors, I have found that there are other people and institutions aware of the violence – e.g., neighbors, friends, relatives, child protective services, and the police – and that earlier interventions may have saved people from greater harm and non-intervention can cost lives. And in my international work in areas where there is armed conflict or high levels of non-state violence, there are always other actors – e.g., countries, officials, and even citizens – who could have intervened to at least mitigate and suspend collective violence, if not end it. Thus, I will consider the critical role of bystanders.

Staub (2019), a social psychologist who survived the Jewish Holocaust as a child, has written extensively about the role of bystanders based on his personal experiences of surviving genocide, his research, and his programs and interventions to promote active bystanders. Bystanders can be inactive, allowing violence to occur, or they can attempt to intervene with perpetrators before, during, or after acts of violence (Lui et al., 2021; Sanderson, 2020). This can involve physically intervening, speaking up, sheltering people, seeking help from others, and offering care and support (Lui et al.; Staub). What are the conditions under which bystanders fade into the background or actively seek to intervene and protect people? I have often asked myself this question about my own responses and encourage readers to do the same (see Box 4.1).

Box 4.1 Being an Active Bystander

1. Recall a time in the past when you wish that you had intervened in a situation but did not do so or were not satisfied with how you responded.
2. Recall a time in the past when you did intervene. What was going on with your body and your thinking? How did you feel at the time?
3. What are the factors that help you to become an active bystander and what are the barriers that inhibit your ability to intervene?
4. Are there particular situations where you feel a responsibility to intervene?
5. What goal might you set for yourself – however small – about being more likely to intervene as an active bystander? What kind of skills or training would be helpful?
6. Are there any steps that you can take to help prepare yourself for future situations where you may want to intervene?

Three conditions that social psychologists have identified that inhibit active bystander interventions are the previously mentioned pluralistic ignorance (we didn't know what was happening and did not want to get involved), diffusion of responsibility (I will wait for someone else to intervene), and embarrassment about standing out or making a mistake in public (Sanderson, 2020; Staub, 2019). However, there has been recent research that challenges the diffusion of responsibility hypothesis, finding that sometimes people are more likely to act when there are more bystanders, a form of strength in numbers (Levine et al., 2019). A key factor that seems to foster bystander interventions when there are many bystanders is the social identities of the bystanders; can they identify with victims (Levine et al.)? This can be challenging as it rubs up against the dehumanization that occurs with violence because when victims are not viewed as being fully human, it is more difficult for bystanders to identify with them. Another motivator for intervention can be when members of the group that is perpetrating the violence do not want their group besmirched by these acts and actively seek to stop them (Levine et al.).

So, what helps to foster active bystander behavior? Empathy seems to be key. When someone is a member of a group that has experienced marginalization, violence, or oppression, it can increase both identification and compassion for others who are targeted (Staub, 2019). And there is greater empathy when there is a resonance between the identity of victims and bystanders (Sanders, 2020). Children who have received love and affection tend to see be able to generate greater compassion, but it is also important to teach them values and the rules of just treatment of others as well as to help them to understand the harmful consequences of violent behavior toward others (Staub). Laws and prohibitions against violence offer some protection against interpersonal violence, including mandated reporting laws that lead to investigations and interventions when there is domestic or elderly violence (Levine et al., 2019). Along with laws and statutes, cultural norms also play an important role in either condemning or in some instances covering up various forms of domestic violence (Xie & Miller, 2018).

Bystander interventions are more likely when there is a belief that intervening will have a positive impact, when it is done with others and when people have developed intervention skills (Sanderson, 2020). Bystander interventions can be encouraged by training programs that stress bystander obligations to intervene, such as college programs to prevent sexual assault on campus (Levine et al., 2019; Sanderson). These programs teach intervention skills and convey that not only are all people obligated to intervene but intervention is the expected norm. Often, there is social norm misperception – the sense that others condone violence when this is not the case – so it is critical to reframe what is normative and expected (Sanderson). This sometimes necessitates changing organizational cultures – e.g., police and colleges – so that bystander interventions are encouraged, appreciated, and validated (Sanderson). Staub (2019) has produced radio shows in Rwanda to promote bystander behavior in the wake of genocide and subsequent ethnic conflict. The programs seek to generate empathy from potential perpetrators and bystanders by telling stories that humanize victims and help listeners to understand the ways that they can intervene in the future, seeking to engender a sense of responsibility and efficacy while offering intervention skills.

Central to bystander interventions is humanizing victims, which in turn relies on helping bystanders and potential perpetrators to access their own humanity. Having "moral exemplars," people from one's own group who stand up and are willing to intervene, helps to humanize not only the targeted group but also the perpetrators by setting an example that can help the group to feel better about itself (Cehajik-Clancy & Bilewicz, 2020). I will discuss the process of mutual rehumanizing further in the section on violence prevention and intervention in the following section.

Consequences of Violence

I have lingered on the types and dynamics of violence as those of us who are practitioners need to understand the experiences of our partners. As I have argued, different levels of violence often merge with one another. I will briefly summarize the common psychosocial consequences of violence. While they are similar to those due to structural oppression, violence adds a unique layer of intensity and lack of safety. The social ecology where violence occurs – which includes the types of violence, its history, and the sociocultural context – also shapes psychosocial reactions in unique ways; it can be difficult to generalize about universal reactions. What is consistent for survivors is feeling in danger and unsafe, often inhabiting an activated, self-protective space in order to survive and to retain, recapture, or reconstitute a minimal sense of control. What I will do is outline themes that appear to be common, although the exact manifestations differ considerably. Most of this section is drawn from my book *Psychosocial capacity building in response to disasters* (2012) unless otherwise noted.

Violence has a psychosocial impact on individuals, families, and communities. These are not separate processes – rather, they all interact and are part of a multidimensional, multilevel process. Individual and family reactions influence collective reactions; community, political, and societal responses to violence profoundly influence the experiences of individuals and families. So, although I will consider them separately, they are part of a recursive, interactive process.

Impact on Individuals

Violence affects all aspects of individual well-being. In general, it affects people's bodies and their health, their thinking, feelings and emotions, behaviors, social relationships, how they view the world, and their sense of meaning. None of these reactions stand alone and what is happening with the body influences thoughts, feelings, and emotions, which leads to certain behaviors. There have been many debates between neurologists, psychiatrists, psychologists, anthropologists, and social workers about how universal or culturally contingent such reactions are. In my professional experiences, the threat of death and destruction wrought by violence universally causes severe and debilitating reactions, but "the idioms of stress are so culturally contingent" (Miller, 2012, p. 89) that the expression of reactions varies considerably across groups with different sociocultural realities and social identities. And even the separation of reactions into these different domains reflects a particular, Western worldview.

Bodies

When we have a fall or cut ourselves, these events are inscribed in our bodies and brains, encoded as embodied memories that help to keep us safe. Such memories are not always conscious, and there has been much written about how they are stored. When there is the threat or experience of violence, a complex interaction of cellular, molecular, neurological, hormonal, and physiological processes – activating the autonomic nervous system with the amygdala at the center and also involving the hippocampus, cortical, thalamic, and brainstem regions – leads to (often unconscious) memories about the signs of danger (Maddox et al., 2019). These encoded memories are activated when there are perceptions of similar threats and lead to elevated heart rate and breathing, the release of stress hormones, lower blood sugar, and complex neurochemical reactions that are experienced as fear (Maddox et al.).

Thus, bodies often have physical reactions after encountering violence as well as in anticipation of future violence; the two often go together. When a new threat of violence is perceived, neurological and endocrinological changes are experienced as preparing for flight or fight. Hypervigilance is often present. Even the anticipation of micro-aggressions can precipitate such reactions. The experience and anticipation of violence are exhausting and can lead to profound fatigue and somatic complaints such as headaches, muscle tension, depressed libido, and a weakened immune system.

Thinking

Bodily reactions affect people's thinking. When the amygdala and associated neuroendocrine systems are lighting up, deliberative thinking in the pre-frontal cortex is dimming, compromising concentration, logic, reasoning, and efficient problem solving. Memory can become distorted or fragmented. When confronted with violence, people can become confused and disoriented. Related to the need to protect oneself from future violence, obsessive-compulsive thinking and rumination can be activated. All of this can lead to hyper-focusing on not only perceived threats but also distortions about their meaning; while trauma survivors are highly attuned to situations that remind them of previous violence, they can also misread or distort situations that mimic prior violent encounters but are more innocuous. For example, having survived a violent encounter with a police officer, a person may react with alarm when passing a parking violation officer in uniform. Such misreading of people and situations can fuel behaviors such as running away or attacking the perceived threat, both of which can escalate a situation and precipitate further violence.

Emotions and Feelings

Emotions stem from bodily reactions affecting neurochemistry and are then read, narrated, and experienced as feelings. Thus, the bodily trauma of experiencing violence affects mood states, as well as the cognitive understanding of those states. Emotions and feelings are integrated as the affective experience of violence: numbing, fear, terror, anger, sadness, and later guilt and remorse. Feelings are both caused by thinking and shape what we think. Thus, a thought such as "I have bad karma and luck and always end up being victimized" can fuel feelings of hopelessness and despair. But as Damasio (2000) in his work on consciousness has argued, feelings often precede conscious thoughts. Who has not experienced a sense of gloom and anguish and while in that state has been unable to generate positive or hopeful thoughts?

Sociocultural context has a profound impact on what people feel and how they express their feelings. We are taught to make sense of our emotional states and our understandings are shaped by collective cultural contexts and experiences. What feelings are within our range of possibility and even the words for feelings are dependent on these contexts (Mesquita, 2022). How others respond to our emotions and feelings – with empathy, compassion, confusion, misunderstanding, or even condemnation – influences what feelings are viewed as being real, understandable, and socially acceptable.

Behaviors

All of the aforementioned – our bodies, thoughts, emotions, and feelings – contribute to our behaviors. Hypervigilance, fear, suspicion, and mistrust in the wake of violence weaken social trust and cohesion and can spawn protective or aggressive behaviors. Constantly being on high alert affects sleep, appetite, energy levels, overall health, and how people behave toward others. Wariness, suspicion, or aggression toward those perceived as threatening are direct responses but frustration, hostility, and brutality toward those who are family and friends, or those in authority, can be secondary consequences of experiencing violence. Other behavioral manifestations are irritability, depression, and withdrawal. Increased use of alcohol and drugs or self-destructive behaviors, such as self-cutting or attempting suicide, are behavioral responses generating cascading problems. Psychiatric disorders resulting from violence can include disassociation, hallucinations, depression, and psychosis.

Social Interactions

Clearly, all of the aforementioned – bodily reactions, thoughts, feelings, and behaviors – affect how people relate to one another. On the positive side, threats of violence can draw people closer to one another as they resist but more often than not, violence causes interpersonal rifts, schisms, and chasms. When dehumanized through violence, it is more difficult to reclaim one's own humanity and to recognize and validate it in others. Strong emotions, ranging from shame to terror, contribute to people isolating themselves from others in response to experiencing violence; this is a tragic consequence as what can help people to withstand and also recover from violence are relationships and social networks. Mistrust is another factor that inhibits social interactions in the wake of violence. I will consider the social impact of violence further in the sections on family and collective consequences.

Meaning-Making and Spirituality

All societies and all people have belief systems that shape thoughts and feelings, structure relationships and social interactions, and guide behaviors, whether secular, spiritual, or religious. When violence occurs, it usually challenges the foundations of these worldviews and values and can undermine internalized beliefs as well as respect for the authority of those viewed as spiritual or meaning-making leaders (e.g., religious leaders, philosophers, politicians, artists). In my work with survivors of violence in many different sociocultural and political contexts, I have frequently heard people question the values and worldviews that sustain their lives; 'this is not what I expected and how could this happen'? Such questions can unravel many aspects of life – trust in society and leaders, the narratives we tell ourselves that sustain one's sense of purpose, duty and obligations, and even the meaning of one's identity.

As with everything, the social ecology in which violence occurs offers important contextual shaping of meaning-making. Some of my Afghan students have told me that they have grown up with violence, expect violence as the norm, and that they even accept that they will experience further violence, particularly if they are women or members of ethnic minority groups. In contrast, domestic U.S. students were stunned and overwhelmed by the events of 9/11 or the coup attempt staged by Donald Trump and his supporters on January 6, 2021, in response to Joseph Biden's electoral victory. They wonder how this could happen in the United States and question their sense of security or the myths and narratives about what kind of society they inhabit, learned from family, school, and society. While in Northern Uganda, despite living in a country continually racked by violence and political instability, people felt traumatized and overwhelmed by the scale of violence unleashed by the LRA and Ugandan government forces. This has not only shaken their faith in and respect for political leaders but has also undermined social trust, social norms and practices, domestic relationships, and confidence in clan elders and leaders.

Identity is another important variable and shapes one's meaning-making of violence. As described in the opening vignette, being Acholi meant a very different experience of the 20-year armed conflict than for other Ugandans, not only literally but also when constructing the meaning of what happened; the armed conflict was not simply a Ugandan conflict but an existential crisis for the Acholi tribe. In the United States, one's racial and ethnic identity is a significant factor in determining how one understands being exposed to violence and political instability, as does socioeconomic class and where one lives. For some, violence is "un-American" and out of the ordinary, while for others, it is both a historical and contemporary reality, as discussed in Chapters 2 and 3.

Trauma

As I mentioned in Chapter 2, I am always ambivalent about writing about trauma for fear of medicalizing or Westernizing human suffering (Summerfield, 2004). This is particularly true of the diagnosis of post-traumatic stress disorder (PTSD), which many have criticized as being Eurocentric and pathologizing (Ager, 1997; Keane et al., 1996; Kirmayer, 1996; Miller, 2006, 2012; Pupavec, 2004; Reyes & Elhai, 2004; Summerfield, 2004). As Charkraborty (1991, p. 1204) states: "A central pattern of [Western] disorders is identified and taken as the standard by which other [local] patterns are seen as minor variations." Although PTSD is often viewed as being a universal bodily response to exposure to life-threatening, violent, or overwhelming events, I have seen many different responses to such events depending on an individual and group's social identities and varied social ecologies. Vietnamese fisherman in Biloxi were exposed to Hurricane Katrina but in my research (Park et al., 2010). I found that they were not overwhelmed or traumatized by the event and even found that it paled in comparison with other stressful times, such as their experiences as "boat people" after the United States withdrew from Vietnam.

However, with these cautions in mind, I think that violence does cause trauma. The American Psychological Association (2022) definition of trauma is as follows:

> Trauma is an emotional response to a terrible event like an accident, rape or natural disaster. Immediately after the event, shock and denial are typical. Longer term reactions include unpredictable emotions, flashbacks, strained relationships and even physical symptoms like headaches or nausea. While these feelings are normal, some people have difficulty moving on with their lives.

There are often other psychosocial problems linked with trauma in the wake of violence, such as drug use, depression, and anxiety (Droždek et al., 2020), I would add hypervigilance, profound fear, difficulty in self-calming, disassociation, emotional flooding, invasive recurring images, and guilt and shame are other manifestations of trauma in response to violence. As I have discussed in Chapters 2 and 3, there is often historical and collective trauma as a consequence of violence. And all of these conditions can beget further conditions – the effects of repeated exposure to violence are cumulative and can be sequential (Droždek et al.).

Once when I was conducting a workshop in the 2000s along with an Acholi Catholic priest in Northern Uganda for women leaders, local officials, health-care workers, police officers, taxi drivers, health-care workers, clan leaders, and religious catechists, we were exploring how the 20-year armed conflict had affected individuals and the community. A woman stood up and shared a terrible incident that she had witnessed during the war – an infant being brutally murdered by the LRA in front of her. She started to cry and all participants appeared to be disassociating – averting their gaze and not making eye contact, twitching, appearing to disassociate. The translator began to cry and was unable to continue. Fortunately, I was able to ask my co-facilitator to talk with the group about his own trauma as well as Acholi rituals of healing and how his Catholic faith could be a comfort at a time like this. When he talked to the group, people listened intently and seemed to calm down. He asked questions about what rituals and practices people still engaged with, which generated sharing and seemed to be empowering. He then asked one of the catechists to lead the group in prayer. We then asked the group if anyone could think of an Acholi song that captured grief and mourning. The woman who had shared her story started to sing and was joined by everyone in the group. We broke for lunch, where participants seemed to regain their composure as we chatted and ate together. I share this brief vignette not because I think that it cured or transformed the trauma that people were carrying but because it illustrates the degree of collective trauma carried by a group of individuals who directly experienced a brutal armed conflict. And I also think that it exemplifies the power of drawing on indigenous rituals, the power of praying, and the empowerment and connection that comes from communal singing and dancing.

Impact on Families

Individual reactions to the violence of course influence family reactions when one or all members of a family have directly been exposed. There is an extensive range of family types and structures – e.g., nuclear, extended, heterosexual, queer, blended, biological, chosen, polyamorous, polygamous, multigenerational, with or without children, and more. Some families consist of people with similar cultural, national, tribal, racial, and national backgrounds while others are multi-racial, cultural, national, and religious. Every family is a mini-sub-culture, with iterative family structures, patterns of interaction and relationships, norms, boundaries, routines, communication styles, worldviews, values, and shared understandings and meanings. And yet within any family, there are often differences in all of these areas between people, generations, and genders.

Exposure to violence can place a strain on all aspects of family life. Traditional roles are upended when people are killed, disappeared, attacked, and sexually assaulted. This also affects relationships, intimacy, trust, and family cohesion. While in some instances, family members share perceptions, emotions, and reactions to the violence, which can increase intimacy and solidarity, exposure to violence can fragment families as everyone is feeling threatened, under extreme stress, and may have different responses and coping mechanisms that are not only varied but may be at odds with one another; one person may be agitated, while another is withdrawn and catatonic, exacerbating one another's difficult and painful reactions. Morgan et al. (2020) citing Henry identify five common marital problems when families encounter war: (1) reestablishing roles with one another; (2) boundary issues, and the dynamic of an emotional pursuer/avoider; (3) intimacy problems; (4) triggers for each family member (which are not necessarily the same); and (5) using different coping mechanisms. Also, sexual intimacy is often affected when rape and sexual assault are present.

As was mentioned earlier in this chapter, violence is already present in some families through IPV and child maltreatment. When violence is exploding outside of families, violence can implode inside a family, escalating an already established pattern. Thus, adults who are already experiencing IPV – often women in heterosexual families – and children are at great risk of mounting violence when the family is exposed to external violence.

Families often have to flee violent situations and therefore can end up in precarious and dangerous situations, such as the many migrants trying to flee violence (and poverty) in Central and South America and from Africa and find themselves making hazardous journeys, living in refugee and concentration camps or in the wild, and being met with vitriol, hostility, and further violence when trying to enter North America or Europe, which, as described in earlier chapters, is a continuation of coloniality and the profound global inequalities it has spawned and is covered in detail in Chapter 9. Involuntary migration also means leaving one's home, community, precious possessions, and one's familiar sociocultural world. This disrupts transitional pathways (Landau, 2007; Landau & Saul, 2004), cutting people off from their past, weakening ties to ancestors and cultural traditions. Schools are closed or children are removed from schools, jobs and sources of livelihood are lost, and critical social networks may fray or vanish.

In Northern Uganda, children were kidnapped by the LRA and forced to be child soldiers, often being made to brutally attack their own families as a form of initiation. Young women were abducted, sexually assaulted, and forced to be concubines, resulting in many having children. If they escaped or were released, they would try to return to their own families with children related to the perpetrators of violence against their families, as described in the opening vignette for this chapter. This can disrupt family interactions and life cycles for generations.

Violence results in death, often sudden, and injury which in turn can lead to families experiencing traumatic loss and traumatic grief, which like other forms of trauma can become stuck and linger (Halpern & Tramontin, 2007). Ochberg (1988) has identified the tasks of traumatic grieving, which include expressing affect, constructing meaning, and re-cathecting with others, all of which are difficult to do when experiencing ongoing violence. When there is a tension between coping/surviving and grieving, survival often takes precedence. This in turn may lead to guilt over not mourning properly as well as survivor's guilt. This can also translate into anger and a desire for revenge. Thus, here is much to grieve and mourn when there is violence and little space or stability for this to occur.

Impact on Communities

When violence occurs, the fate of individuals, families, and communities is inextricably linked. When communities collapse, this buries the hopes, social trust, and social connections of families and individuals who reside there; when people are traumatized, overwhelmed, and undermined, it is difficult for them to contribute to and build a healthy community. Collective trauma is a combination of aggregated individual trauma and the systemic multidimensional and multilayered shock to public and communal cohesion, integrity, and efficacy. Collective trauma, as discussed in Chapter 3, is related to historical trauma and affects collective identity and communal survival.

The impact of violence on communities is shaped by its unique social ecology. This includes the community's history, size, population, location, demographics, infrastructure, resources, system of government, civic associations, public institutions, dynamics, and its cultures. Violence has both a horizontal and a vertical impact on communities. The horizontal consequences are the impact of violence on economic functioning, infrastructure, governance, transportation, medical services, housing and shelter, daily routines, social networking, and the community's collective mood and spirit. There is often a collective sense of helplessness and hopelessness.

The vertical consequences are the severing of connections with a community's past and its vision of its future, what Landau (2007) has termed "transitional pathways." Neighborhoods, public spaces, monuments, and the many domestic artifacts of life are destroyed or lost. Due to a profound, involuntary assault, a way of life is displaced and often not replaced, which includes disruptions with the past as well as truncating future hopes. The present moment for a community (and the same holds true for individuals) relies on its history and past – this gives context and a foundation, a sense of purpose, and shapes expectations for what to expect in the present, which in turn influences its vision of the future. Both the past and an imagined future give the present moment meaning. It is difficult for a community to have confidence for the future when it has lost its connection with its past. This can lead to a communal loss of pride, self-worth, and self-efficacy, which are replaced by pessimism, fear, and social mistrust.

This is not to say that community change is bad and in fact it is often a positive development. When communities have discriminated against groups based on race, ethnicity, gender identities, and religion or based on other factors, it is important that this is resisted, contested, and leads to change. However, the changes wrought by large-scale violence inevitably lead to the disruptions and collective trauma that I have been describing. And these changes affect families, extended families, clans, and individuals as the example I have been using about Northern Uganda illustrates. When security is no longer present, then it is difficult for people to achieve a sense of safety, and when this occurs, it is challenging for people to be able to self-calm, which contributes to an escalating cycle of instability and increased violence.

All of these consequences – horizontal and vertical – can last for years, decades, and generations, as described in Chapter 2 (historical trauma). Once lost, social trust and confidence and belief in leaders and society can be difficult to reestablish. This is particularly true when violence has been sanctioned by the state. Thus, there are cascading social and personal consequences of violence, affecting life courses, family histories and dynamics, and community cohesion and efficacy that go beyond the initial acts of violence, as the effects reverberate even beyond the lifetimes of those who directly experienced it. This is certainly the case with historical and structural violence, where acts of violence are part of a larger pattern of racial, ethnic, and religious violence.

Vicarious Consequences

Working with anyone or any group that has suffered from sociopolitical targeting presents many challenges to responders, and Chapter 10 considers the risks, costs, and ways that workers can protect and care for themselves. This is made more challenging when workers share the same identities as the consumers who they are helping. When there is violence, the risks of vicarious psychosocial consequences are particularly high. I know this from first-hand experience, having suffered from vicarious trauma when working with clients who were murdered by their partners, sometimes in front of their children. Like all forms of trauma, vicarious trauma has the capacity to shape one's life trajectory.

There is a spectrum of vicarious reactions to violence ranging from burnout and compassion fatigue to secondary or vicarious trauma (Miller, 2012). I will briefly describe some broad conceptualizations of how workers are affected when the people who they are helping encounter violence, although I am wary of rigid, diagnostic categories. Often people suffer from a range of reactions that blur discrete categories and people also go through different phases of reactions and are not frozen into a particular status. From my review of the literature and practice experience, I have found that whatever the potential vicarious reactions, what is most important is to help workers prepare for such risks and offer psychosocial support when there is injury, on both the interpersonal and organizational levels.

Burnout occurs to workers in all professions and refers to when people have overdone things or are constantly exposed to psychologically and emotionally difficult stimuli. Workers are more prone to burnout when they are socially and professionally isolated and/or they see little sign of success or progress in achieving their goals in their work (Rosenfeld et al., 2005). When considering the way that violence pierces the membrane of security, safety, and control for victims/survivors, it is not surprising that for those trying to offer empathic/support, there can be feelings of resignation about how humans treat one another, pessimism about one's ability to prevent violence, and disheartenment about the potential for amelioration and full recovery, all of which increase burnout. When burnout becomes extreme, it can lead to compassion fatigue (Adams et al., 2006; Figley, 1995), reducing the capacity for empathic engagement and where a person may lose their will and desire to continue with their work.

When there is violence, workers are not only exposed to the pain of those directly affected but as well to their own anxiety and fear. This is not always secondary as workers might find themselves in an unsafe situation. While compassion fatigue is often viewed as being situational and can be ameliorated by removing or protecting workers from the conditions that cause it (Canfield, 2005), vicarious trauma goes even further because it can transform the person's construction of themselves: who they are, what they have assumed about the world, the values that they hold, their belief in themselves, and their capacity to care for themselves and others (Pearlman & Saakvitne, 1995; Tosone, 2007). One's sense of competency, self-worth, and self-efficacy can be severely undermined (Way et al., 2007). When there is large-scale violence, all of what I have described can happen simultaneously and lead to what I have termed "disaster distress," where the sheer volume and extent of exposure can lead to multiple levels of impairment and existential dread.

Violence Prevention and Amelioration

In the next chapters, I will present a holistic model of intervention for working with people who have experienced historical and contemporary sociopolitical targeting, including those who have been exposed to violence. In this section, I will briefly summarize broad interventions that can help to prevent and ameliorate violence.

As I have argued, societal inequities are significant contributors to intergroup conflict and other forms of violence. Coloniality, extreme economic inequality, and structural and cultural racism, misogyny, and queerphobia create the conditions for discrimination, scapegoating, state/non-state sponsored, institutional, intergroup, and individual violence throughout the world. The specific focus and forms of violence vary considerably across – e.g., ethno-religious oppression against Hazaras in Afghanistan, racism, and police brutality toward BIPOC people in the United States, legislation in Uganda outlawing homosexuality, placing Uighurs in concentration camps in China – but the dynamics of power, supremacy, and privilege are always at play when there is violence at the macro, societal level. And this is linked to violence in communities and within the family as these patterns and dynamics are replicated and also internalized. Working toward equity, social justice, the radical reconstruction of institutions, and revisioning values and reparations are components of a global large-scale violence prevention project. The arc of progress in these areas is often slow and long term, but human service practitioners need to keep the light of this vision in focus and always have it inform our work.

All of the aforementioned forms of oppression involve dehumanizing, and as I have contended, violence is an extreme manifestation of dehumanization. Thus, prevention efforts should focus on love, empathy, and the connections that bind us all together, beginning with how we teach our children (Staub, 2019). I don't believe that this is innate. Children can be taught to feel superior, to be bullies, misogynist, homophobic, and to be violent with one another. And they can also be taught core values of compassion, collaboration, sharing, and responsibility for one another, including becoming active bystanders when they encounter cruelty and viciousness. As discussed in the section on bystanders, this involves a familial or organizational commitment to these values and teaching the skills needed to effectively intervene on behalf of others (Sanderson, 2020; Staub, 2019).

There is a tremendous body of research and literature about resolving and transforming violent intergroup conflict (e.g., Bar-Tal, 2007; Deutsch, 2008; Kelman, 2008; Lederach, 1997; Maynard, 1999; Minow, 2002; Miron & Branscombe, 2008; Stefan, 2008). Related to this is an extensive scholarship on restorative justice (e.g., Leland & Stockwell, 2021; Roche, 2006; Zehr, 2002). From my review of the literature and my own international practice in conflict zones and other areas where there is violence, there is a circle of recovery with four major areas that need to be addressed: (1) social justice; (2) psychosocial healing; (3) peace and reconciliation; and (4) reconstructing society (Miller, 2012) (see Figure 4.3).

As stated earlier, structural violence is a major form of violence and leads to ongoing denial or rights, access to resources, essential goods, and care, which results in death, illness, trauma, and shorter life expectancy (Garran et al., 2021; Mari et al., 2020). Structural violence is entrenched and ongoing and in turn fosters direct, often mass, violence (Mari et al.). Thus, ending structural and direct violence relies on efforts to achieve social justice: human rights, equity in group rights and privileges, reparations for past and current injustices (e.g., slavery, genocide, land appropriation and displacement, ethnic cleansing), proactive and affirmative political, educational and economic development, and a process of restorative justice.

Figure 4.3 Recovering From Intergroup Conflict

Source: "Psychosocial Capacity building . . . " with Columbia U. Press, Joshua L. Miller

Collective recovery and psychosocial healing go hand in hand; there cannot be full collective healing without individual psychosocial healing, and psychosocial healing is accelerated when there is recognition of past wrongs, formal apologies, reparations, and group recovery. Psychosocial healing relies on safety and security, social connections and relationships, having positive social roles that open educational, political, and employment access, strong families, connection to past and present cultural practices and meaning, grieving and mourning losses, and group narratives and aspirations of hope for the future.

Peace and reconciliation are therefore a necessary condition for both social justice and psychosocial healing. With direct, large-scale violence, there needs to be a process of conflict transformation, peace building, truth commissions, and healing rituals and ceremonies. And for both direct and structural violence, there must be efforts to achieve a recovered society, the fourth piece of the circle of recovery: respect for human rights, intergroup equity, social cohesion, and a society where all lives are valued, supported, and respected. This involves perpetrators taking responsibility, apologizing and offering reparations, opportunities for contact and perspective taking, learning skills of violence prevention, community reintegration of all parties, and establishing institutions and mechanisms to prevent future intergroup violence (Leland & Stockwell, 2021; Zehr, 2002). These processes benefit not only victims but also perpetrators and those who stood on the sidelines. Such mechanisms are appropriate for responding to not only contemporary collective violence but also historical violence. All parts of this circle are related to one another, and all are necessary for full recovery from violence to occur.

All of this is part of a process of rehumanizing "the other." Large-scale violence is fueled by leadership that dehumanizes, lighting matches and pouring kerosene on societal tinderboxes. Examples of this abound: President Donald Trump's casting of COVID-19 as the "Chinese Virus," spurring anti-Asian violence, mostly by white people, across the United States was not only incendiary but also ignited by historical and collective racism toward Asians and Asian Pacific Islanders (Cowan, 2021). Indian Prime Minister Narendra Modi's portrayal of Hindu victimhood at the hands of Muslims has spurred anti-Muslim riots, while in nearby Sri Lanka, President Gotabaya Rajapaksa appointed a hardline Buddhist Monk to overhaul the legal system, stirring long-seated animosities by Sinhalese Buddhists against Tamil Hindus and Muslims (Mashal, 2021). An encyclopedia would not have enough room to cover all of the historical and contemporary examples of this dynamic. Mason et al. (2021) have described this process as "activating animus."

The horrific violence unleashed by bad actors points to another important ingredient in prevention and amelioration of violence, moral exemplars (Cehajik-Clancy & Bilewicz, 2020). Non-violence and social justice are furthered by leaders such as Mahatma Gandhi and Martin Luther King Jr. They not only provide a vision for a social movement but also inspire people to be like them. Chehajik-Clancy and Biliwicz give examples of less well-known moral exemplars – e.g., Turks saving Armenians from genocide, Poles aiding Jews during the Jewish Holocaust, and Serbs saving Bosnians during the violent dissolution of Bosnia. In these sorts of situations, people do the right thing despite risking their own lives and facing charges of in-group betrayal, which in turn can influence and inspire other people. As I described in the section on bystanders – bystanders are more likely to actively intervene if they see others who take the lead. When mass violence is perpetrated, morality "downshifts" as the in-group seeks to justify aggression (Cehajik-Clancy & Bilewicz, 2020) while moral leaders contribute to moral uplift. This is partially due to the fact that seeing morally just people who are part of a group can lead to other members of a group feeling better about themselves, which opens up more space for reflection, complex thinking (e.g., less binaries about good and evil people), taking responsibility, and also challenging narratives of the immorality of the out-group.

Lastly, it can be helpful to look at the ingredients that constitute peaceful societies. Coleman and Fry (2021) conducted international comparative research and identified some important factors. I have mentioned how social identities can be constructed in order to divide and oppress, but when there are overarching social identities – e.g., national identities and religious identities – these can help to foster a sense of unity and commonality. Related to that, Coleman and Fry found if there can be greater contact and work together on projects related to economics, ecology, and security in public places, then people realize that they have common interests and goals that transcend their differences. They also stress that developing peaceful norms that deemphasize conflict and violence, including the use of peaceful language in public discourses, are important attributes of peaceful societies. And finally, leadership is vital: it can divide and foment hatred or leaders can be exemplars of respectful, peaceful attempts at compromise and consensus. Helping professionals/volunteers can engage in resistance to violence and oppression while modeling these attributes with collaborators, colleagues, and in our own lives.

Conclusion

Violence is central to and is the most extreme form of sociopolitical targeting and oppression. This chapter considered how violence is defined, the spectrum of violence, and the various categories and types of violence. At one end of the spectrum of violence is collective violence, which includes social, political, and economic violence perpetrated not only by states and governments but also by non-state actors such as militias and cartels. I have argued that all forms of collective violence are often linked and occur at the same time. In addition to collective violence, I considered interpersonal violence, in the home and in the community, and violence toward one's self. Structural violence is ongoing and endemic – fueled by inequality, racism, ethnocentrism, misogyny, and queerphobia – and is seen as normative by groups with power and privilege. It is baked into social, political, and economic institutions and mainstream culture.

How social identities are constructed, the meaning and value of citizenship, and the unequal rights and privileges based on these identities and categories are ingredients of collective violence, and collective violence – whether immediate or institutional – spawn's interpersonal violence. Social identities are central constructs when there is intergroup conflict. Identities and their meanings are constructed through the unique histories and social ecologies of a given location at a specific time, shaping the specific contours of structural and collective violence.

A critical aspect of all forms of violence is the dehumanization of "the other," whether that is one's family or members of a different ethnic, racial, or religious group. Dehumanizing is not static or fixed; there are different phases of dehumanization as well as contexts. Someone may be part of an apparatus that attacks and harms members of another ethnic group while being partnered or a colleague with a member of that same group. The same is true for collective violence – it increases and decreases, lies dormant and is activated, and diminishes and crescendos. It evolves over time and cascades into other countries and communities and one form of violence mutates into another form; e.g., kidnapping and ransom by drug cartels migrate to murders and mutilations.

There are a range of roles when there is collective and interpersonal violence, with three of the most central being perpetrator/aggressor, survivor/victim, and bystander. Sometimes there is asymmetrical violence – such as White violence toward African Americans in the United States, while in other instances, there are cycles of violence, where victims can become perpetrators and vice versa. What can mitigate violence – whether at the societal or local level – are the interventions of bystanders. The chapter considered what constrains active interventions by bystanders and what can promote effective engagement.

I considered the consequences of violence and how it affects individual health, thoughts, feelings and emotions, behaviors, social relationships, worldviews, and the construction of meaning and hope. While trauma is frequently present, it is a complex phenomenon and a trauma diagnosis can be helpful but there are also risks of pathologizing or imposing White Western thinking and categories on other populations, who make up the majority of the world. Violence has consequences for families and communities as well as individuals, and there is an interaction between all levels of impact: collective, family, and individual trauma are inseparable as they intermingle and potentiate reactions in different domains: individual trauma begets family trauma and family trauma when enacted causes trauma in individuals; collective wounds and suffering are manifested in the community but also through individual and family reactions. Violence affects societies, communities, families, and individuals by abrogating transitional pathways with the past, which in turn truncates visions of the future, and also leads to a withering of the latticework of social networks, relations, and institutions.

I considered the risks for workers and volunteers when trying to help individuals and communities afflicted by violence, including compassion fatigue and vicarious trauma. This will be developed further in Chapter 10.

The chapter concluded with a look at broad ways of preventing and ameliorating violence at all levels. This ranged from confronting coloniality, all forms of social supremacy, and the many structural and institutional arrangements that foster societal violence to describing the need and importance of nurturing empathy and morality. Equity, reparations, and restorative justice are related to love and compassion, and I presented a circle of recovery from violence that included social justice, psychosocial healing, peace and reconciliation, and reconstructing society. I also discussed the attributes of non-violent societies. Violence is part of the human condition, but we must be active bystanders in our efforts to thwart violence before it occurs and heal hearts, relationships, and community when it transpires.

The chapter opened with a description of the armed conflict in Northern Uganda and its many consequences. The community is still wracked by collective trauma and the many ways that this is manifested domestically (e.g., IPV), in the community (e.g., land disputes, interpersonal violence, high rates of infant mortality, less respect for religious and clan elders), and its toll on individuals (high rates of suicide, alcoholism, teenage pregnancy). But I have also seen how medical and psychosocial capacity building, as well as community efforts to heal and reconcile – often employing indigenous practices and elements of restorative justice and conflict transformation – have reduced some of the suffering and have contributed to the reconstruction and rebuilding of community. And this gives people a sense of hope, which is critical to recovery from violence.

References

Adams, R.E., Boscarino, J.A., & Figley, C.R. (2006). Compassion fatigue and psychological stress among social workers: A validation study. *American Journal of Orthopsychiatry*, *76*(1): 103–108.

Ager, A. (1997). Tensions in the psychosocial discourse: Implications for the planning of interventions with war-affected populations. *Development in Practice*, *7*(4): 402–407.

American Psychological Association. (2022). *Trauma*. www.apa.org/topics/trauma.

Anderson, J.L. (2021). Is the President of Honduras a narco-trafficker? *The New Yorker*. www.newyorker.com/magazine/2021/11/15/is-the-president-of-honduras-a-narco-trafficker

Aymer, S.R. (2021). *Intimate partner violence*. New York: Rowman & Littlefield Publishers.

Bar-Tal, D. (2007). Sociopsychological foundations of intractable conflicts. *American Behavioral Scientist*, *50*(11): 1430–1454.

Beer, T. (2021, February 11). Trump's policies resulted in the unnecessary deaths of hundreds of thousands of Americans: Lancet report. *Forbes*. www.forbes.com/sites/tommybeer/2021/02/11/trumps-policies-resulted-in-the-unnecessary-deaths-of-hundreds-of-thousands-of-americans-lancet-report/?sh=b44bacf77e8d

Bergman, W., & Crutchfield, R.D. (2009). Racial and ethnic conflict and violence. *International Journal of Conflict and Violence*, *3*(2): 146–153.

Blakemore, E. (2019, March 7). 30,000 people were 'disappeared' in Argentina's dirty war. These women never stopped looking. *History*. www.history.com/news/mothers-plaza-de-mayo-disappeared-children-dirty-war-argentina

Boudreau, T. (2021). Moral injury: What's the use? *The International Journal of Narrative Therapy and Community Work*, *4*: 64–69.

Braithwaite, J., & D'Costa, B. (2016). Cascades across an "extremely violent society": Sri Lanka. *International Journal of Conflict and Violence*, *10*(1): 11–24. www.ijcv.org/index.php/ijcv/article/view/3075/pdf

Bramsen, I. (2017). How violence breeds violence: Micro-dynamics and reciprocity of violent interaction in the Arab Spring uprisings. *International Journal of Conflict and Violence*, *11*: 1–11. DOI: 10.4119/UNIBI/ijcv.625.

Branch, A. (2010). Exploring the roots of LRA violence: Political crisis and ethnic politics in Acholiland. In T. Allen & K. Vlassenroot (Eds.). *The Lord's resistance army: Myth and reality*. New York: Zed Books.

Canfield, J. (2005). Secondarty traumatization, burnout, and vicarious traumatization: A review of the literature as it relates to therapists who treat trauma. *Smith College Studied in Social Work*, *75*(2): 81–101.

Cehajik-Clancy, S., & Bilewicz, M. (2020). Appealing to moral exemplars: Shared perception of morality essential for intergroup reconciliation. *Social Issues and Policy Review*, *14*(1): 217–243. DOI: 10.1111/sipr.12067.

Charkraborty, A. (1991). Culture, colonialism, and psychiatry. *The Lancet*, *337*(8751): 1204–1207.

Coleman, P.T., & Fry, D.P. (2021, June 7). What can we learn from the world's most peaceful societies. *Greater Good Magazine*. https://greatergood.berkeley.edu/article/item/what_can_we_learn_from_the_worlds_most_peaceful_societies
Cowan, J. (2021, February 12). A tense lunar New Year for the Bay area after attacks on Asian-Americans. *The New York Times*. www.nytimes.com/2021/02/12/us/asian-american-racism.html
Damasio, A. (2000). *The feeling of what happens: Body, emotions and the making of consciousness*. London: Vintage Books.
Deutsch, M. (2008). Reconciliation after destructive intergroup conflict. In A. Nadler, T.E. Malloy, & J.D. Fisher (Eds.). *The social psychology of intergroup reconciliation* (pp. 471–486). New York: Oxford University Press.
Droždek, B., Rodenburg, J., & Moyene-Jansen, A. (2020). "Hidden" and diverse long-term impacts of exposure to war and violence. *Frontiers of Psychiatry*, *10*: 975. DOI: 10.3389/fpsyt.2019.00975.
DW. (2017, December 30). Forgotten victims: Polish children abducted during WW II still seeking truth. *Author*. www.dw.com/en/forgotten-victims-polish-children-abducted-during-world-war-ii-still-seeking-truth/a-41981284
Figley, C.R. (1995). Compassion fatigue as secondary traumatic stress disorder: An overview. In C.R. Figley (Ed.). *Compassion fatigue: Coping with secondary traumatic stress disorder in those who treat the traumatized* (pp. 1–20). New York: Brunner-Mazel Publishing.
Garran, A.M., Werkmeister-Rozas, L., Kang, H.K., & Miller, J. (2021). *Racism in the United States: Implications for the helping professions* (3rd ed.). New York: Springer Publishing.
Gerlach, C. (2006). Extremely violent societies: An alternative to the concept of genocide. *Journal of Genocide Research*, *8*(4): 455–471. DOI: 10.1080/14623520601056299.
Halpern, J., & Tramontin, M. (2007). *Disaster mental health: Theory and practice*. Belmont, CA: Thompson Learning.
Illing, S. (2019, April 27). White identity politics is about more than racism: A political scientist about the rise of white identity politics in America. *VOX*. www.vox.com/2019/4/26/18306125/white-identity-politics-trump-racism-ashley-jardina
Kara, S. (2017). *Modern slavery: A global perspective*. New York: Columbia University Press.
Karstedt, S. (2016). Introduction: Extremely violent societies. *International Journal of Conflict and Violence*, *10*(1): 4–9.
Keane, T.M., Kaloupek, D.G., & Weathers, F.W. (1996). Ethnocultural considerations in the assessment of PTSD. In A.J. Marsella, M.J. Friedman, E.T. Gerrity, & R.M. Scurfield (Eds.). *Ethnocultural aspects of posttraumatic stress disorder: Issues, research, and clinical applications* (pp. 183–205). Washington, DC: American Psychological Association.
Kelman, H.C. (2008). Reconciliation from a social-psychological perspective. In A. Nadler, T.E. Malloy, & J.D. Fisher (Eds.). *The social psychology of intergroup reconciliation* (pp. 15–32). New York: Oxford University Press.
Kiconco, A., & Nthakomwa, M. (2018). Marriage for the 'new woman' from the Lord's resistance army: Experiences of ex-abductees in Acholi region of

Uganda. *Women's Studies International Forum*, *68*: 65–74. DOI: 10.1016/j.wsif.2018.02.008.

Kirmayer, L.J. (1996). Confusion of the senses: Implications of ethnocultural variations in somatoform and dissociative disorders. In A.J. Marsella, M.J. Friedman, E.T. Gerrity, & R.M. Scurfield (Eds.). *Ethnocultural aspects of posttraumatic stress disorder: Issues, research, and clinical applications* (pp. 131–164). Washington, DC: American Psychological Association.

Kochenov, D. (2019). *Citizenship*. Cambridge, MA: MIT University Press.

Landau, J. (2007). Enhancing resilience: Communities and families as agents of change. *Family Process*, *41*(1): 351–365.

Landau, J., & Saul, J. (2004). Facilitating family and community resilience in response to major disaster. In F. Walsh & M. McGoldrick (Eds.). *Living beyond loss* (pp. 285–309). New York: W.W. Norton and Co.

Lederach, J.P. (1997). *Building peace: Sustainable reconciliation in divided societies*. Washington, DC: United States Institute of Peace Press.

Leland, W., & Stockwell, A. (2021). Anti-oppressive restorative justice: Behavior analysis in alternatives to policing. *Behavior Analysis in Practice*. DOI: 10.1007/s40617-021-00633-0.

Levine, M., Philpot, R., & Kovalenko, A.G. (2019). Rethinking the bystander effect in violence reduction training programs. *Social Issues and Policy Review*. DOI: 10.1111/sipr.12063.

Lui, P.P., Parikh, K., Katedia, S., & Jouriles, E.N. (2021). Anti-Asian discrimination and Antiracist bystander behaviors amid the COVID-19 outbreak. *Asian American Journal of Psychology*. DOI: 10.1037/aap0000258.

Maddox, S.A., Hartmann, J., Ross, R.A., & Ressler, K.J. (2019). Deconstructing the gestalt mechanisms of fear, threat and trauma memory encoding. *Neuron*, *102*: 60–74.

Mari, S., Bentrovato, D., Durante, F., & Wasserman, J. (2020). Collective victimhood resulting from structural violence. In J.R. Vollhardt (Ed.). *The social psychology of collective victimhood* (pp. 231–251). New York: Oxford University Press.

Mariot, N. (2020). On the role of dehumanization of victims in in the perpetration of mass killings. *Violence: An International Journal*. DOI: 10.1177/2633002420916979.

Mashal, M. (2021, November 6). In a region of strife, India's moral high-ground erodes. *The New York Times*. www.nytimes.com/2021/11/06/world/asia/india-region-muslim-hindu-strife.html

Mason, L., Wronski, J., & Kane, J.V. (2021). Activating animus: The uniquely social roots of Trump support. *American Political Science Review*. DOI: 10.1017/S0003055421000563.

Maynard, K.A. (1999). *Healing communities in conflict: International assistance in complex emergencies*. New York: Columbia University Press.

Melenotte, S. (2020). Perpetrating violence viewed from the perspective of the social sciences: Debates and perspectives. *Violence: An International Journal*. DOI: 10.1177/2633002420924963.

Mesquita, B. (2022). *Between us: How cultures create emotions*. New York, W.W. Norton & Company.

Miller, J. (2006). Waves amidst war: Intercultural challenges while training volunteers to respond to the psychosocial needs of Sri Lankan tsunami survivors. *Brief Treatment and Crisis Intervention*, 6(4): 349–365.

Miller, J., & Schamess, G. (2000). The discourse of denigration and the creation of other. *Journal of Sociology and Social Welfare*, 27(3): 39–62.

Miller, J.L. (2012). *Psychosocial capacity building in response to disasters*. New York: Columbia University Press.

Mills, C.W. (1997). *The racial contract*. Ithaca, NY: Cornell University Press.

Minow, M. (2002). *Breaking the cycles of hatred: Memory, law, and repair*. Princeton, NJ: Princeton University Press.

Miron, A.M., & Branscombe, N.R. (2008). Social categorization, standards of justice, and collective guilt. In A. Nadler, T.E. Malloy, & J.D. Fisher (Eds.). *The social psychology of intergroup reconciliation* (pp. 77–96). New York: Oxford University Press.

Morgan, E., Wieling, E., Hubbard, J., & Dwanyen, L. (2020). Perceptions of war trauma and healing of marital relations among torture-surviving Congolese couples participating in multicouple therapy. *Family Process, 59*(3): 1128–1143. DOI: 10.1111/famp.12487

Mugizi, F.M.P., & Matsumoto, T. (2021). From conflict to conflicts: War-induced displacement, land conflicts, and agricultural productivity in post-war Northern Uganda. *Land Use Policy*, *101*. DOI: 10.1016/j.landusepol.2020.105149.

Nannyonjo, J. (2005). *Conflicts, poverty and human development in Northern Uganda* (WIDER Research Paper, No. 2005 (47)). ISBN 9291907308. The United Nations University World Institute for Development Economics Research (UNU-WIDER), Helsinki.

Neiman, S. (2020, August 11). The enduring harm inflicted by the Lord's Resistance Army. *The New Humanitarian*. https://www.thenewhumanitarian.org/news-feature/2020/08/11/Kony-LRA-Uganda-Congo-CAR

Ochberg, F. (1988). Post-traumatic therapy and victims of violence. In F. Ochberg (Ed.). *Post-traumatic therapy and victims of violence*. New York: Brunner-Mazel Publishing.

Park, Y., Miller, J., & Van, B.C. (2010). "Everything has changed": Narratives of the Vietnamese community in post-Katrina Mississippi. *Journal of Sociology & Social Welfare*, *XXXVII*(3): 79–105.

Pearlman, C.A., & Saakvitne, K.W. (1995). *Trauma and the therapist: Counter-transference and vicarious trauma in psychotherapy with incest survivors*. New York: W.W. Norton and Co.

Perreda, V. (2021). Macabre ceremonies: How Los Zetas produces extreme violence to promote organizational cohesion. *Violence: An International Journal,* 2(2): 278–296. DOI: 10.1177/26330024211059840.

Pierce, C., Carew, J., Pierce-Gonazalez, D., & Wills, D. (1978). An experiment in racism: T.V. commercials. In C. Pierce (Ed.). *Television and education* (pp. 62–88). Beverly Hills, CA: Sage Publishing.

Pupavec, C. (2004). Psychosocial interventions and the demoralization of humanitarianism. *Journal of Biological Science*, *36*: 491–504.

Reveal. (2022. October 15). Buried secrets: America's Indian boarding schools part 1. *The Center for Investigative Reporting*. https://revealnews.org/podcast/indian-boarding-schools-part-one/

Reyes, G., & Elhai, J.D. (2004). Psychosocial interventions in the early stages of disasters. *Psychotherapy, Theory, Research, Practice, Training*, *41*(4): 399–411.

Roche, D. (2006). Dimensions of restorative justice. *Journal of Social Issues*, 2: 217–238.

Rosenfeld, L.B., Caye, J.S., Ayalon, O., & Lahad, M. (2005). *When their world falls apart: Helping families and children manage the effects of disasters*. Silver Springs, MD: NASW Press.

Sanderson, C.A. (2020). *Why we act: Turning bystanders into moral rebels*. Cambridge, MA: Harvard University Press.

Sherwood, H. (2017, October 3). More than 20% of countries have official state religions-survey. *The Guardian*. www.theguardian.com/world/2017/oct/03/more-than-20-percent-countries-have-official-state-religions-pew-survey

Staub, E. (2019). Witnesses/bystanders: The tragic fruits of passivity, the power of bystanders and promoting bystandership in children, adults and groups. *The Journal of Social Issues*. DOI: 10.1111/josi.12351.

Stefan, W.G. (2008). The road to reconciliation. In A. Nadler, T.E. Malloy, & J.D. Fisher (Eds.). *The social psychology of intergroup reconciliation* (pp. 369–394). New York: Oxford University Press.

Sue, D.W., & Spanierman, L.B. (2020). *Microaggressions in everyday life* (2nd ed.). New York: John Wiley and Sons Publishing.

Summerfield, D. (2004). Cross-cultural perspectives on the medicalization of human suffering. In G. Rosen (Ed.). *Post-traumatic stress disorder: Issues and controversies*. New York: John Wiley and Sons Publishing.

Svendsen, L. (2008). *A philosophy of fear*. London: Reaktion Books.

Tosone, C. (2007). Editor's note. *Clinical Social Work Journal*, *35*: 287–288.

Volpato, C., & Licata, L. (2010). Introduction: Collective memories of colonial violence. *International Journal of Conflict and Violence*, *4*(1): 4–10.

Way, I., VanDeusen, K., & Cottrell, T. (2007). Vicarious trauma: Predictors of clinicians disrupted cognitions about self-esteem and self-intimacy. *Journal of Child Sexual Abuse*, *14*(4): 81–98.

World Health Organization. (2002). *World report on violence and health*. Geneva, Switzerland: World Health Organization.

World Health Organization. (2014). *Global status report on violence prevention: 2014*. Geneva, Switzerland: World Health Organization.

Xie, Q., & Miller, J. (2018). Perceptions of Intra-familial child abuse and Intimate parent-child interactions. *Asian Journal of Social Work*, *3*(2): e-ISSN: 0128–1577.

Zehr, H. (2002). *The little book of restorative justice*. Intercourse, PA: Good Books.

5 Liberatory, Decolonial Psychosocial Capacity Building

Guiding Ethical Principles

Introduction

Jessie Thistle was born to an indigenous Canadian teenage mother and a white, drug-addicted father in his early 20s (BBC Outlook, 2020; Thistle, 2019). By age 3, his mother abandoned him and his two younger brothers, he relocated to Toronto with his father, and soon all three children were taken into custody by the state and placed with their paternal grandparents. They endured taunts and violence from white children in school when their indigeneity was revealed, and as a teenager, Jessie became addicted to drugs, broke the law, was homeless, and ended up in jail and then rehab. His grandfather had long ago forced him to leave the home due to his drug use. He was illiterate.

In rehab, he learned to read from another resident. He reconnected with his white grandmother before she died, who made him promise to stop using drugs. He applied to and was accepted at a major university as a student while in his 30s. While studying history, he reconnected with his mother and realized that he wanted to understand indigenous history from an indigenous perspective. He became the top student in the university, was accepted into their Ph.D. program, and then became an assistant professor, with a specialty in indigenous history, particularly focusing on people who live by roadsides because their land had been taken. He discovered that he descended from a lineage of chiefs and tribal elders. He came to realize that his use of drugs was not due to his personal failings but was part of a centuries-old historical process of dispossession, white supremacy, and racial violence. He grasped that "Canadian homelessness" was not the same as "indigenous Canadian homelessness."

How did Jessie become empowered to take control over the direction of his life? What role did reconnecting with his mother, indigenous culture, and his existential re-storying through appreciating his

DOI: 10.4324/9781003021162-5

connections with his ancestors play in his road to well-being? Jessie is an individual, and I am cautious about generalizing from one person. But historical and collective violence and trauma affect individuals and are embodied, internalized by, and enacted through individual lives and perhaps we can learn something from Jessie's story about how to help other people facing historical and collective targeting and violence. I will keep his story in mind as I proceed through this chapter.

The preceding chapters considered the nature of oppression, historical and collective trauma, and exposure to violence. In this chapter, I will present guidelines for liberatory, decolonial psychosocial capacity building. My goal is to offer a scaffolding that practitioners, communities, groups, and tribes can use as a structure, and the next chapter will suggest how specific strategies and interventions can be constructed, erected, and assembled within this framework. When working with people who experience sociocultural oppression, guiding principles are very important precisely because they do not tell us specifically what to do, as interventions should be co-constructed with collaborators to avoid the risk of replicating colonial, Eurocentric hierarchies. While I will suggest some broad interventions in the next chapter, I do not want to fill in too much; I should NOT be prescribing what a given culture, community, and society do to respond to historical and collective trauma, this should be creatively and collaboratively designed and constructed by those who are affected and living within these historical and structural realities. Practitioners and collaborators can draw from a wide range of indigenous and "mainstream" intervention strategies that are consistent with the principles presented in this chapter.

But what about "evidence-based practices?" I appreciate this question, and there is great value in seeking evidence for the efficacy of certain approaches and attempting to ensure, or at least reduce, any iatrogenic affects of specific interventions. What I question is the neutrality and legitimacy of what is considered "evidence-based." As I have been arguing throughout this book, I am skeptical about the notion of impartial universality, particularly in the social sciences and its research and evaluation apparatus. It is not possible to escape the positionality imposed by coloniality and continuing supremacies based on identities, which are established and reinforced by universities, government funders, think tanks, and other institutions that decide what is significant and meaningful, valid and reliable, what should be studied, how it should be studied, who should do the investigating, and who benefits from research. Journals and the entire enterprise of academia act as gatekeepers to ensure that the standards for such "knowledge" are in accordance with the prevailing mores and practices of those societies and groups of people within those societies, who have benefited from coloniality and its devastating global inequities. The voices of members of affected communities too rarely inform the design, methods, and standards of evaluation for programs and interventions that are often conceptualized by others – those with social privileges and resources – for their "benefit."

As I have argued in previous chapters, coloniality and its legacies of identity-based privileges and violence toward targeted groups are central to understanding the lives of people like Jessie, and contributing to decolonization is a central task for the helping professions. One of the biggest challenges is the positionality of helpers, many of whom are white, middle class, based in Western societies, and trained as helping professionals. Professionals are paid for our work and there are rules – e.g., boundaries, limits, epistemologies, and what constitutes evidence – that govern the parameters of intervention. Often, they are presented as protecting clients – and in many ways they do – but they also protect the rights and privileges of workers. While there are important values and skills that are taught in professional training programs, they can also contribute to perpetuating structural violence, social control, and unequal social privileges. Given this, I hope to interrogate not only how helpers who hold power and represent authority, many of whom are differentially socially positioned than the people they are working with, can establish empathy, trust, and relationships that permit meaningful liberatory work to occur. I will begin by summarizing the roots of social oppression, covered in the preceding chapters, and then articulate guiding ethical principles for practice, before moving to a justice-oriented framework that is geared toward decolonizing, liberatory practice in the next chapter.

The Roots of Social Oppression

I have argued in preceding chapters about the power and legacy of coloniality and white supremacy as factors shaping the structure and delivery of psychosocial services today. Some of it is overt, such as the "web of institutional racism" (Garran et al., 2021), but much of it is covert and manifested through informal cultural, social, and professional practices. Insidiously, it is internalized by all who inhabit these social spaces – and we all occupy social spaces mapped and structured by coloniality – which affects interpersonal relationships, identities, self-concepts, and our inner psychic worlds, both conscious and unconscious.

How do coloniality and historical trauma get passed down to people who are sometimes generations removed from the period of acute violence and overt oppression? Weaver and Congress (2010) cite Kellerman who posits four means of transmission: psychodynamic, sociocultural, family systems, and biological. I have covered much of this in Chapter 2 and will briefly recapitulate it here. Psychodynamic refers to how our inner worlds are formed at our ontological beginning and shape our thoughts, feelings, perceptions, understandings, values, and beliefs throughout our life course. Much of psychodynamic theory focuses on early childhood experiences with parents, and this leads to a second transmission pathway – family systems. Parents are molded by their own experiences of their parents, who were shaped by their parents, and so forth. Although I did not have direct exposure to the Jewish Holocaust, I experienced anxious and pessimistic parents, who directly lost relatives and felt existentially threatened by global fascism. I have probably passed some of this down to my children.

The website Transcending Jewish Trauma (2022) maps the impact of collective historical trauma for Jews (Figure 5.1).

At the center of "internalized anti-Semitism" is a sense of terror about unpredictable events that can presage ethnic annihilation and therefore the need to try and exert control whenever possible. A sense of otherness is omnipresent for many Jews, including assimilated Jews, which can lead to a drive for acceptance by others and perfectionism. Other aspects are criticism of self and others, defensiveness, and an ongoing drive for security. Although every group that has encountered historical/collective trauma has experienced unique social conditions and inhabits very different social positions from one another, the map illustrates pathways that illuminate the familial and psychodynamic roots of intergenerational trauma transmission that can be adapted for other groups. This speaks to a third pathway – sociocultural conditions. For example, as a White Jew, I do not experience collective oppression in the United States today (although there is a steady undercurrent of anti-Jewishness in certain parts of society) and my sociocultural conditions are not structurally oppressive as they are for my BIPOC friends and colleagues; I live with White privilege. But, if parents are anxious, secreting hormones that are in response to hypervigilance and alarm, and society continues to be an unsafe place, there are neurobiological affects that begin in utero and are reinforced by parenting behaviors. Like all forms of trauma, historical/collective trauma is embodied and neurobiological. And as with all forms of historical trauma, the sense of collective victimhood can be used to justify aggression toward other

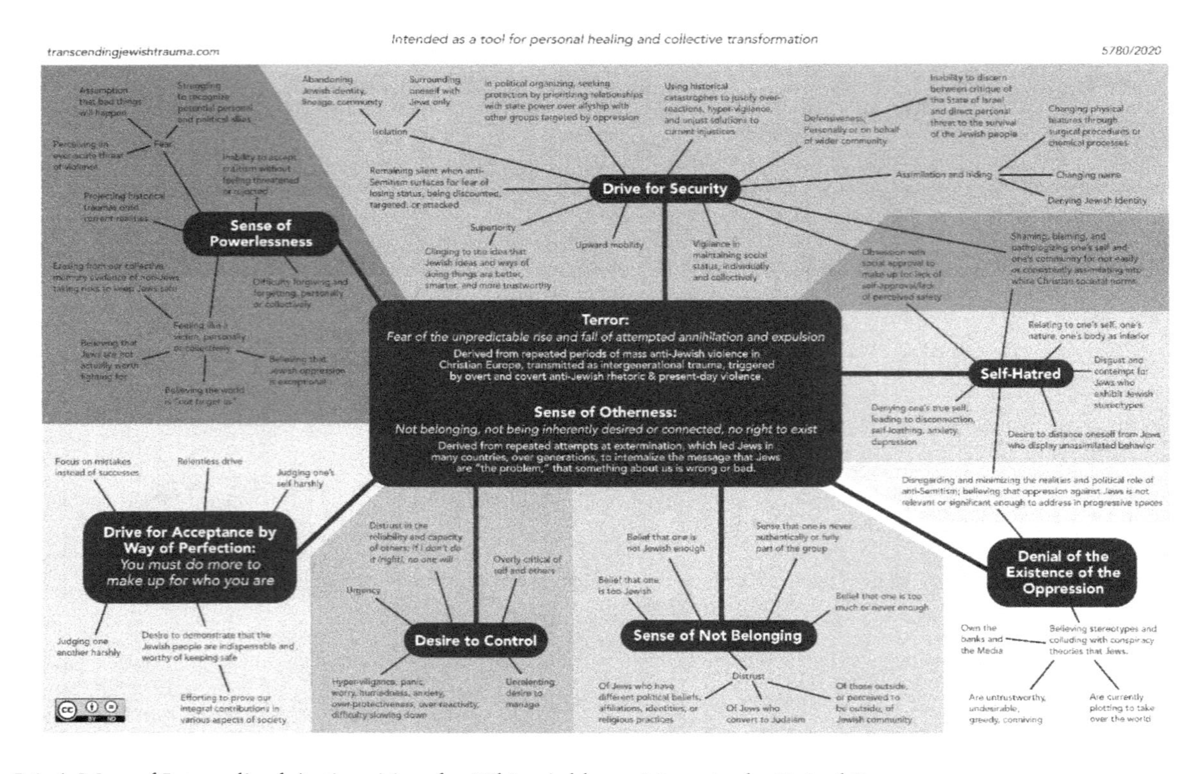

Figure 5.1 A Map of Internalized Antisemitism for White Ashkenazi Jews in the United States

Source: Reprinted with permission from Transcending Jewish Trauma: www.transcendingjewishtrauma.com/map

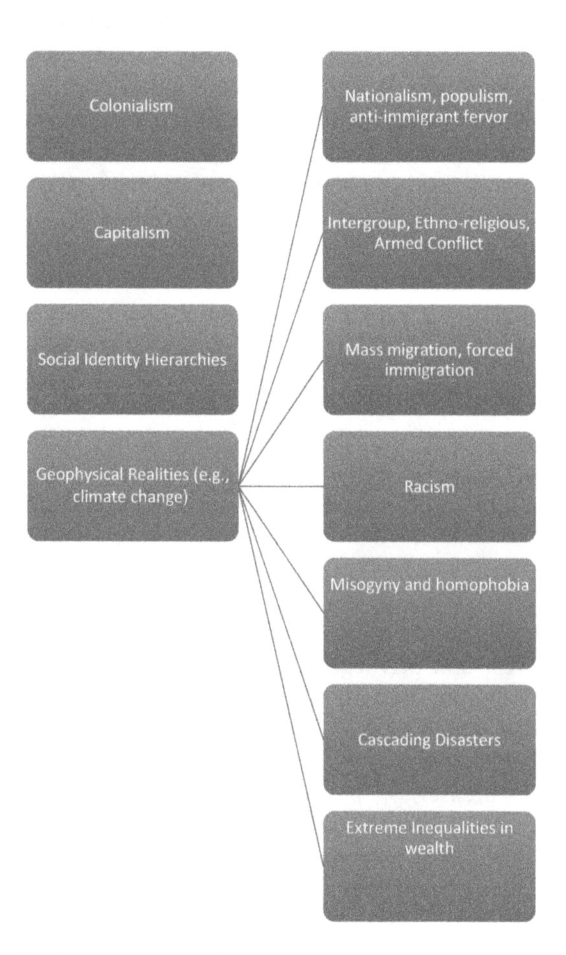

Figure 5.2 The Roots of Social Oppression

ethnic groups (as described in Chapter 4), as has been a significant factor in the intractable intergroup conflict in the Middle East.

Thus, there are many paths of transmission for historical/collective trauma. Figure 5.2 illustrates many of the points developed in the book thus far.

The Soil

The soil for the growth of social oppression is the geophysical realities that shape and constrain social ecologies such as water supplies, suitability of land for grazing and growing, access to ports, topography, and neighboring countries in a region. The interaction of natural landscape with population density and human infrastructure (the economy, political system, cultural practices, roads, electric grids, running water, etc.), forms a social ecology that further contributes to the social dynamics of oppression. Is farmland over-used and yielding insufficient supplies of food? Does the socio-political infrastructure limit economic growth or allow and support it for some and not others? Has climate change turned arable land into deserts? All of these factors, "natural" and human are the environment where the roots of social oppression take hold.

Taproots

Three taproots of social oppression are coloniality, neo-liberal capitalism, and social hierarchies based on constructed social identities.

Coloniality

In Chapter 1, I discussed coloniality, a 600-year-old system of domination by the West that privileged whiteness, wealth, maleness, capitalism, and Christianity over all other sociocultural ways of organizing society. Werkmeister-Rozas in Garran et al. (2021) has fashioned a diagram called The Web of Coloniality of Power, which I have reproduced here (Figure 5.3).

It illustrates how White supremacy, Christianity, patriarchy, and Capitalism joined in a matrix to create enduring inequalities, institutionalized violence, and economic, cultural, political, and social hierarchies and discriminations. This continues to dominate human social arrangements: how labor is paid for or not paid for (e.g., slavery), who receives the profits from other people's labor, what is considered modern and civilized, and the privileging of certain epistemologies, knowledge, and practices. It is important to note that even countries that were not literally colonized by the West – e.g., Thailand and China – still encountered Western political, economic, and cultural dominance (Millner et al., 2021), which persists to this day.

Neo-Liberal Capitalism

The English Political Philosopher John Gray (1998) considered the unique form of capitalism that is taken for granted as the normal economic system today. He noted that commercial systems, including

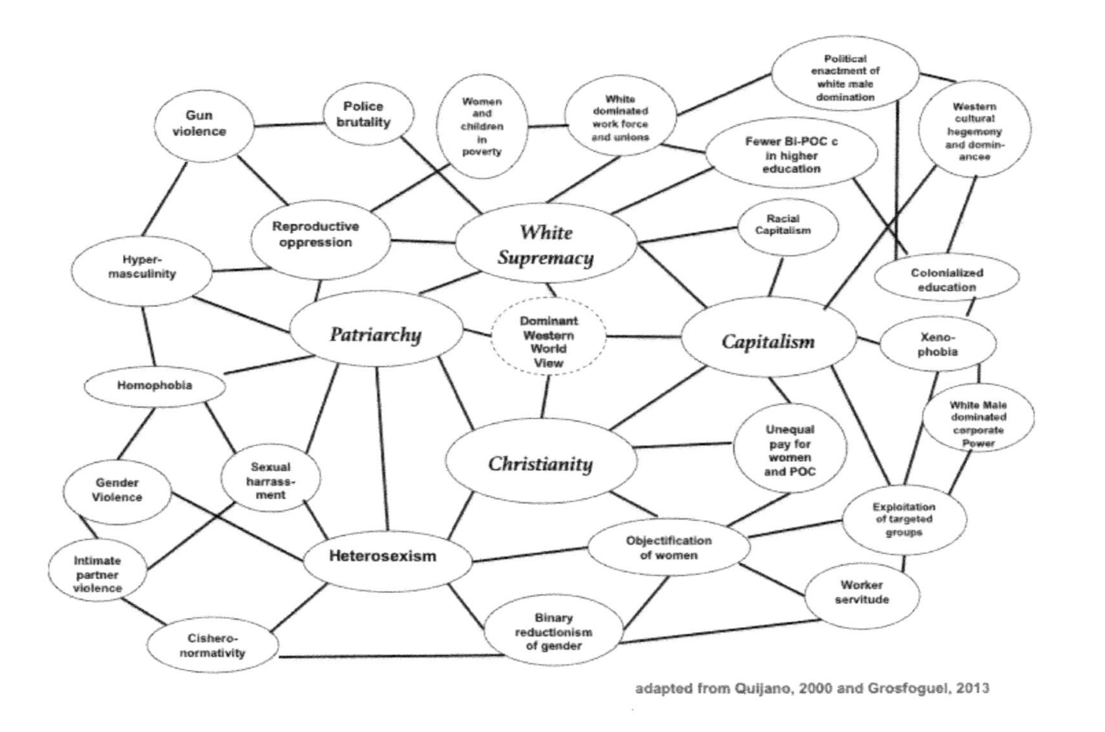

Figure 5.3 Web of Coloniality of Power

Source: Designed by Werkmeister-Rozas and reprinted from Garran et al. (2021). Racism in the United States: Implications for the helping professions. New York: Springer Publishing.

other forms of capitalism, were embedded in social relationships but that neoliberalism, or free-market capitalism, uncoupled this relationship and lionized an unfettered free market without global boundaries, espousing a religion of capital mobility and deregulation, which has devastated local economies, industries, and communities. There have been critiques of capitalism as an economic system for centuries, and Karl Marx in particular described the exploitation of workers inherent in this market structure. However, Gray describes the difference between capitalism that has a partnership with government, as in Scandinavian social democracies, where there are market economies but not market societies, and market societies, where all of social life is geared toward feeding the needs of the market. In such societies, the individual is held responsible for their social fate despite macro-economic forces beyond their control, democracy is fragile and under threat, and there are "byproducts" such as extreme economic inequality, deep and intractable poverty, mass incarceration, and nationalist, populist, anti-immigrant movements and governments. And of course, this is all accompanied by a weakened and tattered system of state support and benefits, further deepening inequality and the suffering of those deemed necessary for sustaining the economic machine but socially expendable. Human rights are minimized, political rights (such as the right to vote) are suppressed, while the right of corporations to pollute and desecrate the environment is enshrined.

Part of the power of neoliberalism is its ubiquity and invisibility (Monbiat, 2016). Many people's eyes glaze over when they hear the term and its values and principles are taken for granted by political and corporate elites; this is the way things are and should be. This sense of "normal" is embraced with religious fervor, justifying massive tax cuts for the wealthy, weakening and destroying trade unions, privatization, outsourcing, and dismantling public services so that they are replaced by competitive private companies, as with the prison-industrial complex in the United States. The exception to this is when markets collapse and then the state is then expected to pick up the tab. Internationally, neoliberalism is propped up and policed by the World Bank, International Monetary Fund, Maastricht Treaty, and the World Trade Organization. The notion of citizens with democratic rights is replaced by that of consumers with money to be spent.

Ultimately, neoliberalism masks the power relations central to coloniality and offers a utopia of products, markets, and customers, where money and profits flow internationally, weakening the power of workers to bargain collectively and the state to regulate corporate abuses and ensure social safety, fairness, and equity. It sustains, maintains, and exacerbates unequal power relations that are instantiated through social identities.

Social Identity Hierarchies

I discussed social identity in previous chapters and will briefly summarize some key points here. Social identity refers to our self-concept that comes from membership in particular social groups (Tafjel, as cited by Garran et al., 2021). Some social identities are chosen – e.g., becoming a Buddhist or a New Englander – but many are foisted upon people, reflecting prevailing social norms and patterns of dominance and supremacy. Cherokee farmers who tried to farm and live like White people, including converting to Christianity, were still constructed as "Indians," by Andrew Jackson and his followers and were dispossessed of their land and forced to move Westward as part of the "trail of tears" (Garran et al.). Social identities are socially constructed, a mixture of chosen and imposed. Some are conscious and some unconscious or taken for granted – e.g., White people not noticing that they are always surrounded by White people or that they are not being stopped by the police in the United States when driving through White neighborhoods. They are also fluid and can change and are shaped by our different historical and social contexts – e.g., the Irish, Italians, and Jews were socially constructed as non-White when they first emigrated to the United States but eventually assimilated and became White. And social identity is not binary, as illustrated by multiracial and gender non-conforming or non-binary people.

Social identities are shaped by history, social structures, and intergroup relationships, which reflect power dynamics. Coloniality and neoliberalism ensure that white people continue to exploit BIPOC folks, men have greater power over women, and cis-gendered, straight people have greater rights than Queer persons; the structure of power relations and group inequalities is unaddressed, and efforts to advocate for the rights of those with fewer rights are dismissed as "identity politics," being "woke," "political correctness," and "cancel culture." Even efforts to educate children and students about the legacies of genocide and slavery are being prohibited by law in some parts of the United States in order to not make White people feel uncomfortable about their privileged group status. Social identity hierarchies are both an outcome of coloniality and neo-liberalism and a contributor, as those with greater power pass laws to ban the discernment of the sources of their supremacy while dismantling laws that attempt to redress historic and contemporary wrongs.

Trunks and Branches

If we were tracing a tree of social oppression, the trunk would consist of White Supremacy, Male dominance, and Cis-gendered heterosexism. Some of the branches would be the following:

- Nationalism, populism, authoritarianism, fascism, nativism, and anti-immigrant fervor.
- Intergroup conflict based on social identities such as nationality, ethnicity, race, and religion: e.g., wars, genocide, ethnic cleansing, and armed conflict.
- Increasing extreme inequalities in wealth, which often correspond to social identities (e.g., race) but that also exist in societies that are relatively homogenous. This is true within nations and between nations.
- Mass migration and forced migration are consequences of coloniality, neoliberalism, climate change, intergroup conflict, other forms of violence, political instability, and economic inequality.
- Modern-day slavery in the form of economic servitude, sexual bondage, human trafficking, abusive domestic labor situations, and often a combination of all of them (Armas, 2010; Kara, 2017).
- Cascading disasters (Miller & Pescaroli, 2018) occur when there is an interaction between the human-caused dynamics described above and geophysical events, such as earthquakes, tsunamis, hurricanes, and floods.

So how can workers and volunteers offering psychosocial support and services respond to all of this?

Guiding Ethical Principles

In many ways, guiding ethical principles are even more important than specific interventions when working with those who are socially targeted. Given all that I have said about historical and collective trauma, violence, and the roots of oppression, great care must be taken to ensure that patterns of supremacy do not reverberate in the helping relationship, that individuals and community members have agency and authority in authoring what they need, that there is cultural and social competency as designed and evaluated by members of the affected group, that Western ways of knowing do not dominate and displace other knowledge and sources of wisdom, and that iatrogenic affects are mitigated. I shared these principles in Chapter 1 but will reiterate and build on them in light of the chapters on historical trauma, collective trauma, and violence before moving to present a model of intervention in the next chapter.

A Commitment to Decolonizing Psychosocial Practice

I have argued that coloniality has dominated societies, shaped interpersonal relationships, governed the structure of psychosocial interventions and the theories that guide them, and has been internalized by all – affected people and those trying to support them – so decolonizing means interrogating, resisting, and negating coloniality. This is a huge task and requires a long-term commitment. Decolonizing involves knowing oneself and the many ways that one is socially positioned, questioning everything that one has been taught professionally and personally, and a willingness to assume a humble, inquisitive, collaborative stance. All assumptions, institutions, structures, theories, practices, and interventions should be scrutinized by a decolonizing gaze.

This is not an abstraction; coloniality has very real consequences for psychosocial well-being. In addition to examples shared in earlier chapters about North American genocide toward indigenous peoples and chattel slavery in the United States, a recent study by Nikalje and Çiftçi (2021) found that Asian Indians living in the United States were still experiencing negative effects from colonialization: cultural shame, feelings of inferiority, valuing lighter skin color, embarrassment about speaking English with an Indian accent, and even feeling a sense of debt for having been colonized, all of which contribute to psychosocial suffering such as depression. Many Asian Americans are disconnected from their ancestral culture and find that a collective orientation, with obligations to the extended family, is pathologized (Millner et al., 2021). While decolonizing is important work for individuals, it is even more effective when done with others: with those who share similar identities and are committed to helping one another to decolonize and with those who have different social identities, histories, experiences, sources of wisdom, and worldviews. But although this may feel like a huge, even overwhelming task, it is not possible to work (without harming) with socially targeted and minoritized populations without making this commitment. The principles that follow this are all part of the decolonizing process.

Radical Transparency

As I discussed in Chapter 1, radical transparency means that workers always share their assumptions, motives, hypothesis, and the basis for their questions and interventions with clients in an open, non-hierarchical fashion (Comas-Diaz & Rivera, 2020; Miller, 2020). This challenges the very heart of how social workers, psychologists, counselors, psychiatrists, and other helping professionals are trained: to rely on diagnosis; to assume that there are patterns, object relations, attachment styles, learned narratives, behaviors, and schemas that clients do not see, understand, or are able to confront on their own. This does not mean that these cannot be helpful constructs, but they should not be imposed on those seeking help and should never be assumed or applied without the active collaboration of consumers. The implication of this is that rather than exerting an expert stance, the helper is not only sharing what they see and think but the sociohistorical context that shapes their perceptions. Conversely, the worker/volunteer is always inviting knowledge and understandings that inform the person being helped. It is important that any helper takes this radically transparent stance, but there is even greater urgency when the worker/volunteer has greater power and privilege due to their social positioning or comes from a very different culture. Collaborators should be viewed as authors and teachers, workers/volunteers as students, or midwives and doulas.

Full Collaboration and Leadership by Affected People

This ethical principle is easier to aspire to than achieve. Due to coloniality, the helper often comes from a group or society with greater wealth and resources, opportunities for professional education, and greater status, whether warranted or not. And they often have institutional power by representing or being members of an agency or organization. When I, a White man from the United States who is professionally educated and a Smith College professor work with people from Uganda, Haiti, Sri Lanka, or China, no matter how much effort I exert not to be placed in the role of expert, it is like swimming upstream. Patterns of interaction and internalizations reflecting coloniality as well as the structure of a helping relationship mitigate against an egalitarian approach.

Thus, one should endeavor to approach this work as a student and a seeker, rather than as an expert. Questions that invite sharing assumptions, understandings, beliefs, experiences, and worldviews of those being helped are an important place to begin. Offering leadership to the affected person in helping them to formulate the problem and identify their questions and inviting them to offer leadership and guidance for the ways that the helper can help works to establish the consumer as the agentic leader of the interpersonal process. This does not mean that the worker/volunteer does not share ideas or suggestions or offer parameters for what they feel capable of providing, but that this is done in the service of the consumer's leadership. It is important to be mindful of how one's identity may reflect violence, both historical and contemporary. Thus, trust may take time to establish, and initial mistrust is normal. Coloniality was an intentional assault on people's language, culture, society, and lives and thus cannot be allayed or undone in a single relationship, but workers can strive to be accountable to this history in how they approach their work.

Working with groups is a structural intervention that makes it more possible for egalitarian collaboration and minimizes imposed professional hierarchies. When working with individuals, the worker has greater power and the person being helped may feel intimidated or unsure of how to assert their needs. When there is a group of affected people, there are social networks, mutual aid, and support, and groups offer a wider pool of knowledge and foster greater creativity.

Paying attention to power, hierarchies (both those that result from history and those that are institutionally structured), social identities, and social locations are central to a collaborative approach. This is an ongoing process and one where there are limits to what one individual can see and perceive. Thus, supervision is essential to the process and if possible, from someone whose social identities are closer to those being served than the helping professional/volunteer. An additional support is to have an accountability circle of people, who share social identities with the affected people, reviewing the psychosocial work to ensure that power and hierarchies are being managed, collaboration is full and genuine, transparency is the norm, and cultural and professional values are not being imposed by the helper.

Situating Individual Problems in a Historical and Sociocultural Context

This is critical because there is always a risk of pathologizing clients when there are historical and structural roots to their problems. And there are always sources of resilience and strength from the community and collectivity as well as important cultural lessons from ancestors and elders. It is a way of externalizing and helping people to feel relieved of feelings like personal shame and guilt over their struggles. This is what happened to Jesse Thistle when he reconnected with his indigenous family, discovering his lineage of chiefs and tribal elders, learning about the historical and sociocultural sources of his suffering, and reconnecting with tribal customs. As he said, "I remembered who I was" (Thistle, 2019).

This principle helps people to feel connected to their history, culture and collectivity, and collective past. Collaborative assessments should include an exploration of a person's collective history and what it was that helped those who came before, or those who are struggling now to survive and thrive.

Integrating Knowledge Bases

As I mentioned in Chapter 1, I use indigenous to mean emanating from the local population that is being helped and reflecting accumulated knowledge, wisdom, and practices from their historical and collective experiences. Western-derived knowledge should be used but carefully and cautiously, ensuring that there are relevant elements not only to apply but also to critically appraise what may be inappropriate or even harmful. For example, attachment is a relevant concept from Attachment Theory – it is universal that babies become attached to their caregivers and the structure of attachment endures over time. But given the profound range of child-rearing styles in different cultures and societies, I am wary of using concepts such as "ambivalent attachment," despite claims by attachment theorists that they have found that their model has universal applicability throughout the world. The research projects that confirmed this were usually designed and implemented by researchers from Western societies who already had an investment in attachment theory. Even if one accepts that ambivalent attachment is universal, how does one deal with an entire generation of indigenous children in Canada, who developed ambivalent attachment through being taken from their parents and forced to go to Eurocentric boarding schools (Thomson et al., 2010). Is that really the same as a child diagnosed with an ambivalent attachment from a White, middle-class family in Manhattan?

Or the notion of "individuation" used in developmental ego psychology is dependent on many factors in the sociocultural environment: in China, I know of many children who sleep with their parents until roughly the age of 10, which is radically different from children who have been given their own cribs and bedrooms from birth. And the developmental transitions from childhood to adolescence to young adulthood are socioculturally specific, dependent on factors such as consumer cultures, job markets, and social expectations for when a person achieves an autonomous life (Modell, 1989). And the very notion of autonomy is much more salient in Western capitalist societies than in those that are more collectively oriented, with extended family and clan obligations.

Far too often, indigenous, Black, and Asian wisdom is seen as inferior or less applicable to the modern world, which is another way that coloniality continues to subjugate collectivities (Millner et al., 2021). As I mentioned in Chapter 1, I endorse Mignolo and Walsh's (2018) notion of "pluriversal" ways of knowing, where there are multiple ways of understanding the world, all valued and without a hierarchy with Western epistemologies at the top.

Centering Indigenous Resilience, Strength, and Beauty

Pluriversality is difficult to achieve even when intentions are good because global economic, social, and cultural systems reflect coloniality and the dominance of the White West. This needs to be actively counter-acted and one way of doing this is to center indigenous and non-Western visions of resilience, strength, and beauty. Western epistemologies, derived from the European Enlightenment, have consistently denigrated not only ways of knowing but have defined the Western notion of personhood as being of a higher order than that of people from Africa, Asia, and South America. This continues both between and within societies. Racism is one obvious way that this is manifested in North America and much of Europe.

An example of this that I already mentioned is the forced attendance for indigenous children at White boarding schools (Adams, 1995; Thomson et al., 2010). These were active attempts to extinguish personhood by forcibly cutting children's hair, forbidding them to speak their language, belittling and prohibiting cultural practices, and teaching in a style that was alien to the students. There were many unreported incidents of physical and sexual abuse of the children. This affected not only the children but also their parents, who felt a sense of shame for not passing down their cultural heritage and undermined their role as parents with their own children; it is a graphic example of severing transitional pathways. This is but one of many examples worldwide of how people were taught that they were not as beautiful as White people, that their cultural practices were inferior, and that the value of their personhood was denigrated. It is not enough to say that this was wrong after decades and centuries of such practices; active efforts must be made to centralize the beauty, strength, and wisdom of people who have survived such attacks, as well as to engage in a meaningful process or reparations. And rather than viewing people through the lens of the problems and dysfunctional behaviors that proliferated through such cultural terrorism, it is essential to recognize the strength and resilience that enabled tribes, ethnic groups, and other collective entities to survive such atrocities.

Non-Neutrality

Given what I have been saying throughout this book, neutrality, a prevalent concept in Western psychotherapy, is not enough. At the very least, it accepts a sociohistorical reality that has harmed and traumatized people and it is often dismissive of the social realities of people's lives and thus harmful. What has been done to socioculturally target, tyrannize, and oppress people was never neutral. And as I have argued, it is not possible in such circumstances to separate psychological and emotional problems and trauma from sociohistorical conditions – in fact, it is pathologizing to reinforce this false dichotomy – then psychosocial interventions should not be neutral; there are historical and systemic injustices that must be remedied as part of the healing process.

Rather than neutrality, there needs to be active validation of what has been done to people, how this may have been internalized as shame and self-doubt, as well as the strength to survive and the potential not only to recover individually but also for collective reclamation. Rather than neutrality, what is called for is advocacy; affected people need to know that those offering help are not standing on the sidelines but are standing by their sides. And as mentioned earlier, it is essential that advocacy follows the leadership of those directly experiencing oppression and to not replicate patterns of coloniality through well-intentioned advocacy that elevates those who are already elevated. What is called for is an intentional approach of anti-oppressive practice (Garran et al., 2021; Morgaine & Capous-Desyllas, 2014), where interpersonal work always involves a critical attention to power dynamics in society, organizations, and between worker and client and recognizing how individual problems are generated in a sociocultural matrix of historical and structural oppression.

Mutual Transformation

There is an asymmetry in the client/helper relationship. One person is dependent, vulnerable, and exposed, while the other is in a protected position of privilege and power. One person is expected to take risks, share their stories, reveal their wounds, and be open emotionally, while the other person can set boundaries and limits about what they disclose and how much they share. This is true whether relationships are structured as case management, therapeutic, or psychosocial capacity building, whether the worker represents a social service organization and is paid or responding as a volunteer. While this dynamic is part of all helping relationships, it is even more the case when working with people experiencing sociocultural oppression, where all social identities are valanced but differentially privileged and targeted.

Intersubjectivity is a clinical movement that encourages mutual disclosure and acknowledges that both people in a helping relationship can and should be transformed (Fort, 2018; Garran et al., 2021). Decolonizing clinical support and intervention relies on all parties being open to change, without one person holding something back because they are the "worker." The same is true for other forms of psychosocial support; there should be mutual openness to transformation. This commitment necessitates a critical, reflexive approach as it contradicts the ways that most psychosocial workers have been trained and what agencies and organizations expect. Thus, it also takes time to unlearn the hierarchical way of relating to those in need and practice. As with many recommendations in this book, it helps to be part of a team of people doing this work together, offering mutual support and critical feedback to one another.

Multi-Level, Multi-Modality

As I have been arguing, individual psychosocial issues for members of groups facing social discrimination and opprobrium cannot be separated from their historical and sociocultural context. Help can come in the form of clinical interventions, but anti-oppressive practice includes groupwork, community organizing and advocacy, and activities that confront structural threats, such as violence from the state directed at certain populations. Local leadership and empowerment and collaboration are central themes in such work.

The structure and values of professional training work against this. Specialization – such as training to become a clinician – has its value, as it can offer deep understanding and skill development within a certain modality. This also means that workers may lack broader skills, such as being able to engage in community organizing or network building. This can be addressed through broadening training programs so that clinicians are not only exposed to theories of community development but are also taught about the ethical obligation to engage in such practice. There is more to this than skill building and familiarity with a professional code of ethics. There is a need to explicitly endorse a decolonial, anti-racism, anti-oppression, social justice value system for *all* activities and types of psychosocial work.

But not everyone will have the same capacity to effectively engage in all aspects of psychosocial work: some are more adept at one on one counseling, others in activism and community organizing, while some are particularly at home with peace building and intergroup reconciliation. One way to address this is to ensure that psychosocial responses are not separate, atomistic interventions but are bundled in multi-need, multi-modality coalitions. And such coalitions must have a large representation of affected people in meaningful leadership roles so that the activities of various helping professionals are not self-directed but rather at the service of those engaged in liberatory struggles.

Jesse Thistle (2019) describes the importance of treatment for drug addiction, but this also included exposure to other people struggling with similar issues in a milieu offering mutual aid and social support. These were important activities but, by his description, would not have transformed his suffering into an understanding of how his personal struggles were part of a larger collective, historical process and the essential need to be connected with other people sharing his identities and experiences.

Know Thyself

Workers and volunteers offering psychosocial interventions come from a range of backgrounds, with an array of social identities. Sometimes these identities are congruent with those experiencing social injustice while there are also workers/volunteers whose mixture of identities is significantly different from those they are trying to support and may tend to be privileged. There are different issues for people carrying different social identities, but there is one maxim that is constant: know thyself. For helping professionals with similar identities to those with whom they are working, it is important to be aware of the potential for being triggered, activated, or overwhelmed by the same issues that the people whom they are supporting are grappling with. I am not talking about what I view as a pathologizing concept – overidentification – identification is a form of empathy and congruence of identities has many benefits. But all helpers must achieve a balance between genuine, deep empathy, and understanding while maintaining sufficient balance, grounding, and equanimity to strategically help affected group members to achieve their goals.

Workers with different identities, particularly those with privilege, need to reflect on what they may take for granted that their collaborators are unable to share: issues like safety, security, access to resources, and seeing themselves mirrored by culture and society in a way that their associates are not. White fragility, a desire to please or feel better about oneself, and stereotyping or essentializing those being supported are all pitfalls for responders with large amounts of social privilege (Garran et al., 2021). Lack of awareness about biases can lead to enacting harmful microaggressions.

Critical self-awareness is essential for all helping professionals. For all workers, regardless of their social identities, it is also important to surface, examine, and interrogate all assumptions about suffering, helping, healing, and recovery that have come from their professional training. Coloniality and all forms of supremacy (e.g., White, male, heterosexual, etc.) are part of the DNA of all societies and all professional training programs. How do they operate today within a given context? How have they been internalized? How are they still manifested in professional practices and codes of ethics? These are the kinds of questions that not only individuals but also affinity groups and coalitions need to ask on a regular basis. I link critical self-awareness with self-care in Chapter 10.

Do No Harm

The final principle is critical – always anticipate and try to avoid any iatrogenic effects of intervention. Intentions and motivations are important, and I assume that all helping professionals have good intentions, but good intentions do not excuse causing harm. All of the principles discussed in this section are ways of guarding against unanticipated negative effects, but there should always be a conscious, intentional assessment of the ways that helping can hurt. Obvious examples of this are trying to help an individual recover from trauma while separating this from situating the trauma in the context of surviving armed conflict, historical legacies of genocide, or everyday encounters with racism. This can lead to people feeling blamed or ashamed of their struggles – which Jesse Thistle (2019) eloquently describes – as if their trauma is due to their own weaknesses or failings. But a less palpable example might be counseling parents to stop allowing their 3 year old to sleep in their bed – which is normative socially and culturally and is consistent with how the helper lives her life – but may undermine a tradition of child rearing that has been part of a range of cultural practices that have sustained a people and connected them with one another as well as with their past.

Conclusion

In this chapter, I have tried to erect a scaffolding for psychosocial work with socially targeted populations by offering 11 guiding ethical principles that I briefly outlined in Chapter 1. I began by considering the roots of social oppression before turning to the guidelines. My hope is that genuine, non-hierarchical collaboration can occur by considering general guidelines for practice without being overly prescriptive about what to offer and how to provide it. In the next chapter, I will consider a range of interventions and modalities but hope that readers will see these as an incomplete menu that helps affected people and helping professionals to creatively craft responses that consider history, coloniality, structural oppression, unique social ecologies, and the social and cultural values of affected people. My hope is that guidelines for intervention and practice reflect the needs, goals, and wishes of those experiencing sociocultural oppression rather than inadvertently replicating patterns of power and discrimination and maintaining privileges that benefit workers more than those being helped.

These are the 11 guiding principles discussed in this chapter:

1. An overt commitment to decolonizing, recognizing that coloniality suffuses all aspects of society and its institutions and practices.
2. A commitment to radical transparency between helper and the those being helped where there is mutual vulnerability and openness to change and transformation.
3. Full collaboration between affected people and helping professionals where the leadership of affected people is intentional and prominent.
4. Situating individual problems in the context of historical and structural causes of oppression and suffering.
5. Integrating a range of knowledge bases that respect and honor indigenous practices.
6. Centering the resilience, strength, and beauty of affected groups and people.
7. Advocacy for all forms of social justice and for the rights and needs of affected people rather than maintaining a stance of neutrality.

8. An ethic of mutual transformation so that risks and vulnerabilities are shared by helpers and those being helped.
9. Engaging in multi-level interventions using a range of modalities that go well beyond the Western prototype of "talk therapy."
10. Workers/volunteers continually working toward developing and maintaining critical self-awareness of assumptions, values, and judgments.
11. Ensuring that all well-intentioned interventions "do no harm."

References

Adams, D.W. (1995). *Education for extinction: American Indians and the boarding school experience 1875–1928*. Topeka, KS: The University of Kansas Press.

Armas, G.V. (2010). Cultural competence in the trauma treatment of Thai survivors of modern-day slavery: The relevance of Buddhist mindfulness practices and healing rituals to transform shame and guilt of forced prostitution. In A. Kalyayjian & D. Eugene (Eds.). *Mass trauma and emotional healing around the world: Rituals and practices for resilience and meaning-making* (pp. 269–285). Santa Barbara, CA: ABC CLIO, LLC.

BBC Outlook. (2020). *A descendent of chiefs: My long journey home*. www.bbc.co.uk/programmes/w3cszdrv

Comas-Diaz, L., & Rivera, E.T. (2020). Conclusion: Liberation psychology-crossing borders into new frontiers. In L. Comas-Diaz & E.T. Rivera (Eds.). *Liberation psychology: Theory, method, practice and social justice* (pp. 283–295). Washington, DC: American Psychological Association Press.

Fort, C.J. (2018). Intersectionality, intersubjectivity and integration: A two-person therapy. *Journal of Psychology and Theology*, *46*(2): 116–121. DOI: 10.1177/0091647118767987.

Garran, A.M., Werkmeister-Rozas, L., Kang, H.K., & Miller, J. (2021). *Racism in the United States: Implications for the helping professions* (3rd ed.). New York: Springer Publishing.

Gray, J. (1998). *False dawn: The delusions of global capitalism*. New York: The New Press.

Kara, S. (2017). *Modern slavery: A global perspective*. New York: Columbia University Press.

Mignolo, W.D., & Walsh, C.E. (2018). *On decoloniality: Concepts, analytics, praxis*. Durham, NC: Duke University Press.

Miller, J.L. (2020). The four pandemics. *Smith College Studies in Social Work*. DOI: 10.1080/00377317.2020.1832944.

Miller, J.L., & Pescaroli, G. (2018). Psychosocial capacity building in response to cascading disasters: A culturally informed approach. *International Journal of Disaster Risk Reduction*, *30*: 164–171. DOI: 10.1016/j.ijdrr.2018.04.018.

Millner, U.C., Maru, M., Ismail, A., & Chakrabarti, U. (2021). Decolonizing mental health practice: Reconstructing an Asian-centric framework through a social justice lens. *Asian American Journal of Psychology*, *12*(4): 333–345. DOI: 10.1037/aap0000268.

Modell, J. (1989). *Into one's own: From youth to adulthood in the United States 1920–1975*. Berkeley, CA: University of California Press.

Monbiat, G. (2016, April 15). Neoliberalism – the ideology at the root of all our problems. *The Guardian*. www.theguardian.com/books/2016/apr/15/neoliberalism-ideology-problem-george-monbiot

Morgaine, K., & Capous-Desyllas, M. (2014). *Anti-oppressive social work practice*. Belmont, CA: Sage Publishing.

Nikalje, A., & Çiftçi, A. (2021, September 30). Colonial mentality, racism, and depressive symptoms: Asian Indians in the United States. *Asian American Journal of Psychology*. DOI: 10.1037/aap0000262.

Thistle, J. (2019). *From the ashes: On being Metis, homeless and finding my way*. Toronto: Simon and Schuster Canada.

Thomson, S., Kopperud, C., & Mehl-Madrona, L. (2010). Healing intergenerational trauma among aboriginal communities. In A. Kalyayjian & D. Eugene (Eds.). *Mass trauma and emotional healing around the world: Rituals and practices for resilience and meaning-making* (pp. 343–360). Santa Barbara, CA: ABC CLIO, LLC.

Transcending Jewish Trauma. (2022). www.transcendingjewishtrauma.com/

Weaver, H., & Congress, E. (2010). The ongoing impact of colonization: Man-made trauma and Native Americans. In A. Kalyayjian & D. Eugene (Eds.). *Mass trauma and emotional healing around the world: Rituals and practices for resilience and meaning-making* (pp. 211–226). Santa Barbara, CA: ABC CLIO, LLC.

6 Liberatory, Decolonizing Psychosocial Capacity Building

A Framework for Collaboration

Introduction

Anthropologist and clinical psychologist Joseph Gone (2021) explored depression and problem drinking on the Fort Belknap Indian Reservation in Montana and interviewed a "cultural traditionalist" named Traveling Thunder. When asked about what caused these problems, Traveling Thunder identified the loss of a time when indigenous peoples lived according to their customs and traditions: "Everything was good because everybody lived according to custom and teachings. And there were no jails, no hospitals. There were no prisons, no insane asylums. There was none of that stuff because everybody lived according to a strict custom." When White people subjugated indigenous peoples in North America, they attempted to destroy this society and culture, forcing their cultural and religious beliefs on others, while introducing an alien market economy. The impact of this reign of terror and communal, social, and cultural genocide contributed to alcoholism, drug abuse, depression, feelings of unworthiness, and suicide. Traveling Thunder added that eventually indigenous peoples reclaimed their heritage, culture, connections with elders and ancestors, and relationship with "the Creator." Gone realized that Traveling Thunder had identified the colonization of American Indians, its inherent racism, theft of lands, and attempted social and cultural erasure as the root cause of today's emotional, psychological, and substance abuse problems; they were not due to individual failings, genetic weaknesses, or inherent interpersonal patterns. I will return to what Gone has shared about Traveling Thunder throughout this chapter.

In previous chapters, I covered sociocultural oppression, historical and collective trauma, and the psychosocial impact of violence and, given all of this, suggested guiding principles for helping professionals

DOI: 10.4324/9781003021162-6

who are working with groups affected by these processes domestically and internationally. In this chapter, I will offer a framework for intervention that I propose with caution and offer with humility; these are ideas distilled from my professional experiences and listening to the voices of people who have experienced coloniality, White supremacy, collective violence, and collective trauma. As I have said in prior chapters, it is important not to offer rigid, proscriptive formulas and intervention protocols but rather to contribute to a polyvocal conversation about psychosocial support and capacity building. To this end, I will examine what decolonial psychosocial practice might look like. I will consider assessment and the helping/collaborative process. The chapter will conclude with evaluation, contesting the mainstream notion of "evidence-based practice."

Decolonial, Liberatory Practice

When Gone (2021) pressed Traveling Thunder to consider if he could imagine using the Indian Health Service's psychiatric services, he described it as part of the Whiteman's war: "[If you] want to [look] good to the Whiteman, then . . . go [to the] White psychiatrists . . . and say, . . . 'Go ahead and rid me of my history, my past, and brainwash me forever so I can be like a Whiteman.' " Why would Traveling Thunder see seeking psychiatric help for problems as part of a war of survival? How does psychiatry destroy history and "brainwash" people?

What is fundamental to Traveling Thunder's argument is the locus of the cause of suffering and psychiatry's notion of personhood. If the heart of suffering is the individual, then the focus of efforts to help people seeks individual causes and solutions, which is at the core of modern psychiatry and psychology as practiced in North America and Europe, where this epistemological understanding and model of intervention originated, and in the rest of the world to where it was exported.

For those trained in this model – which are the vast majority of helping professionals – it is like the water for fish, always there, an invisible context that frames what is "normal" and taken for granted. Within this worldview, helping professionals should of course seek to reduce suffering and enhance well-being by treating an individual's pain and seeking to understand it, using, for example, a psychodynamic, cognitive behavioral, or humanistic lens. And there are many "evidence-based" talk therapies and pharmacological interventions that reduce symptoms, treat pain, and enhance individual functioning and well-being. But what I hear Traveling Thunder saying is that by assuming Western individual psychology as the starting point and imposing this model on all cultures and societies, the wars of colonialism and White supremacy are continuing without bullets, promoting cultural erasure and subjugation.

I believe that this is true not only for indigenous and BIPOC people in North America and Europe but also for non-White people throughout the world; the world's majority. Western psychology as it currently stands perpetuates notions of personhood, suffering, and recovery forced by coloniality and racism (Malherbe et al., 2021). In my work (and friendships) in Sri Lanka, Uganda, China, Haiti, and with BIPOC, immigrant and undocumented clients and students in the United States. I have consistently encountered both the elevation of Western psychology's vision of the individual, family, health, and pathology and have been struck by how poorly it fits with the historical and lived experiences of the people exposed to and "helped" by this model. Central to decolonizing is to move from a White, Western cosmology that privileges the individual, nuclear families, and neoliberal capitalism. As Burrage et al. (2021) put it: "To decolonize itself as a discipline and better serve Indigenous communities, the field of psychology must open up to understandings of trauma, loss, and healing that decentralize the individual, a difficult task given the discipline's psychocentric nature." Millner et al. (2021) recommend that when working with Asian Americans, clinicians honor the lived experiences of their collaborators, focusing on narratives, spirituality, and collective practices. Malherbe et al. (2021) argue that an Afro-centric focus involves collective antiracist struggle and everyday collective resistance, rather than individual therapy, to challenge the Western epistemologies and universal "truths" that decontextualize culture, family, and personhood.

If the individual is the axis of understanding and treatment, then the task is for individuals to work on their internal or relational problems and the historical legacies and social contributors to these problems continue undisturbed (Goodman, 2015; Gone, 2021). This can contribute to pathologizing individuals and self-blame (Beuregard, 2021; Burrage et al., 2021; Goodman, 2015). I don't mean to suggest that individuals should not receive treatment and psychosocial support, but liberatory practice necessitates a shift in gestalt to prioritizing relational, group, collective, and spiritual interventions that recognize the shared network of relationships found in most non-Western cultures and societies (de la Rey & Thompson, 2020; Millner et al., 2021). This means viewing mental health within historical, social, and cultural contexts (Phillips et al., 2015). This will require a great deal of "unlearning" by helping professionals (Adames et al., 2022) as the vast majority of us have been trained to view individual interventions as the paramount form of psychosocial support. This shift in perspective stands in direct opposition to the Diagnostic and Statistical Manual (DSM) of the American Psychiatric Association (Gone, 2021), which is the bible of psychological treatment in much of the world.

Martin-Baro (Phillips et al., 2015), the father of liberation psychology, noted three major tasks for a decolonial psychology: (1) decolonizing everyday experience; (2) utilizing people's virtues; and (3) recovering historical meaning. Inspired by this, I think that there are seven important tasks to keep in focus in this chapter as I sketch what this looks like in practice (the first six named by Adames et al., 2022).

1. **Critical consciousness** (Adames et al., 2022) – There is a need for critical consciousness not only of who we are and who we are working with (Garran et al., 2021) but also of the historical and systemic causes of individual suffering (Goodman, 2015; Gone, 2021).
2. **Cultural authenticity and self-knowledge** (Adames et al., 2022; Gone, 2021) – Assessment, interventions, and evaluation should be guided by those on the inside of the group being helped. They should reflect the vision, world-views, self-definition, personhood, wisdom, and knowledge of those in the group, as they seek to draw on their culture and society and recover their historical memories. This means privileging indigenous and local epistemologies, experiences, and cosmologies (Blume et al., 2020; Burrage et al., 2021).
3. **Balance between acknowledging oppression and losses and offering hope** (Adames et al., 2022; Burrage et al., 2021) – The level of historical/structural oppression should never be minimized and yet hope for the future, even if the flame is small, must be kindled. As mentioned earlier, transitional pathways (Landau, 2007; Landau & Saul, 2004) connect people with their past, but it is also important to maintain connections with the future, particularly through an investment in future generations.
4. **Collectivism** (Adames et al., 2022, Malherbe et al., 2021) – Societies across the globe stress collective ties, connectedness, kinship relationships and obligations to ancestors and future generations, and being part of a tribe or community (Blume et al., 2020; Millner et al., 2021). The minority of the world mostly in Westernized societies and cultures stress individuation and individualism (Heinrich, 2020). One aspect of coloniality has been to impose this model of self and family as a norm for all families and societies.

And yet collective solidarity has been essential for groups facing oppression to unite, survive, and thrive. Rather than starting with the individual and then adding attention to the collective, I recommend reversing this, taking the collective as the starting point.

5. **Strength, beauty, and resistance** (Adames et al., 2022) – An insidious aspect of coloniality is to project Western norms of intelligence, wisdom, strength, and beauty onto all people in the form of racial and ethnic hierarchies. This is done through invidious comparisons and pathologizing, diminishing, and demeaning differences and variations found in others. It also comes from minimizing the structural conditions that privilege White people while focusing on the individual pathologies and failings of members of other racial/ethnic groups. So much effort has been expended in this project that it requires an intentional, continual effort to not only confront it but to actively restore pride, respect, and self-love within communities that may have faced discourses of denigration for decades if not centuries.
6. **Releasing self-blame** (Adames et al., 2022) – This is the corollary of Task 5. Coloniality has relied on blaming victims, justifying terrorism, violence, and enduring inequalities and the privileges of those in power. Releasing blame and restoring pride go hand and hand.
7. **Social justice across all domains, at all levels** (Beuregard, 2021; Phillips et al., 2015) – Social justice is a commitment, a process, and a state of mind. Helping professionals and volunteers should have social justice as a lodestar in everything they do when working with socially targeted groups. It needs to be a central, unwavering, commitment and conceptual navigator for all activities.

Assessment

All psychosocial work involves assessment. In this section, I apply the principles from the previous chapter and the tasks from the prior section of this chapter.

Assessment and Understanding of the Context

Social Ecology

The social ecology of the group being responded to is a critical starting point. As I have said elsewhere, the social ecology includes the unique history of the collectivity, structural and institutional patterns, cultural practices, beliefs and values, social networks and capital, political patterns, the unique dynamics of oppression, and the physical, environmental, and technological infrastructure (Miller, 2012; Miller & Pescaroli, 2018; Park & Miller, 2006). Understanding the social ecology is essential for making sense and meaning of the lives of those being helped and supported (see Figure 1.1).

This assessment includes evaluating the impact of the current form of government and its institutions and practices. What is the economic system and how does it advantage and disadvantage different groups? How much inequality is fostered and maintained through institutions and policies? What form of social welfare, social safety nets, and social services exist? What laws legitimize social targeting and exclusion and what legal protections exist for human rights? What is the nature of intergroup relations, including their histories, inequalities, and power dynamics?

In addition to considering the impact of history and collective traumas, what is happening in the present? Who is safe and unsafe in society? Who do the police protect and who do they attack? Have threats to group members increased or decreased?

Understanding the Group and Community

It is important that outsiders do not read up on ethnic, racial, or national group in order to gain an understanding of the group's culture and practices; this centralizes the outsider as the locus of understanding. Understanding a group by a helping professional/volunteer outside of a group necessitates a collaborative process with those on the inside. The most authoritative voices are those of members of the group and community. However, there can be a tension between supporting a collectivity, clan, and tribal structure and leadership, while also noticing who is absent, marginalized, and decentered from decision making and power. For example, when I work in Northern Uganda, the clan and elder system is predominantly male while many urgent medical and psychosocial issues disproportionately affect women – e.g., maternal and infant health, teenage pregnancy, and domestic violence. How can the local leadership structure, reflecting eons of wisdom and experience be respected while also appreciating the rights of women? (Responses to this question are continued in the following). While it is important for outside helpers not to determine how a group functions nor to impose their own values, it is also vital to not ignore inequalities and exclusions that exist within groups, thus, the necessity of mapping the group and community in a cooperative, complex fashion and to be able to patiently and collaboratively work to resolve these tensions.

A good starting point for this part of the assessment is to chart who identifies with which groups. Of course, people identify with multiple groups – e.g., gender, age cohort, tribe and ethnic group, nationality, and religion. What are the meanings for people of these identifications and which ones hold the most salience as well as the greatest ambivalence? Who is invited into a group, or has an earned or ascribed status within a group, and who is excluded from groups? What characterizes a group and distinguishes it from other groups? How do perspective and context affect this? For example, for people living outside of Afghanistan, refugees from the recent takeover by the Taliban were identified as Afghans. But for Afghan refugees, ethnic identification (e.g., Pashtun, Uzbek, Hazara), tribal affiliation within an ethnic group, and religious affiliation (e.g., Shiite, Sunni) are critical markers and distinguishers. One of my former students was working to help Somali refugees settle and thrive in Maine but was unaware of clan conflicts that had made their way from Somalia to the United States and inadvertently found herself in the center of an intense power struggle between clans.

Who are formal and informal leaders within groups and communities? Who is represented and not represented in planning, negotiations, service provision, and evaluation? Who are the most vulnerable members within groups? What are group members comfortable and uncomfortable with? For example, when I was in Eastern Sri Lanka working with people affected by the Tsunami and civil war, Hindu Tamils were comfortable being taught in groups of men and women while Muslim Tamils preferred to have men and women sitting separately, maintaining this separation in small break-out groups. Thus, what are important collective values and practices? Within this, what is negotiable and non-negotiable? Also, how do group members protect themselves and support one another from sociopolitical assaults?

An important aspect of assessment is to consider the various roles within groups as well as the tasks associated with those roles. When I work in Northern Uganda, there are customary roles in any gathering or training event – spiritual leader, social welfare person, time keeper, and energizer (person who wakes the group up through exercises when things start to lag). How do social markers such as gender, ethnic, tribal, and religious affiliation affect who can and cannot hold certain roles?

As I have mentioned in other chapters, an important concept to consider is personhood (Miller, 2012; Miller & Pescaroli, 2018; Summerfield, 2004). Summerfield has identified some core questions to consider:

What are acceptable reactions to have in response to tragedy?
What is normal and abnormal?
How is distress expressed?
How is help-seeking behavior expressed?
Who do you go to for help?
What constitutes recovery?
What do you want from other people?

In addition to understanding personhood, an assessment should focus on the community's assets and resources, including social, political, economic, and educational capital? What contributes to or threatens group cohesion? What are the outside threats (historical and contemporary) to group members feeling connected to their history, elders, and traditional customs and practices (Gone, 2021)? What important customs and traditions or cultural touchstones have been lost?

Self-Assessment

Any helping professional or volunteer should do a comprehensive self-assessment of their personhood, and much more, but this is a particularly critical task when working with individuals, groups, and communities as an outsider. Failure to do this, despite the best intentions, will most likely lead to an imposition of the helper's values, professional orientation, and power and, if the helper is trained in Western psychosocial practices (e.g., social work, psychology, psychiatry, counseling), will be furthering the Western project of coloniality. Reflecting on what Traveling Thunder said, interventions lacking critical consciousness by helpers may do more harm than good in the long run, as they contribute to scouring out local and indigenous wisdom and practices, replacing them with a Western vision of personhood, healing, recovery, and survivance. Thus, central to the worker's self-assessment is having a critical social awareness.

A starting place for developing critical social awareness is for the helper to explore their own social identities (Abe, 2020; Adames et al., 2022; Garran et al., 2021; Phillips et al., 2015). Which aspects of social identity are most salient, least meaningful? Which are recognized in a person's conscious awareness and which are taken for granted? A power and privilege analysis of the helper's intersectional social identities is called for – which are mirrored and can be taken for granted and which are forged through assertion, claiming, and resistance to oppression. For example, in my teaching, I have often found that White students want to understand the experiences of BIPOC people but are much more resistant to exploring what it means to be White. There are complex reasons for this, including not wanting to view oneself as the beneficiary of unearned privilege, strong feelings that are evoked, such as guilt and shame, and the unending siren call of a society structured to not only reward whiteness but also render it invisible. Structurally, many communities and societies are racially and ethnically segregated so those with power and privilege are often surrounded by people who look, think, and act like them and who access to and command similar resources in their lives. What is also challenging is that much of the information – the DNA that constructed cognitive maps – came from loved family members, trusted teachers, and a steady stream of books, magazines, television shows, films, and social media that reinforce White privilege, dominance, and supremacy. Thus, there is often a lot of unlearning to do. Millner et al. (2021) urge Western practitioners to shift not only from their positionality of coloniality but also from own their own power, privilege, and assumptions if they are to establish credibility with Asian American clients.

So, it is important for the practitioner to reflect on what they learned, where they learned it, and what were implicit values, assumptions, and epistemologies. As I have said in earlier chapters, this includes assumptions about what causes suffering, what constitutes healing, the methods and skills of helping, and the centrality of individual talk therapy. It also means deconstructing the system of service delivery, such as organizations that hire professionals to see a certain number of clients per week, for 50-minute sessions that are often held in the offices of the organization or company where the worker is employed. Organizational settings often replicate coloniality and Whiteness but have the potential to become spaces and drivers that facilitate resistance (Buckingham et al., 2021). Critical social awareness involves surfacing and questioning the most basic tenets of professional practices. This includes boundaries – why are most therapists taught to not have contact with their clients outside of therapy? What are cultural norms that are taken for granted about civility, respect, and professional behavior? As stated earlier, it is also important to question the norm of one-way sharing and unidirectional vulnerability; why should helpers not also be exposed or open to psychosocial transformation?

Critical social awareness also helps workers to explore their collaborator's personhood, worldviews, traditions, and practices without being patronizing, exoticizing, or othering. This leads to examining the helping relationship – what is shared, what is similar, and what is different? Often helpers have identities that garner greater social power and privilege; how will this be managed when working together? How will the power of being a professional, having an organizational base, and representing societal roles and values be navigated? What stereotypes (all people carry stereotypes, particularly those with privilege who have their stereotypes amplified by social structures and dominant social narratives) are held and how will the helper identify and work on their stereotypes? (Garran et al., 2021 have exercises for working on stereotypes). Adames et al., 2022 have found that because of these tensions, clients often prefer to have workers who match their own identities and experiences, which has implications for using a training-of-trainers (TOT) model which will be explored later in this chapter. However, they also found that what accounted for the most success in achieving treatment goals was the workers' cultural humility and competence and their responsiveness to the historical and social realities of those being helped.

I mentioned earlier that local and indigenous knowledge and practices should be prioritized and privileged. One reason for this is that helping professionals with privilege often live in a world of distorted and obfuscated reality (Phillips et al., 2015), for the reasons discussed earlier. Practitioners are often steeped in the mythology of the dominant groups in their societies, or in the triumphalist narratives of their nations, which obscures the reality of the violence and terror of subjugation through coloniality and its impact on socially targeted groups. Thus, not only do they often not see this history and legacy of structural oppression but even if they do, find it challenging to unlearn what they have been taught or stymied about how to work within the constraints of repressive social structures. While those who have been subjected to oppression may have internalized some of the social and psychological pollution to which they have been exposed, they have also been members of collectivities that have contested, resisted, and fought against this tyranny and are able to discern the reality of social oppression more easily than those with greater privilege.

Critical social awareness requires self-reflection not only about values, stereotypes, and assumptions but also about how one has situated oneself and who is helped or excluded by professional positioning. For example, in the United States, does the practitioner take insurance and work with people on Medicaid? We know that many

BIPOC people in the United States with mental health problems end up in the criminal justice system because of racism and lack of care or poor care, not receiving adequate psychosocial support, which is exacerbated by clinicians setting up firewalls that do not "permit" them to work with low-income clients (Rolin et al., 2021).

Assessing the Current Situation

Along with assessing the social ecology, the historical and structural situation of affected groups, and self-assessment by helping professionals and volunteers, it is important to assess the immediate, acute situation and its impact on people. I have intentionally placed this *after* the earlier assessments because often the acute assessment is done first because it is so pressing and is on the helper's radar screen. Much of the literature on disaster mental health takes this approach. But as I have been arguing, this is decontextualized and ahistorical and ignores or minimizes structural realities, which provide the context for assessing the acute situation.

As an illustration, I vividly recall responding to Hurricane Katrina in 2005 days after the storm for the American Red Cross in Biloxi, Mississippi, and with two colleagues – one Chinese American and one African American – trying to engage with outreach with the Vietnamese community, which lived and worked at the epicenter of the storm and was isolated and not receiving emergency services for linguistic, cultural, and structural reasons, such as racism. Survivors were gathering in a Catholic Church and Buddhist Temple, which are adjacent to one another. The three of us felt a sense of urgency – relief supplies were not reaching the community, people were not receiving or understanding public service messages and there were no attempts by responding organizations to consider the community's social organization, cultural practices, immigration experiences, and any sense of Vietnamese personhood. Ultimately, my two colleagues were reassigned (and there was pressure to do the same with me) because they were violating the Red Cross' emphasis on neutrality and were viewed as being too "emotionally involved." The emphasis was on reaching all affected communities equally without attempting to understand the unique socio-historical factors affecting the impact of the storm on particular communities.

Thankfully, two years later, I was able to conduct research with a colleague and student (Park et al., 2010) and found that the community had come together and rebuilt, despite many challenges (e.g., a slump in shrimp fishing, loss of jobs at Casinos, having to move elsewhere to find work, relationship breakups, delays with federal relief, having to rebuild most houses and businesses) and for many community members, the experience of surviving Hurricane Katrina paled in comparison to having survived the war in Vietnam and the process of immigration to the United States (many had been at sea in small boats). These experiences had contributed to forging collective and individual resilience, and the ability to reconstruct a community with rich social networks and shared cultural practices had helped to provide a foundation for survival and even flourishing. I do not want to minimize the terror of surviving the storm, the losses, pain, or suffering, but two years later, the people whom we interviewed felt "everything has changed" due to Hurricane Katrina, but that they and their community were moving on with their lives.

Sometimes affected people are mired in an ongoing struggle with historical and structural oppression, while others are encountering new and immediate threats, and often it is a combination of both. For example, racism in the United States is historical, structural, endemic, and ongoing; this does not mean that there has not been significant progress (e.g., civil rights legislation), but White supremacy and racism still are central to U.S. society. And yet there are also acute situations – the murders and assassinations of Black people by law enforcement in communities around the United States, or the attempts to suppress and nullify democratic electoral processes when there are significant Black and Latino/a voters by Republican legislatures in states that they politically control, or even denying people the right to vote, such as the refusal by Florida's governor and legislature to respect a referendum restoring the vote to convicted felons who served their sentences, many of whom are people of color.

Another example is the Hazaras in Afghanistan, who are Shia Muslims. They have been historically marginalized and targeted by other ethnic groups for their ethnicity and religious beliefs and this continued, even during the Russian and U.S. occupations of Afghanistan. But their experience of brutality, and what is considered by some to be genocide, when the Taliban took control of the country has accelerated and their situation as an ethnic group, with all of its tribes, families, and individuals, has deteriorated and become dire.

Other Aspects of Assessment

While most assessments of critical situations begin with the individual, I would like to start with the collectivity and community. Kretzman and McKnight (1993) took a positive approach to community mapping, underscoring how important it is to recognize assets and sources of strength, which is a good starting point. This includes "hard" assets – such as economic resources, access to healthy and open spaces, sufficient supplies of food, banks and financial institutions, jobs, transportation systems, solid school systems, decent health care, religious and spiritual associations, and honest, responsive, and representative government and its institutions (e.g., police, teachers). Many communities around the world lack these hard assets, but it is important to note what they do have.

There are other more socially oriented assets, such as social networks, civic associations, neighborhoods that are safe and inclusive, and access to local, often informal, political processes. There are also more subjective concepts, such as social capital, social cohesion, and social networks. "Collective efficacy" (Sampson et al., 1997) is another important asset – the capacity of a community, neighborhood, or street – to be able to collectively articulate goals (e.g., safe streets for children) and work together to at least partially achieve these goals. In order to get try and understand the subjective experience of social capital, social cohesion, social networks, and collective efficacy, it can help to ask residents certain questions (Garran et al., 2021):

- What is it like to live in our community? What does it mean to you? How would you describe it to others who have never been there?
- How would you describe relations between different ethnic/racial/religious groups in the community?
- Where does power reside in the community and how is it expressed?
- What are your community's problems and strengths and assets?
- Do you and your family feel safe in the community?
- How do you feel about law enforcement in your community?
- What would you like to see your community become?

These questions help outsiders to collaboratively assess the strengths and challenges of a community and can be asked in order to establish a baseline of community assets and cohesion. Of course, it is important to do this collaboratively with local residents and to have insiders help to cooperatively design and implement any such assessment. When there have been acute incidents, such as an attack, assassination, precipitous decline in safety, or terrorist incidents – then it is important to add questions that examine what has changed, what has been lost and destroyed, what is now missing, and what needs to be rebuilt. This is also an opportunity to consider transitional pathways (Landau, 2007; Landau & Saul, 2004) – how does the current situation connect to what the community *was* and what is the collective vision of the community's *future*?

The next area to assess is the profound impact of oppression and violence on families. There are so many different kinds of families that it is difficult to generalize. As with everything else in this book, I recommend two sources to draw upon: (1) Members of the affected family, recognizing that their needs may not converge and that some information will not be shared in front of other family members – so creativity with creating space to assess the needs of all members is called for, as is an assessment of the family system. (2) Assessing the family system as an outsider runs the risk of imposing the helper's worldview on the family, so it is important to work alongside people who are indigenous to the family's culture or to even step aside and let that person (or persons) conduct the assessment. At the very least an indigenous consultant should review all aspects of a family (as well as community and individual) assessment – who to interview, what questions to ask and not ask, and how to interpret what emerges. Another strategy is to have key community informants describe the overall impact of the social targeting and violence in general terms.

In my experience, relationships within the family are affected in many possible ways. If there are partners in the family, social oppression can bring them closer together as they jointly resist or, conversely, this can drive partner's apart. As mentioned in Chapter 4, structural, collective violence is often internalized and replicated within families. It is also challenging when partners have different reactions – perhaps one being highly activated and the other remaining calm, or minimizing or compartmentalizing. There are also differences in how much people seek traditional knowledge and customs as sources of strength within a family. Established roles for different partners (such as who is the primary breadwinner), as well as expectations for children can be upended by social oppression. My Afghan students, who are women, assumed much more active roles within their families because they were living in the United States and attending a U.S. university and exerted leadership in supporting their families and helping them to escape from Afghanistan after the Taliban takeover. This was a sharp break with traditional role expectations for women in their families, as well as placing people in a younger generation in a role of contributing to and even making decisions with and for their elders. All of these challenges are more likely when there are major disruptions such as forced migration, living in refugee camps, death or severe injury of a family member, and imprisonment, which affects all aspects of family life: roles, routines, expected life cycles, privacy, communication patterns, and the family's relationship to their community and the outside world. Common feelings that circulate within families in such situations are guilt over not having protected other family members, accompanied by grief.

What is key with family assessment is to ascertain what has changed due to current threats and challenges, how family members feel about those changes, and how this has affected family members' meaning-making systems, worldviews, and connections with their community and culture. Such judgments should not be made by outsiders without community collaborators, as mentioned earlier. As stated in earlier chapters, current psychosocial reactions, including trauma, are often inseparable from historical and collective trauma.

Most psychosocial practitioners are familiar with individual assessments; all social and psychological service agencies have their own assessment protocols and in North America, insurance companies have their own assessment procedures, so I will only accent some important aspects that must be attended to when working with people experiencing social oppression. By assessing the sociocultural context, collective/community situation, and family reactions, helping professionals have hopefully begun to establish a necessary context for assessing individuals, who should never be evaluated separately from these milieus, but more is needed.

In Chapter 4, I identified common areas that affect individuals who experience violence and I will only list them here, recommending that the reader refers to the earlier, more in-depth discussion to guide individual assessment: bodily/physical reactions, cognitive/thinking, emotional/feeling, behaviors, social and interpersonal interactions, meaning-making, and spirituality. And I discussed trauma in all of the preceding chapters, distinguishing historical, collective, and structural trauma from the individualistic Western psychiatric notion of PTSD. As with communities and families, I think that it is important when assessing the impact of current oppression to try and understand what has changed from what had been a person's baseline functioning. Even people who are constantly grappling with the affects of historical and collective trauma may present more severe psychosocial distress when confronted with acute, new, and more extreme threats. Some of the signs of this are hyper-alertness and an inability to feel safe and self-calm. Rumination over anticipated threats and difficulty redirecting one's thoughts are also indicators of an acute heightening of distress. And as mentioned earlier, it is important to be attuned to deep sadness, grief, mourning, and symptoms of depression, as well as strong feelings of guilt, shame, anger, rage, hopelessness, and a lack of desire to continue with life.

Lastly, two related areas are important to assess. One is how a person may have internalized historical and social oppression and how this may have become part of their personhood and self-image. The converse of this is also important – how has a person resisted this and through strength, courage, and family and collective support resisted such internalizations? The second area includes the degree of connection, or lack thereof, with ethnic, racial, and cultural pride and history, and accompanying cultural values and practices.

Psychosocial Capacity Building

As with all psychosocial work, the relationship between the helper and their collaborator is central. Although I encourage helping professionals to consider less direct work involving the use of self and to instead employ models such as mentoring/consulting, and training of trainers, the relationship is the foundation for whatever kind of work is being planned. In this section, I will consider building a helping relationship, goal setting, mobilizing resources, methods and modalities of intervention and support, empowering targeted people and groups, mobilizing resources, and evidence and evaluation.

Building a Trusting Relationship

Assuming that the helping professional is an outsider – not from the community that is socially targeted – it is important to not expect trust. There are many reasons for this. Depending on the intersecting social identities of the helper and their collaborators, it is possible, if not likely that the person offering psychosocial support has more social privilege than those being helped. This can be on an international level – the helper comes from a Western or wealthier nation – or within the same country – the helper has privilege due to their identities (e.g., race, ethnicity, socioeconomic class, gender, education). As I have discussed at length, people with greater privilege are more prone to viewing the world in a distorted, obfuscated fashion because their social status has minimized or mitigated disjunctures between them and societies shaped by coloniality, Eurocentrism, and White supremacy. Not only might their collaborators see the reality and dynamics of oppression more clearly, but they may also have an awareness of how difficult it will be for the helping professional/volunteer to understand their world. It is also likely that the helping professional carries assumptions and stereotypes that will surface in the work, reinforcing their lack of understanding of their collaborators and their community. This can also lead to the enactment of microaggressions. Mistrust is furthered by the strong possibility that collaborators may have directly had bad experiences with people with similar identities to the helper or heard from others in their collectivity of bad experiences. Thus, trust is not assumed but needs to be earned, and mistrust surfaced and explored.

There is another dynamic that is the reverse of what I have discussed; due to coloniality, the helper is elevated and endowed with higher social status and prestige. If the helper comes from a majority group or a wealthy, economically developed country, this is reinforced by public discourses, institutional power, and cultural representations. This can feel seductive to the worker/volunteer as they are looked up to and granted authority and expertise. And there are many traditions and practitioners who rely on being granted this influence for their work. But that goes against many of the guiding principles articulated in this book and discussed in the previous chapter.

In addition to all of the challenges to establishing trust that I have discussed, there is also another important question: what are the risks of establishing a trusting relationship? This may sound counterintuitive and as I have said that a trusting relationship is central to psychosocial work but it is important for practitioners to raise this question with themselves and their partners in an authentic, genuine way. We need to ask ourselves if we have done sufficient work on developing a crucial social awareness so that we have insight into our assumptions and how our proposed interventions may reflect power, privilege, and cultural dominance. Is there a risk that a trusting relationship will loosen or replace the collaborator's connection with their community, culture, and history, as Traveling Thunder warned? Is it possible that the helper's own needs – e.g., getting paid, satisfying agency or insurance requirements, and setting limits and boundaries that benefit them – will shape the course of intervention in a way that is not beneficial to the collaborator? Are there aspects of social control or maintaining the social, economic, and political order that the helping relationship embodies or represents? Will the helper sufficiently be available for the long haul, or might they start something that then is dropped or unfinished?

No helping professionals are perfect or have worked out all of their assumptions and biases, and it is not possible to operate completely outside of a societal, institutional, and organizational structure. So what I have shared is not intended to discourage helping professionals from offering help to people who are socially targeted – to the contrary, this book is encouraging that work – but it is important to be aware of the harm that can come from helping in order to minimize this and to work to ensure that consumer's needs are paramount and that the goal is their resilience and flourishing, not completing successful "treatment" on the worker's terms.

How might we mitigate the risks and increase the likelihood that a trusting productive, trusting relationship can be established. This will (and should) take time. It is important for helpers and collaborators to get to know one another and not have a "speed-dating" relationship. What opportunities exist for people having meals or tea together, or informally hanging out without a clear, task-driven agenda? This is not easy for helpers working within an agency structure where there are productivity requirements and clinical assessment expectations. Can there be drop-in groups where collaborators and potential helpers get to know one another and where collaborators also have some choice and agency about who they work with, rather than being assigned an intake or assessment worker?

Part of the getting to know one another phase is the opportunity to share problems, needs, hopes, and expectations with collaborators and for helpers to share who they are, how they approach their work, what psychosocial approaches they draw upon, how flexible they can and cannot be, and how open they are to negotiation and collaboration. When this is done in a group setting, it lessens the pressure for two people to size one another up and it also respects the collective nature of historical and structural oppression. It is not necessary for those seeking help to share personal information in a group that leaves them feeling vulnerable or uncomfortable, but space can be opened for surfacing important themes.

An example of this is when I was working with a regional health authority in North America that wanted to do outreach to a First Nation community to see if the health authority might be able to offer psychosocial services in response to a natural disaster. Two groups met – representatives from the health authority met with tribal leaders and elders. The tribe presented their history, including that of colonization and boarding schools. They identified critical problems that the community was dealing with, including historical, intergenerational trauma from coloniality, racism and forced boarding schools, the consequences of the natural disaster, chemical dependency issues, and concerns about suicide and premature deaths. As one member of the tribe put it, "we cannot separate out the effects of the natural disaster from our historical trauma and the social problems that we are currently facing."

The next step was in another meeting when the health authority presented what they could offer – based on two "evidence-based" intervention protocols, which were rooted in Western disaster responses but tried to be adaptable to a range of cultural contexts. There were questions as well as some skepticism from tribal members, and there were numerous follow-up meetings to see if a partnership would be possible. Tribal members were wary of services being parachuted into their community without cultural humility and a long-term commitment, as well as concerns about the health authority not sufficiently understanding their history, society, community, and cultural practices. There were also apprehensions about sustainability, power dynamics, and how such a partnership could be equitable.

Over time, and with great effort and investment by all parties, the meetings and subsequent training improved relations between the tribe and the health authority although this was not seamless. Some of the principles from the disaster recovery protocols were viewed by the tribe as being helpful and were adapted for their own use. Not only were there social, cultural, and political differences between the health authority and tribe, but there were also goals and objectives that sometimes corresponded but others that reflected the different positionality of the two entities. The tribal leadership was concerned with the welfare of its people and was committed to maintaining traditional cultural values and practices while the health authority wanted to ensure greater recovery from the natural disaster and also had funding and time limitations that shaped what it could and could not offer. The historical project of coloniality could not be undone over a few months or even a few years, and there were understandable tensions between a state agency needing to manage its own budget and resources and a tribal community wanting to exert leadership over what their community members were exposed to. Goodwill by all concerned was helpful, but the differences in sociocultural worlds and notions of personhood presented complex challenges that could be acknowledged but not completely overcome. The example illustrates how important it is to not only be transparent about history, patterns of oppression, current structural threats, and social problems but also demonstrates how challenging it is for power to be negotiated and shared. As Phillips et al. (2015) state: "the presence of conflict and disharmony may be a desirable sign of progress toward justice rather than an undesirable disturbance of enforced peace."

Despite the many challenges, one positive maneuver was that the health authority visited the tribe in their community as guests, having sought an invitation that was then proffered. When applying this to an urban community, I think that it is important that an organization offering help also does outreach in the community, abiding by their terms and respecting the turf of whomever the hosts are – e.g., churches or mosques, community service organizations, schools, and daycare centers. The enduring legacies of coloniality and the soft power of helping professionals are never completely allayed, but they can be at least raised and grappled with when careful attention is paid to them. Such collective engagement can then shape the context for more micro-services and relationships between people. As I stated earlier, mistrust may understandably be the norm and evinces a healthy understanding of risks, differences, and power dynamics that need to be addressed.

Building a trusting relationship is thus a multi-layered, non-linear process and may not be characterized by peace, harmony, and lack of conflict and disagreement. The same factors that I identified in the inter-organizational example that I shared apply to an interpersonal relationship. The key points for developing a trusting relationship are given in Box 6.1.

Box 6.1 Building a Trusting Relationship

- Critical consciousness by the helper and organization offering services
- Empathy for threatening and harmful experiences by members of the targeted group
- Negotiated terms between helping professional and collaborator
- Honoring and prioritizing local and indigenous lived experiences, values, worldviews, epistemologies, and leadership.
- Genuine, equitable, and full partnering with local and indigenous people from the beginning and throughout the process
- Validating local and indigenous territory, turf, and leadership
- Acknowledging and negotiating the complex intersectionality of social identities and positionality at the personal and organizational level

- Articulating and collaboratively exploring potential unintended risks
- Forging relationships at the group and collective levels, as well as between individuals
- Engaging in healing ceremonies and rituals that respond to coloniality, White supremacy, and microaggressions
- Allowing sufficient time and opportunities for the relationship to develop

- Critical consciousness by the helper and organization offering services, including unlearning and discarding the usual ways of conducting business
- Empathy for threatening and harmful experiences by members of the targeted group that the helper may have not encountered and humility about trying to understand them
- Negotiated terms of engagement – the purpose of work together, the worldviews and history that shapes and constrains the work, the hoped-for outcomes, who is part of the process (e.g., extended family, spiritual leaders), power, and control
- Honoring and prioritizing local and indigenous lived experiences, values, worldviews, epistemologies, and leadership
- Genuine, equitable, and full partnering with local and indigenous people from the beginning and throughout the process
- Validating local and indigenous territory, turf, and leadership; helpers as guests and students
- Acknowledging the complex intersectionality of social identities and positionality at the personal and organizational level and negotiating this
- Articulating and collaboratively exploring the potential unintended risks of helping
- Forging relationships at the group and collective levels, as well as between individuals
- Engaging in healing ceremonies and rituals that respond to coloniality, White supremacy, and microaggressions which have occurred and are likely to reoccur
- Understanding that trust and relationship building takes time and is not a linear, seamless process and that impasses, turbulence, and conflict can be signs of genuine engagement

Goal Setting

All of the aforementioned aspects of assessment and relationship building should lead to mutual goal setting. Goals should not be set for agency or insurance forms and purposes; rather, they should be determined by what collaborators want to work on. This also holds true for how problems will be tackled, goals approached, and the criteria for evaluating success (see the following section on evaluation). Goals should reflect the sociocultural milieu of affected people and how they conceptualize psychosocial phenomena and work. If the word goals, and how they are usually conceptualized, are culturally antithetical, then helping professionals should substitute whatever language or ways of understanding the work together are meaningful for partners. What is most important is that there is clarity between the collaborator and helping professional about what is being worked on, priorities, an anticipated map of the terrain to be traveled together, what bodies of knowledge will inform the work, modalities to be used, and understandings about the frequency and length of time.

Mobilizing Resources

An important step toward building trusting relationships is for those offering psychosocial help to demonstrate their commitment to the socially targeted group by mobilizing resources to support the process of healing and recovery. A good starting place for this is to seek to fund the time that affected people put into the process. A fundamental asymmetry is that those offering services are usually paid for their time, while those receiving services are not. And yet coloniality and all forms of identity-based supremacy have created a structural situation where those offering help usually have greater social and economic privileges than those they are trying to support. And for those who are helpers and are also experiencing social targeting, there is often an "identity tax." Examples of this include BIPOC faculty in universities being expected to spend more time on "diversity" or "social justice" committees or find themselves formally and informally advising many students of color, while at the same time trying to manage their teaching and scholarship expectations as they seek to achieve tenure and promotion. And the same faculty or BIPOC workers at a social service or counseling organization are often encountering the same social challenges and threats as the people and communities they are serving.

In the example I shared in the previous section, the health authority had the backing of government, including access to grants and the services of paid staff, while during the planning phase, tribal leaders were volunteering their time. When a graduate program in counseling, psychology, or social work is trying to deal with embedded coloniality and White supremacy and seeks to hear the voices of BIPOC students, who is being compensated, and who is donating their time? Raising and responding to these questions is an initial way to mobilize resources.

With the project of psychosocial capacity building in Northern Uganda, which I have referred to a number of times in this book, there are many examples of the importance of providing resources as part of psychosocial capacity building. Due to coloniality, members of the U.S. team who are offering to help have a much higher standard of living than people in Uganda: salaries, houses or apartments, cars, infrastructure (e.g., paved roads, electricity, water and sewage), access to education, and much more. In contrast, people living in Northern Uganda experienced a 20-year armed conflict, interacting with chronic poverty, and tribal exclusion/targeting by the federal government. The lack of infrastructure, reliance on subsistence farming, absence of industry, and paucity of overall wealth in comparison to the rest of the world are also legacies of colonialism. Another legacy is a history of partisan cronyism, tribal politics, coups, and government repression and violence.

The relative poverty and underdevelopment of Uganda in relation to the former colonial powers continue to be sustained by globalism, neo-liberal capitalism, and geopolitics. While China has filled a gap created wrought by a profound lack of investment by Western powers through its "belt and road" initiatives throughout Africa – building roads, bridges, dams, ports, and power grids – China is also motivated by the use of "soft power" to ensure its access to extracting metals, minerals, and other goods needed to support its economy and population.

What this means is that dedicated health-care workers, local political leaders, women's leaders, religious leaders, clan leaders, and others who are necessary to plan, mobilize, and implement what is needed for psychosocial capacity building and recovery are also experiencing their own struggles to make ends meet, to provide for their families, to stay healthy, and to fulfill their responsibilities to the community. So, if they are expected to be full collaborators with people from the United States who are working to support psychosocial recovery, they need resources that they cannot directly access. Thus, they need to be paid to attend meetings and training and offered support for the time that it will take them to travel by motorcycle over dirt roads to attend these events. Only the members of the U.S. team have the capacity to engage with fund raising through soliciting donations or writing grants. This is yet another example of how goodwill and intentions are insufficient to support recovery from historical and collective trauma and the critical importance of helpers mobilizing resources so that their partners and collaborators can help to heal their own communities.

What about "clients" in "developed" countries engaged in a helping process? If we refer to clients as collaborators, might this open up consideration of their being paid for their time as well as the helping professional? I realize that this might sound radical but when upending the structures of the helping process shaped by coloniality, remuneration for the time of all involved should be open to reflection.

Mobilizing resources for those directly affected by historical and collective violence and trauma also involves advocacy and work to support social welfare policies – whether local, national, or global – that respond to the socioeconomic and political inequalities that accompany historical and structural oppression. Thus, psychosocial support involves simultaneously working directly with individuals, families, and groups to support their recovery and thriving while also seeking to redress the historical and contemporary conditions that caused and sustain pain and suffering. It is not sufficient for responders and helpers to focus on interpersonal engagement and then wall this off from the larger task of mobilizing resources that respond to people's concrete and material needs.

Modalities

Using a decolonizing, liberatory approach means questioning the most basic assumptions that helping professionals have imbibed throughout their training and careers. This includes the central place of talk therapy and similar modalities; the use of self in directly engaging and working with affected people; the value of detached, "objective," "evidence-based" assessment and treatment planning; all involving a mostly unidirectional, hierarchical relationship structure of "worker" and "client"; boundaries and limits that separate out parts of people's lives and isolates "professional work" from other aspects of a person's life. It is only through identifying, interrogating, and dislodging such assumptions and taken-for-granted professional guidelines that helping professionals can move beyond the limitations of psychosocial work grounded in the coloniality of White, Western supremacy. It is an act of decolonizing the consciousness of helping professionals (Phillips et al., 2015).

Talk therapy emerged in Europe in the early 20th century and is rooted throughout the Western world. This has become normalized within White, middle-class culture in the Western world (Smith et al., 2009). It has been emulated and adapted in non-Western contexts such as China and India and is used with people living in Western nations with a range of nationalities, races, ethnicities, cultural patterns, and notions of personhood, but its taproots are distinctly White and Western. As I have stated in earlier chapters, understandings of suffering and its causes, theories of development and treatment, notions of health, recovery, and thriving, and how helping professionals can help people to achieve these end goals are grounded in this limited, Eurocentric view of humanity.

As I grapple with these themes and issues, I too am situated as a White, Western-based practitioner; my mind has also been occluded with the clouds of coloniality, which seem to "naturally" hover in the sky of practice but are actually but one weather pattern among many. Thus, the importance of my seeking knowledge from BIPOC scholars, practitioners, spiritual leaders, and community members, who have resisted coloniality and White, Western hegemony in all aspects of their lives, including how to heal. The range of histories, societies, and cultures that they represent is vast, and thus the modalities of helping and healing vary considerably. This is why, throughout this book, I have been cautious about proscribing specific ways of helping and have instead opted for an ethic of psychosocial work informed by and led by those experiencing social oppression, which leads me to offer broad alternatives to 1:1 talking-based psychosocial practice. This does not mean that the helping professional does not have ideas about how to respond to the consequences of historical and collective oppression and trauma or important knowledge, skills, and insights to offer, but they should be woven into the fabric of healing spun by those directly affected.

Thus, when it comes to the modalities of helping, I recommend that planning for this should be done in teams, where there is no less than 50% membership of people from the directly affected groups and either leadership or equal co-leadership by those group members. If this leads, for example, to setting up 1:1 counseling, then it is important that when establishing this, there is attention to determining what "counseling" means, looks like, how it should be implemented, and what cosmologies, theories, assumptions, and worldviews inform it.

But in my experiences, more often than not, if local, indigenous group members are planning the modalities of helping, talk therapy is often not at the top of the list or even on the list at all. Bryant-Davis

(2008) describes a creative range of activities that can be applied in response to historical and collective trauma: e.g., dance, poetry, journaling, skits, and music. These activities help people to feel safe and connected with one another and to help calm activated endocrine and neurological systems. I have adapted many of them in my work in Northern Uganda and Haiti but when talking to my Chinese colleagues and students about using song and dance in response to mass tragedies in China, there was nearly universal agreement that they would not resonate or be appropriate in this context. Rather calligraphy, mutual aid and support groups, and skills-building activities such as women learning how to do (and sell) traditional embroidery came to the surface.

Training of Trainers

Given this, I strongly recommend that helping professionals consider a TOT model that enhances the capacity of affected people who are insiders to help other people in their group and community. By training a cadre of people who work, live, and are trusted by the affected community, we are building in a greater likelihood of cultural responsiveness and minimizing the chances of replicating a relationship that reinforces coloniality. It is also more likely that such a team will live in the community and therefore have not only a better understanding of how the community works but also greater availability and enhanced sustainability. Helping professionals from the outside can contribute skills, knowledge, and resources, which they may have greater access to. The assumptions and issues that I mentioned earlier – what modalities are emphasized, how boundaries are negotiated and established, the structure of the relationship between the helper and those being helped, the focus and goals of intervention, minimizing risks and avoiding iatrogenic affects, and evaluating the effectiveness of interventions – are co-constructed and are not taken for granted or imposed.

This is why it is so important to have teams of helping professionals and consultants who represent the affected community and place them in leadership roles; without this, the force field of coloniality will usually reassert itself and prevail, much like a gravitational pull. Such teams can plan all aspects of the intervention – from assessment to evaluation – as well as identifying target groups, eligibility for inclusion in the program, timetables, and necessary resources. Having people from the affected community in leadership positions mitigates against feelings of dependency, passivity, and weakness – the group or community is not reliant on outside saviors. Instead, it builds on a tradition and foundation of indigenous leadership and wisdom and reminding people of historical leaders and highlighting that such leadership still exists. It offers an opportunity to enact the principle of strength, beauty, and leadership from the inside, without needing outsiders to validate this.

An example of this is the friendship benches that were developed in Harare, Zimbabwe, and have spread to other parts of the world, including New York and London (Rosenberg, 2019). Friendship benches rely on a TOT model where local residents are trained in basic methods of assessing depression and anxiety and undergo a two-week program in basic problem-solving skills. The benches are portable and can be moved to different neighborhoods. They do not require an appointment and do not have a limit on how long a session will last. It is possible that the helper and those being helped may run into one another in the neighborhood in different roles and capacities. The people dispensing advice have real-life experiences – deep empathy – for what the people seeking help are experiencing. They normalize having psychosocial problems and seeking help and support for them. Preliminary evaluations indicate that friendship benches reach people who may not seek office-based therapy or counseling but that the interventions do reduce anxiety and depression.

But what about dealing with clients who might be suicidal? How is historical and collective trauma assuaged in an impromptu session on a friendship bench? Do the friendship benches do anything to confront the sociocultural conditions that contributed to anxiety and depression? Do they bring people together to form social networks and support groups? Do they connect people with their historical legacies and cultural traditions? Are they reliant on knowledge bases that emanate from the very sources of oppression?

These are but a few of questions that friendship benches can generate. The intention is to create "nontraditional safe spaces in plain view – no strings attached" (Rosenberg, 2019). One way to think about friendship benches is that they are a start, a frontline intervention that challenges traditional helping hierarchies and assemblages. There is no reason that every question that I raised can't be addressed in concert with this early, non-threatening engagement. Suicide assessment can be part of the basic skills training with backup and further assessment and treatment from community members who undergo more specialized, extensive training. There are people who carry cultural knowledge who can offer groups to reconnect people with these sources of cultural wisdom as well as understandings of collective oppression and trauma; how it affects people and how to respond to it. There can be resilience and strength groups that focus on surviving sociocultural targeting and exploring resilience and ways to thrive. The initial friendship group intervention can connect people to mutual aid and support groups, grief and mourning groups, or trauma and anxiety management groups, all led by local people indigenous to the targeted group. Performing arts groups that engage people in cultural practices, such as dancing, drumming, or oral storytelling, is another resource that can further healing social relationships and networks, group cohesion, and cultural connections (O'Neill et al., 2018). Advocacy and lobbying groups can collectively challenge the social conditions of subjugation. All of these possibilities, and more, can be mapped out by the leadership group that is planning how to address community problems and foster community resilience. The friendship benches can be a gateway to a decolonized world of coping and resistance.

Friendship benches are but one model and they work in certain contexts but perhaps are not applicable everywhere. Other examples include Promotoras de Salud, where trusted members of a Chicano community in L.A. are trained in health management and reach out to other people in the community to promote healthier practices: they have linguistic and cultural fluency, know their community, are part of social networks, are aware of community needs and resources, and through their own struggles and achievements can serve as role models of resilience for people whom they reach out to (Falicov et al., 2020), Similarly, Curanderas, who are faith healers in some Mexican villages, who live in their communities and unlike therapists, residents know where they live and can approach them in the evening and on weekends (Lopez personal communication, 2021). Curanderas are part of existing social networks, which is not true of most therapists. These models easily draw on a TOT framework to develop a corps of community counselors, outreach workers, or resident healers. Another model is to train parents and extended family in the effects of historical and collective trauma so that they can support BIPOC adolescents and situate and explicate the trauma from a historical and cultural perspective (O'Neill et al., 2018). This is an intergenerational response to intergenerational trauma and has the potential to foster family pride and cohesion. Prayer groups and other spiritually oriented practices can connect people with a wider theology and philosophy and enhance their sense of pride in their personhood within this cosmology (Blume et al., 2020; Lewis et al., 2021; Millner et al., 2021; Ortega-Williams et al., 2021). A system of mentors, matching younger people with "elders" or older people can be established and serve as a resource that a friendship bench worker or Curandera could draw on and refer people to. Collective emotional healing networks can be established and spawn emotional emancipation circles as well as learning modules to teach about history, culture, and collective oppression (Barlow, 2018). This can be one of a range of collective forms of "psychosocial accompaniment" (Abe, 2020). Resistance cells can provide a platform and edifice for collective contesting of targeting and oppression, from coping with microaggressions at school or the workplace to confronting racially-based police stop-and-frisk programs in a neighborhood. What is important in all of these possibilities is to connect acute encounters with and reactions to oppression with larger historical and collective experiences and the resources, knowledge, and strategies that were generated through these struggles. Adaptation and short-term strategies can be useful to mitigate immediate distress and suffering (Adessky & Freedman, 2005) but without being connected to collective forms of resistance, they run the risk of reinforcing individual culpability for wounds and injuries. Otherwise, workers, even in their efforts to help, are embracing mainstream narratives about individual culpability for the suffering that can marginalize and "other" their clients (Combs & Freedman, 2012).

Box 6.2 Examples of Training-of-Trainers Programs and Groups

Friendship Benches – Trained volunteers from a community sit on a portable bench and have conversations with people who walk by and sit down next to them about life's problems. They can also be a gateway for referral to some of the groups mentioned in the following. The volunteers are trained in anxiety management skills which are then shared with collaborators.

Cultural Practices and Traditions Groups – Elders or those with special skills teach people about cultural practices (e.g., dance, storytelling, drumming, calligraphy) who in turn run cultural activities groups for others within the community.

Resilience and Strength Groups – Community members share and train one another about accessing personal, collective, and historical sources of strength and then divide up and run groups for others in the community. This can be based on stories, people's lives, historical figures, and so on.

Mutual Aid and Support Groups – Group leaders are trained in group dynamics and group facilitation. Some may also be trained in special skills – e.g., embroidery – which are then taught and practiced with group members. Groups can foster social networks, mutual aid with babysitting, shopping, and so on.

Social Advocacy Groups – Community members can share their community organization skills with others, who in turn form cells of resistance that advocate and lobby for important policy, procedural, economic, or political changes.

Grief and Mourning Groups – Facilitators are trained in culturally relevant grief and mourning practices and then work with community members in a group setting. Mourning can be about personal losses as well as collective, historical losses.

Emotional Healing Networks and Trauma and Anxiety Management Groups – While Friendship Benches are more individual and provisional in nature, this could be a resource to refer people to. As with Friendship Benches, facilitators would come from the community of those being served and receive training and supervision not only about anxiety and trauma but also about facilitation and ways to use cultural practices to promote emotional healing and placing emotional reactions in a historical and structural context.

Promotoras de Salud – Community members can be trained to do proactive, health, and psychosocial outreach to community members and either directly respond to their needs or refer them to groups such as the ones mentioned earlier. They build on their linguistic and cultural fluency, know their community, are part of social networks, are aware of community needs and resources, and through their own struggles and achievements serve as role models of resilience for people whom they reach out to.

Curanderas – Spiritual or faith healers can train other community members to be lay spiritual leaders and consult with them as they work with community members and are available for crises as well as ongoing spiritual practice.

Family and Parent Training Groups – Parents can train other parents in culturally appropriate ways of raising children, including ways of building resilience, preparing for how to manage dangerous or oppressive situations, and how to thrive. Elders can also be matched with younger community members and serve as mentors, consultants, and teachers of cultural practices.

With all models, it is important to connect acute situations and reactions with larger historical and collective experiences and the resources, knowledge, and strategies that were generated through these struggles.

As can be seen from these descriptions, the use of groups is recommended for all of the reasons discussed thus far: pooling skills, knowledge, and resources; engaging many people in a collective project which can feel empowering; strengthening social networks; sharing tasks and burdens; embodying empathy by bringing together people with similar experiences; and minimizing personal vulnerability, shame, and isolation. Positive social advocacy, change, and liberation always involve people working in groups together. In many places in the world, people see themselves in their roles in groups and less as autonomous individuals. And yet the majority of helping professionals have been trained to primarily work with individuals, and sometimes couples or families. Individual work has a place in healing and liberation from oppression, but it should not be the starting point. Individuation, individualism, individual vulnerability, personal responsibility, and culpability are all characteristics of neo-liberalism, and the helping professions – which function in a neo-liberal context – reflect this in theory and practice, training and education, how services are delivered, funded, and paid for, in how evaluation is conceptualized and conducted and, in the ways that professional careers are defined, measured, compensated for, and valued. Thus, part of the unlearning process and critical consciousness of helping professionals is to first think of groups before considering working with individuals.

Related to this is to also consider the collective units of family, extended family, clan, and tribe as primary entities to work with. Another aspect of neo-liberalism and Western culture is to place a high value on not only individual achievement but also privacy, individual boundaries, autonomy, and the expectation of control of one's life and the ability to achieve one's goals. In many contexts, these attributes should be valued and respected, but unfortunately, this singular model is applied to many nationalities, ethnic/racial groups, and tribes who do not approach life in this way.

So how can helping professionals figure out who to work with and how to work with them? This question completes the circle begun in this chapter: members of the affected group, who are hopefully now part of planning teams in leadership positions, should help to determine the various ways that services should be delivered – how, what, and to whom. This is not straightforward, and there can be tensions and contradictions, but it is a starting point. However, the collaboration between indigenous people and Western-trained practitioners provides a circle of care and collaboration where such issues can be surfaced, discussed, processed, and sufficiently worked out to allow things to proceed.

An example of this process is the psychosocial capacity-building project in Northern Uganda, referenced numerous times in this book. The major institutions that members of the Acholi tribe have relied on in this psychosocial and medical capacity-building project are health-care workers, government officials, clan leaders and elders, and religious leaders, such as catechists. This has worked well in many ways as sources of information, knowledge and wisdom, and networks of influencers, who can distill and carry interventions to their constituents, who compose a significant part of the community. However, these groups have identified social issues that they are concerned about and wish to address – e.g., increases in teenage pregnancy and concerns about domestic violence – where gender is an important factor. And most of the members of these groups are male!

Many health-care workers are women – roughly about half – and some government officials are women, although they are a small minority, but the vast majority of clan leaders and catechists are male. So, in this instance, the U.S. team identified and assessed the importance of creating spaces where women could have space and safety to speak, identify the complex causes of both domestic violence and teenage pregnancy, and share their views about the sources and solutions to these problems. How could this be approached without undermining the traditional Acholi structures and practices already in place?

The U.S. team approached a specific subset of health-care workers, midwives, who are almost entirely female and who also are involved with the majority of maternal deliveries – so were very immediately in touch with these issues. They were able to be a source of direct information but were also able to map out with the U.S. team focus groups with teenagers – those who became pregnant and those who did not – to better understand the problem. And they recognized the importance of having groups that were entirely female, both because of the nature of the issues but also because of how their society traditionally functions and discusses such issues. This was done in partnership with a female Acholi social worker, who also happened to be on the Acholi board of directors for the overall medical and psychosocial capacity-building project. All of this made it easier to work with other members of the board of directors, mostly male, who quickly and enthusiastically embraced opening this channel of local, teenage understanding of the problem and its solutions.

This is still a work in progress and the tensions between the more traditional structures and this gendered way of understanding and processing may still arise. And what would have happened if the Acholi board of directors had said "no, we do not feel comfortable supporting a group of teenage women," we prefer to go back to our usual sources and networks? This scenario could easily have occurred in many contexts around the world. And given all that I have discussed about coloniality and the importance of indigenous leadership throughout this book, if concerns about this approach had arisen, it may well have represented a way of resisting the influences of modern, Western culture and hegemony that would need to be valued and respected. If the processes that I have been recommending were in place – collaborative teams of helping professionals with indigenous people (in leadership positions) – then a problem-solving process that reflected mutual respect and the primacy of indigenous ways of knowing and being could have been set in motion. And it is this process that is of the highest importance – I don't know where it would lead to and what the outcome would be, but if this process is in motion, I have hope that a decolonial, liberatory effort to offer psychosocial healing and recovery would emerge. It reflects my belief that Western culture and helping professionals, while having important contributions to make to psychosocial work, do not have all of the answers and my trust that indigenous societies, groups, and practices are concerned about the welfare of all group members.

The Power of Narrative

Narratives are part of every culture, society, and epoch, ranging from cave drawings to *War and Peace*. The substance, content, and form of narratives vary as do the means of telling stories, including drawing, storytelling, writing, singing, dancing, drama, film, photography, and other forms of art. All societies and cultures use narratives to establish constituent myths, that construct personhood, identity, collective history, society, and values and offer norms, wisdom, ethics, and guidance to a collectivity (e.g., group, tribe, religion), delineating what is distinctive about the group. Narratives are used at all levels – nation, state, tribe, ethnic/racial group, community, family, and by individuals constructing the story of their lives and identities. Reiss (1987) talked of a "Family Paradigm" – internalized maps to orient the family to what is real, meaningful, and important, including its relationship to the community and wider society. There are also community paradigms – albeit often contested – about origins, values, lifestyle, and the meaning of a municipality or neighborhood, which intersects with the narratives of families who live there (Miller, 2001). Racial, ethnic, and religious groups often have origin stories and narratives – collective paradigms – about what it means to be a member of the group. Sadly, narratives are often imposed on groups, such as Donald Trump's calling Mexican immigrants "criminals, drug dealers and rapists," which is central to the dynamics of racism, White supremacy, and all forms of group-based oppression.

This raises the issue of who controls narratives – how some are privileged while others marginalized, suppressed, and erased – and the power of a socially dominant group (or individual) to author their own narratives or of another group (or individual) to impose a narrative on others (Combs & Freedman, 2012; Garran et al., 2021; Miller, 2001). This leads to what Fricker termed "testimonial injustice" (Weinberg, 2022). As I have been discussing in this book, people such as Jessie Thistle, mentioned in the previous chapter – internalize derogatory, racist, dominant narratives, shaped by coloniality and neoliberalism, which place the emphasis and blame on individual culpability, shrouding White supremacy in invisibility. This problematizes the targets of social oppression and undermines a sense of efficacy for individuals, families, groups, and tribes – the belief that one can achieve goals and have a modicum of control over one's life and community. Thus, the critical importance of shedding or as narrative therapists would say "externalizing" such narratives (Goodman, 2015).

Externalizing refers to the recognition that individuals (and groups) can internalize oppressive, coercive, imposed narratives and view themselves as the problem, rather than seeing the problem as the problem (Combs & Freedman, 2012; White & Epston, 1990). White and Epston recognized that sociocultural forces shape individual and family problems, thus the importance of recognizing the social factors that lead to psychosocial problems and externalizing what has been internalized (Etchison & Kleist, 2000). While narrative therapy has tended to focus on individuals and families, its understandings can be applied to groups as well.

Gone's (2021) description of Traveling Thunder illustrates this point; one should not seek help from Western-trained mental health clinicians but rather return to collective cultural well-springs. He quotes Traveling Thunder as saying (punctuation by Gone): "After we looked around and realized that . . . we left something behind . . . , we started going back to the hills to fast . . . we started going to the sweat lodges to pray . . . we started going to the elders to learn." This eloquently describes the importance of rejecting Western hegemony and recovering historical memory (Gone; Millner et al., 2021; Phillips et al., 2015). This process of recovering historical narratives goes beyond an individual reclaiming a sense of their own story, it infuses one's suffering with the meaning and power of collective beauty, morality, and resilience.

An outsider offering psychosocial support cannot directly offer this unless working collaboratively with group insiders; they/we simply do not have this understanding, knowledge, authority, and credibility. I have urged a collaborative relationship throughout this book that allows for multiple perspectives and shared skills and resources. Narrative therapy offers a way to mitigate against helpers with more social power and privilege inadvertently imposing their worldviews and notion of personhood on others with the concept of "witness groups." Witness groups were initially viewed as people outside of the direct therapeutic process witnessing and commenting on the therapeutic process (Combs & Freedman, 2012), but I am suggesting that they be used to ensure that a collaborative process is guided by indigenous leadership and ways of understanding. For example, if I or an organization is working with a tribe – e.g., from North America, a country in Africa, or in Southeast Asia – there would be a group of indigenous consultants witnessing the work to safeguard the integrity of the process. The same would be applicable to a mainstream clinical program – such as an outreach program or satellite mental health clinic being offered by a hospital to a particular neighborhood or group of people – a witness group would oversee the process: what is being offered, how it is delivered, underlying ethical, and theoretical assumptions and how this helps, or harms, the community being served. I am not talking about a consumer or neighborhood advisory group but rather a leadership group that has the power to direct, modify, or even nullify the process. This offers the capacity to collaboratively and collectively achieve what the family therapist Karl Tomm (quoted by Combs & Freedman, 2012) suggested occurs from externalization: "By externalizing the problem it moves from the victim confronting abuse on their own to the perpetrator also confronting the abuse." And this includes the helping professionals/volunteers confronting their complicity and own internalizations of being a member of a group, society, nation, or profession that has inflicted harm.

Evaluation

Before concluding this chapter, I would like to briefly consider the role of evaluation in a decolonizing, liberatory approach to psychosocial support. One of the main purposes of evaluation in the helping professions is to assess the efficacy of particular interventions and to protect consumers from ineffectual, harmful, or deceptive practices. Practitioners are expected to be guided by evidence-based practices. In Western academia and practice, this has usually translated into quantitative research, funded by grants, conducted by professional researchers and scholars, with the results submitted to peer-reviewed journals in Western nations. Detachment and objectivity are highly valued. As I have been arguing throughout this book, none of this is neutral and reflects epistemological dominance by those who benefitted from coloniality. This does not mean that these scientific methods are only being used by Western nations. China and India, for example, contribute massive amounts of data and articles to scholarly journals. However, I still view this as an outgrowth of coloniality: for a Chinese academic to achieve tenure and promotion, they are encouraged to seek Ph.D.s in Western countries and must publish in highly ranked Western journals, usually in English. Publishing in Mandarin in Chinese scholarly journals is considered second rate and less likely to lead to coveted successful academic careers.

Evaluation is important and is critical to ensuring that meaningful best practices are offered to people and that helping professionals strive for an ethic of "do no harm." What I question is whether there is only one way to do this – the accepted Western scientific way? And I believe that not interrogating and challenging this inflicts harm, as it diminishes and derogates other forms of knowledge production, wisdom, and understanding and yokes those who are targeted and oppressed to a standard developed by those who have oppressed them, what Fricker called "testimonial injustice" (Weinberg, 2022).

In addition to the concern about epistemic privilege and hegemony, there are also other issues. Is it correct to separate and distance evaluation, outsourcing it to an outside evaluator, from the group that is targeted by social oppression and their lived experiences? If group members are experiencing violence, can research that is not connected to or even detracts from protection and intervention be justified? Should insurance companies decide what are valid interventions and whether the people and community receiving them trust them or find them to be helpful? Is it ethical to impose not only epistemology but also a methodology that assumes access to certain resources (e.g., education, grants, language, advanced degrees, academic status), that privileges written evaluation over oral understanding, numbers, and statistical formulas over narratives, creating a hierarchy of what is "fact," what is "true," what is "real," and what is "myth" and "superstition"? Have these standards and methods evolved from a sociocultural and economic vacuum?

People who are members of socially targeted groups do not need the affirmation and legitimacy conferred by members of privileged groups and nations; what is empowering is having the agency to identify, evaluate, and articulate their own needs and opportunities to tap into their own cultural heritages, roots, and practices and to achieve collective efficacy through their own construction of problems, solutions, and evaluation (Gone, 2021). Evaluation may involve rituals, ceremonies, visions, dances, storytelling, photography, and poetry (Smith et al., 2009), which do not easily correspond with what is considered by helping professionals as "evidence" or fit with the current format of scholarly journals. Gone has articulated how in North America indigenous knowledge production relies on traditional teachings, empirical knowledge gained from lived experiences, and revealed knowledge, which includes dreams and visions. How can these sources be shared with others, considered valid, and help to guide the efforts of helping professionals?

I suggested in the previous section how "witness groups" (Combs & Freedman, 2012) composed of people from the affected group can offer greater possibilities for ensuring that indigeneity is not submerged by waves of Western coloniality and supremacy, and I think that the same holds true for evaluation. Community-based Participatory Research (CBPR) is another effective way of conducting research in collaboration with members of socially targeted and marginalized communities (Kang, 2015; Sanchez et al., 2021). This form of research is conducted by members of the community, at times in partnership with academics connected to the community. The researcher should actively be a part of whatever change efforts are taking place in the community and community members involved with all phases and aspects of evaluation. There is a shared commitment to social justice. Kang describes how this means having group discussions to articulate research purposes, questions, methodologies, data analysis, writing, and dissemination.

In this model, the outside academic joins the change-effort group and subsumes her professional needs to that of group members, validating the lived experiences of project members.

Another example of community inclusion is described by Vindevogel et al. (2015) in their work trying to understand what made for resilient youth in war-affected Northern Uganda. This involved a team of Western researchers working with an indigenous Northern Ugandan community using a participatory research approach. They began by meeting and consulting with existing community "structures" – elders, youth in villages, and schools. They invited community representatives "to make a historic timeline of important events in the area and to construct a community map on which relevant resources (schools, roads, health centers, church, etc.) and all households were situated." They conducted what they called a "transect walk," where they visited all households in a village to establish a relationship, seek consent, and gather "sociodemographic information." They employed a Western research notion of ranking but involved indigenous people in the actual process of ranking their results before drawing their conclusions. The results were not only a mixture of factors like eating well and being healthy but also included things like "looking smart" and engaging in farming work, living in a good house, and having a bicycle for transportation. Although the evaluation project was initiated and in broad strokes designed by Western academics and published in a scholarly journal, it is a good example of a partnership between Western researchers and indigenous people, where local voices were heard and amplified through the process.

Ultimately, there is no one way to contest the coloniality of evaluation; rather there are a range of possibilities. In some instances, it should remain completely within indigenous control. In others, an embedded researcher who is part of a community change effort (Kang, 2015) or a collaborative, respectful partnership such as the one described by Vindevogel et al. (2015) between researchers and villagers with radically different lives and personhoods are options. What is most important is to employ a critical consciousness to all aspects of the research project and to not only respect but also elevate the leadership of affected people.

Conclusion

This chapter confronted the hegemony and primacy of Western psychology and its focus on individual psychotherapy as a beginning point of contention for helping professionals working to support groups experiencing oppression. I listed seven tasks for psychosocial interventions, inspired by Adames et al. (2022) and other BIPOC scholars:

1. Honing a critical consciousness
2. Validating, respecting, and elevating cultural authenticity and self-knowledge
3. Balancing losses and acknowledging oppression with offering hope
4. Using the collectivity as the starting point of understanding and intervention
5. Centering the strength and beauty of those who have resisted and continue to resist oppression
6. Releasing self-blame
7. Working toward social justice at all levels, as a commitment, process, and state of mind

I considered the process of assessment, beginning with an understanding of the context of the helping relationship, which includes the social ecology, the targeted group and community, critical self-assessment by the helping professional (of not only their own values and assumptions but also those of their agencies and professions), and assessment of the current situation. Assessment should be grounded in the historical and cultural context of those receiving psychosocial support, not in the usual terms imposed by helping professionals and the organizations that they represent. And I encouraged readers to begin assessments with an understanding of the collectivity, community, and groups, including what foundations and networks of assets already exist. All aspects of assessment are enhanced when conducted by cultural insiders or at the very least, having such people as consultants to outside helping professionals.

The chapter considered the core of what constitutes psychosocial capacity building. Building a trusting relationship is a foundation of psychosocial support, but there are also risks: undermining the collaborators' connection with their history and culture, imposing the helper's worldview and values, meeting the helping professional's needs, as well as those of their organization, and beginning a process that creates dependency or intimacy and not being available for the long haul. I suggested informal, group processes of getting to know one another so that collaborators could question, edit, revise, and even reject the help being proffered. Doing this in groups, rather than individually, reinforces the understanding of the collective nature of the problems. The key points of establishing trusting, helping relationships are summarized in Box 6.2.

Another aspect of psychosocial capacity building is not only to focus on interpersonal, relationally-based use of self but also to actively work to mobilize resources for the affected group. This includes respecting and remunerating the time of affected people and members of their community when engaged in a helping process. I urged readers to consider using modalities that reflect the practices of the affected group rather than the training of the helping professional, which often tilts toward working with individuals. Groups emphasize the collective nature of problems, strengthen social connections, pool resources, reduce individual isolation and self-blame, and model collective solidarity. Even the planning of interventions should be done in teams, where at least 50% of the members are from the affected group. While talk therapy is normative in some cultures as a primary vehicle of recovery, in many societies and cultures, activities are used to bring people together, share burdens, and experience joy. It is important to ground activities in a sociocultural context, so while dancing and singing may be meaningful in some contexts, collective calligraphy and embroidery may be more appropriate in others.

Whenever possible, using a TOT model is preferable as this centralizes people indigenous to their group in the process of healing and recovery. I shared a number of examples of using TOT models: e.g., friendship benches, promitores de salud, curanderas, emotional healing networks, and collective psychosocial accompaniment.

In all cultures and societies, narratives are critical to understanding and responding to adversity, although the form of narrative varies considerably. Oral storytelling, the written word, dance, drama, music, film, and photography are some of the ways that stories can be conveyed. Narratives portray foundational myths and construct personhood and identity, delineating shared group membership and shared histories, while offering ethical and cultural guidance. In societies shaped by coloniality, all narratives are not equal; some are privileged, centralized, and dominant, while others are erased and marginalized. This can lead to people from targeted groups internalizing derogatory narratives about themselves. Externalizing these narratives and tracing them to their structural and historical origins, replacing them with affirming narratives of beauty, strength, and resistance can be liberating. Helping professionals, who are not from the group whom they are working with, can ensure that they do not inadvertently impose their narratives by having witness groups – a kind of indigenous chorus – to ensure cultural, collective, and historical fidelity.

As with all aspects of the helping process, mainstream evaluation is suffused with coloniality. I questioned Western dominance and epistemic hegemony of what is considered valid in research and evaluation, particularly in the form of privileging large-scale, quantitative research. Rather, I argued for a greater plurality of research methods, where indigenous group members control evaluation – what is being studied, how it is being managed, who conducts the research, and what is done with the data. CBPR is one way of including researchers in a group project committed to social justice. As with all aspects of psychosocial capacity building, those who are affected and being studied should be in the driver's seat and not treated as passengers in someone else's vehicle.

References

Abe, J. (2020). Beyond cultural competence, toward social transformation: Liberation psychologies and the practice of cultural humility. *Journal of Social Work Education*, *56*(4): 696–707. DOI: 10.1080/10437797.2019.1661911.

Adames, H.Y., Chavez-Duenas, N.Y., Lewis, J.A., Neville, H.A., French, B.H., Chen, G.A., & Mosley, D.V. (2022). Radical healing in psychotherapy: Addressing the wounds of racism-related stress and trauma. *Psychotherapy*. DOI: 10.1037/pst0000435.

Adessky, R.S., & Freedman, S.A. (2005). Treating survivors of terrorism while adversity continues. In Y. Danieli, D. Brom, & J. Sills (Eds.). *The trauma of terrorism: Sharing knowledge and shared care, an international handbook* (pp. 443–454). Binghamton, NY: The Haworth Press.

Barlow, J.N. (2018). Restoring optimal Black mental health and reversing intergenerational trauma in an era of Black lives matter. *Biography*, *41*(4): 895–908.

Beuregard, E.M. (2021). We should all be marching: Why humanistic psychologists should take action toward social justice. *The Humanist Psychologist*. DOI: 10.1037/hum0000269.

Blume, A.W., Morse, G.S., & Love, C. (2020). Human rights and psychology from indigenous perspectives. In N.S. Rubin & R.L. Flores (Eds.). *The Cambridge handbook of psychology and human rights* (pp. 258–272). Cambridge, UK: Cambridge University Press.

Bryant-Davis, T. (2008). *Thriving in the wake of trauma: A multicultural guide*. Lanham, MD: AltaMira Press.

Buckingham, S. L., et al. (2021). The roles of settings in supporting immigrants' resistance to injustice and oppression: A policy position statement by the society for community research and action. *American Journal of Community Psychology*, *68*: 268–291. DOI: 10.1002/ajcp.12515.

Burrage, R.L., Momper, S.L., & Gone, J.P. (2021). Beyond trauma: Decolonizing understandings of loss and healing in the Indian residential school system of Canada. *Journal of Social Issues*. DOI: 10.1111/josi.12455.

Combs, G., & Freedman, J. (2012). Narrative, post-structuralism, and social justice: Current practices in narrative therapy. *The Counseling Psychologist*, *40*: 1033. DOI: 10.1177/0011000012460662.

de la Rey, C., & Thompson, C.E. (2020). Decolonization and liberation psychology: The case of psychology in South Africa. In N.S. Rubin & R.L. Flores (Eds.). *The Cambridge handbook of psychology and human rights* (pp. 461–474). Cambridge, UK: Cambridge University Press.

Etchison, M., & Kleist, D.M. (2000). Review of narrative therapy: Research and utility. *The Family Journal: Counseling and Therapy for Couples and Families*, *8*(1): 61–66.

Falicov, C., Nino, A., & D'Urso, S. (2020). Expanding possibilities: Flexibility and solidarity with under-resourced immigrant families during the COVID-19 pandemic. *Family Process*, *59*: 865–882.

Garran, A.M., Werkmeister-Rozas, L., Kang, H.K., & Miller, J. (2021). *Racism in the United States: Implications for the helping professions* (3rd ed.). New York: Springer Publishing.

Gone, J.P. (2021). The (post)colonial predicament in community mental health services for American Indians: Explorations in alter-native psy-ence. *American Psychologist*, *76*(9): 1514–1525. DOI: 10.1037/amp0000906.

Goodman, R.D. (2015). A liberatory approach to trauma counseling: Decolonizing our trauma-informed practices. In R.D. Goodman & P.C. Gorski (Eds.). *Decolonizing multicultural counseling through social justice* (pp. 55–72). New York: Springer Publishing.

Heinrich, J. (2020). *The WEIRDest people in the world: How the west became psychologically peculiar and particularly prosperous*. New York: Farrar, Straus & Giroux Publishers.

Kang, H.K. (2015). "We're who we've been waiting for": Intergenerational community organizing for a healthy community. *Journal of Community Practice*, *23*: 126–140. DOI: 10.1080/10705422.2014.983214.

Kretzman, J.P., & McKnight, J.L. (1993). *Building communities from the inside out: A path towards finding and mobilizing a community's assets*. Chicago, IL: ACTA Publications.

Landau, J. (2007). Enhancing resilience: Communities and families as agents of change. *Family Process*, *41*(1): 351–365.

Landau, J., & Saul, J. (2004). Facilitating family and community resilience in response to major disaster. In F. Walsh & M. McGoldrick (Eds.). *Living beyond loss* (pp. 285–309). New York: W.W. Norton and Co.

Lewis, M.E.L., Akhu, A., & Hunter, C.D. (2021). Advancing African American psychology: An exploration of African American College student's definitions and use of spirit in times of stress. *Journal of Black Psychology*, *47*(7): 507–541.

Malherbe, N., Ratele, K., Adams, G., Reddy, G., & Suffla, S. (2021). A decolonial Africa(n)-centered psychology of antiracism. *Review of General Psychology*, *25*(4): 437–450. DOI: 10.1177/10892680211022992.

Miller, J. (2001). Family and community integrity. *The Journal of Sociology & Social Welfare*, *28*(4): 23–44.

Miller, J.L. (2012). *Psychosocial capacity building in response to disasters*. New York: Columbia University Press.

Miller, J.L., & Pescaroli, G. (2018). Psychosocial capacity building in response to cascading disasters: A culturally informed approach. *International Journal of Disaster Risk Reduction*, *30*: 164–171. DOI: 10.1016/j.ijdrr.2018.04.018.

Millner, U.C., Maru, M., Ismail, A., & Chakrabarti, U. (2021). Decolonizing mental health practice: Reconstructing an Asian-centric framework through a social justice lens. *Asian American Journal of Psychology*, *12*(4): 333–345. DOI: 10.1037/aap0000268.

O'Neill, L., Fraser, T., Kitchenham, A., & McDonald, V. (2018). Hidden burdens: A review of intergenerational, historical and complex trauma, implications for indigenous families. *Journal of Child and Adolescent Trauma*, *11*. DOI: 10.1007/s40653-016-0117-9.

Ortega-Williams, A., Beltran, R., Schultz, K., Henderson, Z.R., Colon, L., & Teyra, C. (2021). An integrated historical trauma and posttraumatic growth framework: A cross-cultural exploration. *Journal of Trauma & Dissociation*. DOI: 10.1080/15299732.2020.1869106

Park, Y., & Miller, J. (2006). The social ecology of Hurricane Katrina: Rewriting the discourse of "natural" disasters. *Smith College Studies in Social Work*, *76*(3): 9–24.

Park, Y., Miller, J., & Chau, B. (2010). "Everything has changed": Narratives of the Vietnamese-American community in Biloxi, Mississippi. *Journal of Sociology and Social Welfare*, *XXXVII*(3): 79–105.

Phillips, N.L., Adams, G., & Salther, P.S. (2015). Beyond adaptation: Decolonizing approaches to coping with oppression. *Journal of Social and Political Psychology*, *3*(1): 365–387. DOI: 10.5964/jspp.v3i1.310.

Reiss, D. (1987). *The family's construction of reality*. Cambridge, MA: Harvard University Press.

Rolin, S.A., Jackson, D.S., & Swartz, M.S. (2021). The bridge between racial justice and clinical practice. *Psychiatric Services*, 72(12). 1369. DOI: 10.1176/appi.ps.721204.

Rosenberg, T. (2019, July 22). Depressed? Here's a bench. Talk to me. *The New York Times*. www.nytimes.com/2019/07/22/opinion/depressed-heres-a-bench-talk-to-me.html

Sampson, R.J., Raudenbush, S.W., & Earls, F. (1997). Neighborhoods and violent crime: A multilevel study of community efficacy. *Science*, *277*(5328): 918–924.

Sanchez, V., Sanchez-Youngman, S., Dickson, E., Burgess, E., Haozous, E., Trickett, E., Baker, E., & Wallerstein, N. (2021). CBPR implementation framework for community-academic partnerships. *American Journal of Community Psychology*, *67*: 284–296. DOI: 10.1002/ajcp.12506.

Smith, L., Chambers, D., & Bratini, L. (2009). When oppression is the pathogen: The participatory development of socially just mental health practice. *American Journal of Orthopsychiatry*, *79*(2): 159–168. DOI: 10.1037/a0015353.

Summerfield, D. (2004). Cross-cultural perspectives on the medicalization of human suffering. In G. Rosen (Ed.). *Post-traumatic stress disorder: Issues and controversies*. New York: John Wiley and Sons Publishing.

Vindevogel, S., Ager, A., Schiltz, J., Broekaert, E., & Derluyn, I. (2015). Toward a culturally sensitive conceptualization of resilience: Participatory research with war-affected communities in northern Uganda. *Transcultural Psychiatry*. DOI: 10.1177/1363461514565852.

Weinberg, M. (2022). The supremacy of whiteness in social work ethics. *Ethics and Social Welfare*. DOI: 10.1080/17496535.2022.2058579.

White, M., & Epston, D. (1990). *Narrative ends to therapeutic means*. New York: W.W. Norton and Sons.

7 Responding to Critical Psychosocial Needs

Introduction

In the previous two chapters, I wrote about guiding ethical principles and a framework of intervention for decolonizing liberatory psychosocial capacity building. I emphasized responding to historical and collective trauma, full collaboration with and leadership by people indigenous to the group being supported, and how to avoid the hegemony of White, Eurocentric epistemologies, theories, and helping practices when working domestically and internationally with socially targeted, oppressed, and marginalized groups. A major focus was on developing TOT models that broke from a classical therapy and counseling mold (see Box 6.2). In this chapter, I discuss how this approach can be integrated with direct interventions responding to critical psychosocial needs.

As with other chapters in the book, I endeavor to strike a balance between acknowledging and validating the destructive consequences of social oppression while respecting, honoring, and celebrating sources of strength and resilience. I have also been cautious about being proscriptive about specific interventions and encouraging the evolution of local helping processes rather than universal interventions. In this chapter, I develop what I mentioned in Chapter 1, how Western, "evidence-based" practices can judiciously, carefully, and humbly be integrated with indigenous knowledge and wisdom by helping professionals.

I have been stressing the importance of the unique social ecology for a given group in a specific matrix of time and place in shaping our understanding of the present-day needs of a group. The social ecology also considers the collective history and consequent group trauma experienced by affected people, and how they have resisted and developed ways of survival, using a range of strategies, usually

DOI: 10.4324/9781003021162-7

based on a foundation of traditional, indigenous epistemologies and cultural practices.

There are predictable reactions and consequences to historical and collective trauma, as well as violence, which I covered in the first four chapters, which I have summarized in Figure 7.1.

Historical, Collective and Structural Oppression and Exposure to Violence are overlapping categories and often groups and their members fall into all of these categories. This figure summarizes some of the most common psychosocial consequences that were described in Chapters 2–4. (A full list would be much longer). I have divided reactions up into Individual, Interpersonal/Family and Collective/Community although these are artificial distinctions as reactions cross boundaries and all levels are interrelated.

Individual

- Neurological/allostatic overload
- Anxiety
- Ongoing apprehension and wariness.
- Repetitive, ruminative thoughts
- Complex Trauma
- Avoidance
- Hyperalertness, hypervigilance, and a high state of arousal
- Difficulty with self-calming
- Dysregulated affect
- Emotional flooding
- Repeated triggering and re-experiencing traumatic events
- Wariness, mistrust, suspicion
- Misreading current social situations as being more threatening than they are based on complex trauma.
- Cumulative health stressors
- Somatic complaints
- Eating and sleeping disorders
- Health and medical risks and vulnerability
- Weakened immune system
- Negative consequences for infant and maternal health
- Less access to quality health care

Figure 7.1 Negative Psychosocial Consequences of Historical, Collective, and Structural Oppression and Exposure to Violence

- Depression
- Psychic numbing
- Disturbances of self-organization
- Disassociation
- Negative self-concept
- Depression
- Hopelessness and despair
- Self-cutting
- Suicide risks
- Threats to integrity of belief and meaning-making systems.
- Race-based and other identity based traumatic stress
- Self-blame
- Guilt and shame
- Moral injury
- Remorse

Interpersonal and Family

- Relationship strains
- Difficulty engaging in intimate relationships and emotional distance
- Mistrust of others
- Struggles to maintain boundaries.
- Domestic tension and violence
- Fear for children and concern about ability to keep them safe
- Intergenerational transmission of high levels of anxiety and arousal
- Experiencing microaggressions
- Lost moments of intimacy and joy
- Loss of family hope
- Weakening of family cohesion
- Higher rates of teenage pregnancy
- Role changes and role reversal
- Collective, traumatic grief

Collective and Community

- Lack of educational and economic opportunities
- Threats to adequate shelter and food.

Figure 7.1 (Continued)

- Historical trauma
- Collective trauma
- Cultural erasure and trauma
- Blocking of transitional pathways
- Discriminating against others
- Formal and informal residential segregation
- Formal and informal workplace segregation
- Having to conform to white-dominant group logic and norms in the workplace
- Lack of political power
- Active targeting by institutions of the state – e.g., police, armed forces, border patrols
- Repeated exposure to violence
- Dehumanizing of members of other groups
- Passive bystanders
- Intergroup power struggles and ethnic competition.
- Armed Conflict and war
- Coups
- Undermined social trust and cohesion.
- Being the object rather than author of collective narratives.
- Land disputes

Figure 7.1 (Continued)

There are also broad strategies to respond to these reactions, although they must be offered within a framework of sociocultural integrity; the expression of needs and what is helpful in response has meaning within a unique sociocultural context. For example, I believe that it is a universal benefit to be able to calm oneself when emotionally activated, but as to how we understand what emotional activation looks like and the ways of achieving self-calming vary considerably. I will draw upon research (particularly by BIPOC practitioners), my own international practice experience and protocols developed (mostly by Westerners) from responding to wars and disasters (e.g., Hobfoll et al., 2007; Skills for Psychological recovery – Berkowitz et al., 2010).

Critical Psychosocial Needs

Of course, there are many psychosocial needs in the wake of violence and collective oppression as I have been discussing but I will focus on safety, re-establishing social connections, and the ability to self-calm. Another critical need involves re-establishing HOPE (Hope, Optimism, Power, and Efficacy) and accessing a transcendent sense of meaning and/or spirituality. I emphasize these four areas because they repeatedly have surfaced in research about war and disasters and I consistently encounter them in my psychosocial work. They encompass the five areas that Hobfoll et al. (2007) identified in their seminal article reviewing empirical studies about the most important interventions in mid-term mass trauma interventions: (1) safety; (2) calming; (3) collective and self-efficacy; (4) connectedness; and (5) hope. Berkowitz et al. (2010) in their model Skills for Psychological Recovery identified building problem-solving skills, promoting positive activities, managing reactions, promoting helpful thinking, and rebuilding healthy social connections, which will be covered in this discussion. I have referred to these protocols because they are used in many training and response programs around the world, although they are developed from a Western standpoint. I am focusing on "mid-term" interventions, rather than psychological first aid, which was developed as immediate short-term, crisis interventions in the wake of a catastrophe because social oppression is an ongoing phenomenon and acute incidents are part of a longer-standing, enduring pattern.

I have found that these essential needs transcend cultures and borders although what they *mean* to affected people varies. They are not discrete categories and intersect: e.g., being with other people and feeling connected can enhance safety, and feeling safe makes it easier to sustain social connections. I will also weave in four general approaches that I have found can be adapted for work with communities and individuals from a range of sociocultural contexts: (1) CBT approaches, particularly control-focused behavioral therapy; (2) EMDR; (3) self-calming techniques; and (4) intentional self-care.

Safety and Security

What is central to all forms of collective and historical oppression and all types of violence is that they *intentionally* undermine the safety and security of those being targeted. In the early 20th century, when German imperialists were exploiting the diamond veins of "Southwest Africa" (Namibia), they engaged in genocide against the indigenous Herero and Nama peoples, issuing exterminating orders and forcing them from their land (Hammer, 2021). They also imported members of the Ovambo tribe, from another part of the territory to work their diamond mines, developing a system of forced, conscripted labor that weakened any capacity to feel safe and secure – not allowing workers to construct shelters or wear warm clothes, so that they had to sleep, unprotected, outside on sand dunes where many perished from hypothermia or starvation. The workers were forced to labor seven days a week and were in a perpetual state of instability and unsafety. This dynamic of violence, terror, and shattering any sense of safety and security characterized much of Western coloniality and its abominations, including slavery, forced labor, land theft, breaking up families, internment, ethnic cleansing, genocide, and perpetual subjugation. When the very essence of social oppression and domination is to disrupt security, safety is hard to come by.

It is not as if threatening conditions have evaporated or diminished, they continue for many and thus safety is being sought in an ongoing sociopolitical storm. As I have discussed, historical trauma and ongoing collective trauma are usually intertwined; if there is historical trauma, there is collective trauma and vice versa. In Chapter 2, I considered the intergenerational legacies of being a member of a group that has been historically oppressed and how difficult it is to feel safe and secure in the world, even when not facing immediate threats; the knowledge that your group that was targeted for violence does not fade. Thus, whether the threat is immediate and constant or a historical legacy, or both, members of a socio-politically targeted group often find it difficult to establish a secure foundation of safety. However, facing ongoing threats to self, family, and community presents particular challenges to feeling protected and secure.

And yet safety is essential for psychosocial recovery (Auerbach & Shiro-Gelrud, 2010; Bryant-Davis, 2005; Hobfoll et al., 2007; Miller, 2012). It is the foundation that allows for healing and recovery to occur although this is difficult to achieve when constantly on high alert, being hyper-aroused and activated, feeling a profound sense of social mistrust and a lack of ability to exert control and protect oneself and others. I have come to view safety as a spectrum ranging from being completely unsafe to feeling totally safe, with most people falling along the spectrum. People can feel physically unsafe, socially unsafe, or emotionally unsafe, and often a combination. Even those with privilege and social cushioning have times of feeling unsafe and members or targeted groups have developed ways of creating moments and pockets of safety within a hostile environment. Beverly Tatum (2017) described this in her book *Why are all the Black kids sitting together in the cafeteria*, when a sub-group intentionally self-isolates to buffer themselves from microaggressions and other repeated assaults. While I will always work in the short and long term for the structural changes that lead to safety for all, in practice, there are situations and groups of people where the immediate step of psychosocial support is to help them to achieve relative safety (Box 7.1).

Box 7.1 Assessing Safety

- Is the person or group in immediate danger?
- What is the nature of the threats and hazards and what opportunities for safety exist?
- Are there resources and social supports available that can be mobilized to protect people?
- Are there moments, spaces, and places where people can feel safe, at least temporarily?
- Are there brief times for people to experience joy, pleasure, connection, and meaning?
- Are there people within a targeted group who are safer than others and can offer buffering and protection?
- What has been the history of safety and security for a group and what are expectations for safety?
- What protections are available for decreasing risk?
- How safe or unsafe is the helping professional and what are the implications of this?

For the purposes of this book, a critical factor of safety is one's social identities. Do the police or army target people who look like me? Is my neighborhood being excluded or threatened by others? Am I in a group, or class, or workplace setting where I am the only person who is BIPOC, or Queer, or who speaks with a particular accent?

When trying to ensure safety it is important to consider the following:

- Is the person or group in immediate danger?
- What is the nature of threats and hazards and what opportunities for safety exist?
- Are there resources and social supports available that can be mobilized to protect people?
- Are there moments, spaces, and places where people can feel safe, at least temporarily?
- Are there brief times for people to experience joy, pleasure, connection, and meaning?
- Are there people within a targeted group who are safer than others and can offer buffering and protection?
- What has been the history of safety and security for a group and what are expectations for safety?

- What protections are available for decreasing risk?
- How safe or unsafe is the helping professional and what are the implications of this?

The answers to these questions help to assess how grave the danger is and what possibilities for relative safety are available. Physical safety and psychological safety are closely intertwined, and all forms of threats to safety are profound and challenging, but it can be helpful to distinguish between a physically unsafe situation – e.g., an armed attack on a village – and a psychologically unsafe situation – e.g., the abrogation of human and legal rights. Some relevant dimensions of threat assessment are immediacy, constancy, severity, and likelihood of reoccurrence.

Another important dimension is power and control. For example, in the invasion of Ukraine by Russia in 2022, there is asymmetrical aggression from Russia and overwhelming differentials in military force and capability. But the war is being fought in Ukraine, where there is a government and military troops trying to protect civilians on their home soil. There are also international observers and efforts by the U.N. and other entities to broker a ceasefire, as ineffectual as they are. Refugee camps are notoriously unsafe, but some have U.N. troops, local police, or the presence of NGOs to try and offer a modicum of protection for people. Contrast this with living in an isolated village in a country where militias, White supremacists, or cartels are terrorizing a population and there is no credible force to mitigate this. Often there is a mixture of the aforementioned situations, such as the internally displaced persons camps in Northern Uganda during the 20-year armed conflict between the Ugandan government and the Lord's Resistance Army. While ostensibly the army was there to protect people, they often retreated at night leaving residents in a terrifying and dangerous situation and also engaged in their own atrocities directed at civilians.

Cognitive Behavioral Approaches and Safety

Cognitive behavioral therapies are used to treat anxiety, depression, overwhelming affect, mental illness, substance abuse disorders, eating disorders, and relationship problems (American Psychological Association, 2022). There has been a great deal of research to demonstrate its effectiveness with these disorders and is often what is meant by "evidence-based practice." Some of its core tenets are as follows:

1. Psychological problems are based, in part, on faulty or unhelpful ways of thinking.

2. Psychological problems are based, in part, on learned patterns of unhelpful behavior.
3. People suffering from psychological problems can learn better ways of coping with them, thereby relieving their symptoms and becoming more effective in their lives.

Changes in thinking involve the following:

- Learning to recognize cognitive distortions that create secondary problems in addition to initial threats and trauma and to learn re-evaluation skills to weigh up and appraise the current situation. It is important to be able to discern between adaptive and maladaptive avoidance strategies (Adessky & Freedman, 2005).
- Developing greater metacognition to be able to track one's thought patterns, which then makes it possible to interrupt or alter them.
- Gaining a better understanding of the behaviors and motivations of others, which is also a key component of emotional intelligence.
- Developing and using problem-solving skills to cope with difficult situations.
- Learning to develop a greater sense of confidence in one's efficacy and ability to change patterns.

Changes in behavioral patterns involve the following:

- Trying to work on one's fears, as avoidance is a common and often counterproductive strategy. This can involve controlled exposure and imagining dangerous situations.
- Using role-playing to prepare for potentially problematic interactions with others.
- Learning to calm one's mind and relax one's body, which I will cover in greater detail in the section on self-calming.

CBT techniques often involve homework and exercises, and there is an emphasis on people learning to treat themselves, which is very helpful in dangerous situations where there is usually a paucity of trained clinicians or therapy is not normative or stigmatized. There is also an emphasis on coping skills in the present moment, which is useful for threatening situations.

Although there are strictly behavioral or cognitive therapies, they are usually used in combination with one another. There are many varieties of cognitive behavioral therapies, and rather than describing them all, I will list some of the most common ones and readers can delve into them more deeply if they wish:

- Cognitive processing therapy
- Trauma-informed CBT
- Mindfulness-based CBT
- Dialectical-behavioral therapy
- Acceptance and commitment therapy
- Rational-emotive behavior therapy
- Stress inoculation training
- Functional analytic psychotherapy
- Narrative exposure therapy

There are also CBT treatments for couples and families including:

- Emotionally focused couples' therapy
- Cognitive behavioral therapy for couples
- Cognitive-behavioral family therapy
- Relational life therapy
- Internal family systems therapy
- Functional family therapy
- Behavioral parent training

One therapeutic approach within the umbrella of cognitive behavioral therapies that I have found is particularly useful when safety is still uncertain is control-focused behavioral treatment (CFBT) (Basoglu & Salcioglu, 2011). The approach has certain advantages for the unstable and risky situation: it is brief and can even be delivered in a single session, lay people can be trained in it, it is adaptable to different cultural contexts, and the skills do not have to be disseminated by therapists – they can be communicated by mass media and self-help tools. It seeks to give people a feeling of a greater sense of control through sequenced exposure to the threatening situation rather than "habituation." When there is a lack of control and severe anxiety associated with traumatic events there are often attempts to avoid further exposure – which is warranted in ongoing threat situations – but can be counterproductive when this constricts movement to work, engagement with family, friends, and activities, access to services, and avoiding potential places of restoration. However, discernment between current threats and reactions to previous threats that engender fear and anxiety but are no longer threatening is critical when using this approach. Although it is asking a lot of people, it is helping them to avoid dangerous situations and protect themselves but allows for creating pockets of control and zones of safety within a threatening milieu.

When CFBT interventions occur in groups, there are advantages. It breaks down isolation, fosters social connections, mutual learning, and support, and destigmatizes interventions. Given that social oppression targets groups of people, groups are a collective way of responding and resisting. Many people can be trained at once and can in turn train others. Group members can help other group members to adapt or correct how they are using the model. It also means that there are witnesses to both the risks and the courage to confront them. It also works to break down the barrier between victims and bystanders; in groups, active bystanding can be the norm, as group members share risks and care for one another.

An example of using CFBT is when my colleague and I ran a group for survivors of political oppression that was still ongoing (see Miller & Wang, 2017 for a detailed description of group sessions). I have altered some details to protect people's safety. Group members were LGBTQ activists who had protested for their rights in public places in a country where this was unacceptable. They were the targets of government surveillance, and all had spent time in jail. Their families were often being "visited." A number of them had been arrested at bus stops and other public venues and had developed a fear of being on the street and of traveling. They were also fearful of being confronted or arrested at work or in their huts and had classic trauma responses anticipating this: hyper-alertness, disassociation, triggering and emotional flooding, difficulty concentrating, relationship strains, and a loss of hope.

One technique that we introduced was CFBT to help group members gain greater control over their lives by having an ability to be in public and travel. It was still a dangerous situation – they could be picked up, arrested, and interrogated without warning. There were also risks for the group facilitators who were supporting them. Group members identified being able to walk past places where they had been arrested without having overwhelming panic attacks as a goal. We spent time looking at realistic threats – such as being followed by the police – and more benign places that were triggering – such as bus stops.

We developed a plan where pairs of group members would walk by places that held terror for at least one of them. They started off slowly – going a few blocks away from a triggering bus stop, getting closer step by step, and eventually walking past it together. They eventually did this on their own but were on the phone with their "buddy" as they did this. One group member eventually reported the following:

> I asked one of my friends to go to the bus station with me. We bought some snacks and hung out in the station for quite a while. We chatted. I asked my friend to take my picture, and I chose the nicest one and put it on my Facebook page with the title "A nice day hanging out with my friend at the bus station," and many friends gave me positive feedback, though they may not know why I hung out at this bus station. Their feedback brought me a lot of positive energy and reduced my anxious feelings. The next time I needed to go to the other side of town to attend a meeting. I asked my colleague to take the bus with me. I took a selfie with him and posted it on Facebook again, with the title "First bus ride in 3 months."
>
> (Miller & Wang, 2017)

I share this as an example of how CFBT could be adapted to a dangerous situation, drawing on social supports and trying to carve out safer spaces and the ability to be able to function more fully, despite still living in fear.

Activities to Increase a Sense of Safety

As mentioned earlier, there are many advantages to using CFBT in a group setting and one of the advantages of using activities is that they are also done in groups. They also generate a sense of flow, play, joy, and pleasure which at least temporarily mitigate against the negative thoughts and feelings associated with feeling unsafe. For some people, activities are easier to access and participate in than discussions when they are feeling unsafe. Activities should be culturally syntonic, as I have discussed throughout the book so they help people to connect with their history and cultural practices, which can feel empowering.

The best summary of activities to increase a sense of safety that I have encountered is Thema Bryant-Davis' *Thriving in the wake of trauma* (2005). Embedded in the activities are a range of ways to engage in storytelling. Bryant-Davis outlines a range of activities that can be adapted to an array of cultural contexts (Box 7.2).

Box 7.2 Activities That Foster a Sense of Safety

- Journaling or writing poems about times, places, and people that help a person to feel safe and what small steps can be taken toward feeling safer.
- Movement and dance connect people to one another and their culture and releases a sense of pleasure.
- Drawing, working with clay, and taking photographs and mounting a collage or installation can portray safety and can be shared with other group members.
- Music is often healing and singing together or playing instruments together, such as drumming are powerful activities that can help people to feel safer.
- The use of skits and drama can portray difficult and frightening things in a compelling way. It is always important that there is a healing component to the sketches.
- Focusing on spirituality, and, if appropriate, praying together can help people to find a sense of safety through collective unity and transcendent meaning.
- Being in nature connects people to a wider space and universe and can also pleasurably activate the senses.
- Activism is always empowering and resistance to unsafe conditions, however small or surreptitious helps to create a sense of collective efficacy.

Source: Taken from Thema Bryant-Davis (2005) Thriving in the Wake of Trauma

- Journaling or writing poems about times, places, and people that help a person to feel safe and what small steps can be taken toward feeling safer.
- There are many kinds of movement that can be used to illustrate feeling unsafe and safe. This can be done by assuming certain postures, but I have also found in my work in Uganda that weaving in dancing to workshops addressing collective trauma inevitably connects people to one another and their culture and releases a sense of pleasure.

- Drawing, working with clay, and taking photographs and mounting a collage or installation can portray safety and can be shared with other group members.
- Music is often healing and singing together or playing instruments together, such as drumming are powerful activities that can help people to feel safer. I will consider more about this in the section where I discuss EMDR.
- The use of skits and drama can portray difficult and frightening things in a compelling way. It is always important that there is a healing component to the sketches. I found in my work in Haiti that having groups develop hip-hop songs that told stories about fear and redemption were effective in integrating music, culture, teamwork, and storytelling.
- Focusing on spirituality, and, if appropriate, praying together can help people to find a sense of safety through collective unity and transcendent meaning.
- Being in nature connects people to a wider space and universe and can also pleasurably activate the senses.
- Activism is always empowering and resistance to unsafe conditions, however small or surreptitious helps to create a sense of collective efficacy.

Summary of Key Points About Safety

Safety is essential for psychosocial healing and recovery and yet there are many people who find themselves in ongoing unsafe situations. There is a spectrum of what it means to feel safe, and it is helpful to think of ways that targeted people can at least achieve relative safety or moments of safety. It is very important to assess the nature of the risks and to ensure that interventions do not ever lead to greater peril. Part of the assessment includes the unique risks for people with certain social identities as well as examining what collective means of resistance and buffering are available.

When thinking about creating pockets of safety, it is critical that affected people direct what will lead them to feel safer. Working in groups breaks down social isolation, creates solidarity, enhances social connections and support, and destigmatizes feelings of fear and anxiety. Groups also amplify coping strategies that are shared with others. CBT treatments are often more amenable to short-term interventions and self-directed learning and progress, with CFBT being a specific CBT treatment that lends itself to unsafe situations where there few therapists or psychosocial workers. Activities are also important ways that people can connect with their cultural practices and collectively explore what makes them feel unsafe and ways of creating places of refuge and a sense of efficacy.

Social Connections and Social Support

It is generally acknowledged by most psychosocial theorists and workers that social support is a critical factor in psychosocial recovery and well-being (e.g., Berkowitz et al., 2010; Bryant-Davis, 2005; Christakis & Fowler, 2009; Hobfoll et al., 2007; Miller, 2012). We are all interconnected and interdependent, which is why groups and collective responses to violence and social targeting are so helpful. The expectations about the nature of social relations – both within and outside of families – vary considerably between cultures and societies as do the form that social networks take. It is worth noting that the majority of the world's societies view interconnectedness and an interdependent self as normative, which is at odds with much psychological theory developed in the West.

Historical and collective trauma and being the target of collective violence have the potential to place a great deal of strain on social relations and networks. People are divided into social categories, are often fighting for their own and their family's survival, and are overwhelmed by negative thoughts and feelings. Social trust is a necessary ingredient of significant relationships and trust is battered by exploitation and dehumanization. Existing social divisions can become magnified. And yet communities that have survived historical trauma have often become more tightly knit and cohesive; effective resistance requires collaboration and unity. Thus, social connections can be both a casualty of sociopolitical targeting and the filaments that scaffold collective defiance and recovery.

As with all aspects of psychosocial support and recovery, an assessment and inventory of resources are helpful (Box 7.3).

Box 7.3 Questions About Social Support

- What are the expectations for social support from within the family? From within the community? From secular sources, such as government, civic associations, and NGOs? From religious networks and communities?
- What social networks have endured violence and social oppression and how did they adapt in order to survive?

- What structural factors foster isolation and how have social networks been damaged and lost?
- How is leadership managed to enhance the capacities of social networks and in what ways can leaders undermine social networks?
- What meaningful roles are available to people within collectivities and social networks?
- What internal consequences of structural oppression – e.g., mistrust and overwhelming affect – need to be worked on in order for people to reestablish social networks?
- What are the different types of social relations that people rely on – e.g., family, friends, cultural leaders, spiritual leaders and faith healers, and professionals?
- Who do people go to for emotional support, advice, recreation, financial help, cultural knowledge, and help with navigating a new environment?

There are also other aspects of social networks that should be considered. For example, how large should they be? A large social network offers, in theory, greater resources and opportunities for support and protection. But the larger a social network, often the more diffuse it becomes. Does this lead to weaker ties and trust? The larger a social network, the more challenging it is to intimately know everyone who is in it. This can also risk a greater likelihood of bad actors (e.g., government informers) infiltrating social networks which can be destructive and damaging to the network and its members. Even when this is not actually happening, the fear and suspicion that it might happen can weaken social trust within the social network. In the example I used in the previous section about the LGBTQ activists, infiltration was a very distinct possibility if the core group became larger and it was very important to vet who could be part of the network.

Another variable is how homogenous or heterogenous the network is. Some networks are homogenous in particular ways, such as group members sharing some aspect of social identity – e.g., gender and race/ethnicity. Or the network comes from a particular neighborhood, village, or region. This usually means that there is a greater similarity that can bond group members with one another, reducing the need to explain oneself and cutting down on intentional or unintentional assaults, such as microaggressions. It can also help with preserving cultural unity in the face of threats from globalization and coloniality.

In conversations I have had with Hazara immigrants to the United States, they stressed how important it was for them and their families to be settled in an area with other Hazara families to provide the benefits of a culturally syntonic social network as they navigated a new and at times hostile society and culture. Hobfoll et al. (2007), citing Kinzie et al., note that adolescent refugees from the Khmer Rouge genocide had lower levels of PTSD, substance abuse, and depression when reunited with at least one family member, compared with those not reunited. Social media is another way that homogenous social support groups can form and be maintained. This can be both supportive but also narrow a group's exposure to varied perspectives and important information and reinforce misinformation and negative feelings toward people who are different or think in another way.

On the other hand, more diverse or heterogenous social networks offer a greater variety of perspectives and resources. Most social networks form organically and naturally, but there are times when intentionality can be helpful when considering the most robust and effective social networks to offer support and resist oppression. As with all that has been discussed in this book, it is important for those in the affected group to take leadership in mapping out expansions, contractions, and modifications to social networks. Outside helping professionals can support these efforts and, if asked, help group members to plan and identify network resources. Heaney and Israel (2008) identify four ways that helping professionals can support social networks:

1. Expanding existing network linkages
2. Developing new network linkages
3. Strengthening networks through the use of indigenous and local residents and helpers
4. Enhancing networks through community capacity building and problem solving

To this end, helping professionals can also support a training-of-trainers model to improve the ability of affected people to deepen and expand their social networks. What is critical is to recognize the value and significance of social networks in resisting, healing, and recovery.

Ability to Self-Calm and Manage Strong Emotional Reactions

The ability to self-calm and manage strong emotional reactions is critical for a person to feel that they are regaining a sense of control when they have experienced major disasters (Berkowitz et al., 2010; Bryant-Davis, 2005; Halpern & Tramontin, 2007; Hobfoll et al., 2007; Miller, 2012). The same holds true for members of socio-politically targeted groups. In prior chapters, I have covered a range of thoughts, feelings, behaviors, interpersonal consequences, and other strong reactions to historical and collective oppression and violence. Common feelings such as fear, anger, shame, and humiliation are destabilizing and contribute to depression, suicidality, aggression toward others, and substance abuse. Traumatic reactions include repetitive thoughts, cognitive confusion, emotional flooding, numbing, avoidance, and social withdrawal. Fear of recurring oppression, such as racist incidents, instills a sense of hypervigilance and contributes to sleeplessness (Kang & Burton, 2014). Without having the tools to manage these reactions, people feel overwhelmed, depleted, and lose their sense of efficacy and hope. All of this undermines group cohesion and the collective capacity to effectively resist cultural erasure, social targeting, and the myriad forms of violence and oppression.

Many of the CBT interventions listed in the previous section are attempts to help people to manage such reactions and to gain a better sense of self-control and mastery. And yet most of them rely on a trained professional – usually a therapist – who is able to see a person – usually individually – for a number of sessions. When therapists are available and accessible and therapy is socially and culturally syntonic, such interventions can effectively respond to managing reactions. But as Gone (2021) reported Traveling Thunder as saying, such interventions are often not part of a group's cultural traditions and practices, which could be said by the majority of the world's population. Thus, they are not only perceived as alien but have the iatrogenic potential to undermine practices that have been helpful in the past and may be helpful in the future. And these interventions were incubated in individualist cultures rather than collectivist contexts.

Thus, while the management of overwhelming reactions and strengthening the ability to self-calm is a goal that transcends sociocultural boundaries, the means and ways of achieving this significantly vary. Even the meaning and social construction of reactions differ. Take anger as an example – in some contexts, anger is viewed as a negative, destructive force that also hurts the person carrying it, and psychotherapy is offered to reduce it. It can be experienced as disrespectful, inappropriate, and damaging. Yet, as Beuregard (2021) notes, anger is often understandable and justified given certain social conditions and can fuel and energize social justice movements and sustained resistance. Treating it as an inappropriate or pathological individual reaction can detract from this. I have worked with students from central Asia who have taught me that they view anger as something to hold on to and to not forget the persons or conditions that provoked their anger or try to mitigate or extinguish it; they view this as critical to survival.

Of course, there are destructive aspects of anger – e.g., physiological, emotional, and interpersonal – and there can be constructive elements to it – e.g., social activism and greater in-group cohesion – so perhaps the task is to assess the destructive and constructive dimensions in a nuanced way. But the specific sociocultural context where anger occurs should inform such appraisals and affected people should determine the goals of responding to an emotion such as anger.

So how can helping professionals know what are the best ways to help members of a particular group manage their reactions? Falicov et al. (2020) have offered some guidelines for such efforts. They should be strength-based rather than deficit oriented and start with an ecological/systems orientation so that interventions are never decontextualized. Those seeking help should be viewed as experts about their own lives, culture, and societies and their preferences should guide interventions. Cultural diversity is important, but it is also vital not to overly generalize or stereotype cultural practices and traditions. Services should be located in the community, and there needs to be flexibility about how services are offered, and I would add, how resources are allocated.

These are some different ways that I have observed people managing overwhelming reactions:

- Primarily in urban North America and Europe, through psychotherapy. This includes desensitizing, problem solving, stress inoculation, anxiety management, positive thinking, and other cognitive approaches. But living within a Western context are many subgroups who are wary of therapy and view it as stigmatizing. And there are also psychotherapeutic practices and interventions used by people in non-Western countries and societies.
- Through psychopharmacological interventions, depending on availability and how normative such interventions are.
- In many parts of the world and within certain group cultures, through singing, dancing, drumming, and playing together.
- Journaling, poetry, song writing, photography, and other artist/narrative approaches.
- Through collective religious practices – such as attending churches, mosques, and temples for prayers and services.

- Through mindfulness practices and breathing exercises – some grounded in religious traditions, while others are secular.
- Achieving transcendent meaning about one's circumstances and reactions.
- Working together as activists in social movements and resisting oppression.
- Spending time with family and friends.
- Exercise and body movement, both vigorous and more contemplative, such as yoga and Tai-Chi.
- Exposure to nature.
- Distraction, enjoyment, and engaging in positive activities.
- Self-care – all of the aforementioned can be a form of self-care, but individuals will identify other self-care practices that have sustained them in the past that may not be included on this list.

This is a partial menu that people can draw upon. While some are more familiar within a specific cultural milieu, the specific nature of the reactions and the actual situation are important factors. If someone has just been attacked or is feeling highly mistrustful, asking them to do something in a group may feel too activating and overwhelming. But for others, being alone accentuates ruminative thinking and feeling isolated and unprotected, while being with others, at least in certain contexts and with certain people, can be soothing and comforting. The meaning of boundaries varies considerably between cultures and for people within particular cultural contexts. This is why assessing what people need should be done directly or in collaboration with affected people and cultural insiders.

Mindfulness

I would like to share some basic mindfulness techniques. As with everything else, some will fit better with particular people or different cultural settings than others. I have effectively used all of the techniques on this list with people in China, Uganda, Haiti, Sri Lanka, the UK, and the United States, adapting them with group participants. All can be taught, and there are many resources on the Internet to better understand both their rationale and how to engage with them. There are a range of recommendations for how long some mindfulness techniques should take; I have found that it is important for this to be interactive with a group or person and to not rigidly adhere to a particular time frame. For example, a five-minute body scan might be less effective than a ½ hour scan, but it may be all that there is time for or that a person can tolerate or focus on and it is usually better than nothing.

While mindfulness is more often than not soothing, calming, and healing, this is not always the case, particularly when someone is having strong trauma reactions and is having difficulty with either focusing or is overwhelmed by negative feelings, including dissociation and self-fragmentation. It is important in such situations that people do not close their eyes, but rather attempts are made to help the person to ground themselves in the present moment with their eyes open. It is advisable to go slowly, step by step, and constantly check in with people, gently inviting them to try something and also encouraging them to not do anything that seems too painful, difficult, or triggering. It can be helpful to work out in advance with group members what they can do if activated – e.g., open their eyes, count objects in the room, and focus on their breathing. With that in mind, these are some basic mindfulness techniques that I have used and were inspired by many spiritual practices, teachers, and practitioners

- **Grounding** – With open eyes, a person can be invited to notice what is in their immediate environment – e.g., what their body is touching such as a chair, the room or outside temperature, objects that they can see, and sounds that they can hear. It can be helpful to ask someone to list five things that they can touch, see, hear, and so on. This can aid with bringing a person into the present when they are reexperiencing a frightening or overwhelming incident or situation.
- **Senses** – While this can be part of grounding, in addition, it can be helpful to go through all of the senses, one by one. Sometimes it helps to linger on one sense – such as hearing and noticing sounds as they arise and dissipate. If people can tolerate having their eyes closed, it can be easier to focus on sounds, smells, or tastes, but as mentioned earlier, this should be approached cautiously. If there are birds singing, it can be helpful to focus on them which connects with the mindfulness practice of being in nature, listed below.
- **Body Scan** – Much of the time, systematically noticing what is going on in different places of the body by sequentially paying attention to them is calming and can also allow people to let

Figure 7.2 Summary of Mindfulness Techniques

go of tension being held in certain locations or even to better tolerate pain. Some body scans recommend simply bringing attention to a body region and noticing, while others encourage participants to breathe into tension points – such as stiff shoulders – and to try and release and let go. As with the other techniques, caution is warranted as some people may be triggered by focusing on certain parts of the body; e.g., someone who has been sexually assaulted may find concentrating on particular body regions to be re-triggering or activating. In such situations, selective body scans directed by the affected person are called for.

- **Focusing on the Breath** – This is often part of Buddhist and yogic meditation practices but can be done as a stand-alone technique. Again, there are different approaches. One is to just notice the breath, focusing on the nostrils or on the rising and falling of the chest or belly. For some, placing their hand on their belly and noticing it swelling and diminishing can be a helpful breathing exercise known as "belly breathing." Counting the number of breaths is another way to deepen focus. Additional techniques include trying to slow down the breath – such as slowly counting to five on an in-breath, holding for a second, and then counting a slow exhalation (5–6) and repeating. Some people prefer to focus on breathing with their eyes open and others with their eyes closed. It is normal for people to become distracted and have thoughts or feelings. Most practices recommend noting this – e.g., "thinking" – but not exploring the thoughts and gently trying to return to paying attention to breathing. Tenderness and normalizing distraction are key as it can be easy to feel self-critical or judgmental or to become discouraged.
- **Loving Kindness and Sympathetic Joy for Others** – There are a cluster of mindfulness practices that focus on cultivating feelings of connection, love, compassion, and appreciation of others. They often involve visualizing another person and reciting a mantra – such as may you be happy, may you be healthy, may you be safe, and may you be at ease. Usually, the first person to do this with is oneself – loving and caring for oneself makes it possible to be compassionate with others. However, I have found that with some people and in some cultural contexts,

Figure 7.2 (Continued)

people can have more difficulty doing this with themselves than with others. If this is the case, it is fine to start by focusing on other people. A helpful adaptation is to imagine someone who loves you wishing you good things, such as a parent, friend, or child; seeing yourself through their eyes. Some meditations involve first sending loving kindness to someone who you find easy – such as a partner, parent, or benefactor – then moving to do this with someone who you feel more neutral about, and in some instances eventually with a "difficult person." However, in the interest of self-calming, this last person might be left out as the difficult person may personify the violence and oppression being experienced and it is asking a lot for people who are already activated to feel loving kindness and compassion for such a person. Sympathetic joy is focusing on those with whom we are connected and thinking of something good going on in their lives, and to intentionally feel grateful for that and wish them even greater happiness.

- **Gratitude** – There are many ways for people to focus on what they are grateful for, even in the midst of appalling challenges and lack of safety. This in no way minimizes the threats or the need to resist but there are usually still things to be grateful for. Victor Frankl and Primo Levi wrote about gratitude and finding meaning even when in death camps during World War II. Examples are feeling grateful for people engaged in the same struggle, family, special times in the past, religious beliefs, or basic needs being met such as being able to drink or stay warm, if this is the case. Gratitude mindfulness can be done by using one's imagination or can involve sharing what one is grateful for with others or writing it down. Just as the zones of relative safety mentioned earlier attempt to diffuse the hegemony of threatening situations, focusing on gratitude despite terrible things happening can serve a similar purpose.
- **Altruism** – I have found that this is a form of mindfulness or spiritual practice. Giving to and helping others can stimulate a sense of feeling good about oneself as well as being connected with others. Helping those experiencing the same fears can feel empowering such as older children comforting younger children and in many instances a sense of oneness with others, a collectivity, or community. Altruism not only helps a person

Figure 7.2 (Continued)

with their own reactions but can also transform fear and anxiety into activism.

- **Letting Go and Recommitting** – The late Vietnamese Zen master Thich Nhat Hanh wrote many books and developed many meditations – some of which can be accessed online – that focus on letting go of regret or anger, forgiving yourself (and others only if helpful and appropriate) and recommitting to one's values and intentions. Part of the power of these meditations is that they acknowledge our own frailty, which is helpful as many people suffering oppression struggle with self-blame or regret – e.g., "why didn't I respond to that more forcefully or effectively?" Acknowledging this and letting go also speaks to starting anew, recognizing that falling is not a failure and that there are new chances and opportunities to resist and to try and protect oneself, family, and community.
- **Everyday, Every Moment Mindfulness** – In general, it can be helpful for a person to be living in the moment and to focus on what is going on inside and outside of them. This can cut down on ruminations or negative memories. However, as with other mindfulness practices, it can be unhelpful for people to focus on how activated their bodies are. And in menacing situations, it can raise anxiety to notice how hazardous the environment is, although by being aware it can help a person feel that they are protecting themselves. As with all mindfulness practices, it is important to work with individuals or a group to help them to ascertain what they aspire to be aware of that they will find helpful. I have found that for many people, it does help to notice smells, sights, and sounds as they are walking and that by being intentional about this, it can take people out of their own negative thoughts and feelings.
- **Exposure to the Natural World** – As with feeling safe, exposure to the natural world (if this is safe and accessible) seems to have its own energy of helping to calm a person by synching our biorhythms with those of the planet. Of course, if there are acute dangers, then this might not be possible and safety takes precedence over mindfulness and calming activities. When I was in Sri Lanka after the tsunami and during the civil war, I noticed people of all ages spending time on the beach, sometimes alone and sometimes with others. If they were Tamil and the army

Figure 7.2 (Continued)

was doing sweeps, this was an unsafe situation, but at other times, it appeared to be a source of comfort; despite an overall dangerous situation, there were moments where the natural world could be (relatively) safely accessed.

- **Prayers and Rituals** – As with promoting a sense of safety, engaging in prayers, ceremonies, or rituals with others can contribute to calming roiled emotions through connections with others; connections to culture, history, and the infinite; and through repetitive phrases or practices that have sustained communities for eons.
- **Guided Visualization** – A group facilitator or individual helper can verbally lead people through guided visualizations of soothing places, people who help people to feel secure, or to past moments of peace and comfort (Figure 7.2).

Figure 7.2 (Continued)

There are other mindfulness practices, such as visualizing a safe space or focusing on earth, water, air, and fire, which have been developed by EMDR practitioners, which I will describe in the next section.

EMDR

EMDR stands for Eye Movement Desensitizing and Reprocessing. It was developed to treat trauma, but unlike many therapies, it is less talk oriented and concentrates on helping the brain to process traumatic memories through bilateral stimulation. I was trained in the first level of EMDR and have used it, or parts of it, in a range of international settings. The EMDR community has made a good-faith effort to extend access to EMDR to non-Western cultures and societies and to adapt it from its initial formulation in the West. There have also been extensions of EMDR, most notably for the purposes of this book, by developing ways that it can be used in groups, where it is called EMDR-ITGP (Integrative Group Treatment Protocol) and in more visual, less verbal ways, such as using drawings (Jarero & Artigas, 2008, 2010; Parelli et al., 2019).

EMDR is an "evidence-based" treatment that has been demonstrated to help people to process PTSD and other strong psychological/emotional reactions to traumatic incidents (Jarero & Artigas, 2008, 2010; Parelli et al., 2019). It posits that traumatic memories are stored in the brain, but not in the same areas where memories are accessible to verbal retrieval. Thus, it asks trauma survivors to visualize (or draw) distressing events while applying bilateral stimulation, such as moving a finger from side to side in front of a person's eyes or having a person apply rhythmic taps to different sides of the body. An example of the latter is the "butterfly hug," where people are taught to hug themselves and alternately apply taps to their shoulders.

Some of the extensions of EMDR, such as the group, have been in response to the recognition that disasters often happen where there are few clinicians at all, let alone trained in EMDR. The skills can be trained to others and thus are adaptable to a TOT model.

The group protocol follows much of the protocol for use with individuals and has eight phases (Jarero & Artigas, 2008):

1. Client history, to identify who was affected and how.
2. Preparation for people who will be receiving EMDR, explaining how it will work, and if using props – such as stuffed animals with children – how they will be used. This is when the concept of "safe space" is introduced through either visualization or the use of stuffed animals. Safe spaces can be a place (or a person) where a participant is asked to go when they want to feel secure or if the focus on distressing events proves to be too painful or overwhelming. Establishing the safe space is a critical scaffolding to be erected before embarking on revisiting upsetting events.
3. Assessment involves asking participants to think of parts of disturbing events and for children to draw them and to rank their distress, sometimes using pictures of different levels of distressed faces for people to choose.
4. Desensitization asks children to look at their drawings (or adults to visualize the distressing event) while applying bilateral stimulation.
5. Future vision (replacing visualization) asks people to think about or children to draw adaptive and non-adaptive visions of the future, usually while undergoing bilateral stimulation.
6. A body scan is done with bilateral stimulation.
7. Participants are asked to return to their safe place.
8. Reevaluation of how people are doing and identifying those who might need further intervention.

There are repeated requests for people to rate their distress as they go through most of the steps.

While EMDR began as a treatment for trauma and disaster, it has since been used in places where there is an ongoing "geopolitical crisis" (Jarero & Artigas, 2010), after "intense rocket attacks" on a town (Shapiro et al., 2018) and with groups of women sexually assaulted in the Congo (Allon, 2015), all of which fit with the subject of this book. Full EMDR seeks to reprocess traumatic events, but parts of it, such as the use of a safe space or bilateral stimulation without visualizing traumatic events can be used for soothing (Kahn, personal communication, 2018; Rowe, personal communication, 2022). Visualizing or drawing a safe space is a form of guided mindfulness that can be used when people are distraught or activated and bilateral stimulation can help people to feel empowered or soothed, as I will describe later.

In Northern Uganda, I used the Earth, Water, Air, and Fire intervention after consulting with an EMDR colleague (Kahn, personal communication, 2018) who had used it in Mexico after an earthquake. It is intended to reduce stress and activation levels. She gave me brightly colored wristbands to distribute that had the four elements listed on it. Each element refers to something that helps a person to feel grounded and empowered. Starting upward from the feet, the earth reminds people that they are grounded on the earth and (hopefully) safe at this moment. It also involves grounding activities such as those mentioned earlier in the safety section. I was able to use it in Northern Uganda because by then people were safe, but it is not advisable to focus on an acutely unsafe environment.

Air focuses on breathing and can utilize the breathing exercises that I mentioned in the safety section. Water focuses on how mouths become dry when people are stressed and it encourages people to be mindful of this and to try and generate saliva, which activates the digestive system. I also found that people can drink something if they have difficulty doing this on their own. And fire refers to firing up one's imagination and is a good time to visualize a safe space. So, this intervention draws on a number of mindfulness and EMDR calming techniques.

In the section on safety, I mentioned working with a group of LGBTQI activists who felt unsafe due to government harassment and surveillance. My colleague and I (Miller & Wang, 2017) also discussed the notion of bilateral stimulation with group members. They felt too frightened and activated to want to visualize being arrested and interrogated but did want to use bilateral stimulation to help themselves to feel calm. Together we considered how they could do this when working in an office or if they were being interrogated by the police.

What they decided was to either alternately tap their feet or alternately move their toes while wearing sandals, as they felt that this would not be seen by those who were harassing them. Many group members reported that they used butterfly hugs to calm themselves at night when anxious and the knowledge that they also had a way of soothing themselves while being interrogated was empowering. They viewed it as a form of secret resistance, where their tormentors were not aware that they were taking care of themselves under extreme duress.

My one critique of EMDR is that from what I have read, practitioners start with the notion that they will try and use EMDR with certain populations in different contexts and adapt it so that it is more digestible or amenable. What I think this leaves out is that when working with affected people, EMDR should be offered as one of a number of ways that people can soothe themselves or process trauma and to emphasize that they are in charge of selecting what they feel will be most helpful and also how they want to modify interventions for their purposes.

Summary of Self-Calming and Managing Emotions

The ability to self-calm is important for a range of reasons: alleviating overwhelming distress, helping a person to feel more in control and instilling a sense of efficacy, creating space for hope, and being a necessary component of being able to strategically resist oppression. I considered a range of ways that can help with affective management: psychotherapy and psychopharmacology; dancing, singing, drumming, and playing together; storytelling through oral recitations, journaling, poetry, drawing, song writing, and photography; collective religious practices and finding transcendent meaning; cultivating social relationships; exercise; exposure to nature; and self-care. I cautioned about imposing or privileging interventions that are culturally dystonic and that can alienate, stigmatize, and pathologize people and undermine traditional cultural practices. Affected people should be viewed as the experts about their lives and have agency over what help they want and how they want it.

I went into more detail about mindfulness and EMDR as two forms of intervention that have the potential to be used in different cultural contexts. I described a range of mindfulness practices: grounding, attention to the senses, body scans, focusing on the breath, loving kindness and sympathetic joy, gratitude, altruism, letting go and recommitting, everyday mindfulness, exposure to the natural world, prayers and rituals, and guided visualizations. With EMDR, I applauded its attempts to use groups and work with people encountering sociopolitical oppression. I also encouraged helping professionals to allow people to use parts of it for soothing and to be able to adapt it for their own purposes rather than to be overly rigid in adhering to certain protocols.

Sustaining HOPE – Hope Optimism Power Efficacy

Sustaining hope and optimism that things can improve, despite ongoing threats and setbacks, is an important human need and, I would argue, a necessary component for struggling against sociopolitical oppression. Essentially, it is developing a vision of survival, resistance, and liberation without which struggling against oppression might appear to be futile. Placing this vision in a wider, long-term context of prior struggles (and successes) helps to link the present with the past and future, reopening "transitional pathways" (Landau, 2007; Landau & Saul, 2004) mentioned in previous chapters. In doing this, it is important to acknowledge the on-the-ground reality of oppression while working to sustain hope. Adames et al. (2022) describe this as a "dialectic" between occupying a space of resistance while also envisioning and moving toward "freedom." They caution against not only being trapped by "despair" and "disempowerment" but also not ignoring the reality of the moment by focusing exclusively on a future divorced from what people are facing; there needs to be both active resistance while envisioning hopeful possibilities. They identify some important aspects of this process:

- The importance of developing a critical consciousness that enables individuals and collectivities to actively reflect on their circumstances in order to strategically act on them.
- "Cultural authenticity and self-knowledge," which I have been stressing throughout the book as an essential ingredient in affirming one's cultural wellsprings and protective and healing practices.
- Cultivating hope through imagining possibilities of liberation.
- "Collectivism," which fits with the discussion about the importance of social connections earlier in this chapter. They also stress the need for "counter-spaces" that accentuate beauty and joy and protect against assaults, such as the ones mentioned earlier when I discussed the importance of buffering and empowerment (Tatum, 2017).
- Committing to live "joy-filled lives" through collective strength and resilience.

Implicit in these recommendations is cultivating the belief that people have a sense of collective efficacy, leading to collective empowerment. There are five interrelated ways to generate HOPE:

1. Cultural practices and pride (Blume et al., 2020; Burrage et al., 2021; Gone, 2021; Millner et al., 2021)
2. Collective resistance to oppression (Phillips et al., 2015) and linking this with historical resistance
3. Collective celebration of strength and beauty (Adames et al., 2022; Falicov et al., 2020) and ensuring that there are times of joy, flow, connection, and meaning
4. Collective storying and re-storying (Auerbach & Shiro-Gelrud, 2010; Combs & Freedman, 2012), which I covered in the section about the power of narratives in Chapter 6
5. Achieving spiritual and transcendent meaning (Auerbach & Shiro-Gelrud, 2010), collectively and individually.

I have discussed reconnecting with cultural practices throughout the book; it is like rebuilding a loom from which patterns, practices, and values can be woven and spun. It affirms a collective sense of identity and personhood that mirrors strength and beauty and counteracts the distortions and pathologies of people viewed through the lens of coloniality. This offers a framework for constructing meaning, values by which to live, and honors individual and collective strength and beauty. Reclaiming cultural practices involves collective storytelling that offers alternatives to dominant narratives, recasting history and the meaning of lives and events. These usually include transcendent philosophies, cosmologies, and spiritual taproots. The endurance of cultural traditions despite coloniality is both a foundation for recovery and a symbol of resistance and survival. As Jesse Thistle (2019), mentioned in Chapter 5, through reconnecting with his cultural heritage and learning about the many tribal and community leaders who were part of his lineage, he gained a sense of pride, shedding many negative internalized beliefs about his self-worth that contributed to his drug addiction and homelessness.

But this can be complicated. For example, the Taliban are attempting to reinstall a culture and society in Afghanistan that harkens back to the middle ages and negates and nullifies agency, empowerment, and the personhood of women and condones attacking and tyrannizing ethnic minorities. Culture is not static and viewing it in either or terms – e.g., traditional/modern and indigenous/Western – does not capture its complexity, how it flows and changes, and the hybridity that characterizes many cultures throughout the world.

For example, one of the consequences of the armed conflict in Northern Uganda, combined with COVID, has been a rise in the rate of adolescent pregnancy. After collaboratively running focus groups for adolescent girls and health-care workers with our Ugandan colleagues, a very mixed picture emerged. Reasons for the rise in pregnancy that were shared included lack of parental supervision, lack of access to education for girls, and risks posed by predatory older men. For some, this meant that it was important to return to traditional tribal roles and practices, strengthening the networks of clan and religious leaders (who are mostly men), and reinforcing parental authority. For others, this perspective was viewed as regressive and devaluing of women; girls should be affirmed rather than shamed or pressured to conform to outdated roles shaped not only by culture but by coloniality and poverty. Traditional Acholi culture, sequestered from other parts of the world, no longer exists, and even long ago, there probably were encounters with other cultures and ensuing challenges to its homogeneity. After a 20-year armed conflict, improvements in roads and infrastructure resulting in less isolation from the rest of the country and of course access to the rest of the world through cell phones, the Internet, and social media, there are many cultural cross-currents and adaptations, reflecting greater hybridity and less cultural purity. This in turn weakens traditional social norms, roles, authority, and networks and affects connection to and the meaning of cultural practices.

This does not mean that revisiting and reclaiming traditional Acholi values and practices is not an important component of healing; connection with the past and envisioning a proud and hopeful future is central to this process. But it is unlikely to succeed without adaptation, modification, updating, and integrating it with other cultural and social practices encountered by the tribe, which in turn leads to reconfiguring social identities, roles, and relationships. For example, the health-care network employs many doctors, medical officers, midwives, and nurses trained in Western medicine, and a significant number of the staff are women, which contrasts with more traditional roles of men working outside of the home and women laboring on behalf of and within the family. But this has not negated the important role of traditional birth attendants – women in villages who advise families and young women about sexuality and pregnancy – they still play an influential part in Acholi society at the village level. It has not changed the fact that this is still a clan-based society or that many people still enjoy Acholi drumming and dancing. Thus, responding to historical and collective oppression and trauma entails honoring cultural practices, reclaiming history and re-instilling pride, appreciating and valuing indigenous strength and beauty, engaging in meaning-making and spiritual practices, and doing all of this without trying to recreate a mythical past but rather constructing a meaningful framework for living life in the present that is not defined by coloniality and racism.

Conclusion

In this chapter, I considered universal psychosocial needs for people and groups experiencing oppression and violence: safety, connections with others, being able to manage negative reactions, and maintaining HOPE. Although I have found these needs to be universal in every country, community, and culture where I have worked, I have also learned the way needs are manifested, their meaning, what is helpful to meet them, and who one can turn to for help varies considerably depending on the social ecology and specific context. I carefully considered how to use certain Western methods of intervention – psychotherapy (particularly cognitive behavioral approaches) and psychopharmacology – and how they can be blended and adapted with culturally indigenous interventions. Throughout the chapter, I tried to weave together a range of CBT models, EMDR, mindfulness, and intentional collective self-care.

With safety, I considered how this is a relative concept and that there is never complete safety; rather there is a spectrum of safety. Given this, the task is to help people achieve relative safety – moments and places – despite ongoing threats to overall safety. I particularly focused on CFBT as well as activities that increase a sense of safety. I stressed the importance of social connections and social networks and examined how to enhance and strengthen existing networks as well as build new ones. In the section on managing symptoms and self-calming, I noted that while the goal is constant, the means and ways to manage symptoms vary. I suggested a variety of interventions to achieve self-calming and in particular considered a range of mindfulness techniques and reviewed the efficacy and adaptability of EMDR.

In the next chapter, I will consider resilience, examining what it means in different sociocultural contexts and how to support and foster resilience. I will focus on collective and community resilience as well as family and individual resilience.

References

Adames, H.Y., Chavez-Duenas, N.Y., Lewis, J.A., Neville, H.A., French, B.H., Chen, G.A., & Mosley, D.V. (2022). Radical healing in psychotherapy: Addressing the wounds of racism-related stress and trauma. *Psychotherapy*. DOI: 10.1037/pst0000435.

Adessky, R.S., & Freedman, S.A. (2005). Treating survivors of terrorism while adversity continues. In Y. Danieli, D. Brom, & J. Sills (Eds.). *The trauma of terrorism: Sharing knowledge and shared care, an international handbook* (pp. 443–454). Binghamton, NY: The Haworth Press.

Allon, M. (2015). EMDR group therapy with women who were sexually assaulted in the Congo: *Journal of EMDR Practice and Research*, *9*(1): 28–34. DOI: 10.1891/1933-3196.9.1.28.

American Psychological Association. (2022). *What is cognitive behavioral therapy*. www.apa.org/ptsd-guideline/patients-and-families/cognitive-behavioral

Auerbach, C.F., & Shiro-Gelrud, E. (2010). The Cambodian refugee experience. In A. Kalyayjian & D. Eugene (Eds.). *Mass trauma and emotional healing around the world: Rituals and practices for resilience and meaning-making* (pp. 423–439). Santa Barbara, CA: ABC CLIO, LLC.

Basoglu, M., & Salcioglu, E. (2011). *A mental health care model for mass trauma survivors: Control-focused behavioral treatment of earthquake, war and torture trauma*. New York, NY: Cambridge University Press.

Berkowitz, S., Bryant, R., Brymer, M., Hamblen, J., Jacobs, A., Layne, C., Macy, R., Osofsky, H., Pynoos, R., Ruzek, J., Steinberg, A., Vernberg, E., & Watson, P. (2010). *Skills for psychological recovery field operations guide*. Washington, DC: National Center for PTSD and National Child Traumatic Stress Network.

Beuregard, E.M. (2021). We should all be marching: Why humanistic psychologists should take action toward social justice. *The Humanist Psychologist*. DOI: 10.1037/hum0000269.

Blume, A.W., Morse, G.S., & Love, C. (2020). Human rights and psychology from indigenous perspectives. In N.S. Rubin & R.L. Flores (Eds.). *The Cambridge handbook of psychology and human rights* (pp. 258–272). Cambridge, UK: Cambridge University Press.

Bryant-Davis, T. (2005). *Thriving in the wake of trauma: A multicultural guide*. Westport, CT: Praeger Publishing.

Burrage, R.L., Momper, S.L., & Gone, J.P. (2021). Beyond trauma: Decolonizing understandings of loss and healing in the Indian residential school system of Canada. *Journal of Social Issues*. DOI: 10.1111/josi.12455.

Christakis, N.A., & Fowler, J.H. (2009). *Connected: The surprising power of social networks and how they shape our lives*. New York: Little Brown and Company.

Combs, G., & Freedman, J. (2012). Narrative, post-structuralism, and social justice: Current practices in narrative therapy. *The Counseling Psychologist*, *40*: 1033. DOI: 10.1177/0011000012460662.

Falicov, C., Nino, A., & D'Urso, S. (2020). Expanding possibilities: Flexibility and solidarity with under-resourced immigrant families during the COVID-19 pandemic. *Family Process*, *59*: 865–882.

Gone, J.P. (2021). The (post)colonial predicament in community mental health services for American Indians: Explorations in alter-native psy-ence. *American Psychologist*, *76*(9): 1514–1525. DOI: 10.1037/amp0000906.

Halpern, J., & Tramontin, M. (2007). *Disaster mental health: Theory and practice*. Belmont, CA: Thompson Learning.

Hammer, J. (2021, November 18). The horrors of the diamond boom. *New York Review of Books*, *LXVIII*(18): 31–33. www.nybooks.com/articles/2021/11/18/horrors-of-the-diamond-boom/

Heaney, C.A., & Israel, B.A. (2008). Social networks and social support. In K. Glanz, B.K. Rimer, & K. Viswanath (Eds.). *Health behavior and health education: Theory, research and practice* (4th ed., pp. 189–210). New York: John Wiley and sons.

Hobfoll, S.E., Watson, P., Bell, C.C., Bryant, R.A., Brymer, M.J., Friedman, M.J., Friedman, M., Gersons, B.P.R., De Jong, J.T.V.M., Layne, C.M., Maguen, S., Neria, Y., Norwood, A.E., Pynoos, R.S., Reisman, D., Ruzek, J.I., Shalev, A.Y., Solomon, Z., Steinberg, A.M., & Ursano, R.J. (2007). Five essential elements of immediate and mid-term mass trauma intervention: Empirical evidence. *Psychiatry*, *70*(4): 283–315.

Jarero, I., & Artigas, L. (2008). The EMDR integrative group treatment protocol: Application with child victims of a mass disaster. *The Journal of EMDR Practice and Research*, *2*(2): 97–105.

Jarero, I., & Artigas, L. (2010). The EMDR group treatment protocol: Application with adults during ongoing geopolitical crisis. *The Journal of EMDR Practice and Research*, *4*(4): 148–155.

Kang, H., & Burton, D. (2014). Effects of racial discrimination, childhood trauma, and trauma symptoms on juvenile delinquency in African American incarcerated youth. *Journal of Aggression, Maltreatment & Trauma*, *23*: 1109–1125. DOI: 10.1080/10926771.2014.968272.

Landau, J. (2007). Enhancing resilience: Communities and families as agents of change. *Family Process*, *41*(1): 351–365.

Landau, J., & Saul, J. (2004). Facilitating family and community resilience in response to major disaster. In F. Walsh & M. McGoldrick (Eds.). *Living beyond loss* (pp. 285–309). New York: W.W. Norton and Co.

Miller, J., & Wang, X. (2017). When there are no therapists: A psychoeducational group for people who have experienced social disasters. *Smith College Studies in Social Work*. DOI: 10.1080/00377317.2018.1404293.

Miller, J.L. (2012). *Psychosocial capacity building in response to disasters*. New York: Columbia University Press.

Millner, U.C., Maru, M., Ismail, A., & Chakrabarti, U. (2021). Decolonizing mental health practice: Reconstructing an Asian-centric framework through a social justice lens. *Asian American Journal of Psychology*, *12*(4): 333–345. DOI: 10.1037/aap0000268.

Parelli, S., et al. (2019). EMDR group treatment of children refugees – A field study. *Journal of EMDR Practice and Research*, *13*(2): 143–155.

Phillips, N.L., Adams, G., & Salther, P.S. (2015). Beyond adaptation: Decolonizing approaches to coping with oppression. *Journal of Social and Political Psychology*, *3*(1): 365–387. DOI: 10.5964/jspp.v3i1.310.

Shapiro, E., Laub, B., & Rosenblat, O. (2018). Early EMDR interventions following intense rocket attacks on a town: A randomized clinical trial. *Clinical Neuropsychiatry*, *15*(3): 158–169.

Tatum, B.D. (2017). *Why are all the Black kids sitting together in the cafeteria?* New York: Basic Books.

Thistle, J. (2019). *From the ashes: On being Metis, homeless and finding my way*. Toronto: Simon and Schuster Canada.

8 Collective Resilience While Facing Oppression

Introduction

This entire book has been about collective resilience in the face of historical and contemporary oppression; resilience forged by communities, tribes, and groups sharing social identities in order to survive and thrive despite persistent, often state-sponsored, adversity and violence. Resilience emerged and evolved from cultures, religions, communities, and societies without help from professionals. Resilience is shared, not a set of traits or something carried by some individuals and not others. Resilience has acted as a collective counterweight to economic, political, and social systems that stripped away communal and institutional supports and placed the blame for success or failure, achievements, and struggles on the individual rather than society and its policies and social structures. Resilience is forged in all of the world's major religions, and cultural and spiritual practices long before "resilience" was discovered, studied, written about, and in many ways appropriated by social scientists and helping professionals (Riffle et al., 2020).

In Somalia, there has been an armed virulent armed conflict for over three decades (Terrana et al., 2022). Many families have been shattered and numerous people resettled in refugee camps, where they have experienced social exclusion, discrimination, racism, Islamophobia, xenophobia, unemployment, and lack of access to resources. They have received mental health services based on Western models, grounded in individualized models of resilience and recovery, that do not integrate or even value Somali wisdom and cultural practices (Terrana et al.). As I have argued throughout the book, psychosocial needs are shaped by structural factors, war, and displacement, and yet the very notion of "mental health," particularly from a Western perspective, implies that the locus of the suffering resides in the individual. It is important to respond to individual anguish, pain, and distress, but

DOI: 10.4324/9781003021162-8

does this mean that psychosocial efforts should disproportionately be directed toward individuals, particularly given the structural causes of suffering and how it affects collectivities.

This example, representative of what occurs throughout the world, raises important questions when considering the concept of resilience. The majority of the literature focuses on individual resilience, omitting systemic and structural factors, and it often assumes the need for professional services offered by people who are not from the affected community (Gebhard et al., 2022). It is as if resilience is context free (Serrano-Garcia, 2020), detached from collective histories, current struggles, and the matrix of networks and relationships which exist within communities. Focusing resilience on robust individuals obscures society's institutional obligations and absolves it of causing stress and pain and neglecting to offer the policies, services, laws, and protections that would build collective resilience (Ager, 2013). This deflects attention from social injustice and structural inequality, which is why Serrano-Garcia and others argue for the need to consider "critical resilience," which includes resilience to poverty, racism, and the many forms of oppression considered in this book.

In this chapter, I will discuss resilience to societal oppression, both historical and contemporary, and particularly focus on collective resilience. In earlier chapters, I considered historical and collective trauma, and it is my belief that collective resilience is what emerges in response. As I have said in previous chapters, collective resilience does not negate the hardships and suffering of collective tyranny, but it is important to recognize and appreciate the collective strengths, bonds, and strategies that have emerged from forced immersion in the social tank of oppression. Since the balance of explorations of resilience has been tilted toward individual resilience, I will spend more time considering collective resilience, although I will briefly summarize ideas about what makes families and individuals resilient. Before that, I will look at what is meant by resilience.

Meanings of Resilience

Resilience and suffering are connected; they are different parts of the same circle of human experience. Most cultural myths and religions have stories about loss, tyranny, violence, devastation, and suffering alongside narratives and precepts about ways that people can surmount and overcome these threats. For example, Buddhism's "Four Noble Truths": (1) there is pain and suffering; (2) there is a cause and origin of pain and suffering; (3) there can be the cessation of suffering; and

(4) there is a path that can lead to the end of suffering. Although Buddhism particularly focuses on perceptions and delusions that contribute to suffering, socially engaged Buddhists acknowledge the social causes of suffering and seek to ameliorate them. The Buddhist Monk Thich Nhat Hanh spent his life as a socially engaged Buddhist and understood that responding to the suffering caused by the war in his native Vietnam or institutional racism in the United States involved more than merely meditating, as important as meditation is (Miller, 2012).

A common way of describing resilience is to view it as responding to adversity and trauma through adaptation and eventually thriving (Buckingham & Brodsky, 2021; Lee et al., 2017). Walsh (2020) noted that resilience is forged by navigating suffering and life's setbacks and integrating one's struggles into the tapestry of a life course. Serrano-Garcia (2020), citing Manyena, calls it "bouncing forward."

Resilience is not only an outcome or a set of traits, but it is also a dynamic process, involving the interaction of many psychological, developmental, and sociocultural factors, which evolve and change (Lee et al., 2017; Riffle et al., 2020). Cenat et al. (2021) cite Patel et al., as differentiating between three ways that resilience is understood: (1) process definitions; (2) absence of adverse effects definitions; and (3) range of attributes definitions. Resilience is a process of recovery, leading to fewer adverse effects, and attempting to understand what contributed to this process of recovery. In my clinical experiences, resilience is evolving, never static, nor is it a straight trajectory; it waxes and wanes and there are times, depending on different contexts and situations, where resilience is more or less apparent. For example, when the level of brutality increases and collectivities find it more difficult to "adapt" and "thrive," this does not mean that they are not resilient or have permanently lost their resilience. Thus, it is important not to reify resilience into resilient individuals or communities.

It is also important not to view resilience as only being a characteristic of individuals, families, and communities. When I responded to the Asian Tsunami of 2005 in Sri Lanka six months after, it hit, I was struck by how communities in the South of the country were rebuilding much more quickly than those in the East. Was this because they were more resilient? The tsunami occurred during the Sri Lankan Civil War, which was being fought in the North and the East of the country. The communities in the East were caught between a tsunami and a brutal armed conflict. The South was not experiencing the direct impact of the war – e.g., fighting between the Sri Lankan army and the Tamil Tigers – when the tsunami hit. Also, the population in the South was predominantly Sinhalese, the country's ethnic majority that controls most government, education, and other state institutions, while those in the East were predominantly Tamil, which meant that they were frequently viewed as being suspect and less deserving in the eyes of the government and its army. Not only did this affect where government resources were directed but the East was also a much more dangerous and unstable area, so it was more difficult for international aid organizations to work as effectively in that environment. On the surface, the communities in the South appeared to be more "resilient" than those in the East, not reflecting the intrinsic resilience of the communities but national politics in a time of armed conflict that directed resources and provided greater immediate infrastructure and the ability to rebuild and "adapt" and "thrive." Resilience is not a politically neutral concept (Miller, 2012).

Both building on and in response to individual resilience theorists, there have been theories and scales developed to capture family, collective, and community resilience, which will be discussed in this chapter. According to Erfurth et al. (2021), Williams and Drury wrote about collective resilience in 2009 to describe how people effectively acted as a group in response to emergencies and disasters. Community resilience definitions, in addition to focusing on adaptivity and positive functioning in response to adverse situations, stress how these capacities are networked, shared, and amplified (Cenat et al., 2021; Gil-Rivas & Kilmer, 2016). And while there are strong similarities between collective and community resilience, I will consider what differentiates them in the following section on collective resilience.

I have been using the frame of coloniality throughout this book to understand historical and collective oppression, and it is also a factor when considering resilience. Who gets to define what constitutes resilience and what models of personhood are being used to examine and understand this concept? As Kuecker (2017) asks, how can we escape from "the everlasting condition of having been colonized," which affects how we see, hear, interact, and comprehend, what is considered resilience (p. 206)? He seeks an understanding of resilience that is transmodern, where the global majority breaks out of conceptual straightjackets and transcends world orders imposed by coloniality and considered "modernity," reclaiming their ability to be "actors" not "subordinates."

One way to respond to coloniality is to have affected people determine the meaning of resilience on their terms (Ager, 2013). Ager and his colleagues (Vindevogel et al., 2015) used this approach in Northern Uganda when they worked with local community residents and leaders, including youth, elders, and teachers to develop a concept of youth resilience as part of a participatory research project in the wake of the decades of armed conflict, which I have referred to throughout this book. Rather than imposing universal resilience scales, nearly all developed in the West, they recognized the importance of context and including local people in identifying what *they* thought resilience means and what are its indicators.

Collective Resilience

The terms "collective resilience" and "community resilience" are often used interchangeably, and while they overlap, there are some subtle distinctions. Community resilience usually refers to a geographic community, which may be ethnically/racially/religiously homogenous but can also be heterogeneous. I gave the example of Eastern and Southern Sri Lanka earlier, where Tamils were the predominant ethnic group in the East and Sinhalese in the south, which affected the relationship of communities to the civil war when a tsunami struck and influenced the trajectory of rebuilding and recovery. In contrast, when 9/11 occurred in New York City, it affected one of the most diverse communities in the world, although there were many micro-communities – such as Chinatown – which were more homogenous. Thus, the "community" in community resilience can be small/large, diverse/homogenous, and communities are nested in successively larger communities; therefore, community resilience is part of a rippling social ecology of interacting communities.

Lee et al. (2017) define community resilience as "the collective ability of a specific geographic area or neighborhood to overcome disaster-related stressors through cooperation in order to return to day-to-day life activities as quickly as possible." They note that this refers to a range of "adaptive capacities": infrastructure, economic, ecological, social capital, and networks – aspects of what I have referred to in this book as the social ecology. Lindberg and Swearingen (2020) expand this definition to also include the ability of local groups to adaptively and productively respond to stressors that include social, political, and environmental changes, despite the unpredictability and uncertainty that accompanies such threats; ultimately the ability of a community to thrive despite these challenges. When considering community resilience, it is important to note that every community has assets – tangible, such as vegetable markets and waterways – as well as social, such as leaders, networks, and support groups, as well as formal and informal institutions (Kretzman & McKnight, 1993).

Collective resilience encompasses these definitions of community resilience but can refer to groups and other forms of collectivities – chosen groups such as the community of taxi drivers or firefighters – or groups delineated by shared, intersectional social identities, such as Muslim Tamils living in villages in Eastern Sri Lanka, or in the U.S. national BIPOC empowerment or advocacy groups. Collective resilience can occur, therefore, within collectivities that do not necessarily live in the same localities. Collective resilience has been defined as the ability to withstand or recover from threatening events to the group's survival or well-being through group agency and adaptability (Lyons et al., 2016; Molinaar et al., 2022).

I believe that community and collective resilience are sufficiently similar so that they can be considered together. In the context of social oppression, they both involve shared threats, trauma, and resilience (Ali et al., 2021). They both often involve group members having shared social identities which unite them as targets of oppression but also in their mutual support, advocacy, and resistance. Both community and collective resilience are multidimensional, involving human resources and assets, infrastructure, relational bonds, social networks, social trust, services, economic resources, and shared visions and values. Collective agency and adaptability are central to them both. And both theories of collective and community resilience were sparked by critiques of theories of individual resilience because they placed the onus of surviving and thriving on individuals rather than institutions, policies, and sociopolitical processes (Serrano-Garcia, 2020).

Focusing on individual capacities absolves society of its social responsibilities (Serrano-Garcia, 2020). But as I mentioned earlier, there is also the risk that groups and communities starved of resources or under perennial attack will be viewed as being less resilient because of a preponderance of negative indicators and outcomes. Critical resilience involves not only strengthening individuals, families, and communities but also addressing racism, poverty, sexism, heterosexism, transphobia, and other forms of institutional oppression (Serrano-Garcia).

Core Processes and Attributes of Collective/Community Resilience

In Figure 8.1, I have listed the core processes of collective/community resilience identified by scholars of these concepts. I have grouped them into three areas: (1) attitudes, behaviors, beliefs, and values; (2) resources; and (3) environmental factors, listing the literature that has discussed at least some of these strategies. There are few groups and communities that have all of these attributes, and as I have argued, local histories and social ecologies shape collective resilience, but it is

Attitudes, Behaviors, Beliefs, Values
Awareness of oppression and what can be done to confront it.
Belief in agency and efficacy
Hope that things can improve over time
Adaptability to a changing matrix of threats, conditions, and responses
Connection to historical and cultural values and practices
Caring and connection for group members
Social trust and cohesion
Caring and effective leadership
Opportunities for restoration, joy, and pleasure
Values of equity, inclusion, cooperation, collaboration
Collective action and advocacy
Sharing and reciprocity
Common goals and aspirations
Sense of shared fate with other group members
Willingness to confront oppression at individual, group, and systemic levels and to participate in resistance activities.

Resources
Housing
Jobs
Infrastructure – e.g., roads
Finances and capital
Markets
Education and training
Social networks
Responsive government and local authorities, including law enforcement
Communication and information
Knowledge, skills, and social capital
Supportive and effective institutions and associations, both government and non-government

Environmental Factors
Safety and the ability to protect group members and limit violence
Possibilities for buffering group members from threats
Lack of corruption
Access to nature, recreation, and opportunities for physical activity

Figure 8.1 Core Processes of Community and Collective Resilience

Source: *Cheng et al., 2021*; *Erfurth et al., 2021*; *Edwards et al., 2019*; *Gebhard et al., 2022*; *Gil-Rivas & Kilmer, 2016*; *Lee et al., 2017*; *Lyons et al., 2016*; *Miller, 2012*; *Ntontis et al., 2020*; *Park & Blake, 2020*; *Riffle et al., 2020*; *Ross, 2017*; *Serrano-Garcia, 2020*; *Suyemoto et al., 2022*

worth noting qualities that can be helpful. As mentioned earlier, it is important to involve local people in determining what constitutes resilience within their social ecology and sociocultural context (Ager, 2013; Vindevogel et al., 2015).

I would also like to note that group resilience is not always a positive thing. Collective resilience is not ideological, and thus groups that oppress other groups can also be resilient and will have many of the attributes that I have listed (Lyons et al., 2016).

Social Identities, Social Ties, and Social Capital

Social oppression is directed against groups of people based on the social construction of their identities. Memmi (2000), writing about racism described a four-part process: (1) A group of people is perceived by a majority group as being different (e.g., physically, culturally, spiritually). (2) The majority group places value on those differences – the "other" groups are thought of as being less advanced, less worthy, less trustworthy, less civilized, and not fully human. (3) The negative attributes are generalized to all members of the group. (4) This is used as a justification to dominate, subjugate, and oppress the group. Cheng et al. (2021) illustrate this process, focusing on Asian Americans after Donald Trump scapegoated them for spreading COVID-19, which led to harassment, slurs, and violent attacks: (1) racial scapegoating – Trump called COVID "the Chinese virus"; (2) racial objectification of all Asian Americans groups as being Chinese; (3) denigration of Asian Americans; (4) ostracization; and (5) dehumanization.

As social targeting relies on social identities, so does collective resilience. Having a shared concept of a common fate based on shared social identities can bring people together as they collectively resist oppression (Cheng et al., 2021; Ntontis et al., 2020; Tekin et al., 2021). Experiencing oppression can foster divisiveness, and there is the classic British colonial strategy of fragmenting local populations through "divide and rule," but it can also lead to greater group consciousness and foster social cohesion, ties, and support. This involves developing a collective critical consciousness where identifying structural factors – such as white racism and cultural hegemony – can lead group members to create counter-spaces and to feel better about themselves as they externalize the causes of their predicament (Cheng et al.). This can lead to greater social support and a sense of collective and self-efficacy and respect (Erfurth et al., 2021).

For example, in Oakland, California's Chinatown, there were attacks and robberies by outsiders as Asian American hatred increased

(Morning Edition, 2022). A 64-year-old grandmother had been assaulted, and a 52-year-old woman was shot in the head with a flare gun. There were thefts, carjackings, and a decline in visitors and tourism. In response, a volunteer citizen patrol known as the Blue Angels was established. Wearing dark blue vests, volunteers patrol the neighborhood three days a week, equipped with cameras, walkie-talkies, air horns, and blue umbrellas. If there are crimes, patrol members use their air horns and body cameras and call the police. They are serving as community witnesses and offer residents and shopkeepers collective support and efficacy that increases safety. This in turn has led to the Oakland police department providing a liaison who speaks Cantonese and more police foot patrols. Crime has declined, and the neighborhood feels safer to both residents and visitors.

This example also illustrates how social capital is harnessed, leveraged, and increases with collective efficacy. Gil-Rivas and Kilmer (2016) defined social capital as a group or community effectively collaborating, articulating, and sharing goals and strategies for achieving them, and engaging in collective action, all of which happened in Oakland's Chinatown. The volunteers gave the community a sense not only of safety but also of collective efficacy. Local volunteers used low-tech resources as they visibly connected people and institutions in the community. Their efforts led to other resources coming in from outside of the community – such as the increased police presence. This in turn increased the social capital of the community as visitors returned, which placed more people on the streets, making the neighborhood safer, and increased the economic well-being of local shopkeepers.

Suyemoto et al. (2022) developed a scale called "Resistance and Empowerment of People of Color against Racism" (REAR) based on a sample of BIPOC people in the United States. They found four core strategies:

1. Distancing and validating – staying away from people who won't deal with their internalized racial stereotypes while supporting and validating other people who are the target of discrimination
2. Confronting people interpersonally when they experience microaggressions, including friends and family
3. Participating in activities and organizations that confront not only racism but also other forms of oppression
4. Taking leadership and creating opportunities for resistance against racism directed at all people of color

They found that by engaging in these activities, people felt better about themselves and their racial/ethnic group and developed effective, collaborative approaches.

Meaning-Making and Spirituality

An important component of collective resilience is the group's capacity to find meaning, share it, and in many instances connect or reconnect with transcendent spiritual processes. There is personal meaning-making, situational meaning-making in response to a particular set of circumstances and state of affairs, and a more global, general sense of meaning-making that is consistent and enduring. Park and Blake (2020) have found in their research that when there is a particularly severe critical incident – e.g., beating by the police, attack by a militia, and election of a demagogue – there can be a disconnect between how a person understands the acute situation and their overall view of the world. Trying to reconcile these differences helps with reducing dissonance and reestablishing coherence with how people view the world.

While much has been written about meaning-making after having it shattered by disasters (e.g., Miller, 2012; Park & Blake, 2020; Van Tongeren et al., 2020), Gebhard et al. (2022) note that state-sanctioned violence against groups in the United States has been part of the country's traditions and practices from its inception. Although the level of violence may wax and wane, there is a consistent pattern of social oppression and exclusion. Examples in the United States abound enslavement, genocide, ethnic cleansing, immigration exclusion based on race and religion, Jim Crow, and mob violence abetted by local law enforcement authorities, leading to modern-day police violence toward African Americans, of which there are many recent instances (Garran et al., 2021). Thus, the task is not necessarily reconciling worldviews with personal experiences but rather to reconfigure and develop counter-narratives that refuse to accept the meanings being imposed on a group by others and instead forging one's own story of survival and resistance. Resistance is a critical part of group resilience, empowerment, and survival. This involves "constructing and communicating meaning, risk management, and collective decision-making" (Gerbhard et al.). Meaning-making is more powerful when it is done with others and is part of a collective process (Riffle et al., 2020). By constructing counter-narratives, collective meaning-making helps to name the institutional forces which contribute to state-sanctioned violence, stripping away dominant rationales and obfuscations and giving coherence to collective action (Gebhard et al.).

Spirituality and religion are often important forms meaning-making for many and offer an interpretative framework to make sense of the chaos and violence that surrounds people (Van Tongeren et al., 2020). This can help people to place acute threats and events in the context of both a longer struggle and transcendent meaning. Religious leaders such as Martin Luther King Jr., Malcolm X, Desmond Tutu, and Thich Nhat Han were all at the forefront of struggles against state-sanctioned violence and for civil rights. Spirituality can also help to deindividualize suffering by helping people to make connections with others, including animals and nature.

When facing enduring social oppression, I have found that thinking of other times when people have faced daunting odds and endured threats and violence is part of a spiritual process that expands struggles to an ongoing global struggle for group equity, respect, and justice. It connects me with so many others who have risked and, in far too many instances, lost, their lives as part of a connected human chain of courage and righteousness. For example, the children of Soweto who demonstrated against Apartheid and its manifestations in South Africa in 1976 were part of a movement that forcefully led to the abolition of apartheid 17 years later. Hundreds lost their lives, and many families were devastated; they could not know at the time what their sacrifices would lead to. Collective struggle is part of human existence, and placing contemporary struggles in this context adds a mythic component to resistance, illustrating our human connectedness, which is a component of most religions and spiritual practice.

Collective and Community Resilience Scales

There have been efforts, primarily by Western-based researchers, to develop scales to measure collective resilience. A scale that is often cited by researchers is the Fletcher-Lyons Collective Resilience Scale, which relies on self-reports to measure resilience within groups (Lyons et al., 2016). The scale appears to measure constructs that are related to collective efficacy, which I have discussed a number of times in this book. These are the areas that the scale focuses on – (1) our group is able to respond to challenges when they arise; (2) our group actively seeks to influence the context and environment where it exists; (3) our group is able to obtain what it needs to thrive; (4) our group bounces back from even the most difficult setbacks; (5) our group is able to achieve things; and (6) our group is adaptable. As can be seen, the notion of adaptability and agency are central to the scale's focus.

Cenat et al. (2021) have developed what they call the Transcultural-Community Resilience Scale. This scale was tested in many non-Western contexts – e.g., The Democratic Republic of the Congo, Haiti, Rwanda, and Togo. The core processes that it examines are local knowledge, community networks and relationships, communication, health, governance and leadership, resources, economic investment, preparedness, and mental outlook. The specific questions examine important variables: relying on others in the community; willingness to help others; mutual aid and support; cultural and religious traditions; social trust and cohesion; and access to important and necessary information and resources. As I have been discussing, these are all important factors in community and collective resilience.

As thoughtful as these scales are, I think that there are limitations. The framing of questions betrays assumptions about how groups and communities function and what is important when responding to crises and disasters. Is this how the range of diverse communities would frame resilience? This differs from the approach used by Vindevogel et al. (2015) where they engaged key community constituents to design a scale that fits a local vision of resilience, rather than to come in with a predetermined scale intended to fit all cultures and societies. And neither of the aforementioned scales was specifically intended to measure resilience in the face of ongoing, collective oppression and trauma, which is different than resilience in response to critical incidents.

Although the scales are intended to be used with a range of cultures and communities, they emanate from the West and are part of a Western tendency to try and measure psychosocial processes, in this instance collective resilience, breaking it down into calculable segments. Not every society thinks this way or finds this important to do. It is significant for Western researchers because it allows them to say, with "scientific certainty," which groups are more or less resilient. This makes it easier to lead to published articles in Western journals, which then become the "standard" for researchers to use throughout the world. As I have mentioned earlier, Western scales and the journals that publish them become the template necessary for doctoral students, academics, and researchers in most parts of the world in order to be seen as credible and worthy of validation and promotion, ranging from China to Chile, Kashmir to Kenya, and Peru to the Philippines. Is this a soft version of coloniality? While there are hard aspects to collective resilience (e.g., infrastructure, economic resources), much of it is subjective and determined by a specific group (Molinaar et al., 2022). It is important to be mindful of how all cultures and religious traditions have considered resilience for eons, well before Western psychologists and social scientists began studying it (Riffle et al., 2020).

Collective Resistance as an Aspect of Collective Resilience

As I have discussed, resistance is empowering; rather than being helplessly buffeted by external forces of oppression, a group is acting and demonstrating collective efficacy. I do not want to sugarcoat resistance; it can be draining, stressful, and overwhelming at times. But whether it was the Civil Rights Movement in the United States or the Anti-Apartheid Movement in South Africa, long-term resistance knitted individuals and communities together, offered hope, and in both instances led to significant and meaningful changes.

Serrano-Garcia (2020) cites Gopel and shares five ingredients of successful social activism:

1. Becoming aware of and increasing the visibility of the forces that are causing harm and how negative consequences are manifesting themselves
2. Recognizing how the status quo is not tenable or viable
3. Forming coalitions to identify and engage in new approaches
4. Development of new mechanisms and technologies for change
5. Creating fissures within the existing system – what post-structuralists would describe as problematizing and destabilizing

I will illustrate how these can work by sharing an example from my work as a community organizer in a mid-sized city in the 1990s. I was hired to lead a coalition of business leaders, religious leaders, local politicians and government officials, human service workers, community members, and residents from different sectors and parts of the city, which included leaders of African American and Latino/a (mostly Puerto Rican) neighborhoods. The coalition identified a range of social problems – homelessness, reducing HIV transmission, substance abuse, improving education, and reducing the number of single-parent families. (Remember, this was the 1990s!)

After a few months, leaders from African American and Latino/a communities and a handful of white allies approached me to say that we were not seeing the problem correctly (Step 1). We were concentrating on downstream "social problems" that were a consequence of systemic and structural racism, which was not even mentioned as an important area to address. In fact, the "community leaders" who had created the coalition were middle-class and well-off mostly white men, corporate and civic power brokers, who had "invited" other people into the process. People of color were shut out of the centers of power in the city and felt like appendages to a process that was not addressing the root of the problem (Step 2). This led to a fragmentation of the original coalition and reconfigured coalitions of people seeking racial justice, which also included some progressive White business and media people as well as professionals such as lawyers (Step 3). This was a period of greater confrontation and conflict between the original members of the coalition, which eventually resulted in recasting how major institutions in the city operated– e.g., the United Way (which had an all-white board and had never had a senior staff member of color needed to dramatically change, as did some of the planning and coordinating groups in the city which had adhered to the status quo), leading to mergers, resignations, and institutional restructuring (Steps 4 and 5). This period of instability resulted in a heightened consciousness about racism by municipal elites in the city, and eventually, the United Way hired an African American director and added people of color to its board while creating new structures that supported and provided resources for community activism. Small agencies that were run by and for communities of color finally were funded by the United Way, which had not happened previously.

I do not want to give the impression that this was a revolution; it was not. The city still has many of the same structural inequities and injustices, but within that, it moved the needle. Local BIPOC leaders became more central to municipal decision making and local agencies and organizations serving BIPOC communities received more resources, enabling them not only to better support their communities but also to develop a new cohort of community leaders of color. Some White local businessmen became more sensitized and aware of the enduring and destructive power of racism. It was insufficient but not insignificant.

It is important to note that collective resistance and resilience do not substitute for a need to change social practices and policies (Cheng et al., 2021). Cheng et al. see a tripartite process that leads to what they call "advocacy," which I view as a form of resistance: the first part is the recognition of social discrimination and feeling that this is a common destiny for other people who share similar social identities. This is huge because it relieves a burden for individuals feeling isolated, wondering if this is due to something about them or something that they did, and forges a collective identity. Chen et al. describe how the increase in anti-Asian violence in the wake of President Trump's xenophobic anti-Chinese framing of COVID helped not only Chinese Americans to feel a sense of solidarity but this also extended to Asian Americans in general; this not only strengthened in-group solidarity but also intergroup unity. This illustrates the second part of the process: having a stronger racial/ethnic identity that is informed by a critical consciousness of the relationship of self, group, and society. And the third part of the process is taking collective action in the form of advocacy. Advocacy in the form of protests, collective gatherings, and political activism enhances group solidarity, enhances positive affect, and deepens meaning and having a purpose in life, as well as increasing the self-esteem and confidence of group members. Gebhard et al. (2022) view this as a recursive process of awareness leading to action leading to further reflection, which then leads to taking more action. This is a form of praxis.

Buckingham et al. (2021) find that there is a cyclical process where oppressed people build a sense of community, collectively develop a liberatory vision, heal from the consequences of oppression, and collectively act toward the group's liberation. They term this process the Transtheoretical Model of Empowerment and Resistance. Two core processes are empowerment (and healing) and activities that challenge or undermine structural processes of oppression. They feed one another: feeling empowered energizes people to act and acting is in itself empowering. Resistance seeks to undermine oppressive power while increasing the power of those who are resisting. There are many possible levels and targets of resistance – institutions, laws, and groups and individuals with inordinate degrees of power and privilege used to dominate others. Buckingham et al. go on to say that resistance can be passive or active, organized or unorganized, and overt or covert. The social ecology in which the resistance occurs shapes what means are available and will be most effective. The Civil Rights Movement in the United States employed all of these forms of resistance and in my experience, effective resistance involves different activities that are harnessed in the service of a common collective goal. For people in China, it is difficult to mount overt, active resistance, so covert activities that are under the radar have a greater chance of success.

In order to muster resistance, a group needs to believe that it can accomplish at least some of its goals (Gebhard et al., 2022). This necessitates having adequate information and knowledge and at least some resources that enable resistance. Assets can include places to meet (virtually or in-person), communication channels, safe spaces, and external support. Gebhard et al. note that there need to be resources that facilitate group maintenance – the glue that binds the group together and keeps it going – in addition to tactics to achieve specific aims and goals. As a group worker and community organizer, I learned the hard way how groups can become overwhelmed with conflict, fragment, or stall and get bogged down if there is insufficient attention to group process and cohesion.

Buckingham et al. (2022) focus on the organizational context of resistance. Many organizations replicate the larger processes of oppression in society through emulation (Tilly, 1999); it is like having a form of societal DNA in every institution and organization which are part of the larger social body. Coloniality, White supremacy, and other forms of oppression can easily be part of an organizational culture if critical attention is not brought to bear to prevent this from happening. But the authors point out that just like oppression can be replicated in settings, so can resistance. Some organizations work directly to confront oppression. I view Black Lives Matter, NAACP, and Common Cause as examples of that in the United States. At a more local level, organizations such as the Asian Counseling Referral Center in Seattle were established as institutions of resistance through their mission, board, and range of clinical, empowerment, and advocacy services that they provide to all Asian American communities in the area.

Another way that organizations can support resistance according to Buckingham and Brodsky (2021) is by offering "safe spaces." Tatum (2017) talks about the importance of spaces that buffer members of socially targeted groups, where people can regroup, avoid aggressions from others, and validate and support one another. Examples of this are cultural centers on the campuses of U.S. colleges and universities specifically established for BIPOC students. In such spaces, there is social support and connection as well as pooling of resources to use in collective resistance (Buckingham et al.). They characterize "empowerment settings" as having a culture of growth and community building, creating opportunities for group members to assume multiple roles that include shared leadership positions, and offering peer support and a commitment to the group and individual development. Part of this culture is one of self-reflection and mutual accountability. Although accountability can sound uncomfortable and threatening to some, I have found that accountability can be enacted compassionately, recognizing that everyone has the capacity to make mistakes or harm others, and where respect, mutual recognition, and the willingness to repair and reconstruct relationships are values central to the process. Buckingham et al. list a range of settings where this can occur: community action programs, faith-based organizations (think of the critical role played by churches during the Civil Rights Movement), direct care facilities, municipal entities, and grassroots organizations.

Support and space for healing and regeneration are foundational to resistance. There needs to be time and space and attention devoted to the full spectrum of emotions experienced in resistance to oppression, such as emotional emancipation circles (Gebhard et al., 2022). Self-care (see Chapter 10) is a form of activism. In addition to collective self-care, meditation and mindfulness are radical acts because they help us to unflinchingly focus attention on what is real; Thich Nhat Hanh and Martin Luther King Jr. both recognized that they did more good and less harm when they took time to be mindful and reflect (Zigmond, 2022). Psychoeducation groups are places where self-care can not only be prioritized but self-care strategies can also be shared among group members. It is also an opportunity for facilitators to help group members to identify any resistance that they might hold to self-care, which often comes from people feeling that this is somehow selfish or distracting from the energy needed for the resistance. Self-care not only replenishes and reenergizes people so that they are stronger and more able to resist but helps them to focus and dedicate themselves to future engagement. Psychoeducation groups that generate ideas about self-care can be in person or online (Cheng et al., 2021). In addition, mutual aid and support groups are also a form of self-care and can be combined with psychoeducation. Self-care and its relationship to resistance and resilience cannot be overemphasized.

Supporting Collective Resilience and Resistance

Figure 8.2 summarizes ways that helping professionals/volunteers can support collective resilience and resistance. The most fundamental way that helping professionals can support collective resilience is to not get in the way or undermine it and to ensure that efforts to help are not iatrogenic. Gone's (2021) description of Traveling Thunder's admonition to stay away from Western psychotherapy in order to not give up one's culture and personhood is a dramatic example of an indigenous leader voicing profound concern over mental health interventions by Western-trained practitioners.

The second way to support collective resilience and resistance is to use all of the principles discussed in this book to support the targeted group (summarized in Figure 8.2). A third way to support collective resilience is to connect group members and leaders with information and resources. A fourth way is to help the group to anticipate

1. **Avoiding getting in the way of and undermining indigenous and cultural sources of collective resilience.**
2. **Principles and parameters:**

   - Radical transparency of intentions, orientation, motivation, and possible positive and negative consequences.
   - Engaging collaborators as full participants and leaders and asking them what constitutes resilience.
   - Ensuring time and space to establish trust, recognizing that full trust may never be possible.
   - Critical awareness and self-awareness of power and hierarchy and the role of the state and the positionality of the helping professional
   - Developing the capacity of group members to help one another through the collaborative use of training of trainers.
   - Openness to mutual transformation, learning, and revising one's assumptions about what constitutes resilience.
   - Appreciation of how oppressions interact and the intersectionality of social identities.
   - Recognizing how inner psychological processes, including strengths, are connected to historical and structural factors.
   - Working collaboratively to blend indigenous and external knowledge and practices.
   - Working multisystemically and on multiple levels.
   - Joining with and helping to facilitate social action and advocacy.
   - Working to create space for grief, mourning, buffering, beauty, and collective joy.
   - Helping groups to draw upon and reclaim cultural processes and to construct and establish new processes for healing, reparations, and restorative justice
   - Recovering and constructing narratives of liberation and strength.
   - Drawing on dance, music, stories, art, and other non-talk modalities.
   - Collaborative psychoeducational opportunities to develop skills of self-calming and symptom management.

Figure 8.2 Supporting Psychosocial Resilience

- Validating and encouraging cultural connections and connection with elders and other sources of wisdom.
- Encouraging inclusion and equity within any group.
- Setting goals and evaluating progress using the terms and modalities familiar to the group.
- Helping group members to experience safety and security, even if it is partial and contingent.
- Encouraging and supporting self-care.

3. **Connecting group members with information and resources.**
4. **Working with group members to anticipate future threats and challenges and ways to prepare for them.**
5. **Promoting social policies that offer economic and social support, open life pathways, and protect targeted populations.**
6. **Promoting relational connection and support of group members, including engaging family members, extended family, clans, or others sharing social identities as well as allies of those who are socially targeted**

Figure 8.2 (Continued)

future threats and challenges and how to meet them. A fifth way is to strengthen the immediate social ecology by promoting social policies that will benefit the group (Ager, 2013). And a sixth way is to promote relational connection and support of targeted people, whether that is through engaging family, clans, or others sharing social identities or allies of those who are socially targeted (Edwards et al., 2019).

Although the main focus of this chapter is collective resilience, I will now briefly consider family and individual resilience.

Family Resilience

Families are complex systems, with roles, rules, communication patterns, histories, structures, systems and sub-systems, hierarchies and power, and overt and covert meanings, narratives, and secrets. Families are part of larger systems – such as neighborhoods and communities as well as collective groups based on shared identities. Families are strengthened when they live in communities with "integrity" – communities that foster safety and security, equity, family support, and access to resources – and recursively, when families in a community are resilient this strengthens collective resilience (Miller, 2001). Families are always in flux and have life cycles. Given all of this, families are not stable or fixed, despite enduring patterns of behaviors. Thus, when considering family resilience, it is helpful to view it as a dynamic process, inextricably connected to community and societal policies and processes, and not a set of static or endemic traits.

Exposure to oppression places stress on family resilience. While some forms of oppression are constant and durable, others wax and wane in intensity. Given all of these moving pieces, adaptability is a core aspect of family resilience (Miller, 2012; Walsh, 2003, 2020).

Walsh (2003, 2020) has written extensively about family resilience, and I will summarize some of her key points. She has identified nine key processes of family resilience:

1. Making meaning of adversity.
2. The capacity to maintain or regain a positive outlook despite threats and challenges. This involves a balance between a belief in the family's efficacy to achieve change while also being able to accept what cannot be changed.
3. An ability to connect with spirituality or to find transcendent meaning.
4. Having a balance between stability and flexibility, which together contribute to adaptability.
5. Connection within the family, which involves respect for individual differences and repairing ruptured relationships.
6. Being able to achieve financial security and stability. (This is of course much more challenging when coloniality and racism undermine this capacity.)
7. Clarity of communication.
8. Open emotional expression (As I have discussed throughout this book, the form and content of emotional expression vary considerably between cultures).
9. Being able to engage in creative, collaborative problem solving.

All of these processes require sufficient trust and safety among and between family members. Walsh also stresses the importance of being able to maintain hope and to be able to have a positive outlook about what is possible. Walsh, like Landau (2007) and Landau and Saul (2004), stresses the importance of connections with the past while revisioning the future. In families, revisiting the past can require the excavation of wounds, losses, and betrayals.

Families need to be able to accurately appraise threats to family members, recognizing what poses acute risks and long-term pressures. This can be challenging because the trauma of experiencing social assaults can also lead to triggering and severe reactions even in neutral or benign situations; so being able to sort the difference between trauma reminders and present threats can be important for the sense of safety and security of family members (Gebhard et al., 2022). This capacity can be helped by having a sense of family coherence (Antonosky & Sourani, 1988), where family members mutually share understandings and unite in the face of violence and social exclusion through common meanings, collectively comprehending situations and working out how to manage them. All of this contributes to family adaptability and the capacity to resist oppression.

Individual Resilience

Bonanno (2004) defines individual resilience as the ability to recover from disruptive and destabilizing life events and to be able to maintain healthy life trajectories. He describes the importance of generating optimistic thinking and positive emotions, finding meaning, and having purpose in life. Riffle et al. (2020) view post-traumatic growth as going beyond resilience in that it is transformative in five domains: (1) finding personal strength; (2) seeing new possibilities; (3) achieving positive changes in relationships; (4) having a greater appreciation of life; and (5) spiritual changes and growth.

When considering individual resilience, there is the risk that it is viewed as a set of personal traits that explain why some people thrive while others are overwhelmed. Discussing resilience without placing it in a sociopolitical context runs the risk of blaming individuals for their lack of resilience (Serrano-Garcia, 2020). This can detract from focusing on, critiquing and confronting social injustice (Park et al., 2018). This is why I prefer to think of resilience as the ability to resist the forces of social oppression, working to undermine oppressive power structures (Buckingham & Brodsky, 2021; Gebhard et al., 2022), as it is more active and action oriented. As with all forms of resilience, exposure to threats and access to resources and privileges are major determinants of what is perceived as resilience. Resilient societies, communities, families, and groups all support individual resilience and confronting and mitigating chronic and acute threats and violence, as well as unrestrained inequities are the most significant interventions that will strengthen individual resilience. Social networks are also critical, as described in the section on collective resilience. Transcending feelings of separation and isolation and being able to achieve a greater sense of connection and oneness with others strengthens individual resilience (Miller, 2012).

As with collective and family resilience, research indicates that resilience is heightened when individuals can construct a sense of meaning, including spirituality, in the face of adversity and are able to use this to achieve a higher sense of efficacy (Park & Blake, 2020). Edwards et al. (2019) note that some have found that personal agency, feelings of empowerment, having an internal locus of control, feelings of hopefulness, and optimism are individual-based resilience factors, particularly for those with minoritized identities. While I agree with this, I wonder about cultures where individuals view themselves as being less able to actively influence their fate. Many Westerners may have a greater tendency to focus on exerting control when confronting adversity (Riffle et al., 2020). They also live in environments where they can exert more control – e.g., reliable transportation networks where they can get to places on time and greater phone and Internet infrastructure. Might acceptance of what cannot be changed be another sign of resilience, within the context of cultural meaning and practices? The same is true with personal factors that are said to influence resilience, such as extroversion and emotional disclosure (Riffle et al.). Surely these are signs of resilience in certain cultural contexts while humility, deference, and careful consideration of when, what, and who when disclosing are also signs of resilience. I have found, however, that in many cultural contexts helping others helps oneself and that altruism fosters social connections, a sense of shared predicament, and is actively empowering. In summary, I believe that caution should be exercised when viewing certain individuals as resilient and that the collective and cultural contexts are important determinants.

The Links Between Different Levels of Resilience

In my experience, all levels of resilience interact and influence one another. A number of researchers contend that community/collective resilience is effective because it strengthens individual resilience (e.g., Edwards et al., 2019; Lee et al., 2017; Lyons et al., 2016). I think that the converse is also true, that when individuals are exhibiting resilience, this amps up collective resilience – it is a recursive process.

However, I think that it is limiting to view collective resilience as merely a process that supports individual resilience. Collective resilience also challenges the historical, systemic, and structural forces of oppression, which goes beyond individual well-being. It is not only a form of survival but also leads to collective efficacy, and while radiating out to individuals, it also flows upward, confronting and transforming social institutions – such as the achievements of the Civil Rights Movement in the United States. In my view, different forms of resilience are imbricated within one another while exerting different spheres of influence: e.g., resilient individuals contribute to resilient families, while collective resilience can lead to resilient societies.

Helping professionals should be concerned with all levels of resilience in our work and understand resilience in the terms of those who are being supported. With all levels it is a process rather than a set of traits and resistance to oppression is a key manifestation. Our task is not to get in the way of resilience nor to impose what we believe constitutes resilience, but to enable affected people to tap into their many wellsprings of resilience.

Conclusion

Resilience is a process, not a set of static traits, an interaction between individuals, families, groups, and communities with one another and with the society and culture that they are part of. In this chapter, I have particularly focused on collective resilience while briefly touching on family and individual resilience. With all forms of resilience, it is important to focus on external (e.g., historical and structural) constraints, resources, and pathways to understand what fosters or undermines resilience. Due to the dominance of Western scholars writing about resilience, conducting research, and developing scales, there has been an excessive emphasis on individual and family resilience and only recently a focus on collective resilience. This has led to assumptions about what constitutes resilience based on a narrow slice of human societies and cultures and attempts to measure this vision of resilience through the use of scales. Therefore, it is essential to engage local people when developing an understanding of what resilience means and looks like to them! And it is also important to view resilience as an interactive process where communities, groups, families, and individuals actively confront the sources of oppression that they and their ancestors have encountered and, in the process, become more cohesive, connected, and resilient.

References

Ager, A. (2013). Annual research review: Resilience and child well-being-public policy implications. *Journal of Child Psychology and Psychiatry*, *54*(4): 488–500. DOI: 10.1111/jcpp.12030.

Ali, D.A., Figley, C.R., Tedeschi, R.G., Galarneu, D., & Amara, S. (2021). Shared trauma, resilience, and growth: A roadmap toward transcultural conceptualization. *Psychological Trauma: Theory, Research, Practice, and Policy*. DOI: 10.1037/tra0001044.

Antonosky, A., & Sourani, T. (1988). Family sense of coherence and family adaptation. *Journal of Marriage and Family Therapy*, *50*: 79–82.

Bonanno, G.A. (2004). Loss, trauma and human resilience: Have we underestimated the capacity to thrive after extremely adverse events? *American Psychologist*, *59*(1): 20–28.

Buckingham, S.L., & Brodsky, A.E. (2021). Relative privilege, risk and sense of community: Understanding Latinx immigrant's empowerment and resilience process across the United States. *American Journal of Community Psychology*, *67*: 364–379. DOI: 10.1002/ajcp.12486.

Cenat, J.M., Dalexis, R.D., Derivois, D., Herbert, M., Haljizadeh, S., Kokou-Kpolou, C.K., Guerrier, M., & Rousseau, C. (2021). The transcultural community resilience scale: Psychometric properties and multinational validity in the context of the COVID-19 pandemic. *Frontiers in Psychology*. DOI: 10.3389/fpsyg.2021.713477.

Cheng, H., Kim, H.Y., Reynolds, J.D., Tsong, Y., & Wong, Y.J. (2021). COVID-19 anti-Asian racism: A tripartite model of collective psychosocial resilience. *American Psychologist*, *76*(4): 627–642. DOI: 10.1037/amp0000808.

Edwards, L.L., Bernal, A.T., Hanley, S.M., & Martin, S. (2019). Resilience factors and suicide risk for a sample of transgender clients. *Family Process*, *59*: 1209–1224. DOI: 10.1111/famp.12479.

Erfurth, L.M., Bark, A.S.H., Molenaar, C., Adyin, A.L., & van Dick, R. (2021). "If worse comes to worst, my neighbors come first": Social identity as a collective resilience factor in areas threatened by sea floods. *SN Social Science*. DOI: 10.1007/s43545-021-00284-6.

Garran, A.M., Werkmeister-Rozas, L.M., Kang, H.K., & Miller, J. (2021). *Racism in the United States: Implications for the helping professions* (3rd ed.). New York: Springer Publishing.

Gebhard, K.T., Hargrove, S., Chaudhry, T., Buchwach, S.V., & Cattaneo, L.B. (2022). Building strength for the long haul toward liberation: What psychology can contribute to the resilience of communities targeted by state-sanctioned violence. *American Journal of Community Psychology*. DOI: 10.1002/ajcp.12596.

Gil-Rivas, V., & Kilmer, R.P. (2016). Building community capacity and fostering disaster resilience. *Journal of Clinical Psychology*, 72(12): 1318–1332. DOI: 10.1002/jclp.22281.

Gone, J.P. (2021). The (post)colonial predicament in community mental health services for American Indians: Explorations in alter-Native psy-ence. *American Psychologist*, *76*(9): 1514–1525. DOI: 10.1037/amp0000906.
Kretzman, J.P., & McKnight, J.L. (1993). *Building communities from the inside out: A path towards finding and mobilizing a community's assets.* Chicago, IL: ACTA Publications; Institute for Policy Research.
Kuecker, G.D. (2017). Enchanting transition: A post-colonial perspective. In T. Henfry, G. Maschkowski, & G. Penha-Lopez (Eds.). *Resilience, community action and societal transformation* (pp. 193–210). East Meon, UK: Permanent Publications.
Landau, J. (2007). Enhancing resilience: Communities and families as agents of change. *Family Process*, *41*(1): 351–365.
Landau, J., & Saul, J. (2004). Facilitating family and community resilience in response to major disaster. In F. Walsh & M. McGoldrick (Eds.). *Living beyond loss* (pp. 285–309). New York: Norton Publishing.
Lee, J., Blackmon, B.J., Cochran, D.M., Kar, B., Rehner, T.A., & Gunnel, M.S. (2017). Community resilience, psychological resilience, and depressive symptoms: An examination of the Mississippi Gulf Coast 10 years after Hurricane Katrina and 5 years after the Deepwater Horizon oil spill. *Disaster Medicine and Public Health Preparedness*. DOI: 10.1017/dmp.2017.61.
Lindberg, K., & Swearingen, T. (2020). A reflective thrive-oriented community resilience scale. *American Journal of Community Psychology*, *65*: 467–478. DOI: 10.1002/ajcp.12416.
Lyons, A., Fletcher, G., & Bariola, E. (2016). Assessing the well-being benefits of belonging to resilient groups and communities: Development and testing of the Fletcher-Lyons collective resilience scale (FLCRS). *Group Dynamics, Theory, Research, and Practice*, *20*(2): 65–77. DOI: 10.1037/gdn0000041.
Memmi, A. (2000). *Racism*. Minneapolis, MN: University of Minnesota Press.
Miller, J. (2001). Family and community integrity. *Journal of Sociology and Social Welfare*, *28*(4): 23–44.
Miller, J.L. (2012). *Psychosocial capacity building in response to disasters.* New York: Columbia University Press.
Molinaar, C., Blessin, M., Erfurth, L., & Imhoff, R. (2022). Were we stressed or was it just me? Efforts to disentangle individual and collective resilience within real and imagined stressors. *British Journal of Social Psychology*, *61*: 167–191. DOI: 10.1111/bjso.12475.
Morning Edition. (2022, June 14). As hate crimes against Asian Americans rise, a California neighborhood takes action. *NPR*. www.npr.org/2022/06/14/1104881768/as-hate-crimes-against-asian-americans-rise-a-california-neighborhood-takes-acti
Ntontis, E., Dury, J., Amlot, R., Rubin, C.J., Williams, R., & Saavedra, P. (2020). Collective resilience in the disaster recovery period: Emergent social identity and observed social support are associated with collective efficacy, well-being, and the provision of social support. *British Journal of Social Psychology*, *60*: 1075–1095. DOI: 10.1111/bjso.12434.
Park, C.L., & Blake, E.C. (2020). Resilience and recovery after disasters: The meaning making model. In S.E. Schulenberg (Ed.). *Positive psychological*

approaches to disaster: Meaning, resilience and posttraumatic growth (pp. 9–26). Cham, Switzerland: Springer Nature Switzerland AG.

Park, Y., Crath, R., & Jeffery, D. (2018). Disciplining the risky subject: A discourse analysis of the concept of resilience in social work literature. *Journal of Social Work*. DOI: 10.1177/1468017318792953.

Riffle, O.M., Lewis, P.R., & Tedeschi, R.G. (2020). Post-traumatic growth after disasters. In S.E. Schulenberg (Ed.). *Positive psychological approaches to disaster: Meaning, resilience and posttraumatic growth* (pp. 155–167). Cham, Switzerland: Springer Nature Switzerland AG.

Ross, H. (2017). Linking theory and practice of community resilience. In T. Henfry, G. Maschkowski, & G. Penha-Lopez (Eds.). *Resilience, community action and societal transformation* (pp. 59–62). East Meon, UK: Permanent Publications.

Serrano-Garcia, I. (2020). Resilience, coloniality, and sovereign acts: The role of community activism. *American Journal of Community Psychology*, *65*: 3–1. DOI: 10.1002/ajcp.12415.

Suyemoto, K.L., Abdullah, T., Godon-Decoteau, D., Tahirkheli, N.N., Arbid, N., & Frye, A.A. (2022). Development of the resistance and empowerment against racism (REAR) scale. *Cultural Diversity and Ethnic Minority Psychology*, *28*(1): 58–71. DOI: 10.1037/cdp0000353.

Tatum, B.D. (2017). *Why are all the Black kids sitting together in the cafeteria?* New York: Basic Books.

Tekin, S., Sager, M., Bushey, A., Deng, Y., & Ulig, O.M. (2021). How do people support one another in emergencies? A qualitative exploration of altruistic and prosocial behaviours during COVID 19 pandemic. *Analysis of Social Issues and Public Policy*. DOI: 10.1111/asap.12277.

Terrana, A., Ibrahim, N., Kaiser, B., & Al-Delaimy, W.K. (2022). Foundations of Somali resilience: Collective identity, faith, and community. *Cultural Diversity and Ethnic Minority Psychology*. DOI: 10.1037/cdp0000536.

Tilly, C. (1999). *Durable inequality*. Berkeley, CA: University of California Press.

Van Tongeren, D.R., Aten, J.D., Davis, E.B., Davis, D.E., & Hook, J.N. (2020). Religion, spirituality and meaning making in the wake of disaster. In S.E. Schulenberg (Ed.). *Positive psychological approaches to disaster: Meaning, resilience and posttraumatic growth* (pp. 27–44). Cham, Switzerland: Springer Nature Switzerland AG.

Vindevogel, S., Ager, A., Schiltz, J., Broekaert, E., & Derluyn, I. (2015). Toward a culturally sensitive conceptualization of resilience: Participatory research with war-affected communities in Northern Uganda. *Transcultural Psychiatry*, *52*(3): 1–21.

Walsh, F. (2003). Family resilience: A framework for clinical practice. *Family Process*, *42*(1): 1–18.

Walsh, F. (2020). Loss and resilience in the time of COVID-19: Meaning making, hope, and transcendence. *Family Process*, *59*(3): 898–911. DOI: 10.1111/famp.12588.

Zigmond, D. (2022, July). Meditation is a political act. *Lion's Roar*, *7*(3): 13–15.

9 Psychosocial Support for Immigrants and Refugees

Introduction

In her book *The Spirit Touches You and You Fall Down* (1997), author Anne Fadiman describes a Hmong family who settled in Merced, California, whose infant daughter develops epilepsy in the 1990s. Over the next few years, a tragic drama unfolds as doctors make little or no effort to understand the parents or Hmong culture, often even neglecting to have translators so that the child's parents, who do not speak English, can be informed about their child's condition, treatment recommendations, and what will be needed from them to care for their child. Instead, the family is pathologized as being non-compliant, primitive, and obstructive by the medical staff and at one point the state removes the child from the parent's custody. Not only do the doctors completely ignore the cultural, social, and historical context of how Hmong's parents, their notion of personhood, their cosmology and belief system, and the meaning of extended family and social connections, but they are completely unaware of how they are perceived by the parents: oblivious, incompetent, uncaring, and at times trying to kill their child.

The medical staff are unmindful of, and perhaps uninterested in, how the family was persecuted as an ethnic minority in Laos, were caught up in the U.S. imperial wars and devastation of Southeast Asia, and their harrowing escape from Laos to a squalid refugee camp in Thailand. This preceded the family being "resettled" in the United States, which was a completely alien, unfamiliar, and in many ways hostile environment for them to live in and raise their children. As Fadiman points out, not only did the family experience being strangers in a strange land, mistreatment by the medical and social service system, and having their history and culture ignored, but the process of immigration also upended and inverted their own internal social

DOI: 10.4324/9781003021162-9

system. In a society where elders and grandparents were venerated and powerful, Hmong families found themselves in a situation where grandparents, and many parents, often never learned to speak English while their children did, leading to children serving as translators, often making decisions, while elders were marginalized and diminished, reversing the hierarchy of family roles as they were structured prior to immigration. Traditional family roles and cultural practices, which had served as lodestones and guideposts for Hmong people – who fiercely resisted assimilation to other societies – for many centuries and in many different countries, were undermined, weakened, and disrespected by residents of their new country and eventually became unviable. In the story that Fadiman tells, all of these factors contributed to the child becoming severely compromised cognitively and neurologically, what U.S. doctors called "brain dead."

In this chapter, I will consider the psychosocial milieu of immigrants, refugees, and asylum seekers who are fleeing dangerous, unstable, and untenable situations and find themselves caught in a nightmare twilight zone of non-status, defined as non-persons without rights, as they traverse a world shaped by coloniality and all of its discontents, exacerbated by increasing inequality between and within countries, and further fueled by climate change. As I have written about in this book, the poverty of Africa and the wealth of Europe and North America were not historical accidents, but the consequences of policies of colonization, imposition of Western governance and notions of personhood, and the legacies of enslavement, genocide, ethnic cleansing, and terrorism. With accelerating climate change, people in poor countries continue to bear the burden of the excesses of fuel and carbon use in wealthier nations, experiencing drought, fires, floods, storms, hunger, and starvation (while wealthy countries continue to extract their natural resources, outsourcing low-wage manufacturing to them), and the violence stemming from corruption, co-existing with other tribes in nation-states that were often figments of the imagination of colonial occupiers, and being used as pawns in continuing global conflicts and struggles for supremacy among the most powerful nations. Walia (2021) views the unprecedentedly high numbers of migrants globally as a consequence of the interactions of conquest, capitalism, and climate change. The U.N. High Commissioner for Refugees estimates that there are 100 million forcibly displaced persons in the world, while the International Organization for Migration predicts that this could swell as high as 1.5 billion people over the ensuing decades (McKibben, 2022).

And yet, rather than paying reparations, returning stolen resources and artifacts, and reconfiguring global economic, political, and social systems – reconstructing a non-colonial, non-White supremacist world – wealthy and predominantly White countries are desperately trying to keep immigrants, refugees, and asylum seekers from entering their territory, often finding ways to circumvent international law. Whether it is the United States trying to keep migrants in Mexico or the United Kingdom planning to fly immigrants, who have literally washed up on their shore, to concentration camps in Rwanda, wealthy nations are working overtime to keep people out, often successfully using the threat of immigration as a political and social wedge issue, one that has increasingly spurred the rise of authoritarian, dissembling demagogues in many countries where this was thought to be unimaginable.[1] When immigrants do successfully enter these countries – such as Mexicans who have immigrated to the United States – they are characterized as "criminals," "rapists," and "drug dealers" by President Donald Trump.

In this chapter, I will consider how helping professionals can be supportive of individuals, families, and communities who were socially targeted and oppressed in their countries of origin, have made arduous and hazardous journeys, and have found themselves in countries where they experience many threats and barriers to their well-being, success, and ability to thrive.

Leaving Home

It can be difficult to imagine the many facets of immigration that affect a person's psychosocial well-being for those who have not immigrated, which is the case for many helping professionals. It is even more of an imaginative challenge for many helping professionals who are citizens of wealthy countries to appreciate the experience of being a refugee. In this section, I will sketch out general challenges when having to depart home for another country, whether this is voluntary or not.

In its most basic sense, a person is leaving what is familiar, a sociocultural milieu where it is clear what it means to be a person, and how one conducts oneself and expresses ideas, thoughts, and feelings. Often one is leaving what is known linguistically, culturally, socially, physically, and sensually – familiar smells, sights, sounds, landscapes, streets, and neighborhoods. And immigrants are leaving behind people – family, friends, members of their community, and social networks – who did not immigrate and often their homes and possessions. As well as this, many immigrants are leaving their occupations and may or may not be able to reconstitute this in their new country.

All of these reasons can contribute to a loss of identity and may lead immigrants to reevaluate who they are, their relationships with people in the country being left, and their purpose in life (Carlsson & Sonne, 2018). Immigrants leave behind partners, parents, grandparents, and extended family, often not knowing whether or not they will see them again and at the very least worrying about when and how they will reunite with their family. Particularly for children (although this is also true for adolescents and adults), leaving behind beloved caretakers and other people with whom they have an emotional relationship can lead to a grieving process – will they see these people again, how can they talk about and remember them, and will those left behind be OK (Bragin, 2019)? Immigrants miss many life events – e.g., births of nieces and nephews, weddings, and funerals (Nesteruk, 2018). Such relational disruptions and losses not only affect the life course but can also persist throughout a person's life (Nesteruk). The loss of and breakdown in relationships may affect a person's ability to trust and bond with others throughout life's journey, and the experiences of corrupt government officials can undermine trust in authorities (Carlson and Sonne).

These factors are present even when people have economic, social, political, and educational resources and immigration is a choice that has been made. But often, immigrants leave because they are experiencing terrible things at home: poverty, political and social targeting, military and paramilitary attacks, gang violence, "natural disasters" (e.g., drought, floods, fires, huge storms, rising sea levels), and an absence or lack of a social safety net. They may have experienced racism, ethnic cleansing, genocide, ongoing armed conflict, torture, sexual assault, kidnapping, selling children, and even sexual and labor slavery. It is not surprising that pre-migration oppression is often a precipitating factor in the decision to emigrate (Buckingham et al., 2021). All of these factors can contribute to trauma, sadness, stress, depression, and medical and psychological vulnerability before, during, and after immigration (Bragin, 2019; Buckingham et al., 2021; Mincin et al., 2022; Myers & Patz, 2009; Stoklosa et al., 2021).

The Journey

Some families who have been socially targeted in their home country have a certain amount of capital – e.g., educational and economic. For example, some Sri Lankan Tamils who fled the brutal Sinhalese campaigns to erase their language and culture and who survived a 26-year armed conflict between the Tamil Tigers and Sri Lankan government moved abroad – sometimes to wealthy nations such as Britain and Canada. – and used their education and social connections to establish themselves and formed an educated Tamil diaspora. They may have been able to fly to their new destination and avoid being stopped at the border or spending time in refugee camps. Certainly, there were many Tamil immigrants who did not have the resources and ability to avoid perilous migration journeys but some were able to. This is not to minimize the challenges of their resettlement but to highlight how for most people without human, social, and economic capital, the journey is fraught with threats.

The vast majority of migrants who are members of groups that have been socially targeted at home embark on dangerous, hazardous, odysseys to escape poverty, an increasingly inhospitable and sustainable environment, and persecution; the terror of such passages adds another layer to the stress and trauma of immigration, particularly for refugees, who lack visas and assets. As was mentioned in earlier chapters, all passports are not the same: those from wealthier nations, such as the United States or Germany, have cache and validity in a range of countries, while those from poorer countries (often former "colonies) such as Myanmar, Sudan, and Guatemala find far fewer open doors, particularly into affluent Western nations. Thus, those fleeing the direst situations often do not have a welcoming nation to move to and are left to face death, food insecurity and starvation, the fragmentation of their families and suffering of their children, exploitation, detentions, and uncertainty about where they might eventually find sanctuary and safety. They have to navigate dangerous sea crossings and dystopian land journeys, where they are vulnerable to hostile police, attacks by militias, extortion by smugglers and "coyotes," attacks by pirates, and are vulnerable and unprotected in the face of natural hazards (e.g., excessive heat and cold, dangerous river crossings, facing predatory animals, and exposure to dangerous diseases such as Dengue fever, malaria, and cholera).

The toll of premigration oppression and the perils of the migratory journey add up to many stressors which increase psychosocial and medical vulnerability (Buckingham et al., 2021). There is no safety, security, stability, or certainty. Migrants and refugees have often witnessed or directly experienced human rights abuses at home and during their travels and are exposed to food insecurity and starvation, loss of loved ones, physical and sexual violence, and torture, which includes mental and emotional agony (Hinton & Patel, 2018).

I have been using the terms migrants and refugees interchangeably and part of my reason for doing this is that they are separated by a blurry line. The United Nations High Commission on Refugees [UNHCR] defines refugees as

> a person who is outside his or her country of nationality or habitual residence; has a well-founded fear of being persecuted because of his or her race, religion, nationality, membership of a particular social group or political opinion; and is unable or unwilling to avail him – or herself of the protection of that country, or to return there, for fear of persecution.
>
> (2011)

Immigrants are viewed as voluntarily leaving their countries (Mincin et al., 2022). A foundational principle for refugees is "non-refoulment," not to forcibly return immigrants to the country from where they fled. Their rights when entering a new country include: not to be expelled, not to be punished, and the right to work, housing, education, public relief and assistance, freedom of religion, freedom of movement, and to be issued identity and travel documents. UNHCR defines migrants as people who voluntarily leave their countries for economic, educational, or family reunification purposes and who are (allegedly) still receiving the protections of the government of the country of which they are a citizen. So, by virtue of international law, there is a distinction between a refugee and a migrant. Asylum seekers are refugees who seek sanctuary, protection, and a new life in another country (Mincin et al.).

However, when it comes to considering the situation of a given person or family that has left their home country, there are many places of overlap. People who are members of groups besieged and oppressed within their home countries are often the targets of direct and indirect, formal and informal, and violence and persecution by official and unofficial antagonists, while also being socially oppressed by not having access to jobs, housing, services, and legal protections. Are people in such a situation leaving their home countries "voluntarily" or are they "forced" to leave? It is usually a combination of factors, some of which fit with the UNHCR definition and some of which are outside of it. And when it comes to receiving and protecting refugees, receiving countries go through contortions to honor their international agreements while not allowing refugees into their countries.

Two recent examples come from populist, right-wing, leaders of Western countries – Boris Johnson, former Prime Minister of the

United Kingdom, and Donald Trump, former President of the United States. Johnson's government devised a plan whereby adults landing on the shores of the UK can be flown to Rwanda, where their asylum status will be processed and they will remain in refugee camps during that process. And in the United States, many migrants from Central and South America are being kept in Mexico, while their asylum applications are being processed in the United States. Australia devised a similar plan, sending refugees to Nauru and Papua New Guinea, while many EU countries have placed many asylum seekers in Turkey. What is a common thread is that White, wealthier nations have, for the most part, resisted having refugees and asylum seekers (particularly if they are people of color) enter and resettle in their countries, despite international obligations and have developed partnerships with less-wealthy countries, which they pay to "detain" refugees, rather than have them enter their borders. This cynical ploy is unsurprising, as it ignores the vast global inequalities in wealth and the role that coloniality had in creating this wealth cap. It overlooks how powerful nations, such as the United States, destabilized countries in Central America, helping to create the conditions for refugees or how countries allow migrants to enter their borders when it suits them, such as when needing them do low-wage work that citizens avoid. And this is how refugees are treated; migrants have even fewer rights and options when trying to enter countries where they *might* be able to survive and make a living.

Thus, many migrants and refugees end up in refugee or concentration camps or living on the streets of places along their journey, such as Mexico City, when attempting journeys to new homes. For those who are living in refugee camps, the standards, resources, and safety and security vary considerably. The experience is like treading water for years in a strange and unfamiliar lake, where there are many hazards beneath the surface. All refugee camps, whether for internally or internationally displaced persons, are interregnum situations and leave families in limbo and often at risk. The threats to safety can come from many angles: government or state-sponsored attacks, militia or gang attacks, overcrowding and unhealthy conditions, lack of access to safe water and adequate food, and an overall dearth of law, order, and legal protections. Women and children are particularly vulnerable to violence and sexual assault. Human traffickers prey on people in refugee camps as will be considered below.

Refugee camps often lack adequate educational and medical resources for inhabitants, who are often living in overcrowded, unprotected conditions and have high exposure levels to infectious diseases. People who are placed there might be from rival clans, ethnic groups, gangs, or political parties, leading to internal conflict, violence, and terrorism. Residents have lost access to their homes, possessions, sociocultural worlds, and ability to be self-sufficient. On the one hand, boredom and listlessness are common in refugee camps, while on the other, hypervigilance and alertness are necessary for survival. It is more difficult for partners to experience intimacy and for parents to be able to care for and supervise their children. In clan-based systems, elders often lose some of their respect and authority and connections to cultural customs are often diminished. Even the ability to cook familiar food is constrained.

Despite these hardships, many refugees and migrants exhibit profound resilience and engage in resistance. Reconstructing old routines and developing new practices often take place within the constraints of living in a refugee camp. Residents often look out for one another, band together for sharing and protection, and pool resources. Informal communities, social networks, and rules for living together spring up. In one refugee camp that I visited, women were at high risk of violence and sexual assault when leaving the camp to look for firewood in "the bush," so women banded together and foraged in groups.

Human Trafficking

The United Nations defines human trafficking as

> the recruitment, transportation, transfer, harboring, or receipt of persons by means of the threat or use of force or other forms of coercion, of abduction, of fraud, of deception, of the abuse of power or of a position of vulnerability or the giving or receiving of payments or benefits to achieve the consent of a person having control over another person, for the purpose of exploitation. Exploitation shall include at a minimum the exploitation of the prostitution of others or other forms of sexual exploitation, forced labor or services, slavery or practices similar to slavery, servitude of the removal of organs.
>
> (Kara, 2017, p. 11)

Bryant-Davis and Tummala-Narra (2020, p. 17) describe human trafficking as "the use of force, fraud, or coercion to recruit or obtain a person illegally for the purposes of labor or sexual exploitation." Debt bondage and forced labor are among the types of human trafficking, and often there are overlapping categories – e.g., sexual exploitation and forced prostitution often involve debt bondage (Kara).

I could discuss human trafficking in any section of this chapter or book, as it occurs in home countries, during the migration process and when immigrants are living in a new land. Human trafficking is another consequence of global inequality, extreme poverty, and low social status and capital within countries or around the world. However, the risks of trafficking accelerate during the migratory trip where protections are stripped away and the dangers of predation increase. This leads to greater vulnerability and desperation, which can result in labor and debt bondage, sexual assault and exploitation, and even the selling of children. There are far fewer safeguards against human trafficking – e.g., laws, social networks, visibility to others in a community, parental, and family oversight – while in transit. For example, as Stoklosa et al. (2021) describe, it is much more difficult for parents to exert supervision of their children, and some parents may have died, are incapacitated, or are not part of the journey. People are subject to overwhelming force, coercion, or fraud, made worse by unregulated markets, lack of protective laws and regulations, and the absence of being documented and having legal status and protections. Evacuation centers and refugee camps are not only sites attracting predators but they also group vulnerable people in a visible location and offer insufficient supervision and protection.

Bryant-Davis and Tummala-Narra (2020) – who link the trafficking of children with colonialism and the history of enslavement by Western countries – point out how child sexual trafficking is more likely to occur when children are cut off from their family and their social milieu and are not attending school. Risk factors include poverty, racism, being female, insecure attachments with adults, and unsafe relationships and neighborhoods (and while in transit children are not living in neighborhoods)! Often there are no protective services available, and even in refugee camps, services frequently are not provided in a linguistically and culturally responsive manner.

Enslavement is not a thing of the past, although the mechanisms of capture and control have shifted as has its form: debt bondage, forced labor, and sexual servitude. The Global Slavery Index (2018) estimates that over 40 million people held in modern slavery and nearly 90 million have experienced slavery at some point in their lives. While it is no longer legal, the desperation of people living in a desert of poverty and flooded by structural oppression, the lack of respect and rights of groups of people based on their social identities, and, frankly, the lack of caring by people who are not directly affected by human trafficking allows it to flourish. Poverty, targeted status, migration, the profits gained from human trafficking, lack of protections by authorities, and often victim blaming all contribute to modern-day enslavement (Kara, 2017). It is more common when there are very repressive regimes and if there are conflict situations, leading to the breakdown of social norms and laws (Global Slavery Index).

The New Land

Many who offer psychosocial support to immigrants and refugees once they have arrived in their new countries focus on their trauma due to experiences in the country of origin and the travails of making the journey. This is of course true, and trauma increases the vulnerability of migrants. Those with trauma from their country of origin are more likely to experience "post-migration stress and the ongoing effects of cumulative trauma" (Mincin et al., 2022). But it is even more important to focus on the current sources of oppression that migrants face in their new homes, as these are what they are confronting on an ongoing basis. Often, the reception in the destination country triggers feelings of lack of safety and agency and evokes prior experiences of social targeting.

Garran et al. (2021) describe the process of immigration racism. Immigrants of color, who are the vast majority of refugees and asylum seekers in the United States, experience racism, Islamophobia, and overt hostility from politicians, particularly since Donald Trump was President. They are convenient scapegoats for social problems not of their making and are represented as those who take jobs from U.S. citizens. President Trump characterized immigrants as bringing antisocial behavior, carrying disease, and posing a national security threat (the alleged reason for his "Muslim ban"). J.D. Vance, the Republican candidate for Senator from Ohio in 2022, while campaigning said that President Biden's "open borders" are killing people in Ohio with illicit drugs," while nativist demagogue Tucker Carlson, promulgater of "replacement theory" (White people are intentionally being replaced in the United States by policies increasing immigrants of color), warned Americans that when immigrants join a community, it becomes poorer (Coy, 2022). These are the kinds of narratives that immigrants and refugees from poorer nations, particularly those of color, have to contend with.

Coy (2022), citing a recent book about immigrant contributions to U.S. society – *Streets of gold: America's untold story of immigrant success* by Abramitsky and Bouston – challenges many of these nativist myths. The children of poor immigrants are more likely to move up socioeconomically than native-born children of the same economic strata. While it is true that the first generation of poor immigrants is costlier than those who are native-born, due to their need for government services, this is offset by the economic achievements of the next generation. And rather than taking jobs away from native-born people, immigrants either work in occupations that residents avoid, therefore contributing to the economy, but also add jobs by eventually creating businesses that did not previously exist and that employ domestic workers. Immigrants also tend to move to areas where there are labor shortages and keep the economy going where they have settled.

But the reality of immigrant contributions and accomplishments does not erase the hostility and nativism that they encounter when arriving in a wealthy country. Racism and White supremacy and Islamophobia are common forms of prejudice encountered by immigrants to Western nations. This leads to blatant acts of violence, such as attacks as well as state surveillance and less support and greater hostility from law enforcement. Barajas-Gonzalez et al. (2018) quote the World Health Organization's definition of violence:

> the intentional use of physical force or power, threatened or actual, against one's self, another person, or against a group or community that either results in or has a high likelihood of resulting in injury, death, psychological harm, maldevelopment, or deprivation.

They go on to say how the Trump administration's actions toward immigrants fit this definition. There was an expansion of Immigration and Customs Enforcement activities (and a tone of threat and hostility) more detentions and deportations, and schools and medical facilities became increasingly unsafe as undocumented people were picked up at such sites. As I have mentioned earlier, President Trump repeatedly defamed immigrants as carrying diseases, bringing crime and drugs to the United States, coming from "shithole countries," and encouraging hostility toward immigrants by communities, vigilantism, and government antagonism rather than government support. There was a shift from providing resources to immigrants to hunting them down and incarcerating and deporting them (Vesely et al., 2017). It is difficult to even write this in 2022 without feeling like it is from a dystopian science fiction novel, but there was a policy of intentionally separating children from their families, keeping them in institutions lacking heat, sanitation, and adequate medical care, which certainly contributed to "psychological harm, maldevelopment, or deprivation." And when President Trump regularly referred to COVID-19 by sneeringly calling it the "Chinese virus," deadly attacks against Asian Americans and Asian immigrants escalated, as I have described in earlier chapters. Unsurprisingly, immigrants felt a sense of insecurity and harbored fears of deportation (Buckingham et al., 2021).

But even when there is not a hostile and injurious leader such as Trump at the helm of a country, immigrants and refugees still face many painful challenges. There are high expectations about "fitting in" with the host nation and often a dismissal of cultural practices brought by the immigrants. As Fadiman (1997) describes in the vignette shared at the beginning of the chapter, doctors were skeptical, at times scathing, and repulsed by Hmong practices to help a family's gravely ill child to heal. Due to discrimination and lack of government support, immigrants often have difficulty finding housing and jobs and accessing adequate health care (Buckingham et al., 2021; Carlsson & Sonne, 2018). And when a government is overtly hostile to immigrants, as with the Trump and Orban regimes, parents are fearful about sending children to school and going to health-care facilities because of the risks of deportation (Buckingham et al.).

There is also the stress of obtaining necessary visas and, for some, applying for asylum (Carlsson & Sonne, 2018). This is particularly challenging for immigrants who do not speak the language of their new country, are unfamiliar with its laws and policies, and where they may be encountering officials who are unhelpful or hostile. And they may already be mistrustful of authorities based on their experiences in their country of origin and during their transit. Often there need to be repeated visits to government offices to update one's documents and status which can contribute to anxiety, worry, stress, and an overall feeling of uncertainty (Daftary, 2020). I have heard from immigrants lacking permanent resident status who had to make regular visits to the FBI in the United States, of feeling demeaned, unsafe, disrespected, and undermined during their meeting. They dreaded these "interviews" and some found them to be traumatic.

Vesely et al. (2017) have found that there are four categories of immigrant stressors. The first is the uncertainty, described earlier, and the constant threat of deportation and family separation. The second is structural threats, which they refer to as "ecosystemic," which I have also described earlier, such as difficulty finding jobs and homes, threats from authorities, and hostility from residents and nativist leaders and media figures. This is on top of trauma, some of it even intergenerational, that has been carried by immigrants to their new countries, and is being reactivated and reinforced – the retriggering that I described earlier. The third basket is "lack of navigational capital," which refers to linguistic and cultural barriers and lack of familiarity with the system, as I described earlier. This is made worse by overt harassment and the understandable fears that immigrants and refugees carry. Their fourth category is the "erosion of collectivism and community solidarity":

> We theorize that the stressors of poverty, trauma exposures, discrimination and limited access to resources, coupled with a strongly felt emphasis on self-sufficiency, "making it" in the United States, and general decline of civic engagement and social capital in the United States (Putnam, 1995) can hinder collectivistic ideologies and practices.

Lack of respect for collectivism in individualist societies, which is mirrored in Western psychology and psychosocial practices, has been a major theme in this book.

Before concluding this section, it is important to acknowledge and applaud sources of resilience among immigrants and refugees. Hou et al. (2018) have developed a drive to thrive theory, which argues that when immigrants reestablish the "fabrics" of their daily lives from their country of origin, ranging from reestablishing and adapting daily routines to recreating social and economic networks critical to survival, particularly in a hostile environment, they not only survive but are also able to thrive. This happens by importing cultural practices and routines from the old country, reconstructing social networks and mutual support mechanisms, and actually using the challenge of immigrating to a new country as an opportunity to develop better and healthier lives. Hou et al. describe how even in the barren and bereft refugee camp in Calais, France, at the entrance to the tunnel to the United Kingdom and known as "the jungle," refugees made make-shift homes, created a marketplace with shops and stalls, set up a church and mosque, created schools and playgrounds for children, and even established restaurants serving familiar food, and venues for cultural activities.

Immigrants and refugees have demonstrated the courage to leave what is familiar and to venture out into an unknown world and undertake journeys that they know are perilous and fraught with risk. Many have survived a multitude of threats during their trek and have landed in unfamiliar and hostile environments even when they arrive at their destination. They have evinced creativity and resourcefulness throughout the entire immigration process. And the emphasis on social obligations, social support, and collective well-being – often pathologized in Western cultures – helps immigrants to survive, sustain, and even eventually flourish. The strength and resilience forged in the experience of immigration and in the face of unrelenting structural threats and challenges are not only unrecognized, as in the story of the Hmong immigrants told by Fadiman, but are often experiences that helping professionals in the new land lack. Thus, the challenges of being helpful rather than harmful are discussed in the next section.

Psychosocial Interventions to Support Immigrants and Refugees

In this section, I will discuss some general considerations about interventions for immigrants and refugees, explore some specific models of intervention, and consider unique factors when working with immigrants in refugee camps. All of the interventions discussed in Chapter 7 are relevant for immigrants and refugees and in this section, I will include additional ideas specifically geared toward meeting the psychosocial needs of immigrants and refugees.

In this book, I have frequently discussed the challenges of helping professionals working across social identities and cultures with collaborators. If the helper is not an immigrant then the gap in understanding the collaborator's experiences and knowing what will be helpful widens. There is an impulse in such situations to learn all that one can about the immigrant's culture and how it diverges from that of the helper and this is indeed important to consider. However, one does not truly grasp the inner reality of an immigrant from a significantly different sociocultural world by learning about their culture or even by having worked with some collaborators with similar backgrounds. Helpers in this situation may intellectually grasp some surface elements, but subjective immersion and empathy do not necessarily follow. Even when helpers learn the contours of personhood, there are no stock stories or repeated direct experiences that lead to deep empathic resonance (Mesquita, 2022). Even after learning about words for emotions and how feelings are expressed, and the meaning of family and relationships, the helper is still using their own embodied understandings and feelings to interpret what is being presented to them. Assumptions that may seem obvious to the helper, are not necessarily true for the collaborator (Schick et al., 2018). And this conundrum is heightened when a non-immigrant helper is working with a refugee or asylum seeker. Thus, as I have suggested throughout the book, I urge helpers to be cautious, not to think that we understand experience in the same ways that our collaborators do, and whenever possible, to empower and build the capacity of people from the same sociocultural milieu to serve as the primary helpers, including religious and community leaders, clan elders, and other trusted people in the community. They can best understand the meaning of events, interactions, relationships, and expressions of emotions, what kinds of relationships people seek, and what people would find helpful and unhelpful (Mesquita).

It is understandable that helpers want to focus on trauma –without question, refugees have often had many traumatic-inducing experiences before, during, and after they began their journey. As I have stated earlier, I make a distinction between trauma when viewed through historical, collective, and structural lens and the DSM V diagnoses of PTSD. Schick et al. (2018) have found in their work and research that a PTSD diagnosis is overused by Western practitioners with immigrants and that this is often unhelpful. They note that experiences in the past influence how immigrants appraise the present and future and vice versa – experiences in the new country contribute to revised understandings of one's past. But more than any factor, what affects the immigrant's well-being is what they encounter in their new world – is it welcoming, validating, and supportive or are immigrants dealing with racism, scapegoating, and demonization? And for immigrants from more collectivist cultures, the entire immigration experience affects entire families and clans, and it can be difficult to separate individual well-being from collective well-being. And yet this is exactly what an individual diagnosis of PTSD does – prying the individual from their communal context.

An essential ingredient in treating PTSD is a sense of safety and yet immigrants and refugees often do not feel safe, usually for good reasons. Many immigrants have seen their assumptions about benevolence and fidelity shattered and thus find it difficult to feel safe with others, including helping professionals from a different culture and society (Schick et al., 2018). Focusing on PTSD can also obscure other stress reactions occurring in response to daily life in the host country, such as depression, struggles with identity, personhood, and meaning, and often feelings of guilt or shame (Schick et al.). Lopez-Zeron et al. (2020) refer to this as "acculturative stress." Discrimination, lack of access to resources, and often, in Western societies, a focus on individual self-sufficiency and reliance can undermine collectivist and communal ways of being and support networks (Vesely et al., 2017). So how can helping professionals avoid this and respect the practices and strengths that immigrants carry and not impose our vision of the causes of suffering and how to treat them? For helping professionals, particularly social workers steeped in the mythic lore of Settlement Houses, this involves a shift in perspective. Settlement Houses focused on helping immigrants to learn values and skills that enabled them to adapt and assimilate to their new sociocultural world; the task for helping professionals today is to recognize our own assumptions and limitations and to avoid pressuring immigrants to give up what has sustained them in an effort to conform to not only their new reality but to an unfamiliar psychosocial system of meaning-making. Rather than conforming or acquiescing, immigrants need help with confronting and resisting, under their own leadership.

Chavez-Dueñas et al. (2019) have developed a model that they call HEART – Healing ethno-racial trauma – that has been applied to Latinx immigrant communities. As I described in Chapters 5–7, establishing safety is a critical starting point and Chavez-Duenas et al. add that creating sanctuary zones is a way of supporting safety. The HEART model then moves to acknowledging the sources of ethno-racial trauma – connecting psychological, emotional, and relational suffering to historical and structural conditions, helping immigrants gain a critical consciousness of the dynamics of oppression and how this may have affected them. The model then moves to strengthening survival strategies and skills and connecting individuals, families, and communities to healing cultural traditions. Lastly, the model encourages collective action and resistance leading to psychological liberation.

Given all that I have described in this chapter, I suggest the following strategies for helping professionals/volunteers when working with immigrants and refugees: (1) focusing on thriving and strength; (2) understanding and building on the immigrant's vision of personhood; (3) using a training-of-trainers model; (4) use of collaborator-directed activities; (5) supporting networking, advocacy and resistance; (6) creating opportunities for narrative construction; and (7) judicious use of targeted clinical interventions.

Box 9.1 Psychosocial Interventions With Immigrants, Refugees, and Asylum Seekers

1. **Focusing on strengths**

    - How is the immigrant doing in the present moment?
    - What kinds of threats and stresses are they encountering and how are they managing them?
    - What assets, including relationships, social networks, cultural and spiritual institutions, and inner strengths – e.g.,

beliefs, values, and affect regulation strategies – are supporting and sustaining them?
- What are they most proud of?
- What is most important for them to hold on to and not lose?
- What are they seeking in their lives (their goals) and what progress have they made, as well as what are the roadblocks?
- Were there ancestors who helped to create the conditions for the migration from the homeland?
- Were there NGOs, people, or unknown benefactors who were essential to the immigrant's success?
- What has contributed to their inner sources of strength?
- Were there earlier experiences, or tests and challenges, that helped to prepare them to be so resilient?
- What are some important life lessons and sources of wisdom?
- Are there practices – e.g., praying and meditation – that they draw upon?
- Are there important routines that were helpful in the past and can be useful in the present and future?
- What is their definition of thriving and are there any goals that they have set for themselves (or their family)?

2. **Understanding and building on the immigrant's vision of personhood**

- What are their preferred language, religious beliefs, and practices (Hinton & Patel, 2018)?
- How are problems and suffering understood and conceptualized (Hinton & Patel, 2018)?
- What constitutes sources of stress or a catastrophe (Hinton & Patel, 2018)?
- What are indigenous sources of resilience (Hinton & Patel, 2018)?
- What proverbs, beliefs, and practices contribute to resilience (Hinton & Patel, 2018)?
- Are there important people in the community – e.g., clan or religious leaders – who can speak for the group by articulating important aspects of society, culture, and personhood?

3. **Using a training-of-trainers model**
4. **Fostering and facilitating collaborator-led activities**
5. **Supporting networking, collective support, advocacy, and resistance**
6. **Opening up space for a range of narratives and ways to express narratives**
7. **Judicious and targeted use of clinical interventions**

Focusing on Thriving and Strength

As discussed, the courage, resourcefulness, assets, and strengths of immigrants and refugees are extraordinary. And yet they have suffered structural and sociopolitical oppression and violence before leaving, during their passage, and in their new homeland. Some along the way have been imprisoned or driven into refugee camps and remain there. While the trauma of these experiences can and should be addressed, the platform for offering psychosocial support should be based on a foundation of strength and resilience, with the goal of thriving rather than simply surviving.

Helping professionals can begin by offering space to witness and understand how the immigrant(s) were able to navigate and manage the different parts of their migration. I recommend that the starting point for this is how the immigrant is doing in the present moment. What kinds of threats and stresses are they encountering and how are they managing them? What assets, including relationships, social networks, cultural and spiritual institutions, and inner strengths – e.g., beliefs, values, and affect regulation strategies – are supporting and sustaining them? What are they most proud of? What is most important for them to hold on to and not lose? What are they seeking in their lives (their goals) and what progress have they made, as well as what are the roadblocks?

After establishing the foundation for survival and flourishing, it can be productive to work backward in order to understand the strengths that helped immigrants survive their crossing from their country of origin to their new homes. This is not solely for the benefit of the helper but aids the immigrants to recall and savor the inner and outer resources that carried them through such perilous times. It is critical to follow the immigrant's lead with understanding the collective nature of the process – including their gratitude to family and friends who made the journey possible – either by their accompaniment or by their support and sacrifices. This sense of appreciation often extends beyond people who were directly connected to the immigrant but can go back historically or extend to strangers or unknown persons whose deeds made the successful journey possible. Were there ancestors who helped to create the conditions for the migration from the homeland? Were there NGOs, people, or unknown benefactors who were essential to the immigrant's success?

As important as relationships and external factors are, it is also important to review with the collaborator their inner sources of strength. Was it their belief in God? Were there earlier experiences, or tests and challenges, that helped to prepare them to be so resilient? What are some important life lessons and sources of wisdom? Are there practices – e.g., praying and meditation – that they draw upon? Are there important routines that were helpful in the past and can be useful in the present and future? What is their definition of thriving and are there any goals that they have set for themselves (or their family)?

Much of this book has been about supporting sources of strength and resilience – this is a critical starting place for work with immigrants and can be adapted to the unique challenges of being an immigrant or refugee.

Understanding and Building Upon the Immigrant's Sense of Personhood

I have already discussed how one of the most challenging aspects of immigration is leaving one's familiar sociocultural world, where personhood is clear and often taken for granted, and entering a new sociocultural space with where there are different roles, relationships, identities, practices, values, and even emotions. Mesquita (2022) has written about the difference between viewing emotions as MINE – belonging to me, inside of me waiting to be expressed, and enduring, which is characteristic in Western societies – and OURS – Outside of us and between people, relational and situational, which is more common in most other parts of the world. This is one of the huge differences that many immigrants have to confront, manage, bridge and navigate and part of why trying to help immigrants from collectivist cultures and societies to "express their feelings" is not necessarily helpful and can even be harmful and confusing. There are often different emotion words between cultures and even when the words are the same, they may have very different internal meanings for people.

Thus, it is essential for helping professionals to attempt to understand an immigrant's explanatory system from the inside (Hinton & Patel, 2018) recognizing *that one may never truly grasp this in a deep and empathic way!* Immigrants and refugees have already experienced too many losses – e.g., relationships and social connections, homes and belongings, and a familiar sociocultural world – so it is important to not inadvertently erase or take away their inner meaning-making and feeling structures. And it is important to recognize how a relatively shallow understanding of their history, culture, and stories does not lead to the same kind of profound understandings that accrue from a lifetime of sociocultural immersion.

Although Hinton and Patel (2018) are writing about the use of CBT interventions to respond to trauma – they recognize the importance of attempting to gain an inside understanding by posing some relevant questions:

- What is the language used by group members? I would add that often people come from regions where multiple languages are spoken – e.g., Afghan refugees may have spoken Pashto, Dari, Uzbek, Turkmen, and English – so it is important to learn about which language a person feels most comfortable with when talking about intimate events with a non-family member (as well as which language they prefer when talking with family members).
- What is the groups' religious background? And what is the meaning of religion, both spiritually and socially? For example, my Hazara students were Shia Muslims, which was not only a belief system but also affected how they were treated by Afghans from other ethnic groups.
- Trying to understand how problems are conceptualized and experienced. Is suffering like a physical pain or illness, as opposed to a psychological/emotional problem? What are indigenous words and metaphors that capture this?
- What constitutes a stressor or catastrophe? What are considered normal or abnormal reactions to life events?
- What are indigenous sources of resilience? What proverbs, beliefs, and practices contribute to resilience?
- What are values regarding treatment and intervention by non-family and community members?

Hinton and Patel (2018) are asking these questions to guide their CBT interventions, which assumes that this is a universally beneficial treatment, but they are important questions for all cross-cultural work. I would add are there important people in the community – e.g., clan or religious leaders – who can speak for the group by articulating important aspects of society, culture, and personhood?

Mesquita (2022) discusses how to "unpack emotional incidents." She recommends three steps:

1. How or why did what occurred matter to the immigrant? Mesquita breaks this down into three areas: self-esteem, status, and respectability in the community. What goals and values are at stake? What are the social consequences of what happened?
2. Searching for the best "emotion words." This includes having the immigrant explain what are correct or incorrect emotions to have in such situations. She also recommends exploring how these fit or do not fit with how the immigrant wants to be in the world.
3. Mesquita refers to these interactions as a "dance," where one participant might be dancing a waltz and the other a tango. So what are the next steps of the dance and where are they likely to lead people?

A good example of dancing to different steps is the issue of gratitude. In the West, often adapted from Buddhist traditions, focusing on what one is grateful for and even writing this down in a gratitude journal is considered to be a helpful intervention for people who have experienced stress and trauma. But most gratitude studies have been conducted by White Westerners (Newman, 2019). In more collectivist cultures, gratitude is often viewed as being part of interconnection with others, with a greater emphasis on harmony and honoring others (Newman). Newman cites research has found that being asked to write gratitude letters for many Asian/Asian Americans can leave the writer feeling indebted, guilty, sad, and regretful. So, an intervention that has become quite common among many clinicians and mindfulness practitioners may be very helpful for some, but distressing for others.

Using a Training-of-Trainer's Model

Given what I have said about how difficult it can be for outsider helping professionals to truly grasp the explanatory and meaning-making systems of immigrants from radically different cultures, it is important to strengthen and empower the capacity of community members to take leadership roles with psychosocial healing and well-being. I have already discussed Promotoras de Salud, Friendship benches

Curanderas, Healing Circles, and other models as examples of this in Chapter 6. There is certainly a role for outside helpers in working with indigenous community members to develop models of education, training, and intervention – e.g., there may be expertise in self-soothing or EMDR. And helpers who are indigenous to the host country understand practices and meanings that may be helpful for immigrants *as long as these are not imposed or presented as mandatory*. Thus, in my experience, a partnership between members of the immigrant community and helping professionals from the host country can be beneficial *as long as it is not structured to meet the needs of the helping professional so that they can implement their agenda!* Therefore, it is important that either such efforts are led by members of the immigrant community or at the very least there is an egalitarian partnership.

Collaborator-Led Activities

As I have argued throughout the book, activities and practices that are not viewed through a Western clinical lens can be very powerful means of helping people to feel safe, reduce emotional activation, stimulate a sense of well-being, validate a person's identity and personhood, and strengthen social bonds and relationships. Trauma and displacement have always been part of the human experience, and collective activities not only bring people together in the present but also link them with the wisdom of ancestors and the collective healing practices that have evolved in all societies, cultures, and spiritual traditions. Whether it is sharing meals, praying together, playing together, singing, dancing, and storytelling, engaging in culturally syntonic activities with family, friends, and other community members is affirming, empowering, and healing. It is a connection with the past and reminder of how adversity has been met with strength, endurance, creativity, group solidarity, and collective resistance. It is a reaffirmation and reconstruction of collective personhood in an alien and at times threatening environment. It not only brings people together to celebrate who they are and where they have come from but also offers connections that can form the matrix of collective advocacy and, when necessary, resistance.

One of the biggest challenges for immigrants can be the contrast between social roles and family practices with those of their new environment. Values, behaviors, social norms, and expectations may be out of synch if not in conflict. Some immigrants from an immigrant community have been in the host country longer and have made some adaptations from the cultural practices that they carried; they can often help newer immigrants to understand their new social calculus, bridge norms, learn how to respond to unfamiliar behaviors, and be a repository of potential resources. NGOs such as Catholic Charities and Jewish Family Services in the United States have resettled many refugees from Africa, the Middle East, and recently from Afghanistan. They often hire case managers who share ethnic, cultural, and linguistic identities and can act as mediators and brokers between immigrant families, communities, and the institutions, practices, and new sociocultural world that they are encountering. These case managers know that collective activities that include having fun and savoring relationships in a culturally familiar way are an important mechanism for achieving some of these aims.

The group-activity approach that I am describing can be compatible with the more traditional, Western psychotherapeutic approaches, such as CBT interventions, that I will briefly discuss later, and can be both an important complement and a gateway for more specialized services. What I think is critical is that the activities are initiated and directed by the local community of immigrants. While clinical interventions are often led or directed by professionals from the host country, collective cultural activities offer the possibility of being initiated and directed by immigrants. This is yet another example of how helping professionals can be supportive of indigenous empowerment by *not* assuming the mantle of experts or exerting leadership. Instead, we can help to locate spaces where people can gather and find resources (e.g., food, cooking apparatus, sound systems, developing virtual communication platforms) that enable immigrants to use and share the many strengths and resources that they collectively and individually carry.

Supporting Networking, Advocacy, and Resistance

Immigrants who are alone feel isolated in their new homes; immigrants who connect with other immigrants from their country of origin receive social support and mirroring of their personhood. This should be considered by social service organizations working to resettle immigrants. As I have discussed at length in this book, networking, social support, collective advocacy, and resistance to oppression are powerful ways for socially and politically targeted people to feel validated and contest subjugation. This is particularly important for immigrants and refugees. Not only does this offer sociocultural validation and familiarity, while resisting the threats immigrants are encountering, but it also offers a collective pathway forward in the new land. Immigrants offer many services, resources, and emotional support when they are connected with one another. It is also a way that immigrants can have fun together, as described in the aforementioned section. Thus, helping professionals should work to facilitate the conditions and help to create spaces for such networking to occur.

Narratives

Immigrants carry many stories from all phases of their journey and from well before. They are often painful, sometimes shameful, as well as carrying insight and joy. They help immigrants not only reconstruct their lives and personhood but also revisit and rework their past, better understand the present, and imagine possible futures. Bragin (2019) notes that for immigrant adults and children, who have been exposed to frightening, overwhelming, and "terrible things", it is important to offer opportunities for them to have space to articulate, process, and reflect on what has happened. They might have been victims, perpetrators, or both, and it is important to help them to tolerate the negative thoughts and feelings that they may have about themselves. This allows them to weave together not only their disparate, confusing, and detrimental experiences but to explore and eventually integrate and metabolize the many different aspects of their self and personhood.

I have discussed the uses of storytelling, art, collective song writing, dance and movement, and photographs as different mediums of narrative expression. This often happens organically, in a non-clinical milieu. However, it can also be part of focused treatment interventions. Narrative Exposure Therapy (NET) is an example of this (e.g., Kangaslampi et al., 2015; Neuner et al., 2018; Parelli et al., 2019).

NET is considered a CBT intervention for trauma. It has been used in many international contexts although it views trauma as having enduring characteristics because of being neurobiological in origin and that cultural differences are something to be addressed by minor adaptations of the model (Neuner et al., 2018). While I find that this minimizes the impact of culture in shaping and understanding trauma, NET has been used in a range of countries and has been implemented with people who have survived not only difficult migrations but people in refugee camps and who have been tortured. NET focuses on how there are twin memory tracks when there is trauma: "hot" memories of trauma (neurologically encoded, perceptual, and not accessible verbally) and "cold" memories that are more autobiographical, contextual, and verbally accessible, leading to coherent narrative with temporal and spatial dimensions (Kangaslampi et al., 2015; Neuner et al., 2018). Thus, the goal of NET is integrating the fragmented, activating memories into a person's contextualized life span and hopefully placing them in a context where they do not define all experiences.

On the one hand, NET is a limited vision of how people can use their stories to heal, but its practitioners are open to what they call "downshifting" interventions to trained lay people (Neuner et al., 2018). This means that it can fit with a training-of-trainers model. If this occurs, I believe that it is important to collaborate with those who will provide direct interventions so that they can be modified to fit the culture and personhood of the target group.

Judicious Use of Targeted Clinical Interventions

The preceding suggestions – focusing on thriving and strength; understanding and building on the immigrant's vision of personhood; using a TOT model; use of collaborator-directed activities; supporting networking and advocacy; and narrative construction – address the collective nature of psychosocial difficulties due to immigration and therefore have the broadest impact. They are also responsive to collectivist orientations, respectful of indigenous practices, and recognize the power of group interventions. But there is also a place for clinical interventions with individuals, albeit with a more limited number of people. When engaging in such interventions with an immigrant community, it is important to first have focus groups or "sharing circles" (Montesonti et al., 2021) to engage with local community members on their terms and turf and to use these understand personhood and needs, while also explaining the rationale of any proposed clinical interventions.

As Nickerson (2018) points out, the experience of persecution in one's home country leading to a difficult migration does not necessarily mean that people are left with psychological problems, and, as I have discussed earlier, often speaks to tremendous resilience. She believes in the significance of cognitive appraisals of the situation that help immigrants to interpret what happened to them before, during, and after their immigration journey. CBT approaches work with cognitive understandings and judgments. However, Nickerson urges clinicians to help people learn to modulate, not suppress their emotions, in advance of CBT treatments, which is consistent with what I have suggested in previous chapters. Emotional regulation as well as experiencing a sense of safety and stability are prerequisites for most forms of psychological healing and recovery.

In addition to the many CBT treatments listed and discussed in Chapter 7 and Narrative Exposure Therapy (mentioned earlier), two relevant CBT interventions that are useful when working with immigrants are Culturally Sensitive CBT and Trauma Informed Systems Therapy. Culturally informed family treatment is also an important intervention.

Culturally sensitive CBT posits the importance of understanding a group's explanatory models when considering psychological pathology: causation, the meaning of symptoms, and cures (Hinton & Patel, 2018). It draws on the range of CBT interventions discussed in Chapter 7 but stresses how it is critical to adapt them culturally for the group receiving interventions (Naeem et al., 2010). As mentioned earlier, it assumes the efficacy of CBT treatments for trauma but acknowledges the importance of cultural "bridging" in order to be acceptable and efficacious with populations from different cultures, particularly non-Western populations.

Trauma Informed Systems Therapy, more than most CBT interventions, is cognizant of the importance of a multi-systemic and culturally informed approach. Benson et al. (2018) note the many possible sources of trauma for immigrants and refugees: "direct and indirect acts of violence, physical and sexual abuse, torture, physical injury, loss and family separation, exposure to extreme living conditions, malnutrition, and lack of access to basic resources." They also are sensitive to the range of barriers that immigrants face in their new host country:

> difficulty in accessing services (e.g., transportation, health insurance), a paucity of available linguistically and culturally sensitive care, distrust of authorities and/or systems, stigma, differing cultural models of "mental health" and help seeking, and other priority needs (e.g., financial assistance, food insecurity).

Kaplin et al. (2019) echo this and add forced labor and food and water scarcity as other causes of trauma as well as acculturation stresses and social isolation once immigrants are in their new host country. Thus, Trauma Informed Systems Therapy recognizes that in addition to receiving clinical interventions, there needs to be a more comprehensive plan that includes parents, schools, health-care centers, and religious institutions. And it stresses the importance of cultural humility and cultural competency. What I find impressive is their recognition of the importance of participating in community activities and engaging in dialogues with community members *before* attempting to implement CBT interventions. They also sequence their interventions so that there are interactive, activity-based, group interventions offered in schools to immigrant children leading up to more focused CBT work. Overall, this approach attempts to be organic and respectful of the immigrant's cultural orientations, recognizing the importance of environmental and structural interventions in addition to CBT work, such as cognitive restructuring; CBT is part of a panoply of services.

Trauma Informed Systems Therapy not only understands how important it is to engage with community-based groups and institutions but also works to involve family members, recognizing the profound impact of migration on family structures, roles, and relationships. Thus, it can include in-home family therapy, which fits well with other family-treatment approaches for immigrants. For example, Lopez-Zeron et al. (2020) also note the relevance of acculturative stress and describe the Oregon model of parent management training:

> 1. Encouraging positive parental involvement, 2. Helping parents to work on limit setting, monitoring and supervision in the new environment, 3. Increasing parenting skills which draws upon home cultural practices adapted to the new host country, 4. Encouraging family problem solving.

Ultimately, clinical interventions with immigrants and refugees cannot stand alone; they require helping families to integrate past practices with current realities, draw on community resources and supports, emphasize natural systems and adapting Western models culturally, and are multi-systemic and multi-level. They should be combined with the other practices described earlier and be part of a range of psychosocial interventions.

Working With People in Refugee Camps

All of the sources of vulnerability and types of interventions mentioned in this chapter apply to people in refugee camps, although there are also different challenges that have to be navigated. While immigrants and refugees in new host countries are often encountering racism, Islamophobia, and other forms of social and structural oppression, there is at least a modicum of security in many instances because of arriving, and resources such as "circles of care" and social service supports. In refugee camps, people also experience hostility, cultural marginalization, and clashes between their internal sense of personhood and that of the country where the camps are located. And of course, they are limbo, stuck in the transit phase of the migration experience, sometimes for years and without reasonable hope of moving on to something better.

As I mentioned earlier, part of immigrant resilience in such circumstances is to be able to recreate their sociocultural world, albeit within the confines of a camp. But sources of vulnerability include the many constraints on agency, mobility, and the capacity to support oneself and family. Dependency is structurally reinforced at refugee camps, and people are often living in dense, overcrowded, unhealthy, unsanitary, and hazardous situations, often with inadequate infrastructure and services. Children are frequently not in school or receiving inadequate education. There may be few spaces available for recreation and socializing. There can be violence generated from outside, such as hostile people in the country where the camp is located as well as from the inside, where there may be unresolved feuds, lack of legal and civil protections, and conflicts between clans or gangs. The location of camps is yet another factor, both geographically and politically. Geographically, camps can be found in conditions of flooding, excessive heat, and in areas prone to natural or technological disasters. Overcrowding and exposure to disease are common. Politically, the level of human rights and legal protections in the host country can portend the rights (or lack thereof) of persons living in a given camp. Often there are NGOs working in refugee camps and their missions, resources, and services vary, which of course affects the refugee experience.

In such situations, safety and security are essential and should be a primary goal. Safety includes physical safety, as well as safety from being deported back to the country of origin or being vulnerable to abuse and exploitation. Safety also includes the security of being able to maintain one's personhood and not to feel that it is constantly under threat. It is important to assess with the migrant community who is at greatest risk (e.g., children or young women) and how to protect them.

Focusing on the current reality and what would make life more bearable, manageable, and meaningful is paramount. Much of this depends on the circumstances of arrival, the nature of the camp environment, and the amount of time refugees have spent there or are likely to remain there. One aspect of this is fostering leadership among the refugees, working toward inclusivity for all living in the camp, and empowering residents to determine and direct how to reconstruct the markers and textures of everyday life – e.g., shops, access to culturally familiar food, the ability to worship and practice one's religion, communication networks, recreational practices and opportunities, and access to education (Hou et al., 2018). In my view, focusing on making life more endurable is of greater importance than treating trauma and other psychological consequences from the pre-migration and migration phases of the immigrant's experience. Ventevogel (2018) talks about three different (and at times competing) humanitarian paradigms in such situations – trauma, mental and general health care, and a psychosocial paradigm, which is what I have been emphasizing. This is not to say that it is not possible to integrate aspects of all three paradigms and, in my view, they often can complement one another, but improving daily life should not be secondary to psychological interventions and treatment for trauma and other mental health concerns.

A third critical area when working with refugees in camps is that of generating and maintaining hope. It is normal for refugees in camps to experience waves of hopelessness and despair. There can be short-term hopes – such as improving conditions in the camp – but it is also essential to help refugees in camps to have hope that they will eventually leave the camps and not have to go back to what they fled or end up in an environment that is as hazardous or even worse. Engaging with hope necessitates working on external factors – e.g., understanding visa and immigration requirements, mediating between camp residents, the host country, and possible destination countries, and advocating with NGOs and governments for actions that will break the entropy and stasis. It also involves working with groups, families, and individuals about their own sources of hope (and hopelessness) and exploring what actions they can take to increase their sense of efficacy and forward movement, as well as internal strategies to resist succumbing to despair.

Conclusion

In this chapter, I have discussed unique factors to consider for helping professionals working with immigrants and refugees, building on the values, principles, and interventions discussed in previous chapters. I considered the challenges and threats experienced by immigrants with targeted social identities before, during, and after embarking on their immigration journey, particularly for refugees and asylum seekers. Facing dangerous, unstable, and untenable conditions at home, maneuvering through perilous journeys, and often encountering hostility and structural oppression in their new countries, or being waylaid in refugee camps, destabilizes, demoralizes, and undermines immigrants who leave out of desperation and often lack the resources to travel safely and "legally." And yet immigrants have developed deep reservoirs of strength and resilience and collectively support one another in their efforts to survive and thrive.

Who are considered valid immigrants, possessing valid passports and visas, who are welcomed or spurned and rejected, and who face the most challenges and have access to the fewest resources are all framed by the legacies of colonialism. Coloniality creates a greater likelihood that immigrants will risk their lives while trying to save their lives and encounter the menaces of human trafficking, modern-day slavery, and the perils of refugee and internment camps. And while there is indeed historical and collective trauma, as well as trauma from the immigration experience itself, the negative structural conditions encountered in destination countries are current and paramount to address. I recommended seven strategies to guide helping professionals (see Box 9.1), which build on other psychosocial interventions introduced in earlier chapters. Immigrant strengths, resilience, wisdom, and the shared capacity to resist oppression and coalesce collectively are the foundation for psychosocial support and intervention.

Note

1 A notable exception to this, as I write this book, is how Ukrainian refugees have been enthusiastically welcomed by many countries in Europe and North America after the invasion of their country by Russia, while people from Afghanistan, African nations, and Central and South American nations are actively prevented from entering these same countries.

References

Barajas-Gonzalez, R.G., Ayon, C., & Torres, F. (2018). Applying a community violence framework to understand the impact of immigration enforcement threat on Latino children. *Social Policy Report, 31*(3): 1–24.

Benson, M.A., Abdi, S.M., Miller, A.B., & Ellis, B.H. (2018). Trauma systems therapy for refugee children and their families. In N. Morina & A. Nickerson (Eds.). *Mental health of refugee and conflict-affected populations: Theory, research and clinical practice* (pp. 243–260). New York, Cham, Switzerland: Springer Nature.

Bragin, M. (2019). Myth, memory, and meaning: Understanding and treating adolescents experiencing forced migration, *Journal of Infant, Child, and Adolescent Psychotherapy*. DOI: 10.1080/15289168.2019.1691892.

Bryant-Davis, T., & Tummala-Narra, P. (2020). Cultural oppression and child sex trafficking. In M.C. Stevenson, B.L. Bottoms, & K.C. Burke (Eds.). *The legacy of racism for children: Psychology, law and public policy* (pp. 17–34). New York: Oxford University Press.

Buckingham et al. (2021). The roles of settings in supporting immigrants' resistance to injustice and oppression: A policy position statement by the society for community research and action. *American Journal of Community Psychology, 68*: 268–291. DOI: 10.1002/ajcp.12515.

Carlsson, J., & Sonne, C. (2018). Mental health, pre-migratory trauma and post-migratory stressors among adult refugees. In N. Morina & A. Nickerson (Eds.). *Mental health of refugee and conflict-affected populations: Theory, research and clinical practice* (pp. 15–34). New York, Cham, Switzerland: Springer Nature.

Chavez-Dueñas, N.Y., Adames, H.Y., Perez-Chavez, J.G., & Salas, S.P. (2019). Healing ethno-racial trauma in Latinx immigrant communities: Cultivating hope, resistance, and action. *American Psychologist, 74*(1): 49–62. DOI: 10.1037/amp0000289

Coy, P. (2022, July 17). Many children of immigrants rise to the top. *The New York Times*, Opinion Section, p. 8.

Daftary, A.M.H. (2020). Living with uncertainty: Perceptions of well-being among Latinx young adults in immigrant family systems. *Family Relations, 69*: 51–62. DOI: 10.1111/fare.12407.

Fadiman, A. (1997). *The spirit catches you and you fall down: A Hmong child, her American doctors, and the collision of two cultures.* New York: Farrar, Straus and Giroux.

Garran, A.M., Werkmeister-Rozas, L.M., Kang, H.K., & Miller, J. (2021). *Racism in the United States: Implications for the helping professions* (3rd ed.). New York: Springer Publishing.

Global Slavery Index. (2018). *Walk free foundation.* www.globalslaveryindex.org/?campaign_id=37&emc=edit_rr_20211002&instance_id=41871&nl=race%2Frelated®i_id=261671&segment_id=70522&te=1&user_id=c40644cf79330c01b71cc3ebdbcb62f9

Hinton, D.E., & Patel, A. (2018). Culturally sensitive CBT for refugees: Key dimensions. In N. Morina & A. Nickerson (Eds.). *Mental health of refugee and conflict-affected populations: Theory, research and clinical practice* (pp. 201–219). Cham, Switzerland: Springer Nature.

Hou, W.K., Hall, B.J., & Hobfall, S.E. (2018). Drive to thrive: A theory of resilience following loss. In N. Morina & A. Nickerson (Eds.). *Mental health of refugee and conflict-affected populations: Theory, research and clinical practice* (pp. 111–134). New York, Cham, Switzerland: Springer Nature.

Kangaslampi, S., Garoff, F., & Peltonen, K. (2015). Narrative exposure therapy for immigrant children traumatized by war: Study protocol for a randomized controlled trial of effectiveness and mechanisms of change. *BMC Psychiatry, 15*. DOI: 10.1186/s12888-015-0520-z.

Kaplin, D., Parente, K., & Santacroce, F.A. (2019). A review of the use of trauma systems therapy to treat refugee children. *Adolescents, and Families, Journal of Infant, Child, and Adolescent Psychotherapy, 18*(4): 417–431. DOI: 10.1080/15289168.2019.1687220.

Kara, S. (2017). *Modern slavery: A global approach.* New York: Columbia University Press.

Lopez-Zeron, G., Parra-Cardona, J.R., & Yeh, H.H. (2020). Addressing immigration-related stress in a culturally adapted parenting intervention for Mexican-origin immigrants: Initial positive effects and key areas of improvement. *Family Process, 59*: 1094–1112. DOI: 10.1111/famp.12481.

McKibben, B. (2022). Where will we live? *The New York Review of Books*. www.nybooks.com/articles/2022/10/06/where-will-we-live-climate-change-mckibben/

Mesquita, B. (2022). *Between us: How cultures create emotions*. New York, W.W. Norton & Company.

Mincin, J., Khetarpal, R., & Steiner, J. (2022). Protecting vulnerable populations: COVID-19 pandemic, mental health, and refugees and asylees. *Journal of Emergency Management*, *20*(9): 9–17.

Montesonti, S., Fitzpatrick, K., Azimi, T., McGee, T., Fayant, B., & Albert, L. (2021). Exploring indigenous ways of coping after a wildfire disaster in Northern Alberta, Canada. *Qualitative Health Research*, *31*(8): 1472–1485. DOI: 10.1177/10497323211009194.

Myers, S.S., & Patz, J.A. (2009). Emerging threats to human health from global environmental change. *Annual Review of Environment and Resources*. DOI: 10.1146/annurev.environ.033108.102650.

Naeem, F., Waheed, W., Gobbi, M., Ayub, M., & Kingdon, D. (2010). Preliminary evaluation of culturally sensitive CBT for depression in Pakistan: Findings from developing culturally-sensitive CBT project (DCCP). *Behavioural and Cognitive Psychotherapy*, *39*: 165–173. DOI: 10.1017/S1352465810000822.

Nesteruk, O. (2018). Immigrants coping with transnational deaths and bereavement: The influence of migratory loss and anticipatory grief. *Family Process*, *57*(4): 1012–1928. DOI: 10.1111/famp.12336.

Neuner, F., Elbert, T., & Schauer, M. (2018). Narrative exposure therapy as a treatment for traumatized refugees and post-conflict populations. In N. Morina & A. Nickerson (Eds.). *Mental health of refugee and conflict-affected populations: Theory, research and clinical practice* (pp. 183–198). New York, Cham, Switzerland: Springer Nature.

Newman, K.M. (2019). How cultural differences shape your gratitude. *Greater Good Magazine*. https://greatergood.berkeley.edu/article/item/how_cultural_differences_shape_your_gratitude

Nickerson, A. (2018). Pathways to recovery: Psychological mechanisms underlying refugee menta health. In N. Morina & A. Nickerson (Eds.). *Mental health of refugee and conflict-affected populations: Theory, research and clinical practice* (pp. 91–109). New York, Cham, Switzerland: Springer Nature.

Parelli, S., et al. (2019). EMDR group treatment of children refugees – A field study. *Journal of EMDR Practice and Research*, *13*(2): 143–155.

Putnam, R.D. (1995). Bowling alone: America's declining social capital. *Journal of Democracy*, *6*(1): 65–78.

Schick, M., Morina, N., Schnyder, U., & Maier, T. (2018). Clinical considerations in the psychological treatment of refugees. In N. Morina & A. Nickerson (Eds.). *Mental health of refugee and conflict-affected populations: Theory, research and clinical practice* (pp. 283–303). New York, Cham, Switzerland: Springer Nature.

Stoklosa, H., Burns, C.J., Karan, A., Lyman, M., Morley, N., Tadee, R., & Goodwin, E. (2021). Mitigating trafficking of migrants and children through disaster reduction: Insights from the Thailand flood. *International Journal of Disaster Risk Reduction*, *60*. DOI: 10.1016/j.ijdrr.2021.102268.

United Nations High Commission for Refugees. (2011). *The 1951 convention related to the status of refugees and its 1967 protocol*. Geneva, Switzerland: Author.

Ventevogel, P. (2018). Interventions for mental health and psychosocial support in complex humanitarian emergencies: Moving towards consensus in policy and action? In N. Morina & A. Nickerson (Eds.). *Mental health of refugee and conflict-affected populations: Theory, research and clinical practice* (pp. 155–180). New York, Cham, Switzerland: Springer Nature.

Vesely, C.K., Letiecq, B.L., & Goodman, R.D. (2017). Immigrant family resilience in context: Using a community-based approach to build a new conceptual model. *Journal of Family Theory & Review*, *9*: 93–10. DOI: 10.1111/jftr.12177.

Walia, H. (2021). *Border & rule: Global migration, capitalism and the rise of racist nationalism*. Chicago: Haymarket Books.

10 Collective and Individual Self-Care and Critical Awareness

Introduction

Helping professionals who engage in the kind of work described in this book do so because of our genuine desire to help people who are suffering due to social targeting and oppression. This is rooted in compassion, caring about people, and also a commitment to contribute to a more socially-just world. Caring for oneself is an important part of social justice work. It should not be separated from caring for others, nor should it take place in isolation. Historical, collective, and structural oppression are collective forces; individual self-care should be integrated into collective self-care. There is a relationship between self-care and self-awareness; one needs to have a meta-awareness of self to plan a self-care regime that will be effective, and when we engage in self-care, we become more self-aware. Self-awareness is also critical for helping professionals/volunteers working with people who are socially targeted, regardless of the helper's social identity.

Self-awareness, or reflexivity, which refers to self-awareness in the moment, can also be part of a collective and communal process and is enhanced and deepened when done in concert with others. There is, of course, value in pursuing an individual self-care regime that involves individual goals, tasks, projects, and activities. And sometimes an individual's self-care/self-awareness plan necessitates temporarily uncoupling oneself from deep engagement with others and collective social justice agendas. But often, working with others enhances everyone's self-care/self-awareness. For some people, caring for oneself is more challenging than caring for others. Although much of the literature on self-care emphasizes social support, it tends, like most Western-oriented psychosocial explorations, to emphasize the individual at the expense of the collectivity, while for most people in the world, individual well-being is inextricably intertwined with family and collective

DOI: 10.4324/9781003021162-10

well-being. In this chapter, I will attempt to integrate individual and collective self-care and awareness strategies.

I have written about self-care (e.g., Miller, 2012, 2016), taught about it in my classes on racism and when responding to disasters, and worked on self-care with many colleagues in a range of countries (e.g., China, Haiti, Sri Lanka, Uganda, the United States, and Canada), as well as engaging in self-care with others in the many crisis and emergency teams that I am part of. I will draw on these experiences for this chapter but will also infuse my ideas and experiences with more recent scholarship on this topic. I will integrate this with self-awareness and developing a critical consciousness – not only about how to care for oneself but also how to do less harm to others. I discussed critical consciousness/awareness in the chapters on psychosocial interventions but will develop its relationship to self-care in this chapter. This involves recognition of the salience of social identities and the sociocultural contexts that produce them, affecting what we are vulnerable to and activated by, the impact we have on colleagues and collaborators, and how we respond when triggered.

In this chapter, I will begin with a review of risks and challenges for helping professionals engaged in the type of work described in this book. I will then move to consider how workers and volunteers can be more proactive in preparing for self-care, including ways that organizations and collectivities can contribute to this process. I will also discuss self-care strategies that can be enacted in and adapted to a range of sociocultural contexts as well as ways to expand and deepen critical consciousness, drawing on the Critical Conversations model. I will conclude with a description of the witness to witness (W2W) program (Weingarten et al., 2020) and their collaboration with the Migrants Clinicians Network, a specific program that aligns with many of the values and principles discussed in this book, integrating an understanding of structural oppression and social identities in a model of self-care for helping professionals.

Risks for Helping Professionals

All helping professionals, regardless of whom they work with, face risks of empathic overload, burnout, compassion fatigue, and secondary and vicarious trauma. There is no one cause of this but rather involves a constellation of interacting factors. Three major factors are worker vulnerabilities, the nature of client's suffering and the level of social oppression that they experience, and the availability of supports: organizational, collective, community, family, friends, and social networks All helping professionals carry vulnerabilities, but they range in nature and degree due to a number of factors: our own personal histories, our social identities and experiences in the world, the type of work that we do, our age and experience, the struggles and pain of our collaborators, and our relationship to them, including how much we identify with them and share some of their experiences (Miller, 2012). Related to this is the level of our empathic engagement with and investment in our collaborators and hoped-for outcomes; the greater the investment in a person or a particular result, the higher likelihood of profound discouragement when things do not go well.

While this is true for all helping professionals and volunteers, it is significantly magnified when our partners have experienced historical trauma and structural exclusion and violence in the present. Some helping professionals share social identities with their collaborators and have experienced and continue to experience the same levels of historical and systemic oppression. This can be a boon for understanding the experiences of partners from the inside, can contribute to greater investment in both helping the collaborator and changing the conditions that harm them, and deepens empathy. But it also ups the ante for identification with collaborators' suffering and can contribute to shared collective trauma. Ali et al. (2021) describe "shared trauma," when both helpers and their collaborators are exposed to the same conditions. Their model is a diagram with three concentric, overlapping circles – direct trauma, indirect trauma, and cultural features. The direct trauma circle highlights PTSD and microtraumas. The indirect trauma circle (connoting the worker) lists factors such as compassion fatigue and secondary trauma. And the cultural features circle contains collective trauma, continuous trauma, historical trauma, the collective context, and the salience of having particular social identities within this cultural context. Interactions within these overlapping circles contribute to shared trauma.

Trauma is not all that is shared; there is also shared marginalization, disrespect, lack of access to resources, and pathways for upward mobility. This involves more than merely a shared cultural context; there is a social, political, and economic order and hierarchy which includes but is not limited to culture. But their key point is relevant – that workers with certain social identities and experiences have "double exposure," based on their relationship with their clients and own, similar experiences with subjugation and domination. This can also mean, however, that there is greater critical awareness of the factors and dynamics of domination and their impact and of one's place in the social order and sociocultural matrix. In my experience, people with privilege – whether by virtue of race, ethnicity, religion, gender and cis-gender, sexual orientation, and economic status – struggle with this. Although there may be moments of understanding and recognition, the societal defaults of power and privilege often make it difficult to maintain a consistent critical consciousness. Even when helping professionals with many privileged social identities have done a lot of personal and collective work and soul searching, it is less embodied, saturated, and metabolized into one's sense of personhood than for those experiencing social oppression on a daily basis, and there inevitably are areas of ignorance and obfuscation – it is an ongoing struggle to maintain the critical consciousness necessary to regularly discern the forces of social disempowerment and domination.

Other risk factors for workers include social isolation from families, friends, colleagues, and organizations and having an overly idealistic view of what is achievable and how soon things can change. Isolation can include isolation from one's culture, community, and feeling cut off from one's collective history and cultural heritage. As mentioned earlier, the level of empathy and emotional investment in collaborators contributes to distress, particularly when one is invested in a particular outcome. Commitment is an important motivator and sustains helping professionals, but investment can contribute to a helping professional/volunteer experiencing disappointment, sorrow, and longing for what was not achieved. This is true of all human relationships but when working non-stop with groups of targeted people experiencing social oppression, it can accentuate that the world is a cruel, unfair, violent, and dangerous place. It is helpful to find a balance between knowing how dreadful things can be without being submerged in a whirlpool of hopelessness and deep pessimism. When helping professionals are profoundly distressed or even wounded, they are less effective.

With this in mind, I would like to briefly consider some common conceptualizations of the ways that helping professionals/volunteers may be affected by their work.

1. **Burnout** – Burnout is a catchall term that refers to helping professionals feeling overwhelmed, tired, pessimistic, professionally and socially isolated, and feeling disillusioned with their work, agency, and the world in general (Miller, 2012). It can negatively affect interpersonal relationships, physical, emotional, and mental health, and the ability of workers to invest in and find meaning in their work. While burnout is often viewed as residing within an individual, there is also collective burnout – when members of an

organization or community feel overwhelmed by a steady barrage of stressors and setbacks and lose confidence in their efforts and efficacy. Helping professionals working for organizations where they carry heavy caseloads, earn meager salaries, and are saddled with excessive bureaucratic responsibilities often suffer from collective burnout.

2. **Compassion Fatigue (CF)** – This concept was coined by Charles Figley (1995) and subsequently developed by him with collaborators (Ali et al., 2021). While related to burnout, compassion fatigue is viewed as being more severe and is shaped by how "traumatic stress, secondary traumatic stress, and cumulative stress affect helping professionals" (Ali et al.). It is characterized by feeling an overwhelming sense of responsibility for clients and their suffering that can lead to reduced capacity for empathic engagement (Adams et al., 2006; Miller, 2012). CF is also not solely an individual malaise but can also be a collective response to overwhelming conditions. Entire villages and communities, enduring the legacies of historical trauma, and encountering relentless oppression are vulnerable to CF, particularly when cut off from cultural practices and wellsprings of strength.
3. **Vicarious Trauma (VT) and Secondary Trauma (ST)** – Pearlman and Saakvitne (1995) developed the concept of vicarious trauma, which can afflict helping professionals who are empathically engaged with people experiencing trauma, particularly when there is an identification with the trauma stories. VT can contribute to cognitive distortions and severe emotional reactions that can lead to a transformation of a person's sense of self (Miller, 2012). Secondary trauma is characterized by a more sudden onset than CF and VT (Ali et al., 2021). Secondary trauma symptoms for the helping professional can be similar to and even as severe as those of the person who directly experienced the trauma.

While burnout, CF, VT, and ST are common categories used to understand the reactions of helping professionals working with people who directly experienced trauma, I have wondered about how conceptually relevant they are to understanding sources of stress for helping professionals and volunteers around the world. Like most psychological concepts, they were developed by Western psychotherapists, reflecting a particular, not universal, sociocultural context. The varying constructions of personhood, radically different notions of what work means, and how it is integrated into other aspects of one's life surely influence how helping professionals and volunteers react when exposed to trauma, what these reactions mean, and what will be helpful in response to them.

It becomes even more complicated when considering the reactions of helping professionals engaged with communities suffering from historical and collective trauma. In many contexts, as I have tried to describe in this book, the boundary and distinction between being a worker and a client, collaborator, partner, or consumer is often less fixed and does not necessarily fit with a Western system of mental health delivery, where roles are more separate and distinct. All of the concepts described in this section evolved from and can be applied to this particular sociocultural context and can be partially adapted to other societies and cultures, but I question whether they are the best way to approach support for helpers with a range of social identities working in a varied terrain of worldviews, values, expectations, and beliefs. Perhaps, it is useful to understand them broadly but to recognize that people helping other people are prone to experiencing distress, even trauma, sometimes shared trauma, but not to get too caught up in trying to use them as diagnostic categories, but rather to examine the particular distress of a helper or group of helpers contextually and to seek their leadership in understanding and responding to their anguish.

As mentioned earlier in this chapter, the causes of psychosocial distress for helpers are multifaceted and interactive. Many factors stem from historical, social, cultural, and organizational arrangements and processes. Thus, in considering how to protect helpers from possible negative consequences of their work, it is important to devise collective strategies, as well as to fortify individual resilience.

Individual and Collective Self-Care

Individual and collective self-care when facing historical trauma and sociocultural targeting and oppression is essential, and yet it is important that helping professionals/volunteers collectively and creatively find their own specific ways to nurture and protect themselves while engaging in their work. In this section, I will consider broad strategies that are not prescriptive, but that hopefully open space for this critical work.

It is predictable that the forms of oppression described in this book have detrimental and destructive consequences for many people and this extends to helping professionals/volunteers. How can we anticipate this and prepare in a meaningful way? An initial step for people engaged in collective action and resistance or working for clinical and social justice organizations is to imagine potential threats to well-being. Things never go as planned, goals are rarely fully achieved, and progress can be partial and incomplete. There are backlashes and downturns to progress. And yet oppression is unrelenting. Given this, I recommend that for anyone or any group involved in this type of work, the risks and hazards are clearly articulated and openly discussed. This is not meant to be a deflating or negative exercise but rather a part of the process of liberation; anticipating factors outside of the group/individual's control and proactively thinking about mitigation strategies.

Schreiber et al. (2019) developed an anticipate, plan, and deter risk and resilience model to help protect health-care workers responding to an Ebola outbreak. The anticipate part involves reviewing the types of challenges and negative psychosocial consequences that such workers face. One way to do this is for people to visualize what they will encounter, which can lead to desensitizing, as well as reducing the element of shock and surprise by normalizing a challenging environment. Out of this preparation, responders are encouraged to develop a personal resilience plan, identifying what a person anticipates as being particularly challenging and then planning for how to respond to these challenges. Part of the plan involves self-monitoring, so that a worker can be aware of when they are at risk, involving a self-triage system utilizing a mobile app.

While this model was developed for use by hierarchical organizations where workers are responding to medical emergencies, there are aspects of it that can be adapted for helping professionals engaged in anti-oppression work. Whether within a formal organization or as a practice of a collectivity or community, there can be group discussions about anticipated risks and negative consequences associated with helping. Such discussions can draw on the shared experiences and accrued wisdom of group participants. They can be informal meetings that seek to extract lessons from participants or can be facilitated and even have manuals that summarize core lessons that the group has learned from past work. There is no one structure that works for everyone in all situations.

By bringing people together to engage in group prediction and problem solving, not only is there a greater chance of identifying potential pitfalls and devising creative strategies, but the actual *process* of doing this is also a preventative strategy. Social isolation is a risk factor. As discussed in earlier chapters, historical and collective trauma are often internalized by individuals, who blame themselves for bad thoughts, behaviors, judgments, and decisions, leading to individual guilt, shame, remorse, and suffering. This can happen to helping professionals/volunteers and by planning and preparing for psychosocial threats, group social ties are strengthened, social isolation reduced, and individual guilt and shame mitigated by sharing with others. It also helps to establish and strengthen social networks and support systems that are in themselves protective edifices and networks that can help workers to withstand and respond to psychosocial challenges.

Affinity groups can be established in advance, as can buddy systems. Lines of communication can be elucidated as well as clarifying where to go and what to do if someone is suffering. Psychosocial auditing, rather than being strictly a self-directed activity, can be shared by group members, looking out for and supporting one another. Groups can anticipate the need to build in expectations for individual and collective opportunities for relaxation, recreation, release of tension, and experiencing joy, in the context of what I have discussed about differences in personhood, family structure, and expectations and norms for non-familial relationships.

I am cautious about being prescriptive about how this should be enacted for helping professionals/volunteers and would rather encourage groups of helping professionals to engage in such planning while leaving the specific process and strategies to be developed by group members. Group members can grapple with important issues, such as boundaries, setting limits, expectations about the intensity of engagement, and needs for rest, relaxation, and family time. This is also true for devising mechanisms of accountability to oneself and other group members, as well as leadership, mechanisms for resolving disagreements and conflict, and protocols for worker engagement with collaborators, and for ensuring self-care. After briefly considering the ethical obligations of organizations in supporting self-care, I will consider an audit that can be used by individuals and groups to build in self-care and protection for workers/volunteers.

Organizational Ethics and Considerations

Most helping professionals work or volunteer for organizations. The responsibility for self-care does not solely rest with individuals and a huge factor is how organizations structure possibilities for self-care; constructing a culture of self-care, or, in far too many instances, undermining it. I worked for many years in different organizations that encouraged self-care, while structurally creating conditions (e.g., workloads, special assignments, too many meetings, a culture of over-working) where self-care was difficult and nearly impossible to achieve. While many agencies and schools that employ and train helping professionals encourage employees and students to engage in self-care, in addition to high workloads, many policies and regulations make self-care difficult to achieve and maintain. In agencies, high caseloads and overwhelming expectations for documentation and labyrinthian agency protocols create worker stress and anxiety, rather than helping staff to find ways to reduce them. While this is often done in the service of productivity, it undermines efficiency and quality, lowers morale, and contributes to high staff turnover. In professional schools, high course loads and overwhelming and unrealistic academic assignments inhibit, rather than enhance, learning.

In order for helping professionals to be able to have a reservoir of compassion, commitment, and empathy to work with their collaborators, they must be able to care for themselves and organizations have an ethnical obligation to ensure this. This can take the form of devolving authority and decision making so that there are fewer directives and less hierarchy and greater ground-level responsibility and empowerment. There are important ways that organizations can protect workers and encourage self-care: ensuring adequate supervision, balancing work assignments, schedules that allow for breaks and recreation, in-service training to prepare workers for stresses and that help them to identify problems, and fostering peer support.

Creating spaces for affinity groups and paying attention to identity taxes, levied on employees and staff due to their social identities, are important interventions. What I mean by identity taxes are the differential expectations due to someone's social identities: e.g., working with clients who do not speak the predominant language and having to translate and interpret as part of their work. This can be not only due to work assignments that reinforce this but also come from the employee's social justice commitments and feelings of responsibility toward clients with particular or shared social identities. Many of my colleagues of color put in extra time formally and informally mentoring students of color, not only due to being sought out by students but also due to their sense of solidarity and responsibility.

It is also important to address structural oppression within the organization, which is expressed in a range of ways: values and assumptions about theories and practices, cultural values favoring communication styles of dominant groups, norms about what is considered to be "professional," and the numerous formal and informal ways that societal oppression is replicated within the organization (Garran et al., 2021). Organizations need mechanisms to address formal and informal patterns of discrimination, including micro-aggressions. It is critical to pay attention to staffing patterns, hierarchies of privilege reflected in organizational charts, and ensuring staff, consumer, and community representation on boards of directors. Garran et al. have developed an organizational audit for dislodging White supremacy and racism and becoming a racially just organization, which can also be used for identifying other forms of power and oppression. I have adapted their major categories for the topic of this chapter:

- Explicit commitment to social justice in the organizational mission statement
- Analyzing staffing patterns, including hierarchies reflecting privileged social identities in positions of higher power and status.
- Opportunities for mentoring and organizational advancement for people with targeted and minoritized social identities
- Affinity groups that create spaces for staff with different social identities
- Analyzing the range of identity taxes experienced by employees and mitigating them
- Analyzing how organizational power is structured and distributed
- Analyzing commitments to social justice in all organizational departments and publications
- Reviewing curricula, policies, and conceptual and treatment models for historical legacies of oppression and current oppressive practices and developing plans to address them
- Allocating organizational resources, including financial, toward reparative social justice initiatives
- Having ongoing discussions within the organization in large and small groups to consider how to address inequities and social oppression within the agency
- Training opportunities for all staff about different manifestations of privilege and oppression and how to address them
- Developing mechanisms to hear narratives, feedback, and the voices of minoritized clients, staff, and community members
- Developing intra and inter-agency alliances to challenge oppressive policies and practices
- Envisioning and developing a transformative, liberatory organizational culture and environment
- Developing mechanisms to address microaggressions and other forms of identity-based interpersonal ruptures and impasses
- Developing mechanisms to address and adjudicate inequitable policies and practices that have the trust and support of employees and/or students

An organizational commitment to identifying, understanding, and addressing these domains is a form of organizational commitment to the well-being of its employees and the people whom they serve.

One of my mentors, the late sociologist and social worker Richard Cloward, often argued that society and its organizations will not make the necessary changes to ensure equity and social justice; they reflect the historical, social, political, and economic conditions in which they were created. When there have been significant changes on behalf of marginalized groups – whether changes in laws and policies or in agency regulations – they have come from the demands of those seeking change. Whether through social movements, such as the Civil Rights and Welfare Rights movements in the United States, or through unionization of employees, dissensus and power struggles are often how meaningful change occurs. As he often told me: "it is a jungle out there" unless socially targeted groups and those with less political power collectively demand changes, create the conditions for change to occur, and develop mechanisms and safeguards to preserve what has been won. To create socially just organizations where collective care of employees is the norm, beneficence is a bonus but often insufficient; active engagement and resistance are needed. And be prepared for resistance and backlash, which are inevitable when there is genuine social change!

Individual and Collective Self-Care Audit

There are a number of domains requiring attention in order to engage in individual and collective self-care. Butler et al. (2019 have identified six: physical, professional, relational, emotional, psychological, and spiritual. I have written about seven self-care activities that roughly map onto these domains: exercise, mindfulness, relational connections, altruism and activism, finding meaning, pleasure and enjoyment, and deepening self-reflection and awareness (Miller, 2016). When writing about helping professionals responding to disasters, I developed an audit to help with self-care (Miller, 2012). I have expanded it here to have a greater collective focus and for application for helping professionals/volunteers engaged with social justice-anti-oppression work. It delineates areas to consider but as I have consistently argued, it should be adapted, revised, and reworked to meet the needs of people from a wide range of sociocultural contexts (see Figure 10.1).

Rather than be prescriptive, I have asked questions in ten areas, so that helping professionals can consider them with colleagues, friends, and others involved with the collective struggle of liberation and all of

1. **Investment** – What are the professional and personal goals of those engaging in liberatory, decolonial, anti-oppressive practice? What are likely impediments to achieving these goals, including forces of repression and lack of societal support, and what are roadblocks, obstacles, and possible sources of backlash? How will individuals and the group manage the affect that comes with this investment and engagement, which can include fear, anger, guilt, sadness, and possible triggering of historical/collective/personal trauma? What boundaries and limits will be helpful and how can group members help one another with this?
2. **Empathic Engagement and Identification** – What are salient social identities for individuals and group members engaged in this work? Who might the helping professionals or collective group members identify and disidentify with? What tools are available to aid with self and collective monitoring of reactions? What are individual and collective strategies for managing reactions?
3. **Supervision, Consultation, and Social Support** – How can people from inside and outside of the group offer support and consultation? Who is considered trustworthy and who is not? What kinds of affinity, support, mutual aid, and psychoeducational groups can be established? How can group members look after one another in a way that feels supportive and not restrictive? How can family members, colleagues, and friends be part of this process?
4. **Meeting Basic Needs** – How will individuals and group members ensure that they are able to do their work while eating sustaining food, getting adequate rest and sleep, and be able to pay bills and make ends meet? What collective mechanisms of mutual aid and support can be established to foster sharing and pooling of resources and to ensure that the group is caring for all of its members?
5. **Physical Activity** – How will individuals and group members build some form of physical activity in their lives? What are minimal and ideal exercise routines? How will individuals and group members maintain their routines during times of high workload and stress? What can be done collectively in this domain (e.g., group walks, runs, or sports) and how can the group ensure that all members have opportunities to engage in this fundamental form of self-care?

Figure 10.1 Self and Collective Care Audit

6. **Joy and Pleasure** – What gives individuals and groups joy and pleasure? How can these be integrated into the demanding work that people are engaged with? What kinds of recreational activities would contribute to this? How can access to nature and beauty be part of everyone's lives? How can meaningful time with family and friends be preserved and cherished?
7. **Meaning and Mindfulness** – What practices give individuals and groups meaning? What helps to broaden and expand perspectives so that the important work that people are engaged in is understood within a larger circle of history and being? Are there culturally relevant mindfulness practices that people can engage in to increase self-awareness, contribute to balance and equanimity, and help with managing strong emotions and reactions?
8. **Connections With Others** – Who are important people to individuals and the collective? What are people's social needs and who can best respond to specific needs? What are formal and informal sources of social support? How can people best connect in person and virtually?
9. **Help When Wounded** – How can individuals recognize when they are wounded and how will group members help with this process? What healing practices have meaning for individuals and groups? What resources are available to promote well-being and thriving? What is available personally, within the family, within the community, and collectivity and professionally?
10. **Altruism and Strengthening Resilience** – How can all of these practices be combined to strengthen individual and group resilience? How can altruism and commitment be a source of meaning and hope in the face of confronting oppression?
11. **Engaging in Activism, Advocacy, and Resistance** – Actively trying to change the conditions that contribute to inequality and oppression is empowering and empowerment is part of the self-care toolbox. What this means concretely varies depending on sociocultural contexts. There are many ways to engage with these activities, and from a self-care vantage point, it is important to strike a balance between taking action and periodically taking breaks and invoking the other forms of self-care.

Figure 10.1 (Continued)

its attendant risks. Readers are encouraged to add other domains and questions that will help them and their partners to engage in effective self-care.

Self-Awareness and Reflexivity

It may appear odd to include self-awareness and reflexivity in a chapter on self-care, but I think that they are related. As I have discussed throughout the book, coloniality, historical and collective trauma, and contemporary structural oppression cannot be resolved by traditional clinical approaches. There is a cost to the imposition of Western psychology and psychotherapy on people throughout the world and I would argue that helping professionals/volunteers are often part of this project. Helping professionals are engaged in their (our) work for admirable reasons and many of the risks to worker well-being described in this chapter happen because of that commitment and investment. Therefore, if those seeking to offer psychosocial support are contributing to harm and furthering oppression, it is injurious to the helper as well as their collaborators.

For helping professionals with mostly dominant identities (e.g., white, middle class, straight, cis-gender), the risk is that they continue to maintain cognitive distortions about the people with whom they are working – misunderstanding their personhood, culture, and what they need to reduce suffering and thrive – and imposing their own values and worldviews on others. People with dominant identities may blame themselves for this, if they are aware of it, and have feelings of guilt and shame. Or, they may dig in, justify their approaches, and become defensive when challenged, which is a secondary wound for people with targeted identities who observe or interact with these dynamics. Critical self-awareness can help with this and lead to greater insight, deeper empathy, and better collaboration.

For helping professionals with minoritized identities (e.g., BIPOC, poor, queer, transgender), there is often a profound cost to helping others who experience oppression, as I have described earlier, including the risk of shared trauma (Ali et al., 2021). There can also be feelings of guilt and shame, as well as anger, sadness, alienation, and isolation. Critical self-awareness can help with recognizing historical and collective threats and losses which may be internalized and hopefully can be externalized.

An area that benefits from critical self-awareness is self-compassion. Much has been written about the benefits of this. Compassion can be directed inwardly toward oneself and outwardly toward others

(Neff, 2021). Neff suggests that self-compassion can help to counteract stereotypes, assist people when dealing with feelings of guilt and shame, and reduce burnout. This is true for many people. However, Womack and Watson-Singleton have done research with Black students at Spelman College and asked about self-compassion in response to experiencing racism (Suttie, 2022). Self-compassion did not seem to be helpful in reducing psychological harm in response to racism because it was perceived as shifting the focus from society to oneself, although reducing self-judgment was productive. The researchers encourage further studies to see if and how self-compassion practices can be adapted for a positive impact in Black communities. This illustrates the importance of identity, sociocultural context, and critical consciousness to subtly discern when a broad concept such as self-compassion is useful or not depending upon how it is understood and the person and their context.

Critical consciousness aids helping professionals/volunteers to untangle how historical and structural forces are internalized and shape interpersonal relationships, including those involving psychosocial support and capacity building. It can lead to greater cohesion between helpers and collaborators and partners. It also encourages greater accountability and taking of responsibility by those who may have caused harm, as well as compassion toward self and others when this occurs. Greater critical consciousness helps helping professionals/volunteers committed to social justice to have the tools to individually and collectively dismantle internalized sources of privilege and oppression, which are impediments to change. It contributes to liberatory psychosocial work and makes it less likely that helping professionals will harm others and when they do, that there are opportunities for repair and reconstruction of relationships. Thus, engaging in this work is a form of self and collective care.

A group of my colleagues – Peggy O'Neill, Hye-Kyung Kang, Annemarie Gockel, Nnamdi Pole, and Maria del Mar Fariña – have been working on developing and studying the use of critical conversations to further critical consciousness. I will describe and draw on their work, as well as from my racial justice work with Ann Marie Garran, Lisa Werkmeister-Rozas, and Hye-Kyung Kang (Garran et al., 2021).

What is meant by critical consciousness? O'Neill (2016, p. 626) has defined it as the "intentional cultivation of self-awareness in context that attends to the dynamics of power in relationships and the structural environment invoking action toward social justice." She goes on to describe three elements of this process. The first is cultivating self-awareness, which includes awareness of one's social identities and how this situates and positions a person in society, which also contributes to recognizing differences, when they exist, with collaborators with different social identities. The second step is critical reflexivity, which is the capacity to self-observe one's assumptions and actions in interactions with others as they are occurring, which includes perceptions, biases, the nature of oppression, and how power and privilege are made manifest. The third step is critical reflection, which involves reviewing how one's work with partners was influenced by assumptions, interpersonal and structural power (and I would add historical inheritances), and consistently appraising one's adherence to social justice values and commitments.

All of these steps can be done by individuals on their own, and this is an important part of self-awareness and self-care but is even more effective when done with others in groups (Garran et al., 2021; Gockel et al., 2022; Kang & O'Neill, 2018; O'Neill & Farina, 2018; O'Neill et al., 2021). Groups can be structured for people with different social identities or they can offer affinity spaces for people with similar social identities; both are valuable. Heterogenous groups offer the opportunity to not only understand oneself and for this to occur in a milieu of people with very different experiences. This benefit also comes with risks, as there can be micro- and macro-aggressions, misunderstandings and conflict, and pain and alienation. Affinity groups offer spaces for support, buffering from ongoing oppression, strategizing about resistance and survival strategies, and engaging in culturally congruent healing practices. All groups should be infused with love, care, respect, taking responsibility, and norms of accountability.

The critical conversations model involves a structured, facilitated conversation where "power dynamics in a social context are illuminated and examined in the moment and subsequently reflected upon to foster development of critical consciousness and reflection" (Kang & O'Neill, 2018, p. 188). The conversations are a social justice intervention that focuses on the interface of multiple levels of power, privilege, and oppression – structural (historical), personal, and interpersonal. And the conversations are intended to lead to action, which as a self-care strategy is efficacious and empowering. There are four themes in a critical conversation that interact in real time: critical self-awareness, recognition of how social positions shape interactions, critical awareness of social structure and how it is internalized, and viewing the conversation as a learning opportunity for all. What is notable is the importance of critical reflection leading to social action, taking place in real time (and hopefully leading to subsequent ongoing critical reflection) (O'Neill et al., 2021). It is hoped that in this group intervention, participants engage in individual and group reflection, critical thinking and awareness, uncovering of assumptions, and helping participants to examine their roles and responsibilities in perpetuating or challenging social inequities. The model encourages space for respectful sharing of differences and disagreements, curiosity, and openness to deep listening, reflection, and a willingness to change on behalf of one's commitment to social justice. The conversations help participants to understand the complex dance of good intentions leading to bad impacts (Gockel et al., 2022).

The critical conversations model has been tested with undergraduate students from large state universities and small liberal arts colleges, graduate social work faculty in multiple programs, and interdisciplinary faculty teaching in undergraduate and graduate programs and recently is being tested as a pedagogical tool with college/university physicist educators. It also has been adapted to supervision, helping supervisors and supervisees to identify dynamics of racism, prejudice, power, and privilege in the supervisory relationship and by helping both to critically reflect on the direct work done by the helping professionals with their collaborators (O'Neill & Farina, 2018).

Critical self-awareness is essential to doing the kind of work described in this book. It protects partners from the iatrogenic effects of well-intentioned helping professionals but, as I have argued in this section, also empowers the helping professionals. Working with people resisting historical and contemporary oppression requires the collaboration of many people and systems and the critical conversations model enhances the possibility of cohesion within such collaborations. Self-care, both individual and collective, and critical consciousness are closely related and should be practiced together.

The Witness to Witness Model

I am using the W2W (Weingarten et al., 2020) as an illustration of a self-care and mutual support model that has been used with the Migrant's Clinician Network, in collaboration with the American Family Therapy Association (AFTA), that is commensurate with the values expressed in this book and the issues raised in this chapter, including models such as the critical conversations model. It takes an intersectional approach, recognizes the power of structural oppression on helpers and collaborators, and has developed a comprehensive self-care program for clinicians. Although this book is not only intended for clinicians, I believe that the program can be adapted to support community members and workers as well as volunteers and para-professionals.

Much of the psychosocial work described in this chapter involves deep listening and witnessing. The W2W approach begins with the premise that there are "four witness positions": (1) empowered and aware; (2) empowered and unaware; (3) disempowered and unaware; and (4) disempowered and aware (Weingarten et al., 2020). The first position means that the witness/helping person understands the historical and structural forces in play as they offer psychosocial support. Not only does a person feel competent and effective but they are also less likely to do harmful things. This is not true of the second position, where a person feels empowered and thinks that they understand what they are witnessing yet is unaware of the complex factors that contribute to a person's distress; this is where well-intentioned harm can occur. The helper in this position may have power and privilege and is perceived by others as such. Throughout the book, I have described the risks of helping professionals with dominant identities imposing their values and worldviews on others, which occurs in this witness position. In position 3, Weingarten et al. believe that the combination of unawareness and disempowerment leads to a form of dereliction of duty, effectively abandoning the collaborator. In position 4, the helper understands what they are witnessing but might lack clarity about what to do or lack resources to effectively intervene. All of the positions evoke different reactions when helping others: position 1 is received as being attuned and helpful, position 2 can feel critical and hurtful, position 3 can seem withdrawn and passive, and position 4 can contribute to confusion and uncertainty. Ultimately, having workers move to position 1 is the goal.

The actual program involves a psychoeducation segment that can be delivered via archived webinars (Weingarten et al., 2020). Following this, AFTA volunteers offer three to four individual sessions to the clinician. This involves listening to and understanding the challenges faced by the clinician as they do their work, engaging in an assessment of the colleague's past and current assets and resources, and identifying roadblocks to accessing those resources and ways to address them. This leads to developing a "personal toolkit" for the worker/volunteer to be able to manage the stress of their work. During COVID, the program added two components: peer consultation groups and organizational consultations to help supervisors and managers to foster "trauma sensitive and resilience hardy work environments" (p. 886).

There are many valuable aspects to this program, including a recognition of the potential for moral injury sustained by helpers who are witnessing terrible things while not being able to do the right thing in the moment (Weingarten et al., 2020). This evolved from the terrible stress endured by health-care workers during the early stages of COVID. On the Migrant Clinicians Website, there are descriptions of the W2W program and downloadable handouts (www.migrantclinician.org/our-work-building-health-provider-capacity/witness-witness-w2w.html), including one on moral injury, developed by Weingarten. The handout stresses remembering one's good intentions, noticing body sensations and negative self-talk, and encourages people to develop a buddy system. Kindness to oneself and others, expressing appreciation, and self-care are encouraged.

Another impressive feature is the recognition of the need to take an intersectional perspective, recognizing the destructive power of structural oppression. There is a detailed handout on the website that describes microaggressions, offering the history and meaning of the term. There are then a series of suggested steps that people who have committed microaggressions can take as well as a handout that discusses how witnesses to and targets of microaggressions can respond.

The W2W model brings together many of the concepts discussed in this book and chapter: the interplay of structural factors and internal suffering, the capacity for helping professionals with dominant identities and trained in dominant paradigms to impose their misunderstandings on to other people, and the need for critical consciousness to both engage in this type of work and as an ingredient of self-care. In my view, it can be adapted to a more collective context where communal care is the focus. And while the steps and protocols are very helpful, engaging leadership of those who are affected in adapting and even redesigning such protocols to meet their unique needs based on their personhood, identities, and sociocultural contexts should be encouraged.

Conclusion

This chapter considered how workers and volunteers offering psychosocial capacity building and support to people and communities experiencing sociopolitical targeting can care for themselves and others. It covered factors that contribute to overall worker stress, burnout, compassion fatigue, and vicarious and secondary trauma. I discussed how the interaction of worker vulnerabilities, the nature of suffering experienced by collaborators, the availability of supports, and the investment in partners and specific intervention outcomes are contributing factors that can undermine the well-being of workers and volunteers. When helping professionals/volunteers share social identities with their collaborators/partners and have also experienced historical trauma and are encountering structural oppression and interpersonal aggression, empathy and understanding are greater but the risks increase. As with earlier chapters, although recognizing the value of some of the concepts relating to worker distress that I described, I interrogated their universality, having been developed within a specific professional and cultural milieu, and questioned the assumption that they are relevant to helpers living and working in very different sociocultural contexts.

I explored how individuals and groups can try to anticipate risks and prepare to engage in self and collective care. This included a self and collective care audit (Figure 10.1). I also explored the role of organizations in undermining worker/volunteer well-being and considered ways that workplaces can offer greater support for self-care and their ethical obligations to protect workers/volunteers. The chapter concluded with two case examples: the critical conversations model that fosters critical consciousness using a group intervention and the W2W program, which has developed protocols for worker self-care that recognizes the significance of structural oppression and social identities. As I have argued in this chapter, self-care and critical awareness of self and others are intertwined and indispensable for helping professionals doing the work described in this book.

References

Adams, R.E., Boscarino, J.A., & Figley, C.R. (2006). Compassion fatigue and psychological stress among social workers: A validation study. *American Journal of Orthopsychiatry*, *761*: 103–108.

Ali, D.A., Figley, C.R., Tedeschi, R.G., Galarneu, D., & Amara, S. (2021). Shared trauma, resilience, and growth: A roadmap toward transcultural conceptualization. *Psychological Trauma: Theory, Research, Practice, and Policy*. DOI: 10.1037/tra0001044.

Butler, L.D., Mercer, K.A., McClain-Meeder, K., Horne, D.M., & Dudley, M. (2019). Six domains of self-care: Attending to the whole person. *Journal of Human Behavior in the Social Environment*, *29*(1): 107–124. DOI: 10.1080/10911359.2018.1482483.

Figley, C.R. (1995). Compassion fatigue as a secondary traumatic stress disorder in those who treat the traumatized. In C.R. Figley (Ed.). *Compassion fatigue: Coping with secondary traumatic stress disorder in those who treat the traumatized*. New York: Brunner/Mazel Publishing.

Garran, A.M., Werkmeister-Rozas, L., Kang, H.K., & Miller, J.L. (2021). *Racism in the United States: Implications for the helping professions* (3rd ed.). New York: Springer Publishing.

Gockel, A., O'Neill, P., & Pole, N. (2022). Social justice conversations: Using critical conversations to unpack oppression. *Families in Society*. DOI: 10.1177/10443894211062647.

Kang, H.K., & O'Neill, P. (2018). Teaching note – Constructing critical conversations: A model for facilitating classroom dialogue for critical learning. *Journal of Social Work Education*, *54*(1): 187–193. DOI: 10.1080/10437797.2017.1341857.

Miller, J.L. (2012). *Psychosocial capacity building in response to disasters*. New York: Columbia University Press.

Miller, J.L. (2016). Seven self-care strategies. *Reflections*, *21*(1): 52–58.

Neff, K. (2021, June 13). Four ways that self-compassion can help you fight for social justice. *Greater Good Magazine*. https://greatergood.berkeley.edu/article/item/four_ways_self_compassion_can_help_you_fight_for_social_justice?utm_source=Greater+Good+Science+Center&utm_campaign=2a5cd3e1ec-EMAIL_CAMPAIGN_GG_Newsletter_June_15_2021&utm_medium=email&utm_term=0_5ae73e326e-2a5cd3e1ec-74212343

O'Neill, M. (2016). Applying critical consciousness and evidence-based practice decision making: A framework for clinical social work practice. *Journal of Social Work Education*, *51*: 624–637. DOI: 10.1080/10437797.2015.1076285.

O'Neill, M., Gockel, A., & Pole, N. (2021). Critical conversations: A dialogic approach to developing critical consciousness. *Journal of the Society for Social Work and Research*. DOI: 10.1086/718634.

O'Neill, P., & Farina, M.D.M. (2018). Constructing critical conversations in social work supervision: Creating change. *Clinical Social Work Journal*, *46*: 298–309. DOI: 10.1007/s10615-018-0681-6.

Pearlman, C.A., & Saakvitne, K.W. (1995). *Trauma and the therapist: Counter-transference and vicarious trauma in psychotherapy with incest survivors*. New York: W.W. Norton & Co.

Schreiber, M., Cates, D.S., Formanski, S., & King, M. (2019). Maximizing the resilience of healthcare workers in multi-hazard events: Lessons from the 2014–2015 Ebola response in Africa. *Military Medicine*, *184*(3/4): 114–120.

Suttie, J. (2022, January 11). Can self-compassion increase resilience in the face of discrimination? *Greater Good Magazine*. https://greatergood.berkeley.edu/article/item/can_self_compassion_increase_resilience_in_the_face_of_discrimination?utm_source=Greater+Good+Science+Center&utm_campaign=4ca8afa91dEMAIL_CAMPAIGN_GG_Newsletter_January_6_2021_COPY_0&utm_medium=email&utm_term=0_5ae73e326e-4ca8afa91d-74212343

Weingarten, K., Gavlven-Duran, A.R., D'Urso, S., & Garcia, D. (2020). The witness to witness program: Helpers in the context of the Covid-19 pandemic. *Family Process*, *59*(3). DOI: 10.1111/famp.12580.

Afterword

I wrote this book between 2020 and 2022 in the midst of the COVID global pandemic, living in Northampton, Massachusetts, and London, England. Both countries are wealthy in comparison with other nations, and both have dim and dismal histories of colonization, genocide, slavery, and White supremacy. London glitters with steel, glass, and electricity, while many residents of Great Britain's former colonies live in poverty, travel on dirt roads, and have had many of their resources extracted and appropriated. Both countries became wealthier due to the enslavement of people from Africa and through genocidal policies directed at indigenous populations. These legacies continue to haunt the helping professions.

At the time of this writing, 1/3 of Pakistan is under water due to unprecedented flooding and many parts of East Africa are experiencing food shortages due to drought. Both are viewed as consequences of climate change and are likely to continue or get worse. This is another legacy of coloniality, where people in wealthy, industrialized countries spew the majority of carbon into the atmosphere which contributes to threatening, possibly unlivable circumstances in those parts of the world that were colonized and exploited. Pakistan is thought to contribute 1% of global carbon emissions and the same is true for the entire region of sub-Saharan Africa, while the United States contributes roughly 28%. The ravages and inequities of coloniality continue their malignant manifestations through the patterns and dynamics of global warming.

It is an understatement to say that the time of COVID was tumultuous. Unsurprisingly, COVID differentially affected communities and countries depending on many factors: access to resources such as information and vaccines, health-care infrastructure, wealth and poverty, people's living and work conditions, constructive or destructive political leadership, and the many inequalities and sources of oppression that are the legacies of coloniality and modern-day racism and oppression. Where were vaccines produced, who could afford them, and which countries were prioritized for distribution? While there have been pandemics throughout history, this felt like a particularly bleak time. Will this continue to exacerbate the patterns and divisions discussed throughout this book or can this be an opportunity to reimagine how we live, and how helping professionals/volunteers practice?

While there have been terrible cruelties inflicted upon people throughout history, it is dispiriting to see how much suffering persists in today's world. Wars and armed conflict are occurring in many places. In addition to this, climate change, poverty, and global inequality have combined to become a worldwide cascading disaster, contributing to an unprecedented wave of forced migration, as battered and desperate people struggle to reach the gated communities of the developed world. Far too many do not survive and only a small number penetrate the legal and military armadas protecting the wealthier nations of the world. Will this continue to fuel nativism, racism, and authoritarianism or can it lead to a rethinking of the mutual relationships, rights, and obligations that must be shared?

I wish that I believed that the winds of positive change are on the horizon, but there are storm clouds gathering in many parts of the world. Major military conflicts are not only occurring but even more threatening and devastating wars may be waiting in the wings, with less adherence to basic norms of human rights and compassion and the threat of the use of nuclear weapons a harrowing, hovering specter. Autocracies, right-wing populism and racism, dictatorships, and repression (and even fascism) have spread like cancer throughout many countries, including the world's most powerful nations. Slavery is not a past abomination but a modern-day reality for far too many. Increasingly, some political parties and leaders question the project of democracy. Corporations wield even greater power, while the ability of the state to regulate and control them diminishes. And unlike other violent and tumultuous eras, the planet is on a downward spiral, as it overheats, oceans rise, communities are flooded, storms increase, water supplies dry up, and crops fail, all of this contributing to death, suffering, and seismic human migration and relocations.

I share this, not to end the book with an apocalyptic vision, but to acknowledge the environment in which it is written, which influences, constrains, and determines the nature of human suffering and provides the context in which helping professionals/volunteers try to intervene. I am not a philosopher, historian, spiritual leader, or politician; I am a social worker and helping professional, groping to understand the forces that shape our lives and our work, ultimately trying to figure out how people in my profession can do the most good and the least harm, while working for equity and justice. Is it possible that the bankruptcy of the legacies of coloniality, the excesses of capitalism, and the existential threats posed by environmental assault and climate change to global survival may herald a reimagining of how we live and remind us of other ways of being, co-existing, and living that were repressed, dismissed, and marginalized? I hope so.

Ultimately, we need to do what we can and do it in concert with others. Throughout the book, I have focused on the ways that communities and peoples have survived the direst of circumstances and the collective spiritual, metaphysical and existential wisdom that endured and evolved. These are wellsprings from which we can try to draw, as we confront the many challenges which we face. We are not separate from one another or the planet, but rather all in this together. Our past has been characterized by exploitation and domination; we need to pivot to greater collaboration, mutual respect and love, and a sense of harmony with the earth. This also includes reparations within and between countries, as those most harmed by coloniality are least able to withstand its present-day effects.

Helping professionals/volunteers not only need to be part of an ethic of love, compassion, and care but should use our work and positions to accelerate these ideals. We need clarity about our life-affirming values, ethical commitment to justice and equity, and to recognize and cherish the many ways of being, knowing, and healing that are available from different parts of the world, but far too often pushed to the margins. We are not the experts, but rather witnesses and accompanists – supporting people who have been historically and collectively subjugated to reclaim and re-envision cultural practices, sources of wisdom and strength, amplifying their voices, while dimming the power of the destructive forces that they/we face and which continue to divide us. We are not bystanders and the imagined social distance between helpers and those being helped is a social construction, an alienating outgrowth of coloniality; we all have a stake in redressing centuries of collective exploitation and trauma and our biggest asset and mechanism for change is how we decide to practice in concert with one another.

The arc of history may tilt toward greater justice, but the road is never straight and unimpeded. There are periods of progress and times of regression and repression. Social movements have often generated the social waves which have led to greater human rights and dignity.

Sometimes they begin as small ripples, joining with other streams before exerting a tidal pull on society. In the wake of the horror of World War II, there were social movements to end colonial empires, foster, and respect the rights of racially oppressed people, women's rights, LGBT rights, and much more, which were part of global freedom struggles. All were imperfect movements and none completely achieved their goals but their impact on the lives of millions, if not billions of people were profound. My mentor Richard Cloward once told me that you cannot manufacture social movements – they occur due to a constellation of factors that come together at a certain point in time. But it is important to keep the pilot light burning so that when there is sufficient fuel for a social movement to ignite, we can light the flame of peace, equity, and justice. Despite all of the threats and challenges that I have discussed, it is important for helping professionals to keep the pilot light burning. We not only need to react when there is injustice but also shine a beacon illuminating the world that we and our partners want to inhabit.

I have written this book for all of my colleagues, students, and collaborators who have been affected by coloniality and social oppression but also for me, my family, and all who have appeared to have benefitted – knowingly or not – from the privileges and wealth accrued to some. The sense of entitlement, of being above and away from the fray, and of security is part of the illusion that helps to sustain the devastating cycle of dehumanization and destruction that disrupts lives and may destroy us all. With privilege, there is often a lack of empathy, and while large swathes of the world are submerged or are burning, those living in wealthier, more secure locations can exhibit what the environmental writer David Wallace-Wells has termed "sociopathic indifference."

The agencies and organizations and their policies, which structure and reinforce this distorted thinking, are part of the cages that helping professionals need to escape from, at least in the form that they currently exist. If there is a sense of urgency in what I am saying, it is because I passionately believe that time is running out and that unless helping professionals/volunteers radically and rapidly change how we practice, we risk being the *hindering* professions, complicit in social control, class and racial divisions, and the downward, death spiral of the planet. We have choices to make, and although there are huge, macro forces that appear to be overwhelming, we can live and practice differently. This requires a sense of hope and a belief that we can contribute to a global reckoning and reimagining. As Pauline Boss, who has written about ambiguous loss, said, "without hope, apathy fills the void." Neither we nor our collaborators can afford to be apathetic. To paraphrase the great saxophonist, composer, and spiritual avatar John Coltrane, whether it is in the realm of music, society, or politics, if we can imagine something to be better, then we need to do all what we can to make it better. Collectively, we can pool our different assets and sources of knowledge and understanding, igniting many pilot lights of social justice!

Index

Note: Page numbers in *italics* indicate a figure or box on the corresponding page.

Printed in the USA
CPSIA information can be obtained
at www.ICGtesting.com
LVHW011235150324
774517LV00048B/2343

9 780367 897949